HIKE LIST

NORTH (WEBER COUNTY)

1 Ben Lomond
2 Ogden River Parkway
3 Mount Ogden (via Snowbasin Gondola)
4 Malans Peak (via Taylor Canyon)
5 Waterfall Canyon

NORTH (DAVIS COUNTY)

6 Adams Canyon
7 Thurston Peak
8 Farmington Creek Trail
9 Frary Peak
10 Kenny Creek Trail

CENTRAL (SALT LAKE COUNTY)

11 Mormon Pioneer Trail
12 Emigration Canyon Ridgeline
13 City Creek Canyon
14 Red Butte Garden
15 The Living Room (with Red Butte Extension)
16 Lambs Canyon
17 Mount Aire
18 Grandeur Peak
19 Desolation Trail to Salt Lake Overlook
20 Gobblers Knob (via Alexander Basin)
21 M
(i
22 N
23 Mount Olympus
24 Dog Lake
25 Desolation Lake
26 Mount Raymond (via Butler Fork)
27 Doughnut Falls
28 Lake Blanche
29 Broads Fork Twin Peaks
30 Willow Heights
31 Ferguson Canyon
32 Jordan River Parkway
33 Great Western Trail (Guardsman Pass to Clayton Peak)
34 Lake Solitude (via the Silver Lake Interpretive Trail)
35 Brighton Lakes
36 Sunset Peak
37 Cecret Lake
38 White Pine Lake
39 Pfeifferhorn (via Red Pine Lake)
40 American Fork Twin Peaks
41 Bells Canyon
42 Lone Peak (via Jacobs Ladder)

(List continues on next page)

MENASHA RIDGE PRESS
Birmingham, Alabama

60 HIKES WITHIN 60 MILES

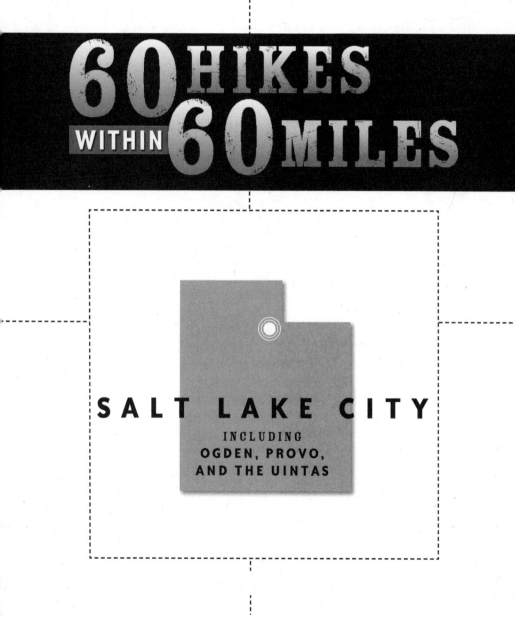

SALT LAKE CITY

INCLUDING
OGDEN, PROVO,
AND THE UINTAS

GREG WITT

DISCLAIMER

This book is meant only as a guide to select trails in the Salt Lake City area and does not guarantee hiker safety in any way—you hike at your own risk. Neither Menasha Ridge Press nor Greg Witt is liable for property loss or damage, personal injury, or death that result in any way from accessing or hiking the trails described in the following pages. Please be aware that hikers have been injured in the Salt Lake City area. Be especially cautious when walking on or near boulders, steep inclines, and drop-offs, and do not attempt to explore terrain that may be beyond your abilities. To help ensure an uneventful hike, please read carefully the introduction to this book, and perhaps get further safety information and guidance from other sources. Familiarize yourself thoroughly with the areas you intend to visit before venturing out. Ask questions, and prepare for the unforeseen. Familiarize yourself with current weather reports, maps of the area you intend to visit, and any relevant park regulations.

Printed in the United States of America
Published by Menasha Ridge Press
Distributed by Publishers Group West
First edition, first printing

 Printed on recycled paper

Library of Congress Cataloging-in-Publication Data

Witt, Greg, 1952–
60 hikes within 60 miles: Salt Lake City, including Ogden, Provo, and the Uintas/
Greg Witt.—1st ed.
p. cm.
Includes index.
ISBN-13: 978-0-89732-956-9
ISBN-10: 0-89732-956-2
1. Hiking—Utah—Salt Lake City Region—Guidebooks. 2. Salt Lake City Region (Utah)—Guidebooks. I. Title. II. Title: Sixty hikes within sixty miles.

GV199.42.U73W58 2008
796.5109792—dc22

2008010539

Text and cover design by Steveco International
Cover photograph © Willie Holdman
Author photograph © Celeste Elain Witt
Other interior photographs © Greg Witt except as follows: page xvi, David Crowther/iStock Photo.com; page 51, Renee Lee/iStockPhoto.com; page 146, Frank Leung/iStockPhoto.com; page 161, Roy Breslawski/iStockPhoto.com; page 166, Sharon Day/iStockPhoto.com; page 178, Michael Madsen/iStockPhoto.com; page 212, Ahmad Asgharzadeh/iStockPhoto.com; page 236, Mark A. Philbrick/Brigham Young University; page 274, Helaman Abacherli/iStockPhoto.com
Cartography and elevation profiles by Scott McGrew and Greg Witt
Indexing by Jan Mucciarone

Menasha Ridge Press
P.O. Box 43673
Birmingham, Alabama 35243
www.menasharidge.com

TABLE OF CONTENTS

ACKNOWLEDGMENTS

A project of this magnitude goes from concept to print with the contributions of many. I'm thankful to Russell Helms at Menasha Ridge Press, who approached me about writing a Salt Lake City hiking guide. I was somewhat reluctant at first, but through his encouragement, vision, and support, *60 Hikes* has become a reality.

Thanks to Sheryl McGlochlin, whose energy and enthusiasm are infectious. She's introduced many of these hikes to hundreds of locals and is always anxious to share a favorite hike with friends like me.

I'm appreciative of Helene Liebman and her associates at Weber Pathways, who have created a hiking legacy for the Ogden area through their efforts to promote, plan, and preserve trails.

I'm grateful to Alan and Kristine Colledge, with whom I have shared gallons of Gatorade and miles of terrain across the Wasatch, the Colorado Plateau, and the Grand Canyon.

Thanks to my parents, Bud and Claire Witt, who took me on hikes in Mill Creek Canyon and Brighton as a toddler. Later, they led me to discover the Sierra Nevada and many national parks on fabulous cross-country road trips.

I've met hundreds of hikers along the trail. Sometimes our exchange was nothing more than "g'morning" or "hello." But often these newfound friends would share their experiences with me—identifying a wildflower, reporting on a moose sighting, or telling me about a favorite waterfall just up the canyon. Their insights and love of the outdoors have enriched my life and are woven into every hike in this book.

Many of those trail acquaintances were members of the Wasatch Mountain Club, an organization of dedicated volunteers who love to explore the scenic wonders of the area mountains. They also deserve much of the credit for improving the quality of the outdoor experience through preservation of wild lands and providing access to these pristine reaches.

Special thanks to many hiking friends who have provided ideas, encouragement, and support along the way, including Phil Schow, Mark McGuire, Bart Hamatake, Bruce Bown, Ben Adcock, Peter Tennis, David Crowther, Jim Rasband, Vaughn Armstrong, Jim McDonald, Mary Baxter, Jack Welch, Al Christy, Jim Driggs, Harlan Hatfield, and Dennis Hoagland.

I always cherish the time I've spent on these and other Utah trails with my children, Heather, Blair, Lindsey, Dallin, and Tessa. I look forward to sharing many more trail miles with my grandchildren, Hannah, Isaac, Alden, and Grant.

My deepest gratitude goes to my wife, Elain, my best friend and eternal trail companion. Her sustaining belief, encouragement, and love have guided me through this project and every other aspect of my life. She joined me on many of these hikes, but I wish she could have joined me on every one. If she had, this would have been a far more elaborate book.

—GREG WITT

ABOUT THE AUTHOR

GREG WITT has lived the adventures he writes about and shares with audiences around the world. His journeys have taken him to every corner of the globe. He has guided mountaineering expeditions in the Alps and Andes and paddled wild rivers in the Americas. He has dropped teams of adventurers into golden slot canyons; trudged through deep jungles in Africa, Central America, and Asia; and guided archaeological expeditions across the parched Arabian Peninsula. His passion for adventure has always focused on sharing his experience with others.

After earning degrees from the University of California and Brigham Young University, Greg had an early career in human-resources management. But because he prefers high adventure to the high-rise, he traded his wing tips for hiking boots decades ago and has never looked back.

Some weeks, Greg hikes more miles than he drives, which means he wears out his boots faster than he wears out his tires. He has crossed the Grand Canyon on foot many times, climbed Colorado's three highest peaks in three days, and in a recent summer in the Alps he hiked more than 700 miles and gained nearly 100,000 vertical feet of elevation—the equivalent of climbing Everest nine times.

Now he leads readers on the most breathtaking hikes and exciting outdoor adventures on the globe. He comes ready to discuss the geology, history, archaeology, weather patterns, culture, flora, and fauna of the exciting locales he loves. Other titles include *Exploring Havasupai* and *Ultimate Adventures: A Rough Guide to Adventure Travel.*

Greg's research and exploration continue to uncover surprising adventures just waiting to be experienced. If you join him, you can be guaranteed a phenomenal journey.

FOREWORD

Welcome to Menasha Ridge Press's *60 Hikes within 60 Miles,* a series designed to provide hikers with the information they need to find and hike the very best trails surrounding metropolitan areas.

Our strategy is simple: First, find a hiker who knows the area and loves to hike. Second, ask that person to spend a year researching the most popular and very best trails around. And third, have that person describe each trail in terms of difficulty, scenery, condition, elevation change, and other categories of information that are important to hikers. "Pretend you've just completed a hike and met up with other hikers at the trailhead," we told each author. "Imagine their questions, be clear in your answers."

An experienced hiker and writer, Greg Witt has selected 60 of the best hikes in and around the Salt Lake metropolitan area. From the wilderness lakes and rocky peaks of the Wasatch Range and Uinta Mountains to a suburban stroll along the Jordan River Parkway, Witt provides hikers (and walkers) with a great variety of outings—and all within roughly 60 miles of Salt Lake City.

You'll get more out of this book if you take a moment to read the Introduction explaining how to read the trail listings. The "Topographic Maps" section will help you understand how useful topos are on a hike, and will also tell you where to get them. And though this is a "where-to," not a "how-to" guide, readers who have not hiked extensively will find the Introduction of particular value.

As much for the opportunity to free the spirit as well as to free the body, let these hikes elevate you above the urban hurry.

All the best,
The Editors at Menasha Ridge Press

PREFACE

Alaska is our biggest, buggiest, boggiest state. Texas remains our largest unfrozen state. But mountainous Utah, if ironed out flat, would take up more space on a map than either.

—Edward Abbey

With mountains on every side, it's easy to see why the Salt Lake Valley offers a greater variety of dramatic and awe-inspiring day hikes than any major metropolitan area in the United States. Nestled below the western flank of the Rockies, Salt Lake City provides ready access to a stunning array of alpine lakes, snow-draped mountain peaks, fragrant evergreen forests, deep canyon waterfalls, granite towers, and flowered cirques.

Within 60 miles of Salt Lake City there are thousands of square miles of national forest, national wilderness areas, state parks, and designated recreation areas to explore. But it takes accurate and dependable information to select the best hiking adventure for you. Within minutes of a bustling urban center, you can immerse yourself in the history of early miners, the Pony Express, the Donner Party, or Mormon pioneers. With a little planning you can summit one of a dozen 11,000-foot peaks sprinkled throughout the region. You can find solitude in flickering aspen groves, shaded canyons, and pristine wilderness. Whether you're lacing up boots, stepping into running shoes, or strapping on snowshoes, Salt Lake City is a premier destination for hikers.

ABOUT THE HIKES

It would have been easy to catalog 60 hikes near Salt Lake City from the hundreds of hiking trails in the area. But the ultimate challenge in writing *60 Hikes* was to pinpoint the *absolute best* of those hikes—the most enjoyable, inspiring, intriguing, and accessible hikes. You'll quickly discover that every hike has an

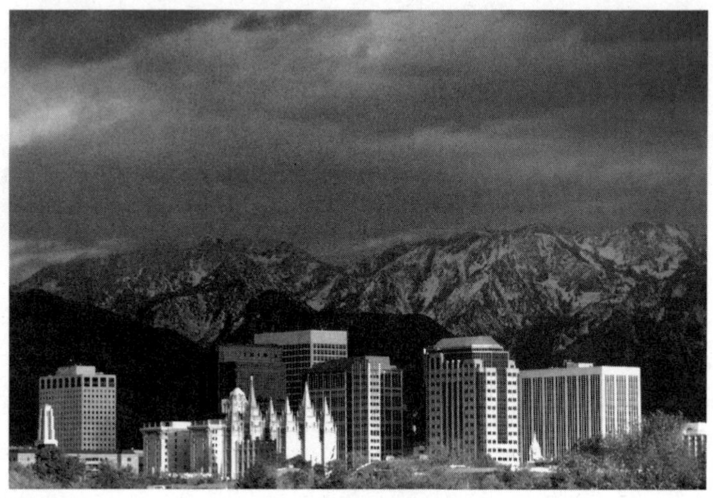

The Wasatch Mountains loom over the Salt Lake City skyline.

unforgettable highlight—a "wow factor." Every hike has a memorable destination, a glistening lake, a mesmerizing stream, a breathtaking view, or a soothing canyon.

The 60 hikes that made the list had to captivate the attention of young hikers and challenge the endurance of seasoned hikers. The hikes needed to reflect the diversity of the mountain, valley, and canyon terrain found in the area. With rising fuel costs, I wanted to reveal hikes that were nearby and easily accessible to the 1.7 million people who live within 60 miles of Salt Lake City.

Faced with the challenge of selecting the best 60 hikes in the Salt Lake area, I assembled a powerful and compelling list in less than an hour. But the book really demanded a more rigorous process. So I distributed my best-hikes list to dozens of area hikers, rangers, scoutmasters, youth leaders, mountain bikers, rock climbers, dog walkers, trails advocates, and city recreation officials. I sought their suggestions on which hikes to include, asking them to advise which route offered the best trailhead access and best overall experience. Their input was exciting to receive and proved invaluable. Surprisingly, there was a high level of consensus on which hikes to include; in fact, the 60 hikes included here are about 90 percent consistent with my original list.

In order to present the most accurate information possible, I rehiked each trail to take distance measurements, GPS coordinates, elevations, and clarify trail markings. The goal was simple: create a trustworthy, authoritative trail guide that would provide years of valuable hiking pleasure.

Just 60 hikes? Hardly. At last count it was closer to 120 hikes organized into 60 profiles. Most of the 60 hikes—indeed, most Wasatch trails—are interconnected. Each hike profile describes a particular route but also allows for options, extensions, and spur trails. In addition, the Nearby Activities mentioned at the end of most trail descriptions often reveal short hikes leading to hidden waterfalls, short interpretive trails, or points of historic or geologic interest. Most of these activities consist of short walks that are less than 1 mile round-trip, while the 60 hikes are 1 mile or more in length. If you're a novice hiker and want to build your speed and stamina, you may want to start with some of the Nearby Activities.

The 60 hikes appeal to a wide variety of skill levels and interests. Of the featured 60 hikes, about 31 percent are considered easy, 47 percent are moderate, and 22 percent are difficult. The hikes range in distance from 1 mile on Buffalo Peak to 16 miles on Ben Lomond. Elevation gain ranges from just 58 feet on the Jordan River Parkway to 5,460 feet on Lone Peak. All the hikes are normally done as day hikes, although many can also be enjoyed as an overnight backpacking trip. You'll find that *60 Hikes* has something for everybody.

REGIONS

The hikes are organized by area in relation to Salt Lake City—north, central, south, east, and west. Conveniently, those areas also match county lines, since most of the county boundaries are defined by mountain ridges. Most of the 60 hikes are in the Wasatch Mountains, which run north and south, with the vast majority of the area's population living on the slopes and valleys to the west of the range. Within each county, hikes are organized from north to south. Here's a quick overview of each region:

NORTH (WEBER COUNTY) The hikes in Weber County are easily accessed from Ogden, about 35 miles north of Salt Lake City. Ogden's historical roots as a junction on the intercontinental railroad have been overshadowed in recent years by its emergence as a center of outdoor recreation. The alpine peaks that hosted downhill and super G events in the 2002 Winter Olympic Games are also great hiking destinations in the summer. Favorite Weber County hikes include Ben Lomond on the north and beautiful Waterfall Canyon, which can be accessed just minutes from the city center.

NORTH (DAVIS COUNTY) Davis County lies immediately north of Salt Lake City. It's traditionally been known for farming communities such as Bountiful, Farmington, and Fruit Heights, which rest on the alluvial plain at the base of smaller Wasatch peaks. But it also offers some great canyon hikes, such as Farmington Canyon and Adams Canyon. Davis County has more square miles of Great Salt Lake than it has land area, and Antelope Island is the ideal place to explore the wonders of the Great Salt Lake on dry ground.

CENTRAL (SALT LAKE COUNTY) It's fitting that more than half of the 60 hikes are located right in Salt Lake County. These hikes offer easy access to glacial canyons, alpine lakes, and snow-capped peaks. You'll be amazed how close wilderness areas are to the heart of the city. Salt Lake's pioneer history unfolds along celebrated trails and the Pony Express route. In *60 Hikes,* you'll find adventure waiting in each of the seven canyons that have shaped, nourished, powered, and built Salt Lake City since 1847. Most hikers can find enough hiking opportunities in Big Cottonwood Canyon alone to feed their passion for a year or more. Some of the more popular hikes in the central Wasatch include Grandeur Peak, Brighton Lakes, and Doughnut Falls.

SOUTH (UTAH COUNTY) To the south of Salt Lake City, the Mount Timpanogos massif watches over Utah County. Dozens of canyons flank "Timp," and waterfalls cascade down all sides. Provo Canyon and American Fork Canyon offer exceptional year-round outdoor recreation opportunities. While Timp is arguably the best hike in northern Utah, don't overlook other Utah County jewels, such as Silver Lake and Stewart Falls.

WEST (TOOELE COUNTY) With so much to enjoy in the Wasatch, you can see why most locals overlook the desert to the west. But the Stansbury Mountains and the Deseret Peak Wilderness Area, with its rugged terrain and 11,031-foot centerpiece, simply can't be ignored. Views stretch across the Bonneville Salt Flats and into Nevada. It's a straight shot out Interstate 80, just 35 miles to the west.

EAST (SUMMIT COUNTY) The Uinta Mountains, home to Utah's highest peaks, lie directly east of Salt Lake City, beyond the Wasatch Mountains. The scenic Mirror Lake Highway provides easy access to picturesque basins and forests of spruce and fir. You can climb 11,943-foot Bald Mountain in less than an hour or spend days on end in the alpine heaven known as Naturalist Basin.

Let *60 Hikes* be a starting point. Let it inspire your own adventure on a road less traveled. Maybe you'll discover a hidden waterfall or encounter a mysterious field of white columbine. Wasatch trails are notoriously unmarked, and maybe with enough experience you'll discover you don't need trail signs to have a great hike. If a family of moose is blocking the trail, you may find a parallel trail over the ridge. If the trailhead parking lot is full, you can often take a shorter, steeper trail to the summit from another trailhead. The possibilities are endless, and you'll have the time of your life exploring them. See you on the trail.

HIKING RECOMMENDATIONS

AUTHOR'S PICKS

HIKES OF 1 TO 3 MILES

HIKES OF 3 TO 6 MILES

HIKES OF 3 TO 6 MILES *(continued)*

HIKES OF 6 TO 9 MILES

HIKES OF MORE THAN 9 MILES

HIKES OF MORE THAN 9 MILES *(continued)*

STEEP HIKES

HIKES NEAR STREAMS AND RIVERS

HIKES NEAR STREAMS AND RIVERS *(continued)*

HIKES WITH LAKES

HIGH-ALTITUDE HIKES (MORE THAN 10,000 FEET)

HIGH-ALTITUDE HIKES (MORE THAN 10,000 FEET) *(continued)*

58 Lofty Lake Loop (page 254)
42 Lone Peak (via Jacobs Ladder) (page 183)
26 Mount Raymond (via Butler Fork) (page 121)
46 Mount Timpanogos (via the Timpooneke Trail) (page 202)
57 Naturalist Basin (page 250)
39 Pfeifferhorn (via Red Pine Lake) (page 171)
36 Sunset Peak (page 159)
38 White Pine Lake (page 167)

HIKES WITH SCRAMBLING OR CLIMBING

40 American Fork Twin Peaks (page 175)
44 Box Elder Peak (page 194)
29 Broads Fork Twin Peaks (page 133)
27 Doughnut Falls (page 125)
42 Lone Peak (via Jacobs Ladder) (page 183)
23 Mount Olympus (page 109)
26 Mount Raymond (via Butler Fork) (page 121)
39 Pfeifferhorn (via Red Pine Lake) (page 171)

BEST TRAILS FOR MOUNTAIN BIKING

1 Ben Lomond (page 16)
25 Desolation Lake (page 117)
24 Dog Lake (page 113)
12 Emigration Canyon Ridgeline (page 65)
18 Grandeur Peak (page 89)
34 Lake Solitude (via the Silver Lake Interpretive Trail) (page 151)
21 Mill Creek to Park City Overlook (including Murdock Peak) (page 101)
11 Mormon Pioneer Trail (page 60)
3 Mount Ogden (via Snowbasin Gondola) (page 24)
55 Stansbury Island Trail (page 240)
38 White Pine Lake (page 167)

BEST TRAILS FOR BICYCLING

13 City Creek Canyon (page 69)
32 Jordan River Parkway (page 143)
2 Ogden River Parkway (page 20)
50 Provo River Parkway (page 218)

HIKES WITH WATERFALLS

6 Adams Canyon (page 38)
49 Battle Creek Falls (page 214)
41 Bells Canyon (page 179)

HIKES WITH WATERFALLS *(continued)*

BEST WINTER HIKES

HIKES WITH HISTORY

BEST HIKES FOR CHILDREN

BEST HIKES FOR CHILDREN *(continued)*

13 City Creek Canyon (page 69)
27 Doughnut Falls (page 125)
59 Fehr Lake Trail (page 258)
32 Jordan River Parkway (page 143)
34 Lake Solitude (via the Silver Lake Interpretive Trail) (page 151)
3 Mount Ogden (via Snowbasin Gondola) (page 24)
2 Ogden River Parkway (page 20)
50 Provo River Parkway (page 218)
14 Red Butte Garden (page 73)
48 Stewart Falls (page 210)
36 Sunset Peak (page 159)
30 Willow Heights (page 137)
54 Y Mountain (page 234)

BEST HIKES FOR DOGS

49 Battle Creek Falls (page 214)
52 Buffalo Peak (page 226)
13 City Creek Canyon (page 69)
56 Deseret Peak (page 244)
19 Desolation Trail to Salt Lake Overlook (page 93)
12 Emigration Canyon Ridgeline (page 65)
31 Ferguson Canyon (page 140)
59 Fehr Lake Trail (page 258)
18 Grandeur Peak (page 89)
33 Great Western Trail (Guardsman Pass to Clayton Peak) (page 147)
32 Jordan River Parkway (page 143)
58 Lofty Lake Loop (page 254)
21 Mill Creek to Park City Overlook (including Murdock Peak) (page 101)
17 Mount Aire (page 85)
57 Naturalist Basin (page 250)
22 Neffs Canyon (page 105)
2 Ogden River Parkway (page 20)
50 Provo River Parkway (page 218)
48 Stewart Falls (page 210)
15 The Living Room (with Red Butte Extension) (page 77)

POPULAR TRAILS

60 Bald Mountain (page 262)
35 Brighton Lakes (page 156)
37 Cecret Lake (page 163)
13 City Creek Canyon (page 69)
19 Desolation Trail to Salt Lake Overlook (page 93)

POPULAR TRAILS *(continued)*

HIKES TO HIGH SUMMITS (MORE THAN 11,000 FEET)

HIKES WITH SWEEPING VIEWS

HIKES WITH SWEEPING VIEWS *(continued)*

YEAR-ROUND HIKES

BEST HIKES FOR SOLITUDE

BEST HIKES FOR WILDLIFE

BEST HIKES FOR WILDFLOWERS

BEST FOR REGULAR WORKOUTS

SCENIC HIKES

SCENIC HIKES *(continued)*

BEST TRAILS FOR RUNNERS

60 HIKES
WITHIN 60 MILES

SALT LAKE CITY

INCLUDING

OGDEN, PROVO,

AND THE UINTAS

INTRODUCTION

Welcome to *60 Hikes within 60 Miles: Salt Lake City*! If you're new to hiking or even if you're a seasoned trailsmith, take a few minutes to read the following introduction. We explain how this book is organized and how to use it.

HOW TO USE THIS GUIDEBOOK

THE OVERVIEW MAP AND OVERVIEW-MAP KEY

Use the overview map on the inside front cover to assess the exact locations of each hike's primary trailhead. Each hike's number appears on the overview map, on the map key facing the overview map, and in the table of contents. As you flip through the book, a hike's full profile is easy to locate by watching for the hike number at the top of most right-hand pages. The book is organized by region, as indicated in the table of contents. A map legend that details the symbols found on trail maps appears on the inside back cover.

REGIONAL MAPS

The book is divided into regions, and prefacing each regional section is an overview map of that region. The regional map provides more detail than the overview map, bringing you closer to the hike.

TRAIL MAPS

Each hike contains a detailed map that shows the trailhead, the route, significant features, facilities, and topographic landmarks such as creeks, overlooks, and peaks. The author gathered map data by carrying a Garmin eTrex Legend GPS unit while hiking. This data was downloaded into DeLorme's Topo USA digital mapping program and processed by expert cartographers to produce the highly accurate maps found in this book. Each trailhead's GPS coordinates are included with each profile (see next page).

In addition to using a GPS, the author measured most trails with a measuring wheel to provide accurate distance measurements. One benefit of a measuring wheel it that it achieves greater accuracy than a GPS on steep trails with short switchbacks or in deep canyons where a satellite signal is not always obtainable.

ELEVATION PROFILES

Corresponding directly to the trail map, each hike contains a detailed elevation profile. The elevation profile provides a quick look at the trail from the side, enabling you to visualize how the trail rises and falls. Key points along the way are labeled. Note the number of feet between each tick mark on the vertical axis (the height scale). To avoid making flat hikes look steep and steep hikes appear flat, height scales are used throughout the book to provide an accurate image of the hike's climbing difficulty.

GPS TRAILHEAD COORDINATES

To collect accurate map data, each trail was hiked with a handheld GPS unit. Data collected was then downloaded and plotted onto a digital USGS topo map. In addition to rendering a highly specific trail outline, this book also includes the GPS coordinates for each trailhead in two formats: latitude–longitude and UTM. Latitude/longitude coordinates tell you where you are by locating a point west (latitude) of the 0° meridian line that passes through Greenwich, England, and north or south of the 0° (longitude) line that belts the Earth, aka the equator.

Topographic maps show latitude–longitude as well as UTM grid lines. Known as UTM coordinates, the numbers index a specific point using a grid method. The survey datum used to arrive at the coordinates in this book is WGS84 (versus NAD27 or WGS83). For readers who own a GPS unit, whether handheld or onboard a vehicle, the latitude–longitude or UTM coordinates provided on the first page of each hike may be entered into the GPS unit. Just make sure your GPS unit is set to navigate using WGS84 datum. Now you can navigate directly to the trailhead.

Most trailheads begin in parking areas and can be reached by car, but some hikes still require a short walk to reach the trailhead from a parking area. In those cases a handheld unit is necessary to continue the GPS navigation process. That said, readers can easily access all trailheads in this book by using the directions given, the overview map, and the trail map, which shows at least one major road leading into the area. But for those who enjoy using the latest GPS technology to navigate, the necessary data has been provided. A brief explanation of the UTM coordinates from Ben Lomond (Hike 1, page 16) follows.

UTM Zone	**12T**
Easting	**0424749**
Northing	**4574693**

The UTM zone number 12 refers to one of the 60 vertical zones of the Universal Transverse Mercator (UTM) projection. Each zone is 6 degrees wide. The UTM zone letter T refers to one of the 20 horizontal zones that span from 80 degrees south to

84 degrees north. The easting number **0424749** indicates in meters how far east or west a point is from the central meridian of the zone. Increasing easting coordinates on a topo map or on your GPS screen indicate that you are moving east; decreasing easting coordinates indicate you are moving west. The northing number **4574693** references in meters how far you are from the equator. Above and below the equator, increasing northing coordinates indicate you are traveling north; decreasing northing coordinates indicate you are traveling south. To learn more about how to enhance your outdoor experiences with GPS technology, refer to *GPS Outdoors: A Practical Guide for Outdoor Enthusiasts* (Menasha Ridge Press).

HIKE DESCRIPTIONS

Each hike contains seven key items: an "In Brief" description of the trail, a Key At-a-Glance Information box, directions to the trail, trailhead coordinates, a trail map, an elevation profile, and a trail description; the majority of hikes also include recommended nearby activities. Combined, the maps and information provide a clear method to assess each trail from the comfort of your favorite reading chair.

IN BRIEF

A "taste of the trail." Think of this section as a snapshot focused on the historical landmarks, beautiful vistas, and other sights you may encounter on the hike.

KEY AT-A-GLANCE INFORMATION

The information in the Key At-a-Glance boxes (and, in some cases, following the main trail description) gives you a quick idea of the statistics and specifics of each hike.

LENGTH The length of the trail from start to finish (total distance traveled). There may be options to shorten or extend the hikes, but the mileage corresponds to the described hike. Consult the hike description to help decide how to customize the hike for your ability or time constraints.

ELEVATION GAIN The difference in feet of elevation from the lowest point on the trail to the highest point. For most hikes in the mountains, this will be from the trailhead (lowest point) to the summit, lake, or waterfall destination.

CONFIGURATION A description of what the trail might look like from overhead. Trails can be loops, out-and-backs (trails on which one enters and leaves along the same path), one-ways, or include optional spurs.

DIFFICULTY The degree of effort an "average" hiker should expect on a given hike. For simplicity, the trails are rated as "easy," "moderate," or "difficult."

SCENERY A short summary of the attractions offered by the hike and what to expect in terms of plant life, wildlife, natural wonders, and historic features.

EXPOSURE A quick check of how much sun you can expect on your shoulders during the hike.

TRAFFIC Indicates how busy the trail might be on an average day. Trail traffic, of course, varies from day to day and season to season. Weekend days typically see the most visitors.

TRAIL SURFACE Indicates whether the trail surface is paved, rocky, gravel, dirt, boardwalk, or a mixture of elements.

HIKING TIME The length of time it takes to hike the trail. A slow but steady hiker will average 2 to 3 miles an hour, depending on the terrain.

WATER REQUIREMENTS Indicates a reasonable amount of water to be carried by each hiker. This amount can vary based on the daytime temperature and the availability of drinking water on the trail. Nearby sources of water that can be purified are also indicated.

SEASON Identifies the best time of year to hike the trail, taking into consideration trailhead access, trail conditions, and weather. An early spring snowmelt or an early fall snowstorm is always a possibility and could affect these suggestions somewhat.

ACCESS A notation of any fees or permits that may be needed to access the trail or park at the trailhead.

Mill Creek Canyon is a fee area in cooperation with Salt Lake County, requiring a charge of $2.25 per vehicle as you leave the canyon. If you plan to visit the canyon frequently each year, it is worth buying the $25 annual pass.

American Fork Canyon and the Alpine Loop Scenic Backway in Utah County are part of the Recreation Fee Demonstration and require a fee paid at the entrance stations. A 1- to 3-day pass is $3, a 14-day pass is $10, and an annual pass is $25. Golden Eagle, Golden Age, and Golden Access passports are honored. Cave-tour fees at Timpanogos Caves National Monument are $7 per adult, $5 for juniors (ages 6 to 15), and $3 for children (ages 3 to 5), and are separate from the recreation fee paid to enter the canyon.

The Mirror Lake Scenic Highway in the Uintas is also a Recreation Fee Demonstration area for trail and campground users. Passes may be purchased at the Kamas Ranger Station or at several self-service fee stations along the highway. A daily pass is $3, a weekly pass is $6, and an annual pass is $25. Golden Eagle, Golden Age, and Golden Access passports are honored.

Antelope Island State Park is the home of Frary Peak (Hike 9) and many other great day hikes. The park admission fee is $9 per vehicle or $6 for walk-ins and cyclists.

The hiking trails accessed through Red Butte Garden (Hike 14) require a paid admission of $6 for adults and $4 for children and seniors.

MAPS Here you'll find a list of maps that show the topography of the trail, including USGS topo quads (7.5-minute series) and Trails Illustrated maps.

FACILITIES What to expect in terms of restrooms and water at the trailhead or nearby.

DOGS You'll want to know the applicable regulations for each hike. Dogs are not permitted in some protected watershed canyons, such as Big Cottonwood and Little Cottonwood. Mill Creek Canyon requires that dogs be leashed on even-numbered days.

SPECIAL COMMENTS These include insider info or special considerations about the trail, access, warnings, or ideas to enhance your hiking experience.

DIRECTIONS

Used in conjunction with the overview map, the driving directions will help you locate each trailhead from nearby interstate highway exits. Once you arrive at the trailhead, park only in designated areas.

GPS TRAILHEAD COORDINATES

The trailhead coordinates can be used in addition to the driving directions if you enter the coordinates into your GPS unit before you set out.

DESCRIPTION

The trail description is the heart of each hike. Here, the authors provide a summary of the trail's essence and highlight any special traits the hike has to offer. The route is clearly outlined, including landmarks, side trips, and possible alternate routes along the way. Ultimately, the hike description will help you choose which hikes are best for you.

NEARBY ACTIVITIES

Look here for information on nearby activities or points of interest. This includes parks, short interpretive trails, hidden waterfalls near the highway, historical sites, museums, and restaurants.

WEATHER

Salt Lake City delivers a wide range of temperatures and climatic conditions in its dry four-season climate. While weather is often the single most important factor in deciding when to enjoy any given hike, many of the 60 hikes can be enjoyed year-round. However, most of the hikes in this guide are located within the Wasatch and Uinta mountain ranges, and in many cases trailheads are not accessible, trails are covered with snow, and avalanche dangers are present.

Because many of the hikes in the Wasatch and the Uintas are at high elevation, you'll find that in their short season, some of these hikes offer a great way to beat the heat on the valley floor. As a rule of thumb, the temperature decreases about three to five degrees with every 1,000 feet of elevation gained.

Average Temperature **Years on Record: 48**

	Year	Jan	Feb	Mar	Apr	May	Jun
°F	52	28	34	42	50	59	69

		Jul	Aug	Sep	Oct	Nov	Dec
°F		78	76	66	53	40	30

Average High Temperature **Years on Record: 48**

	Year	Jan	Feb	Mar	Apr	May	Jun
°F	64	37	43	52	62	72	83

		Jul	Aug	Sep	Oct	Nov	Dec
°F		92	90	80	66	50	39

Average Low Temperature **Years on Record: 48**

	Year	Jan	Feb	Mar	Apr	May	Jun
°F	40	20	24	31	38	46	54

		Jul	Aug	Sep	Oct	Nov	Dec
°F		62	61	51	40	30	22

Average Precipitation **Years on Record: 48**

	Year	Jan	Feb	Mar	Apr	May	Jun
in.	15.6	1.3	1.2	1.8	2	1.8	0.9

		Jul	Aug	Sep	Oct	Nov	Dec
in.		0.7	0.8	1.1	1.3	1.3	1.3

Average Snowfall **Years on Record: 65**

	Year	Jan	Feb	Mar	Apr	May	Jun
in.	57.9	13.5	9.4	9.4	5	0.6	–

		Jul	Aug	Sep	Oct	Nov	Dec
in.		–	–	0.1	1.3	6.6	12

WATER

How much is enough? Well, one simple physiological fact should convince you to err on the side of excess when deciding how much water to pack: a hiker working hard in 90-degree heat needs approximately 10 quarts of fluid per day. That's 2.5 gallons—12 large water bottles or 16 small ones. In other words, pack along one or two bottles even for short hikes.

Some hikers and backpackers hit the trail prepared to purify water found along the route. This method, while less dangerous than drinking it untreated, comes with risks. Purifiers with ceramic filters are the safest. Many hikers pack along the slightly distasteful tetraglycine–hydroperiodide tablets to debug water (sold under the names Potable Aqua, Coughlan's, and others).

Probably the most common waterborne "bug" that hikers face is *Giardia lamblia,* which may not hit until one to four weeks after ingestion. Common symptoms include diarrhea, abdominal pain, bloating, cramping, nausea, and vomiting. Other parasites to worry about include *E. coli* and *Cryptosporidium,* both of which are harder to kill than giardia.

For most people, the pleasures of hiking make carrying water a relatively minor price to pay to remain healthy. If you're tempted to drink "found water," do so only if you understand the risks involved. Better yet, hydrate prior to your hike, carry (and drink) six ounces of water for every mile you plan to hike, and hydrate after the hike.

CLOTHING

For most hikes in the summer season, your choice of trail clothing can vary widely and is really more a matter of personal preference. Shorts or long pants? Long-sleeve or short-sleeve shirt? Those are probably decisions you'll make the morning of the hike without much thought. For longer, more strenuous hikes, you may want to consider synthetic moisture-wicking fabric instead of the trusty cotton T-shirt that retains moisture and can even lead to hypothermia if the temperature drops quickly. It's a good idea to pack a lightweight fleece or an extra outer layer for higher elevations or in case there is a surprise drop in temperature.

When it comes to footwear, comfort and personal preference should be your guide. Since these are all day hikes and don't require a heavy pack, you may find that a lightweight trail shoe is your best bet. Tennis shoes may be sufficient for paved trails and short hikes of less than 3 miles. For longer hikes and those involving steep, rocky terrain, you'll want to consider a hiking shoe that has a thicker, firmer sole that offers more support.

THE TEN ESSENTIALS

One of the first rules of hiking is to be prepared for anything. The simplest way to be prepared is to carry the "Ten Essentials." In addition to carrying the items listed below, you need to know how to use them, especially navigation items. Always consider worst-case scenarios such as getting lost, hiking back in the dark, broken gear (for example, a broken hip strap on your pack or a water filter that gets plugged), twisting an ankle, or a brutal thunderstorm. The items listed below don't cost a lot of money, don't take up much room in a pack, and don't weigh much, but they might just save your life.

Water: durable bottles and water treatment, like iodine or a filter
Map: preferably a topo map and a trail map with a route description
Compass: a high-quality compass
First-aid kit: a good-quality kit including first-aid instructions
Knife: a multitool device with pliers is best
Light: flashlight or headlamp with extra bulbs and batteries
Fire: windproof matches or lighter and fire starter
Extra food: you should always have food in your pack when you've finished hiking
Extra clothes: rain protection, warm layers, gloves, warm hat
Sun protection: sunglasses, lip balm, sunblock, sun hat

FIRST-AID KIT

A typical first-aid kit may contain more items than you think necessary. These are just the basics. Prepackaged kits in waterproof bags (Atwater Carey and Adventure Medical make a variety of kits) are available. Even though quite a few items are listed here, they pack down into a small space:

Ace bandages or Spenco joint wraps
Antibiotic ointment (Neosporin or the generic equivalent)
Aspirin or acetaminophen
Band-Aids
Benadryl or the generic equivalent, diphenhydramine (in case of allergic reactions)
Butterfly-closure bandages
Epinephrine in a prefilled syringe (for people known to have severe allergic reactions to such things as bee stings)
Gauze (one roll)
Gauze compress pads (a half-dozen 4- x 4-inch pads)
Hydrogen peroxide or iodine
Insect repellent
Matches or pocket lighter
Moleskin/Spenco "Second Skin"
Sunscreen
Whistle (it's more effective in signaling rescuers than your voice)

HIKING WITH CHILDREN

No one is too young for a hike in the outdoors. Be mindful, though. Flat, short, and shaded trails are best with an infant. Toddlers who have not quite mastered walking can still tag along, riding on an adult's back in a child carrier. Use common sense to judge a child's capacity to hike a particular trail, and be ready for the child to tire quickly and need to be carried.

When packing for the hike, remember the child's needs as well as your own. Make sure children are adequately clothed for the weather, have proper shoes, and are protected from the sun with sunscreen. Kids dehydrate quickly, so make sure you have plenty of fluids for everyone. To assist an adult with determining which trails are suitable for children, a list of hike recommendations for children is provided on pages xxiv–xxv.

GENERAL SAFETY

To some potential hikers, mountain peaks, canyons, and wilderness areas seem inordinately perilous. It is the fear of the unknown that causes this anxiety. No doubt, potentially dangerous situations can occur outdoors, but if you use sound judgment and prepare yourself before hitting the trail, you'll be much safer in the backcountry than in most urban areas. Look at a backcountry hike as a fascinating chance to discover the unknown rather than a chance for potential disaster. Here are a few tips to make your trip safer and easier.

- **Always carry food and water, whether you plan to go overnight or not. Food will give you energy, help keep you warm, and sustain you in an emergency situation until help arrives. You never know if you will have a stream nearby when you become thirsty. Bring potable water or treat water before drinking it from a stream. Boil or filter all found water before drinking it.**
- **Stay on designated trails. Most hikers get lost when they leave the path. Even on the most clearly marked trails, there is usually a point where you have to stop and consider which direction to head. If you become disoriented, don't panic. As soon as you think you may be off-track, stop, assess your current direction, and then retrace your steps back to the point where you went awry. Using map, compass, this book, and keeping in mind what you have passed thus far, reorient yourself, and trust your judgment on which way to continue. If you become absolutely unsure of how to continue, return to your vehicle the way you came in. Should you become completely lost and have no idea how to return to the trailhead, remaining in place along the trail and waiting for help is most often the best option for adults and always the best option for children.**
- **Be especially careful when crossing streams. Whether you are fording the stream or crossing on a log, make every step count. If you have any doubt about maintaining your balance on a foot log, ford the stream instead. When fording a stream, use a trekking pole or stout stick for balance and face upstream as you cross. If a stream seems too deep to ford, turn back. Whatever is on the other side is not worth risking your life.**

- **Be careful at overlooks. While these areas may provide spectacular views, they are potentially hazardous. Stay back from the edge of outcrops and be absolutely sure of your footing; a misstep can mean a nasty and possibly fatal fall.**
- **Standing dead trees and storm-damaged living trees pose a hazard to hikers and tent campers. These trees may have loose or broken limbs that could fall at any time. When choosing a spot to rest or camp, look up.**
- **Know the symptoms of hypothermia. Shivering and forgetfulness are the two most common indicators of this insipid killer. Hypothermia can occur at any elevation, even in the summer, especially when the hiker is wearing lightweight cotton clothing. If symptoms arise, get the victim shelter, hot liquids, and dry clothes or a dry sleeping bag.**
- **Take along your brain. A cool, calculating mind is the single most important piece of equipment you'll ever need on the trail. Think before you act. Watch your step. Plan ahead. Avoiding accidents before they happen is the best recipe for a rewarding and relaxing hike.**

NATURAL HAZARDS

The two most deadly natural hazards in Utah are lightning and avalanche. The best way, and really the only way, to protect yourself from these hazards is to avoid the areas and conditions where they are most likely to occur. Although many of the chapters in this book identify areas that are particularly avalanche or lightning prone, you should always observe posted warnings, check weather advisories, watch local conditions, and use a healthy dose of common sense before venturing into the backcountry.

LIGHTNING

Most summer hikes in the Wasatch take place in favorable weather under cloud-free skies; still, afternoon thunderstorms can always roll in. If you see a storm approaching, or if you can see lightning or hear thunder, the risk is already present. Louder or more frequent thunder means lightning activity is approaching, increasing the risk for lightning injury or death. If the time delay between seeing the lightning and hearing the thunder is less than 30 seconds, you are in danger.

No place is absolutely safe from the threat of lightning, but some places are safer than others. Seek covered shelter as quickly as possible. Avoid being on, or near, ridgelines, mountain peaks, exposed slopes, open fields, isolated trees, communications towers, ski-lift supports, metal fences, or water.

AVALANCHE

While climbers, backcountry skiers, and snowmobilers are the most likely avalanche victims in Utah, snowshoers and recreational hikers can also be at risk. Avalanches can occur on any slope given the right snow conditions. Hikers should observe avalanche warnings and check local avalanche advisory services before entering the backcountry in wintertime. Avalanches are most likely to occur in areas where avalanches have occurred in the past, particularly near steep, barren slopes and in the presence of avalanche-scarred terrain.

MOUNTAIN LIONS

As more people get into the outdoors and encroach upon wildlife habitat, human encounters with mountain lions, or cougars, are bound to increase. Although sightings of this elusive species are extremely rare, mountain lions live throughout the Wasatch and Uinta mountains. Mountain lions are not likely to attack an adult human, but in the event of an encounter with one, give it a chance to escape before advancing. You can often scare it off by making yourself as big and loud as you can. Try growling, baring your teeth, raising your arms, or fanning out your jacket. Never crouch down or turn your back on the animal. Don't run away, since that can trigger the cat's chasing instincts. Lastly, if there are young children nearby, keep them close and even put one on your shoulders if you can.

BEARS

Black bears, the only bear species found in Utah, are relatively common in mountain forests. Although they are more likely to be found near campgrounds in search of food, they can also be seen on backcountry trails. Generally, they avoid contact with people, and will usually run away. If you come upon a bear by surprise, avoid cornering the animal or coming between a cub and its mother. Back away slowly, and make loud noises to scare it away.

MOOSE

Sightings of moose in Wasatch meadows and canyon drainages are common and generally quite enjoyable. It's a good time to pull out your camera. While moose aren't aggressive, they can charge when they perceive a threat. Do not approach the moose or make any aggressive movements that could make it see you as a threat.

SNAKES

Rattlesnakes are most common on dry, south-facing foothill slopes, where they enjoy sunning themselves on the trail. It's not uncommon to nearly step on the snake before you see it. Rattlesnakes aren't aggressive and will usually slither off if given a chance. If the snake won't move out of your way as you approach, you can usually get it to move by tossing a rock or stick in its direction.

MOSQUITOES

Mosquitoes are not a significant problem for hikers on sunlit Wasatch mountain trails, but cases of West Nile virus have been reported in Utah. Since West Nile virus is primarily spread by the bite of an infected mosquito, you should consider using a mosquito repellent with DEET or Picaridin, especially from dusk to dawn, when mosquitoes are most active.

TOPOGRAPHIC MAPS

The maps in this book have been produced with great care and, used with the hiking directions, will direct you to the trail and help you stay on course. However, you will find superior detail and valuable information in the United States Geological Survey's 7.5-minute series topographic maps. Topo maps are available online in many locations, including a well-known free service at **terraserver.microsoft.com.** Another free service with fast click-and-drag browsing is located at **www.topofinder.com.** You can view and print topos of the entire United States from these Web sites, and view aerial photographs of the same area at terraserver. Several online services such as **www.trails.com** charge annual fees for additional features such as shaded relief, which makes the topography stand out more. If you expect to print out many topo maps each year, it might be worth paying for shaded-relief topo maps. The downside to USGS topos is that many of them are outdated, having been created 20 to 30 years ago. But they still provide excellent topographic detail.

Digital topographic-map programs such as DeLorme's Topo USA enable you to review topo maps of the entire United States on your PC. You can also gather your own GPS data while hiking with a GPS unit, then download the data onto the software and plot your own hikes.

If you're new to hiking, you might be wondering, "What's a topographic map?" In short, a topo indicates not only linear distance but elevation as well, using contour lines. Contour lines spread across the map like dozens of intricate spider webs. Each line represents a particular elevation, and at the base of each topo, a contour's interval designation is given. If the contour interval is 20 feet, then the distance between each contour line is 20 feet. Follow five contour lines up on the same map, and the elevation has increased by 100 feet.

Let's assume that the 7.5-minute series topo reads "Contour Interval 40 feet," that the short trail we'll be hiking is two inches in length on the map, and that it crosses five contour lines from beginning to end. What do we know? Well, because the linear scale of this series is 2,000 feet to the inch (roughly two and three-quarters inches representing 1 mile), we know our trail is approximately four-fifths of a mile long (2 inches are 4,000 feet). But we also know we'll be climbing or descending 200 vertical feet (five contour lines are 40 feet each) over that distance. And the elevation designations written on occasional contour lines will tell us if we're heading up or down.

In addition to the outdoor shops listed in the Appendix, you'll find topos at major universities and some public libraries, where you might try photocopying the ones you need to avoid the cost of buying them. But if you want your own and can't find them locally, visit the United States Geological Survey Web site at **topomaps.usgs.gov.**

TRAIL ETIQUETTE

Whether you're on a city, county, state, or national park trail, always remember that great care and resources (from nature as well as from your tax dollars) have gone into creating these trails. Treat the trail, wildlife, and fellow hikers with respect.

- **Hike on open trails only. Respect trail and road closures (ask if not sure), avoid possible trespassing on private land, and obtain all permits and authorization as required. Also, leave gates as you found them or as marked.**
- **Leave only footprints. Be sensitive to the ground beneath you. This also means staying on the existing trail and not blazing any new trails. Be sure to pack out what you pack in. No one likes to see the trash someone else has left behind.**
- **Never spook animals. An unannounced approach, a sudden movement, or a loud noise startles most animals. A surprised animal can be dangerous to you, to others, and to themselves. Give them plenty of space.**
- **Plan ahead. Know your equipment, your ability, and the area in which you are hiking—and prepare accordingly. Be self-sufficient at all times; carry necessary supplies for changes in weather or other conditions. A well-executed trip is a satisfaction to you and to others.**
- **Be courteous to other hikers, bikers, equestrians, and others you encounter on the trails.**

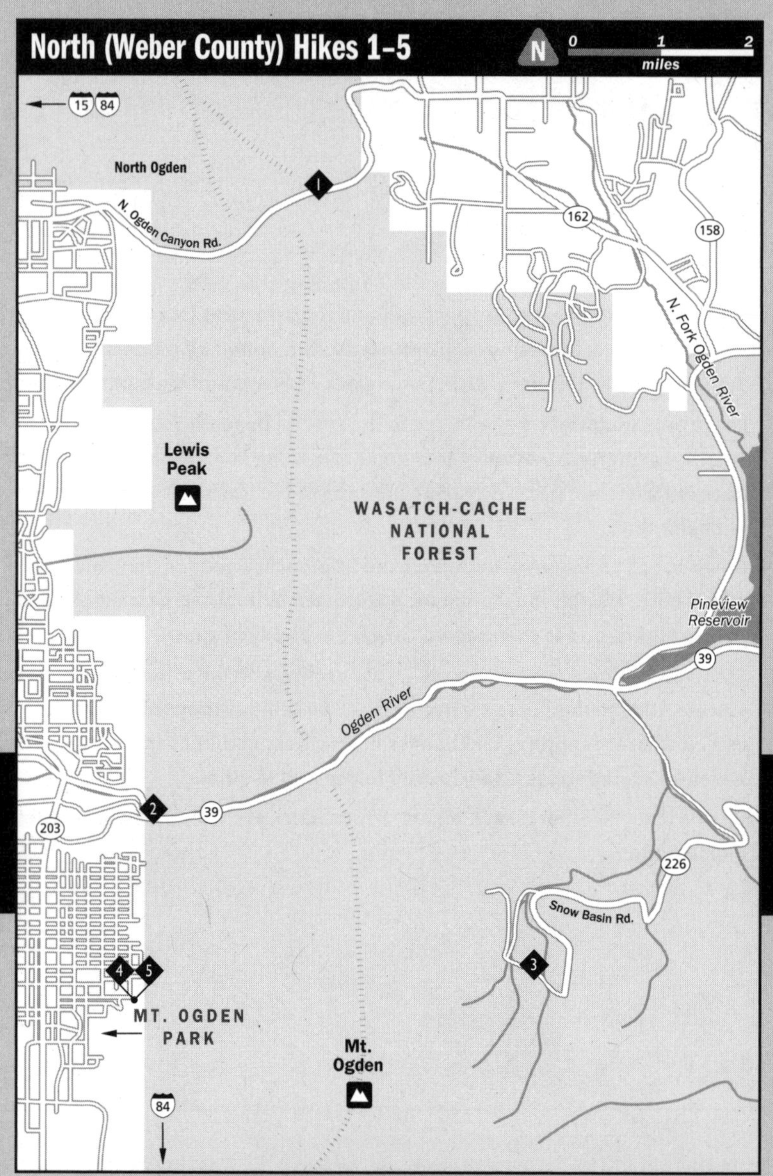
North (Weber County) Hikes 1–5
N
0
1
2
miles
15
84
North Ogden
N. Ogden Canyon Rd.
162
158
N. Fork Ogden River
Lewis Peak
WASATCH-CACHE NATIONAL FOREST
Pineview Reservoir
39
Ogden River
203
39
226
Snow Basin Rd.
MT. OGDEN PARK
Mt. Ogden
84

NORTH (WEBER COUNTY)

01 BEN LOMOND

KEY AT-A-GLANCE INFORMATION

LENGTH: 16 miles round-trip

ELEVATION GAIN: 3,532 feet

ELEVATION AT TRAILHEAD: 6,180 feet

CONFIGURATION: Out-and-back

DIFFICULTY: Difficult

SCENERY: Views of Ogden Valley and Great Salt Lake along the ridgeline, with panoramic views from the summit

EXPOSURE: Partially shaded to saddle; unshaded from saddle to summit

TRAFFIC: Light

TRAIL SURFACE: Dirt with rock near the summit

HIKING TIME: 8–9 hours

WATER REQUIREMENTS: 2–3 liters. No water on or near the trail.

SEASON: Late spring through early fall

ACCESS: No fees for access or parking

MAPS: USGS North Ogden

FACILITIES: Restrooms at trailhead but no water.

DOGS: On leash

SPECIAL COMMENTS: This is a long, dry trail. Come prepared with adequate water, food, and sun protection.

IN BRIEF

Ben Lomond has the longest, most gentle gradient of any summit trail in the Wasatch. Along the way you're treated to continuous and commanding views in all directions, with a diverse range of vegetation and wildlife.

DESCRIPTION

The best known of the northern Wasatch peaks dominates the skyline over North Ogden. An early pioneer named the peak Ben Lomond because it reminded her of Ben Lomond, a mountain in her native Scotland. Years later, W. W. Hodkinson, who lived in Ogden as a young man, drew inspiration from Ben Lomond when he founded Paramount Pictures in 1914. Hodkinson designed the familiar logo of a towering snow-capped peak.

While several routes lead to the Ben Lomond summit, the North Skyline Trail (which is also a section of the Great Western Trail) offers a particularly scenic and varied ascent. Although the North Skyline Trail is a bit longer than the other trails that ascend from the east, it is well traveled, reliable, and offers a wider variety of views along the route, both to the east and west.

From the North Ogden Divide trailhead, cross North Ogden Canyon Road and start

GPS Trailhead Coordinates

UTM Zone (WGS84) 12T

Easting 0424749

Northing 4574693

Latitude N 41° 19' 14.2"

Longitude W 111° 53' 56.0"

Directions →

Take Interstate 15 north from Salt Lake City to 12th Street in Ogden (Exit 344). Go east on 12th Street for 2.3 miles to Washington Boulevard. Turn left on Washington Boulevard (US 89) and go north for 5.1 miles to 31st Street. Turn right on 31st Street and continue for 4.1 miles to the North Ogden Divide trailhead parking area on the right.

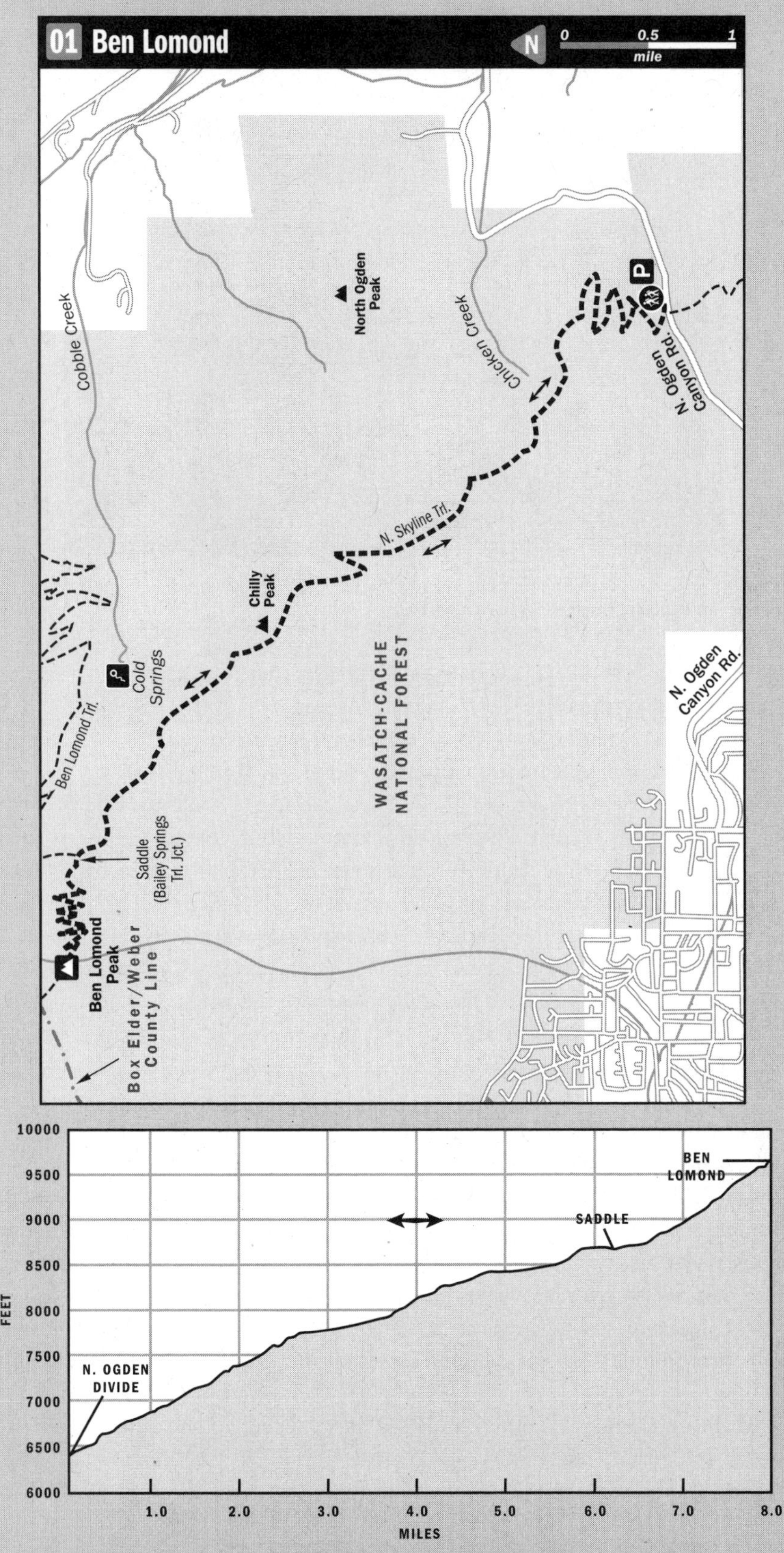

01 Ben Lomond
N
0
0.5
1
mile
Cobble Creek
North Ogden Peak
Chicken Creek
P
N. Ogden Canyon Rd.
N. Skyline Trl.
Chilly Peak
Cold Springs
Ben Lomond Trl.
WASATCH-CACHE NATIONAL FOREST
N. Ogden Canyon Rd.
Saddle (Bailey Springs Trl. Jct.)
Ben Lomond Peak
Box Elder/Weber County Line
10000
9500
9000
8500
8000
7500
7000
6500
6000
FEET
BEN LOMOND
SADDLE
N. OGDEN DIVIDE
1.0
2.0
3.0
4.0
5.0
6.0
7.0
8.0
MILES

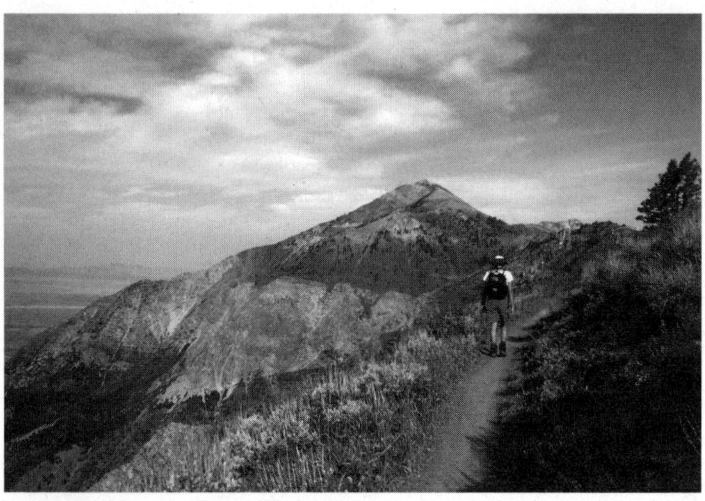

Ben Lomond's summit from the western ridge trail

your way up a series of 12 sweeping switchbacks that lead up the north side of the mountain over the course of 2.5 miles. As you ascend through a dense cover of Gambel oak, maple, and curly-leaf mountain mahogany, watch out for rattlesnakes that enjoy sunning themselves on the south-facing trail.

Beyond the switchbacks, you'll enter a long traverse along the ridge's eastern slope where aspens, bent by heavy snow accumulation, continually lean to the east. This section of trail leads through deer brush (a mountain shrub found throughout the West) and offers generous views of Ogden Valley to the east. Soon the trail enters mature stands of fir and spruce, which provide some shade. Along this ridge you'll have views stretching from Morgan County in the south to 9,979-foot Naomi Peak near the Idaho border in the north.

At 4.2 miles from the trailhead and an elevation of 8,240 feet, the trail crosses to the west side of the ridge and delivers your first view of the Ben Lomond summit to the northwest. The trail continues straight ahead in a northwest direction for another 2.3 miles, gaining just over 500 feet in elevation on slopes blanketed with deer brush and dotted with limber pine.

Arriving at the Bailey Springs Trail junction, commonly known as the saddle, you'll find a large wooden sign with a map showing other trails on the mountain, trail distances, and various points of interest. From this saddle the trail continues to the northwest with the summit in clear view. You're most likely to see mountain goats on rocky slopes at these higher elevations. Above the windswept saddle, krummholz limber pine and subalpine fir dot the grassy slopes, along with lupine.

In the remaining 1.5 miles and 900 vertical feet to the summit, the trail steepens somewhat, but never enough to become grueling. The final summit approach is accomplished with a well-crafted chain of 28 short switchbacks through outcroppings of quartzite, slate, and schist. The well-established trail will take you right to the summit without ever having to scramble, boulder-hop, or bushwhack.

Once on the 9,712-foot summit, the views stretch out in all directions, with Willard Bay and the Great Salt Lake being the dominant features to the west. Directly to your north is Willard Peak, which at 9,764 feet is the highest point in Weber County and a tad higher than Ben Lomond—a fact that comes as a surprise to many hikers. A straightforward traverse along a good trail to the north can lead you on to Willard Peak, adding several hours onto an already long day.

Ben Lomond is a classic northern Utah climb: thoroughly enjoyable, yet very different from the southern Wasatch peaks with their high-elevation trailheads and canyon approaches. On the long descent, come prepared with enough water to keep you hydrated. The afternoon sun beats down on the dry, unshaded, south-facing switchbacks that return you to the trailhead.

NEARBY ACTIVITIES

The Ogden Nature Center is a 152-acre wildlife sanctuary and education center located at 966 West 12th Street in Ogden. The land is home to mule deer, pheasants, fox, and migrating birds. More than 1.5 miles of walking trails make the sanctuary and ponds accessible. The visitor center features hands-on exhibits, an observation beehive, and The Nest gift shop, with nature-related gifts for all ages. For events and information, call the Ogden Nature Center at (801) 621-7595 or visit online at **www.ogdennaturecenter.org.**

02 OGDEN RIVER PARKWAY

KEY AT-A-GLANCE INFORMATION

LENGTH: 3.4 miles one-way (recommended portion, 2 miles one-way)
ELEVATION GAIN: –132 feet (recommended portion, –73 feet)
ELEVATION AT TRAILHEAD: 4,432 feet
CONFIGURATION: One-way or out-and-back
DIFFICULTY: Easy
SCENERY: River, parks, and mountain views
EXPOSURE: Mostly shaded
TRAFFIC: Moderate
TRAIL SURFACE: Asphalt
HIKING TIME: 1–2 hours
WATER REQUIREMENTS: 0.5 liters
SEASON: Year-round
ACCESS: Trail may be used from 1 hour before sunrise to 1 hour after sunset.
MAPS: USGS Ogden
FACILITIES: Restrooms, water, and other services are available at the trailhead and at various parks along the way.
DOGS: On leash
SPECIAL COMMENTS: No skateboarding, horses, or motorized vehicles are permitted on the parkway. Bicycle speed limit is 10 mph.

GPS Trailhead Coordinates

UTM Zone (WGS84) 12T
Easting 0422109
Northing 4565444
Latitude N 41° 14' 12.1"
Longitude W 111° 55' 46.4"

IN BRIEF

Ogden River emerges from Ogden Canyon, cuts through Ogden, and flows west toward the Great Salt Lake. Along the way, the Ogden River Parkway connects many of Ogden's most popular parks and recreational venues. The parkway currently extends 3.4 miles, but the most scenic and enjoyable section is the first 1.4 miles, from the mouth of Ogden Canyon to the Ogden Botanical Gardens.

DESCRIPTION

As it emerges from the mouth of Ogden Canyon, the Ogden River still thinks it's a mountain stream. It tumbles and careens off of large boulders, its banks lined with the quaking aspens and bigtooth maples common to mountain tributaries. But as it enters the city limits, the river becomes more urban. Its pace slows and the boulders give way to dirt banks. Towering cottonwoods—characteristic of desert streams—replace the aspens and maples. The Ogden River Parkway parallels the river and captures the transformation.

The best place to start a walk along the parkway is at the canyon mouth trailhead

Directions

Take I-15 north from Salt Lake City to UT 401/21st Street (Exit 343) in Ogden. Curve right and continue east for 3.2 miles to Harrison Boulevard (UT 203). Turn left on Harrison Boulevard and continue north for 0.8 miles to Canyon Road (UT 39). Turn right on Canyon Road and continue east toward the mouth of Ogden Canyon for 1 mile. At Valley Drive (1700 South) turn right, then enter the Rainbow Gardens parking lot to the left. The trailhead is across the street at the corner of Valley Drive and Park Boulevard (1900 East).

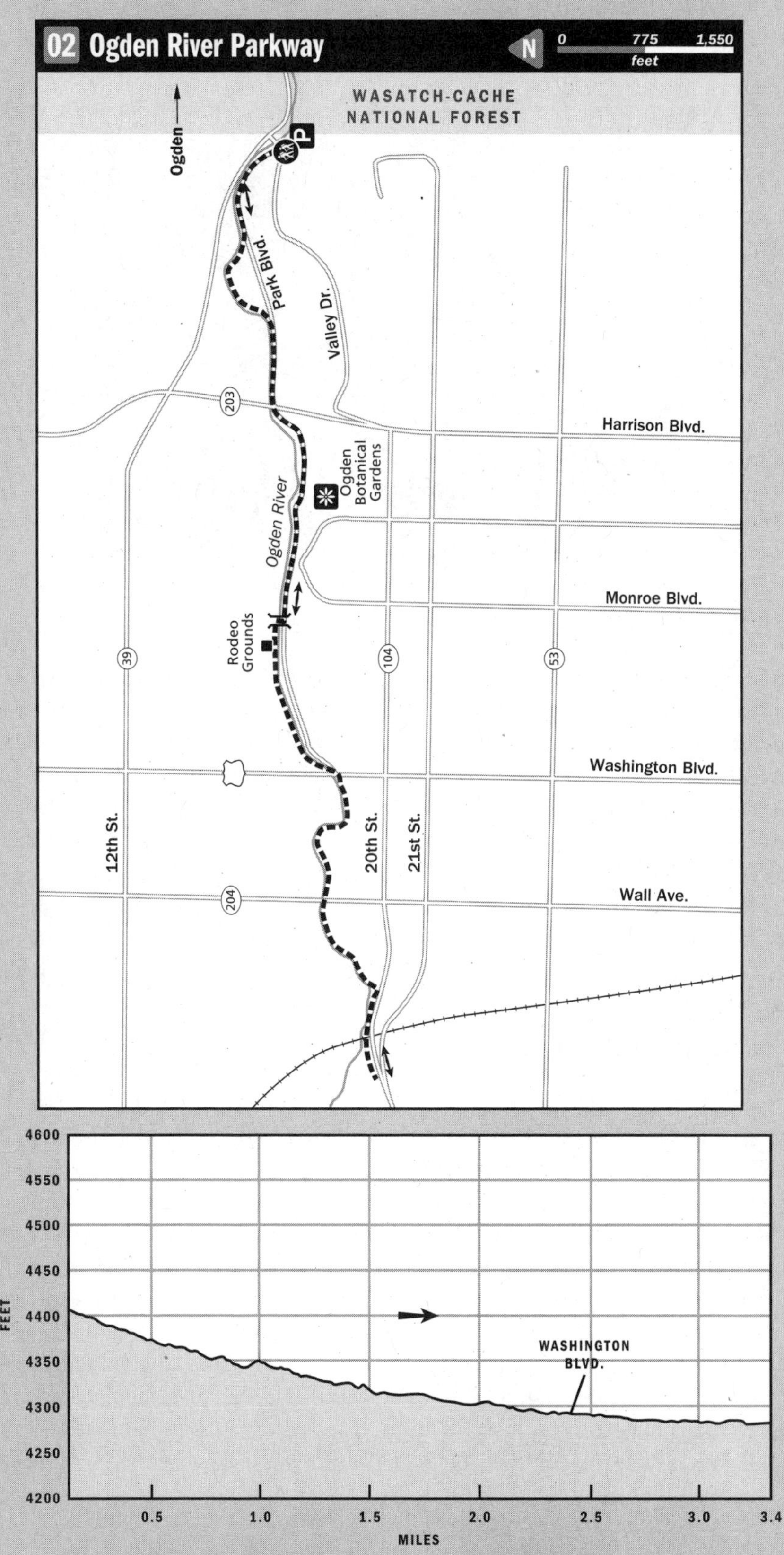
02 Ogden River Parkway
N
0
775
1,550
feet
WASATCH-CACHE
NATIONAL FOREST
Ogden
P
Park Blvd.
Valley Dr.
203
Harrison Blvd.
Ogden Botanical Gardens
Ogden River
Monroe Blvd.
Rodeo Grounds
39
104
53
Washington Blvd.
12th St.
20th St.
21st St.
204
Wall Ave.
4600
4550
4500
4450
4400
4350
4300
4250
4200
FEET
WASHINGTON BLVD.
0.5
1.0
1.5
2.0
2.5
3.0
3.4
MILES

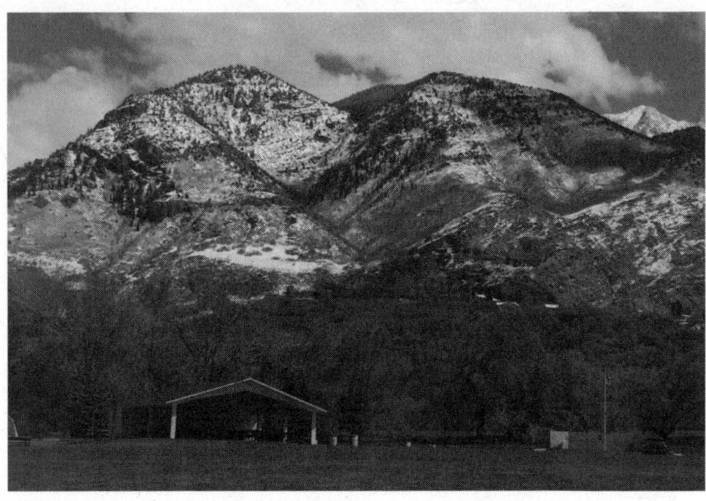

Mount Ogden from the Big Dee Sports Park

across the street from the Rainbow Gardens complex. Rainbow Gardens has been a traditional Ogden resort and recreation area since 1895. With no parking at the trailhead, you may want to park your car in the large parking lot at Rainbow Gardens, stop by the gift shop for water and trail snacks, and use the restrooms.

While it is officially designated as a multiuse trail, the Ogden River Parkway does not allow skateboards or horses. In addition, bicycles have a 10 mph speed limit, which encourages the more avid and aggressive cyclists to go elsewhere.

For the first 0.3 miles, the trail is pinned between the river on the right and Park Boulevard on the left. Then the street diverges from the trail, while the path continues to hug the river. The trail stays close to the river throughout, providing frequent opportunities to access the water.

The trail's upper portion maintains a playful, parklike recreational feel. For the first 2.5 miles, until the parkway crosses Washington Boulevard (US 89), the trail and river link a continuous series of parks, playgrounds, sports fields, George S. Eccles Dinosaur Park, a skateboard park, a rodeo arena, El Monte Golf Course, and Ogden Botanical Gardens.

Park benches every 100 feet or so provide plenty of opportunities to sit and enjoy the river or take a break for a picnic. The string of parks and recreation areas also offers easy access to drinking water and restrooms along the asphalt trail.

At 1 mile from the trailhead, the trail forks. Stay to the right on the river side. At 1.4 miles, you'll arrive at the beautiful Ogden Botanical Gardens. Here you'll have access to water, a public phone, restrooms, and a covered picnic area, making it an ideal spot to stop for a rest, enjoy the gardens, have a picnic, or start back to the trailhead.

If you decide to continue beyond the botanical gardens, the river slows and the parkway takes on an older, more run-down feeling. It passes junkyards,

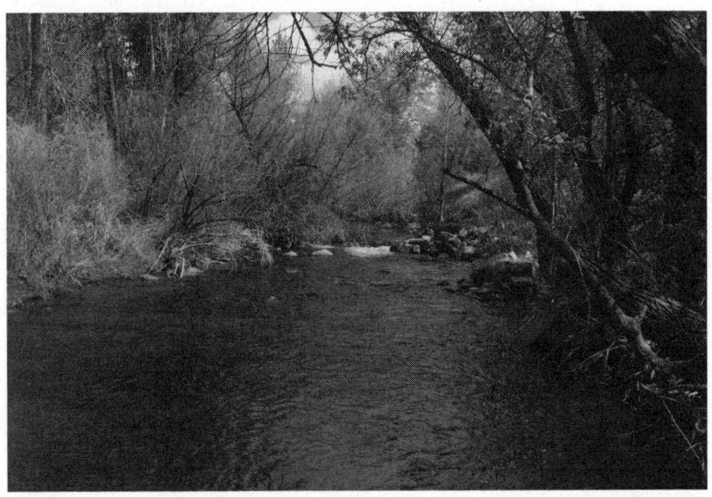

Ogden River

brickyards, old motels, and public storage units. Although the trail still stays close to the river, it's often bound by a fence on both sides. The trail finally crosses over a large railroad yard at the 20th Street Bridge, continues around the 21st Street Pond, and then joins the Weber River Parkway at the confluence of the Ogden and Weber rivers in a scenic, shaded setting. From the trailhead to the 20th Street Bridge is 3.4 miles one-way. But you'll find most of the trail's vibrancy and scenic enjoyment in the first 2 miles, making the Botanical Gardens a recommended turnaround point.

The Ogden River merges with the Weber River just east of I-15 and flows another 10 miles, flattening into a wetlands delta that empties into the Great Salt Lake. At the Ogden River Parkway trailhead, hikers can also easily connect with the Bonneville Shoreline Trail for access to some of Mount Ogden's most popular trails.

NEARBY ACTIVITIES

The Ogden Botanical Gardens are on the Ogden River Parkway 1.4 miles downriver (west) from the trailhead at 1750 Monroe Boulevard. An extension program of Utah State University, the gardens feature more than 11 acres of landscaped grounds. They offer classes, clinics, and facilities for weddings and large group events. The gardens are open to the public year-round. For additional information, call (801) 399-8080.

03 MOUNT OGDEN (via Snowbasin Gondola)

KEY AT-A-GLANCE INFORMATION

LENGTH: 3.1 miles round-trip
ELEVATION GAIN: 862 feet on foot, plus 2,310 feet by gondola
ELEVATION AT NEEDLES GONDOLA BASE: 6,415 feet
ELEVATION AT NEEDLES LODGE: 8,710 feet
CONFIGURATION: Out-and-back
DIFFICULTY: Easy
SCENERY: Glacial bowl, ridgeline, and great views on all sides
EXPOSURE: Fully exposed to sun
TRAFFIC: Moderate
TRAIL SURFACE: Dirt and rock
HIKING TIME: 2–2.5 hours
WATER REQUIREMENTS: 1 liter
SEASON: Summer
ACCESS: Hike lies on U.S. Forest Service land accessed through the Snowbasin Ski Resort. You must purchase a ticket to ride the gondola to the Needles Lodge.
MAPS: USGS Snowbasin, Ogden
FACILITIES: Restrooms, water, phones, equipment rentals, dining, and shopping are available at the base in Grizzly Center and at Earl's Lodge. Restrooms, water, and phones available at Needles Lodge.

See additional information at end of Description, page 27.

GPS Trailhead Coordinates

UTM Zone (WGS84) 12T
Easting 0428035
Northing 4563013
Latitude–Longitude: See page 27

IN BRIEF

You'll gain most of your elevation on the gondola ride, which tops out near a glacial cirque. From there, it's just 20 minutes to the ridgeline. A faint trail follows the ridgeline to the summit, offering sweeping views in all directions.

DESCRIPTION

As with many of Utah's ski resorts, Snowbasin has an appeal that extends far beyond ski season. Summer is a great time to play in the mountains and take advantage of a beautiful setting with available resort features. The same slopes that challenged skiers in the downhill and super-G events at the 2002 Olympic Winter Games test the skills of hikers and mountain bikers in the summer.

You can climb to Mount Ogden's summit from Beus Canyon or Malans Basin on its western slopes. You can also start at the base of the Snowbasin Resort and hike your way up slopes of Douglas-fir and white fir, although much of the route takes you along resort service roads (4 miles one-way from the resort to the summit).

Directions

Take I-15 north from Salt Lake City to US 89 (Exit 324) in Farmington, leading to I-84 east. Continue north on US 89 for 10.5 miles to I-84. Veer right onto I-84 going east toward Morgan. Go 4.4 miles to Mountain Green/Huntsville (Exit 92). At the off-ramp, turn left to cross under I-84, and turn right onto UT 167 toward Snowbasin. Continue on UT 167 for 1.5 miles as it turns left toward Huntsville. At 7 miles from the I-84 exit, turn left onto UT 226 and continue 3.3 miles to the main parking area. The Needles Gondola departs from the area in front of Grizzly Center.

03 Mt. Ogden (via Snowbasin Gondola)

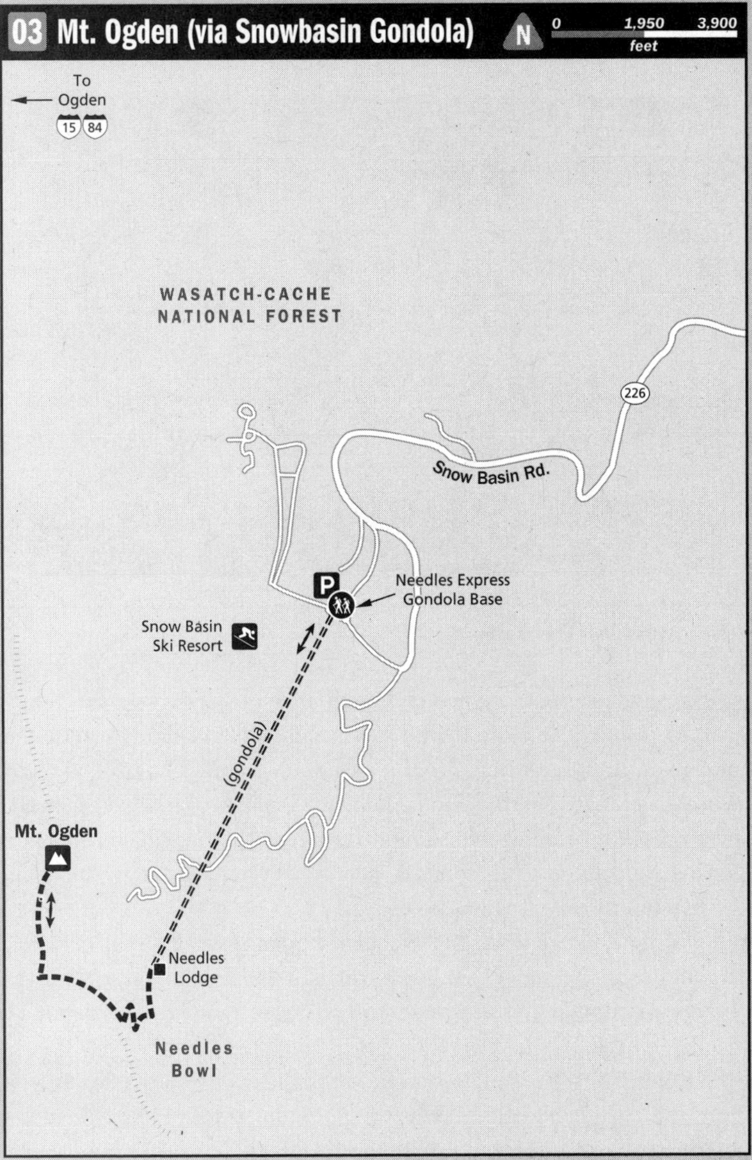

N
0
1,950
3,900
feet
To Ogden
15
84
WASATCH-CACHE NATIONAL FOREST
226
Snow Basin Rd.
P
Needles Express Gondola Base
Snow Basin Ski Resort
(gondola)
Mt. Ogden
Needles Lodge
Needles Bowl

9800
9600
9400
9200
9000
8800
8600
8400
8200
FEET
MT. OGDEN
0.25
0.5
0.75
1.0
1.25
1.5
MILES

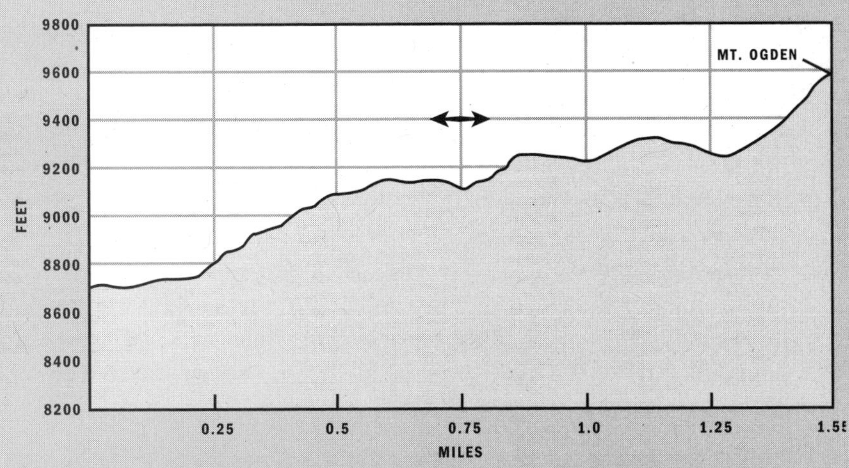

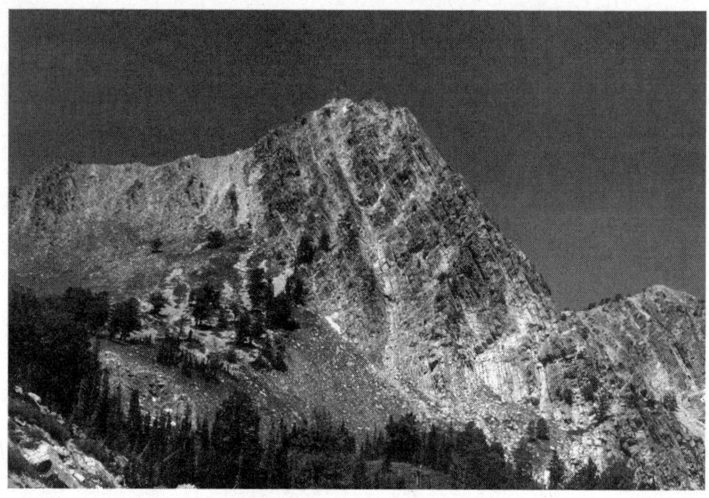

Mount Ogden viewed from Snowbasin

By riding the gondola to the Needles Lodge at 8,710 feet, you can hike to the summit and back in a little more than 2 hours and still have time for mountain biking, an afternoon round of disc golf, or a mountain picnic. The hike to the summit from the Needles Lodge is also a good choice for families or less experienced hikers who want to reach a recognizable summit on a trail that matches their experience levels. During the summer the gondola operates Friday, Saturday, and Sunday. If you hike up, you can ride down at no charge.

After the gondola reaches the Needles Lodge, exit the platform and then turn left, following the signs that lead you to the Needles Loop Trail and the Cirque Practice Loop to the southwest. You will take the Cirque Practice Loop to the right.

At 0.2 miles from the Needles Lodge on the Cirque Practice Loop, you'll see a sign pointing to the Needles Cirque trail to the ridge. Here you depart the mountain-bike trail for a footpath. Follow this faint trail as it switchbacks up this grassy cirque to the ridge. Deer frequently graze in this cirque, and a large patch of snow often remains until midsummer.

Once at the 9,062-foot saddle, you'll enjoy good views looking down Beus Canyon to your west, beyond Hill Air Force Base and stretching far beyond the Great Salt Lake. Mount Ogden lies along the ridgeline to the north and can be recognized by the communications towers on its summit. At this saddle, three unnamed peaks or knolls comprise the ridgeline between you and the Mount Ogden summit.

A faint trail follows a gentle contour along the western slopes of these first two knolls. Below, you'll see the Beus Canyon Trail winding its way up the dry slopes. Along this part of the trail, you'll be hiking on slopes covered with sage and dotted with an occasional limber pine or subalpine fir. Rattlesnakes frequently bask in the sun on this section of trail, so keep your eyes wide open.

After you round the second knoll, the faint trail has all but vanished. You have two options at this point: drop to a lower visible trail to the left of the third knoll, or ascend the sage slope, crossing over the saddle on the south of the third knoll and arriving at the saddle to the south of Mount Ogden from the east. Most hikers favor crossing the saddle at this point. As you descend the eastern slope of this third knoll, you arrive at a service road and a concrete bunker that shields some propane tanks.

From here, follow the steep service road that leads to the summit. At 0.2 miles along the service road, take a marked foot trail to your right that ascends the rocky slope to capture the summit. On the 9,572-foot summit you'll be just a few feet higher than the helipad to your west. You'll have great views in all directions, with some wonderful direct views of Ben Lomond peak to the north and Pineview Reservoir to the east.

ADDITIONAL AT-A-GLANCE INFORMATION

DOGS: Not permitted on gondola

SPECIAL COMMENTS: The Snowbasin Gondola achieves 2,310 feet of vertical lift in about 1.7 miles. In summer, the leisurely ride takes about 18 minutes, in ski season about 15 minutes.

NEEDLES GONDOLA BASE LATITUDE–LONGITUDE: N 41° 12' 56.7"; W 111° 51' 26.3"

NEEDLES LODGE LATITUDE–LONGITUDE: N 41° 11' 37.0"; W 111° 52' 26.4"

NEARBY ACTIVITIES

Snowbasin's summer activities include an 18-hole disc golf course and 25 miles of hiking and mountain-biking trails. Special events include moonlit gondola rides and star parties, summer concerts, guided mountain-bike rides and races, outdoor learning excursions, and award-winning dining. Call Snowbasin at (801) 620-1000 or visit **www.snowbasin.com** for events and schedules.

04 MALANS PEAK (via Taylor Canyon)

KEY AT-A-GLANCE INFORMATION

LENGTH: 5 miles round-trip
ELEVATION GAIN: 2,200 feet
ELEVATION AT TRAILHEAD: 4,780 feet
CONFIGURATION: Out-and-back
DIFFICULTY: Moderate
SCENERY: Deep canyon, natural spring, and exceptional views
EXPOSURE: Mostly shaded above the bench
TRAFFIC: Bench trails are busy, while the trail from Taylor Canyon to Malans Peak is uncrowded.
TRAIL SURFACE: Dirt and rock
HIKING TIME: 2–3 hours
WATER REQUIREMENTS: 1 liter (water from Malans Springs is safe at the source)
SEASON: Year-round. Negligible avalanche risk in lower Taylor Canyon.
ACCESS: Hikable year-round. No fee for parking or trailhead access. Trailhead parking lot and gates close at dusk.
MAPS: USGS Ogden
FACILITIES: No restrooms or water at trailhead
DOGS: On leash
SPECIAL COMMENTS: A deep canyon, a natural spring, and sweeping views reward those who climb Malans Peak.

GPS Trailhead Coordinates

UTM Zone (WGS84) 12T
Easting 0421827
Northing 4562632
Latitude N 41° 12' 38.65"
Longitude W 111° 55' 55.04"

IN BRIEF

In just under 2.5 miles, you go from city neighborhoods to brushy bench to a deep canyon and spring-fed creek. Ascending the steep slope, you're rewarded with one of the best views in the area.

DESCRIPTION

Some might claim that Malans Peak really isn't a peak at all, just a rocky outcropping in the foothills of Mount Ogden's western slopes. But the commanding views and the wooded trail leading up the northern slope make this a satisfying hike and a worthwhile destination. You can most easily reach Malans Peak from Taylor Canyon, the large canyon on the north side of Mount Ogden, starting at the east end of 27th Street in Ogden.

The peak was named for Bartholomew "Tim" Malan, a prominent Ogdenite. In 1892, Malan and his family carved a road up Taylor Canyon, where they built Malan Heights Hotel in the basin between Malans Peak and Mount Ogden. Malan hauled visitors to the hotel in a wagon with a trailing "poke stick" to keep it from rolling backward. Guests received panoramic

Directions

Take I-15 north from Salt Lake City to 31st Street in Ogden (Exit 341A). Go east on 31st Street for 1.1 mile to Washington Boulevard (US 89) and turn left. Go north 0.1 mile to 30th Street and turn right. Continue east on 30th Street for 1.3 miles to Tyler Avenue (1300 East) and turn left. Go north on Tyler Avenue for 0.1 mile to 29th Street and turn right. Continue east on 29th Street for 0.7 miles and turn right into the trailhead parking lot at the end of 29th Street. Look for the trailhead at the south end of the parking lot.

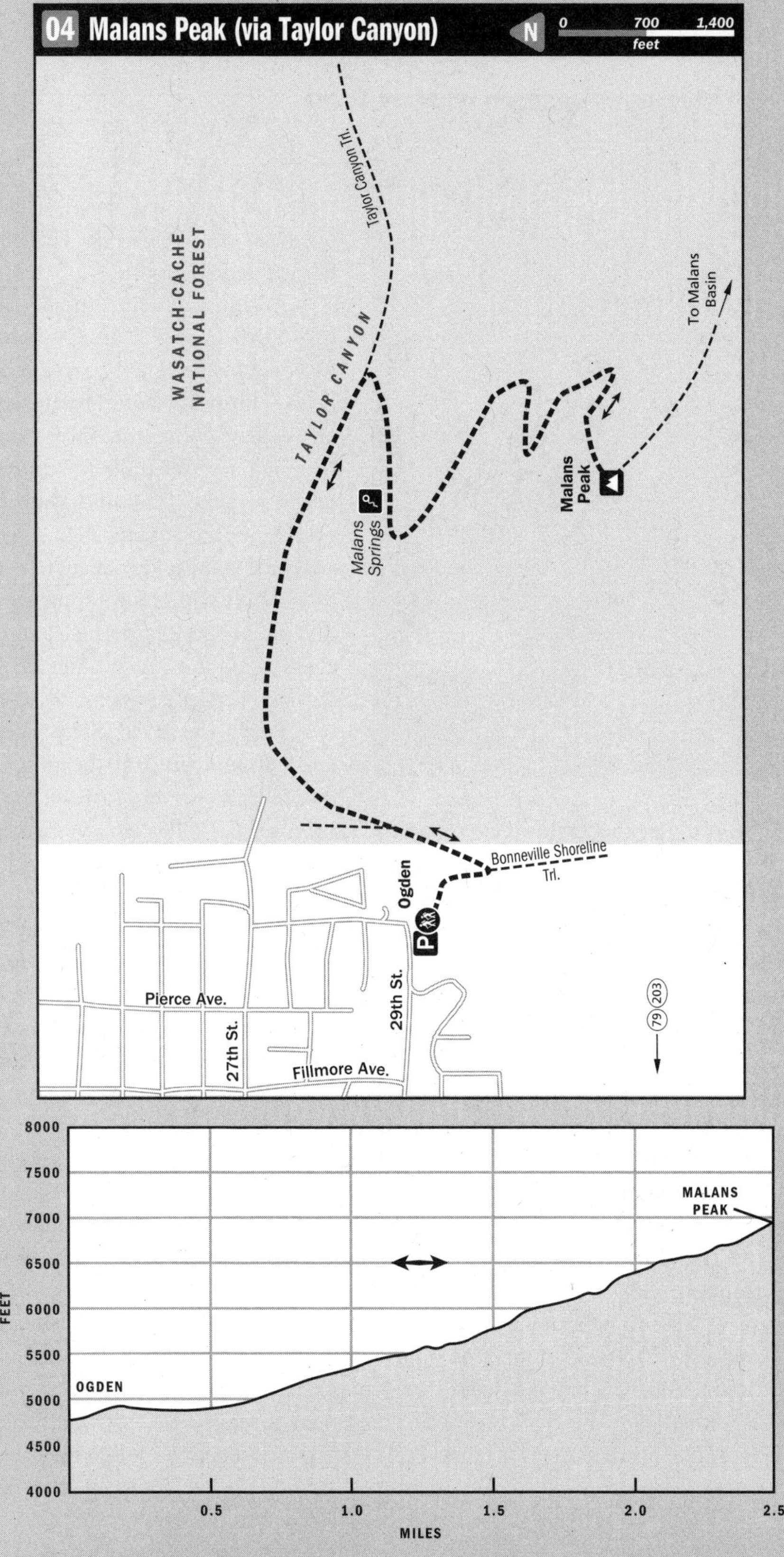
04 Malans Peak (via Taylor Canyon)
N
0
700
1,400
feet
Taylor Canyon Trl.
WASATCH-CACHE NATIONAL FOREST
To Malans Basin
TAYLOR CANYON
Malans Peak
Malans Springs
Bonneville Shoreline Trl.
Ogden
Pierce Ave.
27th St.
29th St.
Fillmore Ave.
79
203
8000
7500
7000
6500
6000
5500
5000
4500
4000
FEET
MALANS PEAK
OGDEN
0.5
1.0
1.5
2.0
2.5
MILES

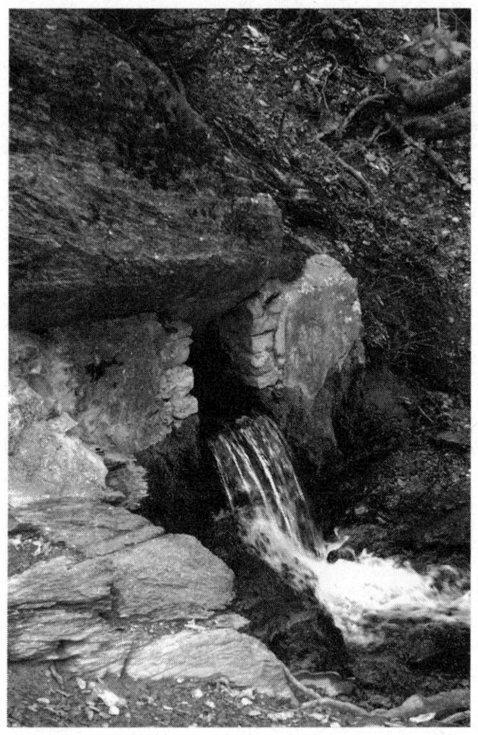

Malans Springs

views, lodging, and meals, including steak, for $6 a week. The hotel burned down in 1906.

Taylor Canyon, which leads to the Malans Peak Trail, is easily accessed from the 29th Street trailhead. This trailhead is also a popular access point for the Mount Ogden Exercise Trail, the Bonneville Shoreline Trail, and Waterfall Canyon (Hike 5, page 32). Joggers and mountain bikers regularly use this network of trails. While often dry and exposed to the sun, the paths along the bench quickly lead to deep, shaded canyons.

From the 29th Street trailhead, follow the trail heading up the hillside to the east with the signs pointing to the Taylor Canyon South Trail. After 0.2 miles, you've reached the Bonneville Shoreline Trail, gained a quick 100 feet of elevation, and been given a good overview of Ogden and the Great Salt Lake. At this junction, turn left and follow the sign leading to Taylor Canyon. After 100 yards along the wide Bonneville Shoreline Trail, the route to Taylor Canyon veers off and up to the right.

The trail leads through sage and Gambel oak into the mouth of Taylor Canyon and up a dry creekbed. At 0.6 miles from the trailhead, the path crosses a bridge to the north side of the creekbed. Soon after, you're engulfed in a beautiful canyon with conifers lining the side slopes. While you may see mountain bikers along the bench trails and even up into Taylor Canyon, few make it into this lush section of the canyon.

Continuing up the canyon, you'll notice that the dry creek suddenly runs with water, but only for about 0.2 miles along the canyon floor before going underground. After several minutes of creekside companionship, you'll see the creek descending from its source about 100 feet up the canyon wall. The creekbed is generally dry above the point where the spring enters.

About 100 feet beyond where the creek reaches the canyon floor, you'll cross a bridge over the dry creekbed. This begins a series of steep switchbacks leading up the north slope of Malans Peak. Along the ascent, you'll see the spring as it emerges from the wall of the canyon.

Continue your climb up the shaded steep slope of Gambel oak sprinkled with spruce and fir. Along the way, and in the bottom of the canyon, you may see deer and an occasional raccoon or porcupine.

At the rocky crest of Malans Peak the trees thin, opening up wide-angle views of the Great Salt Lake and peaks to the north and south. Looking back down the canyon slope, you've just ascended 1,400 vertical feet in about 1.2 miles, but the view makes every step worth it.

NEARBY ACTIVITIES

Ogden is a vibrant hub for year-round outdoor and indoor recreation. The Salomon Center (338 23rd Street; [801] 399-5862; **www.salomoncenter.com**) is a high-adventure downtown sports complex with a vertical wind tunnel that simulates freefall skydiving, an indoor surf wave, and a huge climbing wall. The center also features 32 bowling lanes, billiards, a 55,000-square-foot gym, arcades, bumper cars, and restaurants.

05 WATERFALL CANYON

KEY AT-A-GLANCE INFORMATION

LENGTH: 2.6 miles
ELEVATION GAIN: 1,492 feet
ELEVATION AT TRAILHEAD: 4,780 feet
CONFIGURATION: Out-and-back
DIFFICULTY: Moderate
SCENERY: Spectacular waterfall in a deep canyon
EXPOSURE: Mostly shaded above bench trails
TRAFFIC: Busy on bench trails; moderate on upper trail
TRAIL SURFACE: Dirt and rock, becoming mostly rock near the waterfall
HIKING TIME: 1.5–2 hours
WATER REQUIREMENTS: 1 liter
SEASON: Year-round. Negligible avalanche risk in Waterfall Canyon
ACCESS: Located on private property. No fee for parking or trailhead access. Trailhead parking lot and gates close at dusk.
MAPS: USGS Ogden
FACILITIES: No restrooms or water at trailhead
DOGS: On leash
SPECIAL COMMENTS: Can also be combined with Malans Peak as a scenic loop hike

GPS Trailhead Coordinates

UTM Zone (WGS84) 12T
Easting 0421827
Northing 4562632
Latitude N 41° 12' 38.65"
Longitude W 111° 55' 55.04"

IN BRIEF

A beautiful hike, the Waterfall Canyon trail follows a creek up a deep canyon to a breathtaking surprise. Area hikers love the steep, short trail, while trail runners and mountain bikers use the lower trail network, which connects the canyon with the Bonneville Shoreline Trail and other city trailheads.

DESCRIPTION

The dozens of canyons that flank the foothills of the Wasatch Front are full of surprises. Some are dry and some are wet, and you can't always be sure which is which from the valley below. As you walk along the dry bench trails above Ogden's eastern hillside, you would never suspect a 200-foot waterfall to be spraying down a rock face just minutes up the trail.

The 29th Street trailhead provides the easiest access to Waterfall Canyon. This trailhead is also a popular access point for the Mount Ogden Exercise Trail, the Bonneville Shoreline Trail, Taylor Canyon, and Malans Peak (see Hike 4, page 28).

From the 29th Street trailhead, follow the trail heading up the hillside to the east

Directions →

Take I-15 north from Salt Lake City to 31st Street in Ogden (Exit 341A). Go east on 31st Street for 1.1 mile to Washington Boulevard (US 89) and turn left. Go north 0.1 mile to 30th Street and turn right. Continue east on 30th Street for 1.3 miles to Tyler Avenue and turn left. Go north on Tyler Avenue for 0.1 mile to 29th Street and turn right. Continue east on 29th Street for 0.7 miles and turn right into the trailhead parking lot at the end of 29th Street. The trailhead is at the south end of the parking lot.

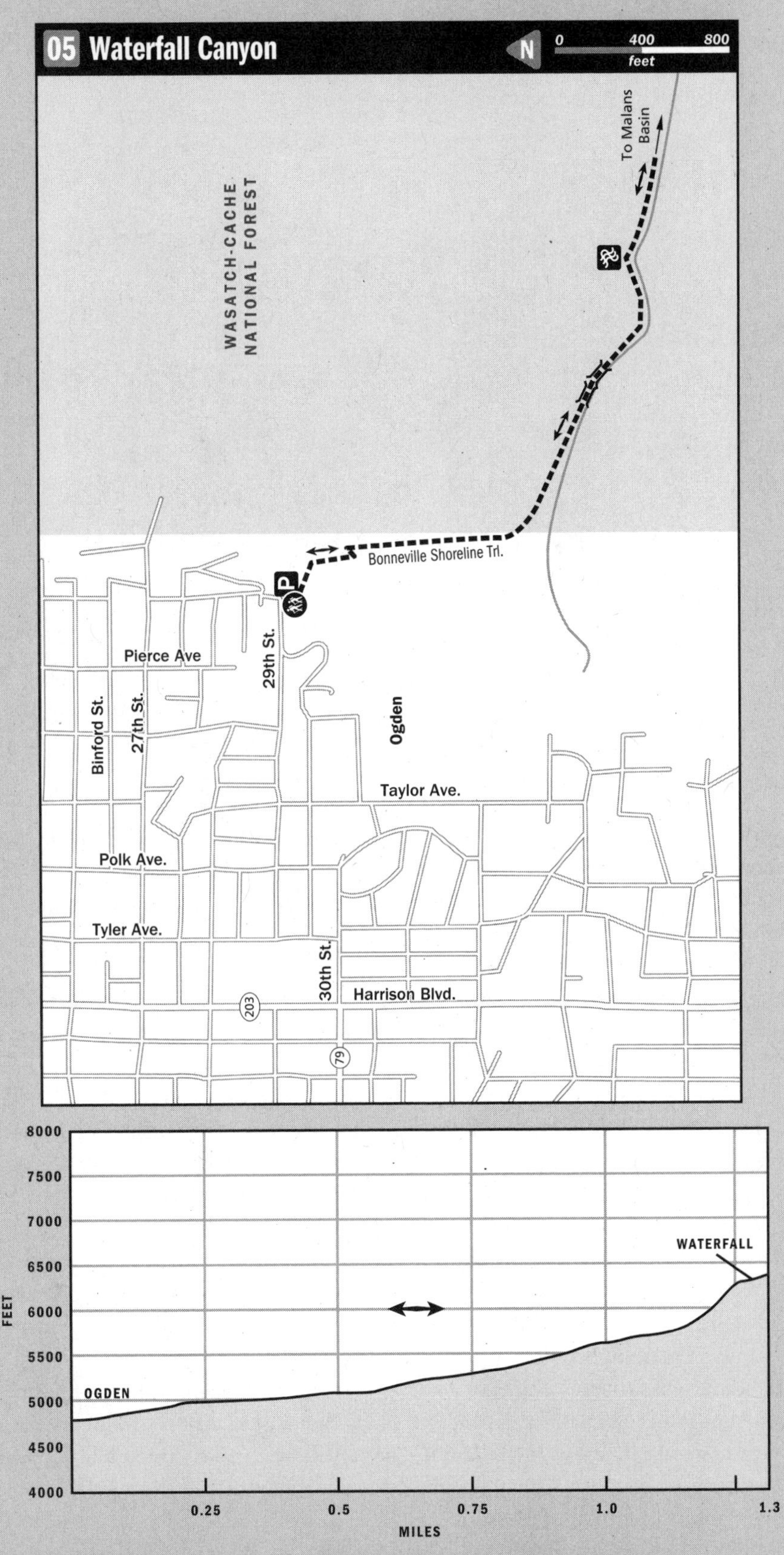
05 Waterfall Canyon
N
0
400
800
feet
To Malans Basin
WASATCH-CACHE NATIONAL FOREST
Bonneville Shoreline Trl.
P
Pierce Ave
29th St.
Binford St.
27th St.
Ogden
Taylor Ave.
Polk Ave.
Tyler Ave.
30th St.
Harrison Blvd.
203
79
8000
7500
7000
6500
6000
5500
5000
4500
4000
FEET
WATERFALL
OGDEN
0.25
0.5
0.75
1.0
1.3
MILES

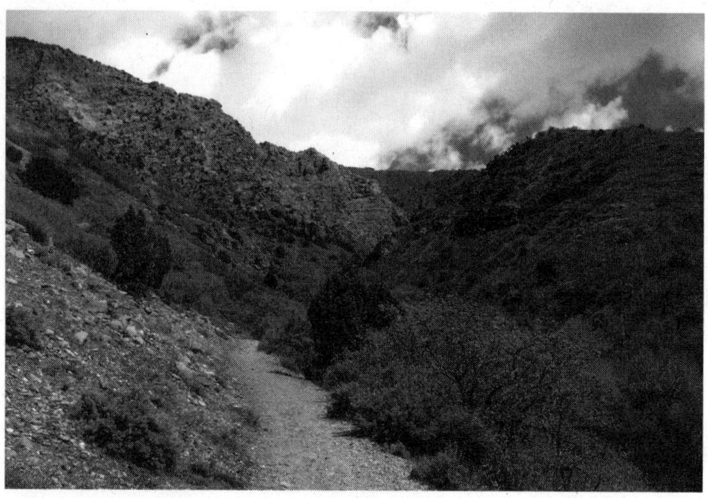

Mouth of Waterfall Canyon

with the signs pointing to the Taylor Canyon South Trail. Upon reaching the Bonneville Shoreline Trail at 0.2 miles, take a sharp right and continue south along the wide trail. This portion of the trail is often shadeless and hot in the summer.

At 0.5 miles, the path turns east into Waterfall Canyon and begins a steep ascent of the northern slope of Malans Peak. After another 0.2 miles you'll come to a bridge on the right with a sign that points to Strong's Canyon. You can either cross the wooden bridge and take an immediate left or take the faint trail up the north side of the creek.

Within another 100 feet you'll pass a second bridge. Again, you can follow the trail up either side of the creek. The trails on both sides of the creek are equally beautiful and comparable in terrain. They both stay within 5 to 10 feet of the creek, so getting lost is never a problem.

After crossing the bridges, the trail becomes more rocky and may even become a little difficult for small children and less agile hikers. But at this point the waterfall appears and you'll immediately forget the steep climb.

A scramble up a talus slope leads to the base of the waterfall. Its height and the narrowness of the canyon make it almost impossible to photograph the entire waterfall. You'll be tempted to climb the rocks on the canyon wall opposite the falls to get the perfect picture, but these crags can be dangerous. Also keep in mind that as a guest on private property, you should stay on the trail and protect the canyon's natural beauty.

If you're full of energy, make a longer scenic loop hike by climbing the steep, rocky slope to the right of the waterfall. This drainage leads up to Malans Basin, on to Malans Peak, then down Taylor Canyon. If you make this 5-mile loop, do it in a counterclockwise direction: you can more safely ascend the rocky drainage above the waterfall than descend it.

Waterfall Canyon

NEARBY ACTIVITIES

Just a mile down the hillside from Waterfall Canyon, you'll find Weber State University. The 12,000-seat Dee Events Center hosts Weber State sports, concerts, and other campus and community events. For tickets and event information, call (801) 626-6500.

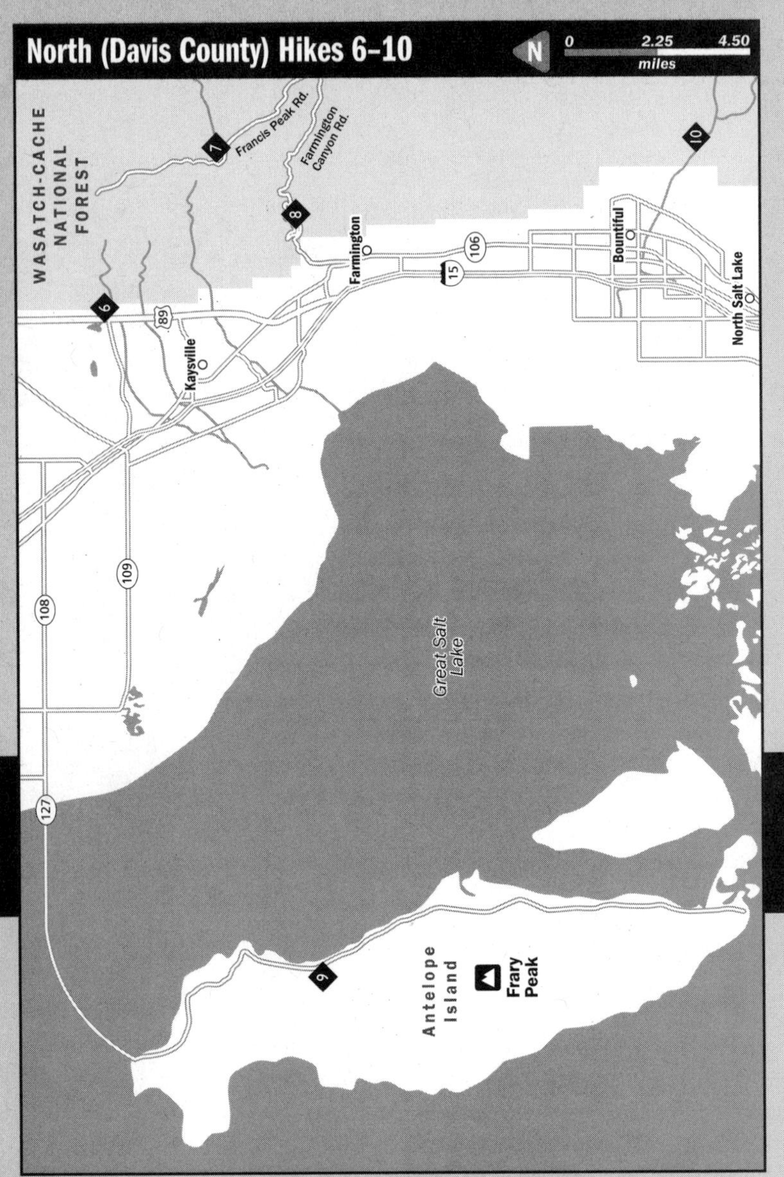
North (Davis County) Hikes 6–10
N
0
2.25
4.50
miles
WASATCH-CACHE NATIONAL FOREST
Francis Peak Rd.
Farmington Canyon Rd.
Farmington
Bountiful
North Salt Lake
Kaysville
106
15
89
108
109
127
Great Salt Lake
Antelope Island
Frary Peak
6
7
8
9
10

NORTH (DAVIS COUNTY)

06 ADAMS CANYON

KEY AT-A-GLANCE INFORMATION

LENGTH: 3.6 miles round-trip
ELEVATION GAIN: 1,268 feet
ELEVATION AT TRAILHEAD: 4,832 feet
CONFIGURATION: Out-and-back
DIFFICULTY: Moderate
SCENERY: Valley views, deep-canyon stream, and waterfall
EXPOSURE: Partially shaded initially, then mostly shaded in the canyon
TRAFFIC: Moderate
TRAIL SURFACE: Dirt and rock
HIKING TIME: 2–3 hours
WATER REQUIREMENTS: 1 liter
SEASON: Year-round
ACCESS: No fees for trailhead parking or access. Adams Canyon is in the Wasatch-Cache National Forest.
MAPS: USGS Kaysville and Peterson
FACILITIES: No restrooms or water at trailhead
DOGS: On leash
SPECIAL COMMENTS: Adams Canyon is especially beautiful in late spring as the creek swells with snowmelt.

GPS Trailhead Coordinates

UTM Zone (WGS84) 12T
Easting 0423552
Northing 4546556
Latitude N 41° 03' 58.8"
Longitude W 111° 54' 34.8"

IN BRIEF

From the valley floor, Adams Canyon appears no different from any other ordinary canyon along the Wasatch Front. But once inside, you'll find a deep canyon filled with white fir, a tumbling creek, and a stunning waterfall waiting at the end of the trail.

DESCRIPTION

Locals have done a good job of keeping Adams Canyon a secret. No signs at the trailhead indicate where you are or that you can even access the canyon. The canyon's name (Adams Canyon) differs from the name of the creek (North Fork Holmes Creek), which only makes it more anonymous. Even the spectacular waterfall at the end of the hike is nameless. Still, locals count this as a favorite hike, enjoying the canyon's deep-forest setting, vibrant mountain stream, and plunging waterfall.

From the northeast corner of the large parking area, take the trail leading along the fence through a thicket of Gambel oak. After 100 yards the path turns left up a steep slope and follows a series of switchbacks up the hillside. This part of the trail cuts through the sandy slopes of the Lake Bonneville

Directions

From Salt Lake City take Interstate 15 north to US 89/NB Ogden (Exit 324). Continue north on US 89 for 5.7 miles to Oak Hills Drive. Crossing Oak Hills Drive, continue north on US 89 another 0.3 miles and turn right onto the Eastside Drive frontage road. Continue south for 0.3 miles on Eastside Drive to the trailhead parking lot on the left. The unmarked parking area is at the northeast corner of Eastside Drive and Canyon Creek Drive (350 North).

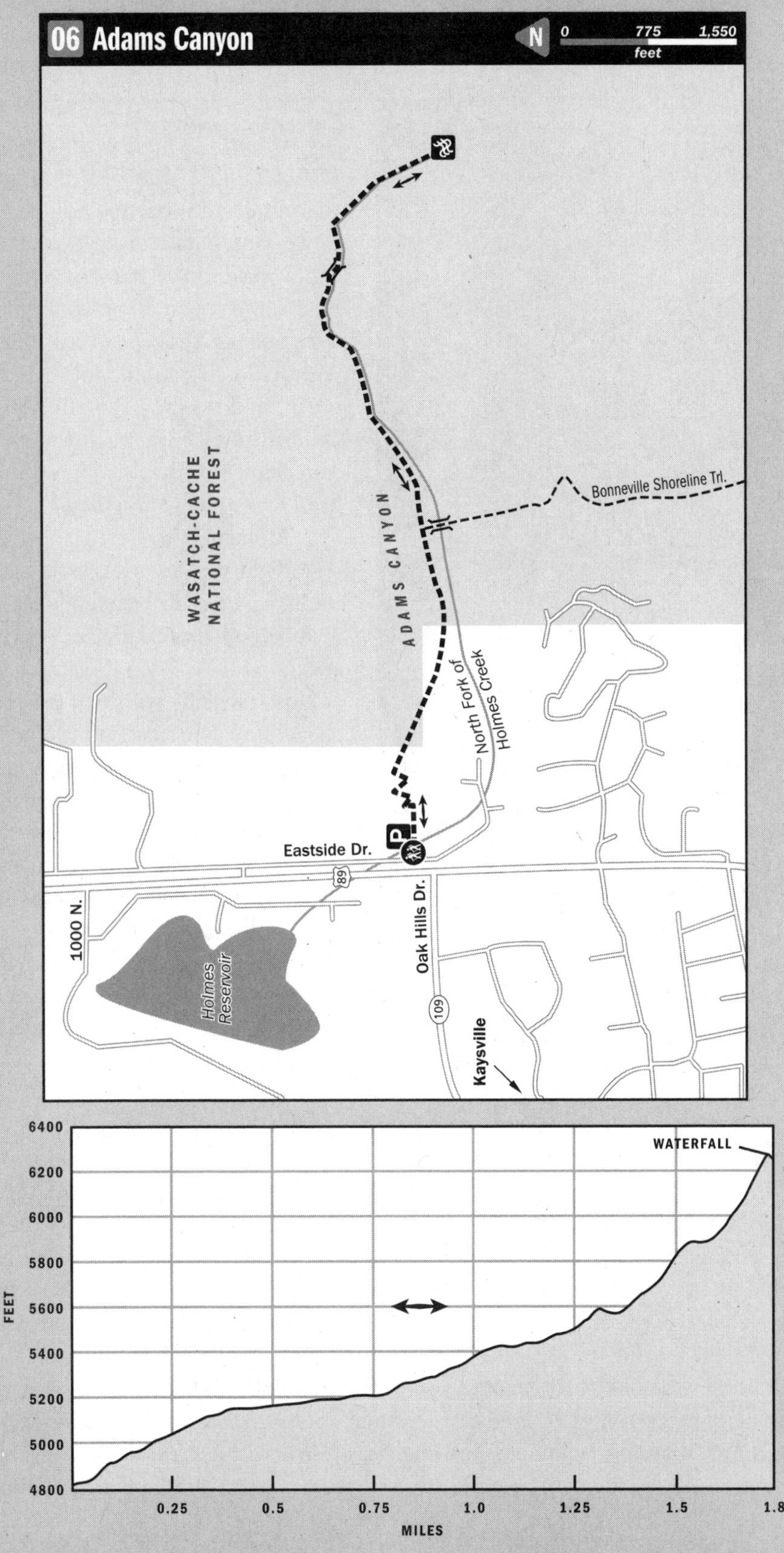

06 Adams Canyon
N
0
775
1,550
feet
WASATCH-CACHE NATIONAL FOREST
ADAMS CANYON
Bonneville Shoreline Trl.
North Fork of Holmes Creek
P
Eastside Dr.
89
Oak Hills Dr.
1000 N.
Holmes Reservoir
109
Kaysville
6400
6200
6000
5800
5600
5400
5200
5000
4800
FEET
WATERFALL
0.25
0.5
0.75
1.0
1.25
1.5
1.8
MILES

Waterfall in Adams Canyon

shoreline and is particularly prone to erosion. Stay on the trail to avoid making the problem worse. At 0.2 miles you come to a quick overlook of the Great Salt Lake with views of mountains to the north and south. This overlook demonstrates how much the view can change with just a few hundred feet of elevation gain.

Along the first part of the hike, you might well see a snake sunning itself on the trail. Frequent visitors include bull snakes, gopher snakes, and rattlers. Avoid surprising them at close range by watching the trail ahead; you can create a little noise to send them safely slithering into the underbrush. You might also glimpse deer, which often graze on the lower slopes, especially in winter.

At 0.5 miles, the trail curves to the left and begins to enter the mouth of Adams Canyon. From the partially shaded slopes of oak on the north side of the canyon, you can see the towering conifers that cover its south side. Soon you become aware of the creek below on the canyon floor. At 0.7 miles, another trail bends to the right and descends to a footbridge that crosses the creek. This is the Bonneville Shoreline Trail, which continues south. Stay on the trail straight ahead as it leads up Adams Canyon and along the bank of the north fork of Holmes Creek.

As you ascend the canyon, the trail steepens and becomes rockier. Holmes Creek is a fast-dropping stream with dozens of cascades and tumbles. The trail manages to parallel the creek's steep gradient as it winds around rocks and trees. White fir trees, most with trunks two feet in diameter, provide ample shade.

At 1.4 miles, the trail crosses from the north to the south side of the creek on a rickety wooden footbridge. Soon you pass several fire rings and primitive campsites. At one point, a huge slab of rock the size of a school bus blocks the trail as it meets the stream. Circumvent the rock most easily by climbing around on the right top side of the slab.

In the last 0.4 miles leading up to the waterfall you'll find several steep sections of the creek with large cascades that could be appropriately considered waterfalls. In spring, abundant snowmelt easily triples the creek's flow, making these cascades particularly scenic. Beyond them, a bit of scrambling around

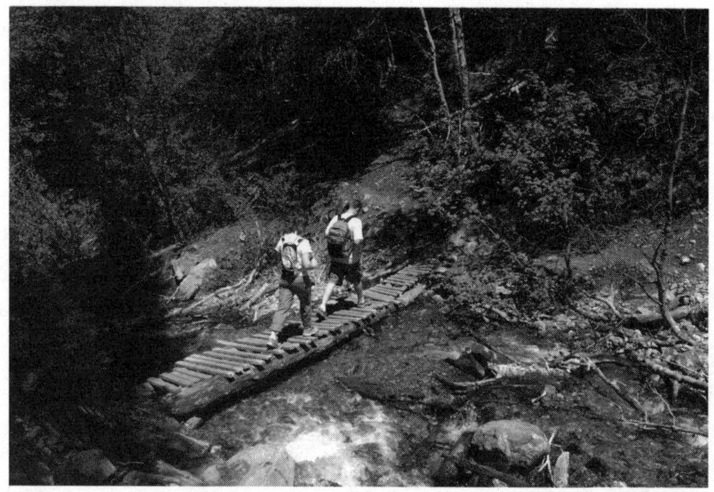

Footbridge crossing Holmes Creek

rocks and tree trunks is required before arriving at the rock cliff that forms the backdrop for the waterfall. One last crossing of the creek will take you to the base of the falls, where you can enjoy the sight and rest on a nearby rock or ledge. Throughout most of the year, you can easily cross the creek by stepping on large rocks, but in the surge of spring snowmelt, plan to get your feet wet.

NEARBY ACTIVITIES

Cherry Hill Resort and Waterpark is located off US 89 at 1325 South Main in Fruit Heights, just 4 miles from the Adams Canyon trailhead. The resort features camping facilities, a water park, miniature golf, batting cages, a climbing wall, and other family-oriented activities. The campground is open year-round, while the recreational portion of the resort is open April 1 through September 15. Call (801) 451-5379 for information and reservations.

07 THURSTON PEAK

KEY AT-A-GLANCE INFORMATION

LENGTH: 8.6 miles
ELEVATION GAIN: 706 feet
ELEVATION AT TRAILHEAD: 9,187 feet
CONFIGURATION: Out-and-back
DIFFICULTY: Moderate
SCENERY: Excellent views in all directions
EXPOSURE: Full exposure to sun
TRAFFIC: Light
TRAIL SURFACE: Dirt and rock
HIKING TIME: 4–5.5 hours
WATER REQUIREMENTS: 1–2 liters. No water is available on the trail.
SEASON: Late spring, summer, early fall
ACCESS: No fees for access or parking. The entire trail lies within the Wasatch-Cache National Forest.
MAPS: USGS Peterson
FACILITIES: No restrooms or water at the trailhead
DOGS: Permitted
SPECIAL COMMENTS: Most people in the valley below recognize Francis Peak by the radar installation that looks like two giant golf balls. But the higher Thurston Peak to the north is generally unknown.

GPS Trailhead Coordinates

UTM Zone (WGS84) 12T
Easting 0429542
Northing 4542174
Latitude N 41° 01' 39.8"
Longitude W 111° 50' 17.0"

IN BRIEF

Thurston Peak, at 9,706 feet, straddles the Davis and Morgan county line and is the tallest peak in each county. The ridge route from Francis Peak to Thurston Peak offers nonstop views of the valleys below and far beyond. High alpine vegetation and wildlife come together in a remote setting.

DESCRIPTION

A trail that begins at a federal radar installation and follows a dirt road for half the distance to the summit may not sound like a remote wilderness experience. And a summit that's just 519 feet higher than the trailhead elevation may not sound like the kind of challenge you hoped for. But the high alpine setting, with expansive views every step of the way, quickly erases any prejudices you may have brought to the hike. The section of trail from Francis Peak to Thurston Peak is also part of the Great Western Trail, a continuous corridor of trails that stretches from Canada to Mexico and traverses some

Directions

Take I-15 north from Salt Lake City to Farmington (Exit 322) and continue north 0.6 miles to State Street (UT 106). Turn right and go east 0.2 miles to Main Street. Turn left on Main Street and continue north 0.6 miles to 600 North. Turn left on 600 North and continue east for 0.1 mile to 100 East and turn left. Continue north on 100 East as it turns into Farmington Canyon Road. Continue up Farmington Canyon Road for 8 miles to a junction with two gates. Drive through the left gate and follow the road for 4.3 miles to the locked gate below the Francis Peak radar installation. Park on the side of the road below the gate.

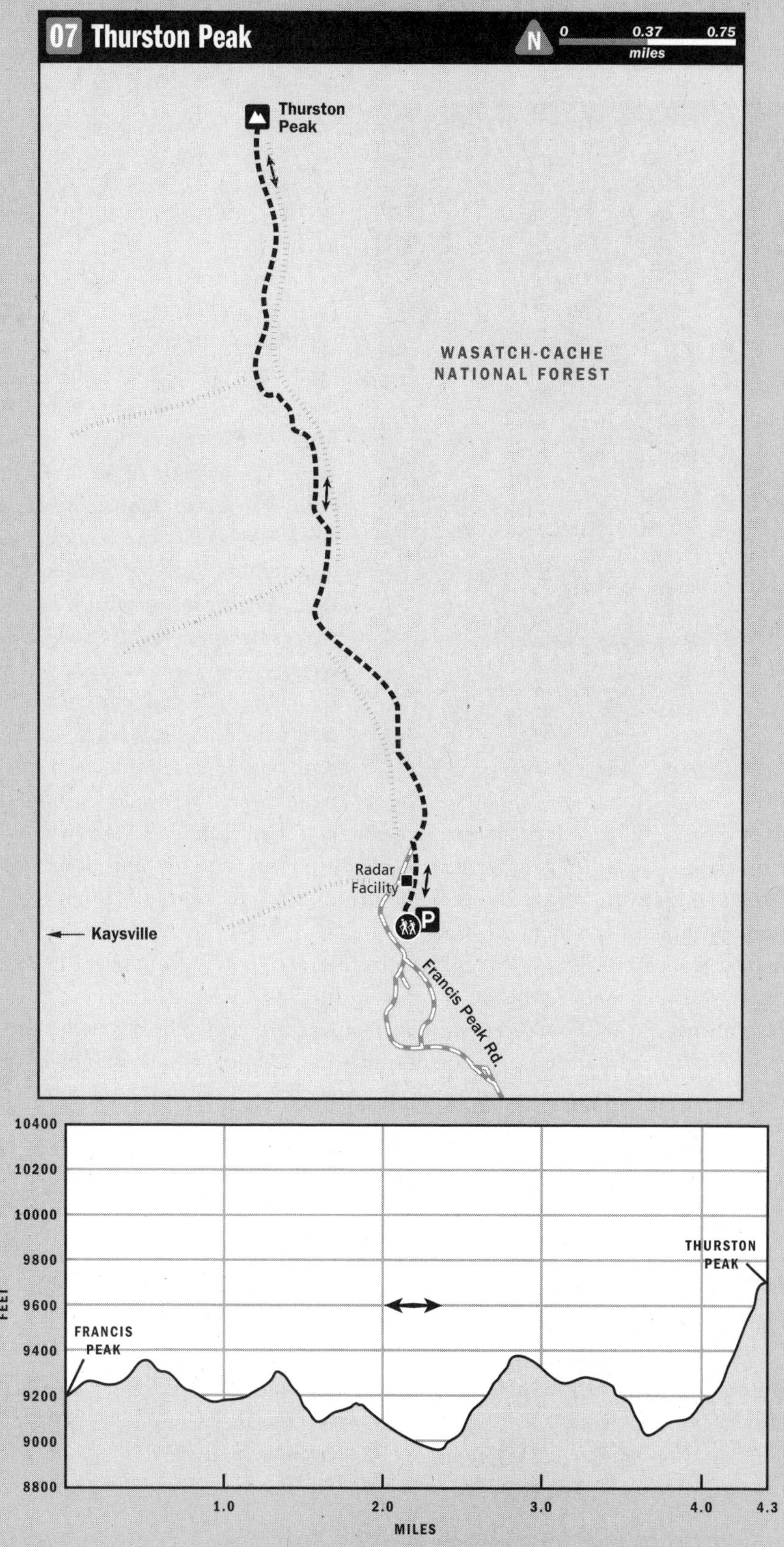
07 Thurston Peak
N
0
0.37
0.75
miles
Thurston
Peak
WASATCH-CACHE
NATIONAL FOREST
Radar
Facility
P
Kaysville
Francis Peak Rd.
10400
10200
10000
9800
9600
9400
9200
9000
8800
FEET
FRANCIS
PEAK
THURSTON
PEAK
1.0
2.0
3.0
4.0
4.3
MILES

THURSTON
PEAK
THOMAS J. THURSTON
1805 – 1885
NAMED IN HONOR OF
THOMAS JEFFERSON
THURSTON, A CENTER-
VILLE RESIDENT, WHO
VIEWED THE VIRGIN
VALLEY OF MORGAN
FROM THE SUMMIT
OF THE MOUNTAINS
IN 1852 AND RECOG-
NIZED ITS POTENTIAL
FOR COLONIZATION.
REALIZING ITS DIS-
ADVANTAGE WAS ITS
INACCESSIBILITY. IN
1855 THURSTON INFLU-
ENCED OTHERS TO
ASSIST HIM TO CARVE
A PASSABLE WAGON
ROAD THROUGH WEBER
CANYON. HE WAS AMONG
THE FIRST TO SETTLE
IN MORGAN VALLEY
MORGAN CO. HISTORICAL
SOCIETY
MORGAN CO. COMMISSIONERS
DAVIS CO. COMMISSIONERS

Summit monument on Thurston Peak

of the most spectacular scenery in the West.

From the locked gate on the road leading up to the radar installation at the top of Francis Peak (elevation 9,547 feet), take the dirt road to the right that follows the more level contour along the eastern slope of Francis Peak. This road stays close to the ridge for much of the way, although it generally skirts the smaller peaks by taking a gentler route along the western slopes, favoring the Davis County side.

Once the road ends, a narrow trail continues along the ridgeline. Rather than ascending each of the small, unnamed peaks along the way, it dips along the slope to an elevation as low as 9,000 feet. Even though the maximum elevation gain is only 706 feet, the repeated ups and downs produce a cumulative gain of about 3,000 feet, certainly a good workout for a round-trip hike of less than 10 miles.

The slopes are largely covered with sage and dotted with wind-mangled subalpine fir and limber pine. In the late spring and early summer, wildflowers appear as fast as the snow can melt. Large snow drifts generally cover the slopes throughout the spring and occasionally into July. Although you'll find no precipitous drop-offs, expect to traverse some steep slopes and approach potentially unstable snow cornices with caution.

The saddle immediately south of Thurston Peak is at an elevation just under 9,100 feet, one of the lower levels of the entire trail. At this point, the trail skirts Thurston Peak's western slope and continues to the north. To reach the summit, leave the main trail and either find a poorly defined trail or make your own way for the remaining 0.3 miles. Pink-and-black marbled granite, which comprises the summit, also dots this slope.

The wildlife along the ridge, like that of other high alpine regions, includes marmots and cliff swallows that nest in the rocky outcroppings. Deer graze in the higher meadows and slopes in the summer, and butterflies abound in the spring.

A granite marker and plaque at the summit honors Thomas Jefferson Thurston, who first viewed the Morgan Valley to the east in 1852. The inspiring

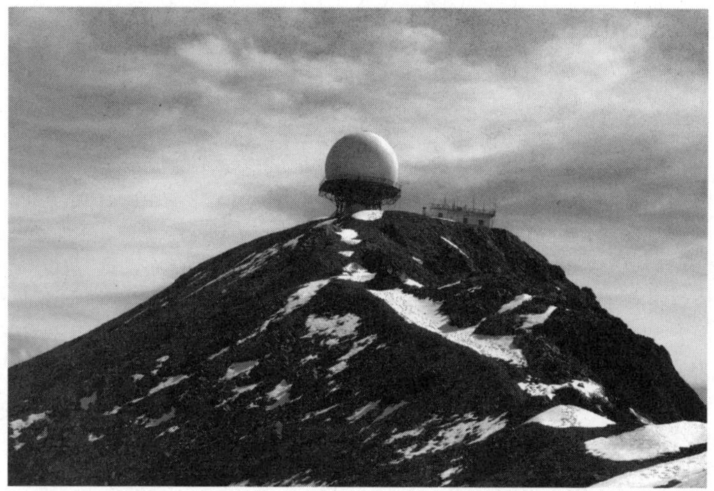

Radar installation on Francis Peak

view led him to build a wagon road through Weber Canyon to access Morgan Valley, where he settled in 1855. The views from the summit are breathtaking in all directions, extending far beyond the valleys and the Great Salt Lake to distant mountains and ranges to the east and west.

NEARBY ACTIVITIES

The Farmington Bay Waterfowl Management Area offers excellent bird-watching and biking trails. More than 200 species of waterfowl, songbirds, and raptors visit this area during the migration and nesting season. Nesting begins in early March for Canada geese and great blue herons; bald eagles winter in the area. The main entrance is located southwest of Farmington at 1325 West Glover Lane. Open 8 a.m. to 5 p.m. daily; call (801) 451-7386 for information.

08 FARMINGTON CREEK TRAIL

KEY AT-A-GLANCE INFORMATION

LENGTH: 3.2 miles round-trip
ELEVATION GAIN: 1,178 feet
ELEVATION AT FARMINGTON CREEK: 5,245 feet
ELEVATION AT SUNSET CAMPGROUND: 6,423 feet
CONFIGURATION: Out-and-back or one-way with shuttle vehicle
DIFFICULTY: Moderate
SCENERY: Canyon views, stream, and waterfall
EXPOSURE: Partially shaded
TRAFFIC: Light
TRAIL SURFACE: Dirt and rock
HIKING TIME: 2.5–3 hours round-trip
WATER REQUIREMENTS: 1–1.5 liters
SEASON: Best in spring and fall
ACCESS: No fees for parking or access. Trail lies within Wasatch-Cache National Forest.
MAPS: USGS Bountiful Peak, Peterson
FACILITIES: No restrooms or water at trailhead. Vault toilet at Sunset Campground
DOGS: On leash
SPECIAL COMMENTS: Farmington Creek Trail is also called the Sunset Trail, since it ends at the Sunset Campground.

GPS Trailhead Coordinates

UTM Zone (WGS84) 12T

Easting 0427135; Northing 4539153

Farmington Creek (lower trailhead):

N 41° 00' 01.1"; W 111° 51' 59.0"

Sunset Campground (upper trailhead):

N 41° 00' 08.2"; W 111° 50' 24.0"

IN BRIEF

The trail follows Farmington Creek, the largest stream or river in Davis County, up a broad canyon to a primitive Forest Service campground. A plunging 40-foot waterfall near the top of the trail and expansive view of the canyon make Farmington Canyon a rewarding destination, especially in spring and fall.

DESCRIPTION

Farmington Creek cuts through a wide canyon fed by several tributary creeks and springs. By the time it reaches the lower canyon, the water flow is substantial enough that it's probably outgrown its simple creek designation. The Farmington Creek Trail makes a steady ascent along the south slope of the canyon and provides great views of the canyon and the creek below. Although the road above the trail receives year-round recreational use by ATVs, snowmobiles, and hunters, the trail below remains relatively quiet.

Directions

From Salt Lake City take I-15 north to Farmington (Exit 322) and continue north 0.6 miles to State Street. Turn right and go east 0.2 miles to Main Street (UT 106). Turn left on Main Street and continue north 0.6 miles to 600 North. Turn left on 600 North and continue east for 0.1 mile to 100 East and turn left. Continue north on 100 East as it turns into Farmington Canyon Road. Continue up Farmington Canyon Road for 1.6 miles to a dirt parking area on the right at the point where the pavement ends. Sunset Campground, the upper end of the trail, is another 5 miles up Farmington Canyon Road (and a handy spot to park a second car if you want to make this a one-way hike).

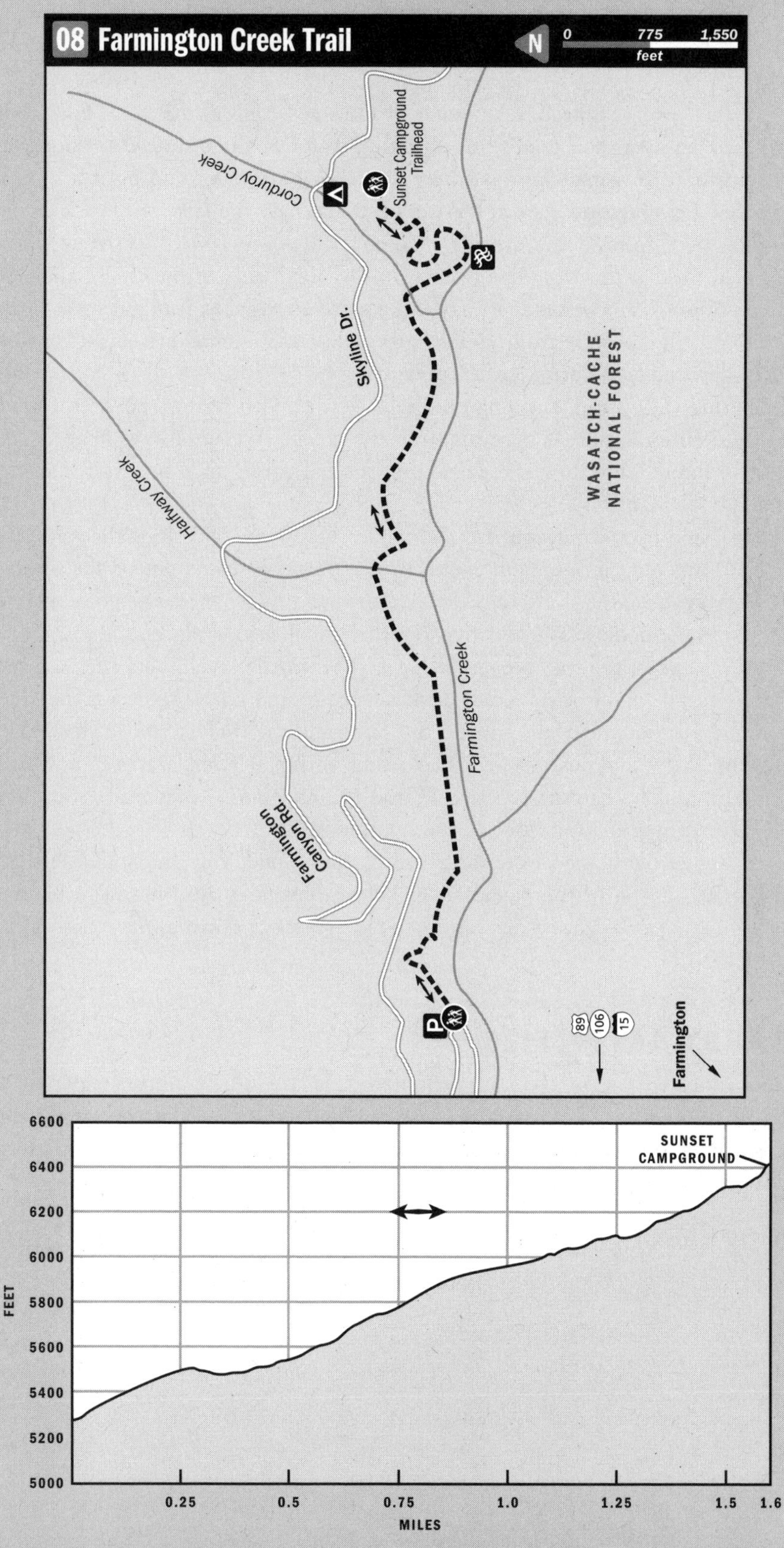
08 Farmington Creek Trail
N
0
775
1,550
feet
Corduroy Creek
Sunset Campground Trailhead
Skyline Dr.
Halfway Creek
WASATCH-CACHE NATIONAL FOREST
Farmington Creek
Farmington Canyon Rd.
89
106
15
Farmington
6600
6400
6200
6000
5800
5600
5400
5200
5000
FEET
SUNSET CAMPGROUND
0.25
0.5
0.75
1.0
1.25
1.5
1.6
MILES

At the lower trailhead, take either of the steep trails at the north end of the small parking area. You won't find drinking water at the trailhead or along the trail, but there are small springs where you can draw water and purify. You can also access Farmington Creek at the trailhead and near the falls.

The hike follows the creek's gradient and stays 100 to 200 feet above the creek most of the way. The trail is on the north side of the creek, and with the exception of a few stands of oak, hikers are exposed to sunlight most of the way. Along the 1.6-mile trail, you'll cross at least four small creeks and springs as they descend into Farmington Creek.

During the spring, Farmington Creek gushes with water, and even though the trail is often hundreds of yards from the creek, you can always hear its roar below. In the fall, the flow is reduced, but the fall colors and cooler air make for an equally pleasant hike.

Deer and foxes are frequently sighted in the canyon and along the trail. Also watch for two old cars—one on the north side of the trail, and one on the south—that plunged over the cliff from the road above nearly 50 years ago, and have made the thick underbrush near the trail their final rusting place.

At 1.3 miles, the trail comes within 50 feet of the creek, near the base of a broad waterfall. A steep spur trail enables sure-footed hikers to access the creek below the 40-foot waterfall. Beyond the waterfall, the trail ascends a steep slope to the north by a series of switchbacks and within 0.3 miles arrives at Sunset Campground. The Farmington Creek Trail (number 1621) enters the southwest side of the campground on one of the small loops.

Although there is no water at Sunset Campground, you can enjoy the shade and a snack at one of the picnic tables before returning. And if you've planned ahead, you may even have a car waiting to take you back down to the mouth of the canyon.

NEARBY ACTIVITIES

Lagoon, located just off I-15 in Farmington, is the largest amusement park in Utah, with 35 rides, a water park, historic Pioneer Village, live entertainment, shops, games, and restaurants. For a schedule and events, call (800) 748-5246 or visit **www.lagoonpark.com.**

FRARY PEAK 09

IN BRIEF

Ascend to the summit of the largest island in the Great Salt Lake. You'll find spectacular vistas and excellent wildlife viewing in a surprisingly distinctive geologic zone and natural habitat. The hike offers the best chance in Utah of spotting bighorn sheep.

KEY AT-A-GLANCE INFORMATION

LENGTH: 6.6 miles round-trip
ELEVATION GAIN: 2,068 feet
ELEVATION AT TRAILHEAD: 4,528 feet
CONFIGURATION: Out-and-back
DIFFICULTY: Moderate
SCENERY: Superb 360-degree summit views of Great Salt Lake, valley, and surrounding peaks. Good opportunities to see bison, bighorn sheep, and pronghorn antelope.
EXPOSURE: Full sun; no shade
TRAFFIC: Moderate
TRAIL SURFACE: Dirt and rock
HIKING TIME: 3½–6 hours
WATER REQUIREMENTS: 1–2 liters depending on weather. No water available on trail.
SEASON: Year-round. Snow may cover trail in winter.
ACCESS: September 15–April 14, 9 a.m.–5 p.m.; April 15–September 14, 9 a.m.–6 p.m. Pay entrance fee of $9 per vehicle at the state park gate before crossing the causeway.
MAPS: USGS Antelope Island, Antelope Island North
FACILITIES: No restrooms or water at trailhead. Nearest public facilities are at park visitor center 7 miles north of trailhead.
DOGS: No dogs are allowed on trail.

DESCRIPTION

At only 6,596 feet in elevation, Frary Peak really isn't much by Utah standards. But it may be the most unusual summit in the state. Located on Antelope Island in the Great Salt Lake, the peak rises 2,400 feet above the surrounding salt flats. Its location was intriguing enough that Kit Carson and John C. Fremont made the first Anglo exploration of the island in 1845. The entire island is a high-desert grassland that provides a hospitable habitat for migrating birds, bighorn sheep, pronghorn antelope, and a herd of more than 500 bison.

You'll find the trail consistently well marked and easy to follow. From the trailhead it winds its way quickly up the island's grassy

Directions

From Salt Lake City, take I-15 north to Syracuse (Exit 232). At the off-ramp, turn left (west) and take UT 108 (known locally as Antelope Drive or 1700 South) west for 6.7 miles to the Antelope Island entrance gate. Continue along the 6.8-mile causeway (UT 127) to Antelope Island. Once on the island, veer left at the RANCH sign and continue for 0.6 miles to Garr Ranch Road. Turn left on Garr Ranch Road and continue 5.2 miles down the east side of the island. Turn right at the "Frary trailhead" sign. Follow this paved road 0.5 miles up the island's eastern slope to the large dirt parking area. The trailhead is at the parking lot's southwest corner.

GPS Trailhead Coordinates

UTM Zone (WGS84) 12T
Easting 0398818
Northing 4538762
Latitude N 40° 59' 37.4"
Longitude W 112° 12' 09.1"

09 Frary Peak

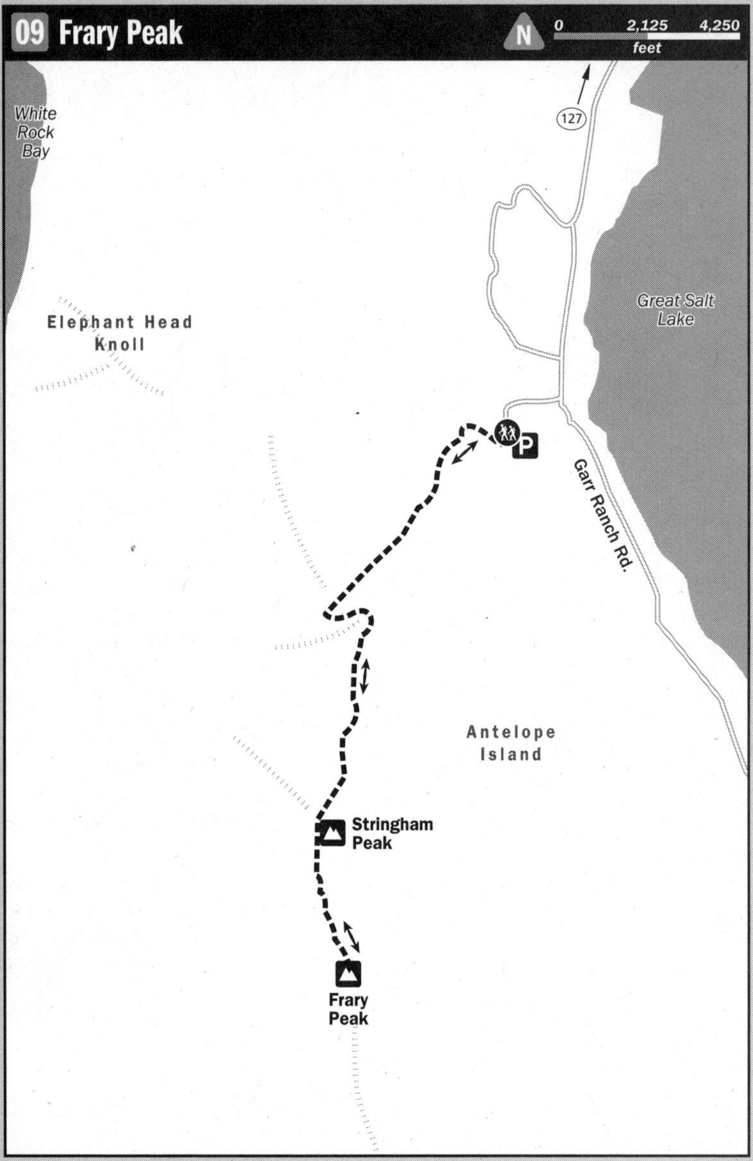

N
0 2,125 4,250
feet

127
White Rock Bay
Elephant Head Knoll
Great Salt Lake
Garr Ranch Rd.
Antelope Island
Stringham Peak
Frary Peak

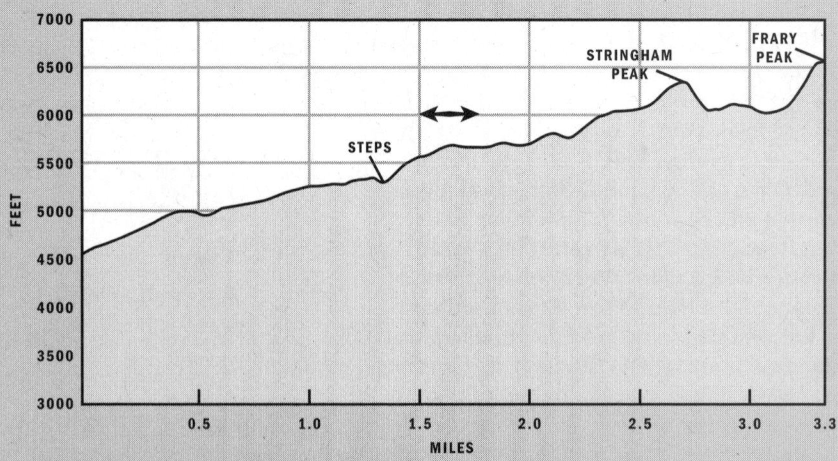

An antelope gazes over the Great Salt Lake.

eastern slopes. Don't be intimidated by the first mile's steep terrain, since the trail climbs more gradually once you hit the ridgeline. At 0.7 miles you'll pass the Dooley Knob trail junction and arrive at the island ridgeline for first views to the west.

From this lower ridgeline, the trail crosses to the island's western side and follows a fairly gentle contour along the western slopes for most of the way to the summit. As the trail begins to descend the slope and move toward the prominent Elephant Head knoll on the western shore, you might even begin to wonder if you're on the right trail. Soon, at 1.2 miles, you'll see a set of wooden steps that lead up and to the east through the rocky escarpment. These steps quickly bring you back to the ridgeline and some expansive views to both the east and west. The trail continues through grassy meadows to cross the rounded slopes of Stringham Peak (elevation 6,374 feet), capped by a large communications tower.

From Stringham Peak you have a clear view of the craggy Frary Peak summit just 0.6 miles and about 15 minutes ahead to the south. At this point you might be tempted to follow the faint trail along the ridgeline straight ahead, but you're really much better off staying on the main trail as it descends to the right along the western slopes, losing about 150 feet of elevation. You'll soon regain the elevation loss by climbing a long flight of wooden steps that leads back up to the ridge.

The higher slopes are blanketed with big sagebrush and an occasional juniper tree, not large enough to create much shade. A short scramble up a steep slope soon brings you to the rocky, beige outcropping that is Frary Peak. The summit's flat rock provides an ideal place to sit down, enjoy lunch, and take in the views in all directions. Directly to the west, Bountiful Peak and the Wasatch Range are reflected in the Great Salt Lake. Forty miles to the southwest, you'll spot the easily recognizable Desert Peak (11,031 feet). On a clear day, you can even see Ibapah Peak (12,087 feet) nearly 120 miles to the southwest.

The rocky slopes near the summit also provide a good place to watch for bighorn sheep. The Utah Department of Wildlife introduced a herd of 22 bighorn to the island in 1996, as a nursery herd that could supply animals to other areas of the state. With few natural predators the bighorn population on the island has grown to 160, and portions of the herd are frequently exported. If you don't happen to see a bighorn, you'll certainly see their clumps of wool along the trail.

Nearly 200 pronghorn antelope and 350 deer graze the island's slopes and rangelands. But Antelope Island's most famous residents are the bison, often found grazing along the trail. The twelve animals introduced in 1893 as part of a private ranch and hunting preserve formed the foundation for today's free-roaming herd of 500 to 700.

Antelope Island plays host to millions of migratory birds each year. The Great Salt Lake's brine flies and brine shrimp provide a primary food source for many of the area's 250 bird species.

Along the trail, you'll often spot western meadowlarks, yellow-headed blackbirds, and various raptors. Chukars nest year-round on the island, concealed in rocks or in the brush near the trail.

Although you'll find no water on the trail, Antelope Island's 40 major freshwater springs, primarily on the eastern slopes, produce 36 million gallons of water annually and support much of the island's wildlife and vegetation. The island's geology exposes some of the oldest rocks on Earth in the 2.7 billion-year-old Farmington Canyon complex. Along the trail you'll also see granite, limestone outcroppings, and shale.

Range grasses such as purple threeawn cover most of the lower meadows and slopes. Common wildflowers along the trail include fiddleneck, a bristly annual with yellow flowers, and the vernal daisy.

Frary Peak is an ideal hike in the early spring when most of the higher mountain trails are still covered in snow. Summer can be grueling on the shadeless trail, so bring plenty of water. Fall brings more pleasant hiking conditions, along with migrating raptors, pronghorn harems, and more-frequent buck deer sightings. Throughout the year, Frary Peak offers exceptional views surrounded by a surprising and continually varying array of wildlife.

Note: The trail is closed for a month or more in the spring during the bighorn-sheep lambing season. Verify accessibility in advance; call (801) 725-9263.

NEARBY ACTIVITIES

The Antelope Island State Park Visitor Center at the island's north end is open year-round. There, you'll find exhibits, a bookstore, restrooms, and a video presentation on the island's natural and human history. Knowledgeable rangers provide interpretive assistance and suggestions on wildlife viewing. Popular events offered throughout the year center around bird migrations and the annual bison roundup. Look for the day-use facility and primitive campgrounds on the north side of the island. The day-use area offers covered picnic tables, drinking water, restrooms, and showers for those wanting to take a dip in the Great Salt Lake's buoyant water.

IN BRIEF

This steep trail follows three separate mountain springs through deep woods and open meadows, finally arriving at a 100-year-old miner's cabin. The trail is as popular with deer and moose as it is with humans.

KEY AT-A-GLANCE INFORMATION

LENGTH: 4.5 miles round-trip
ELEVATION GAIN: 2,217 feet
ELEVATION AT TRAILHEAD: 5,247 feet
CONFIGURATION: Out-and-back
DIFFICULTY: Moderate
SCENERY: Valley views, creeks, and spring-fed mountain meadows
EXPOSURE: Mostly shaded
TRAFFIC: Light
TRAIL SURFACE: Dirt
HIKING TIME: 2.5–3.5 hours
WATER REQUIREMENTS: 1–2 liters
SEASON: Spring, summer, fall
ACCESS: Fee of $2 payable at Mueller Park Entrance. Gate closes at 10 p.m.
MAPS: USGS Fort Douglas
FACILITIES: Restrooms and water at the trailhead parking area
DOGS: On leash
SPECIAL COMMENTS: With thick underbrush and a narrow trail, you'll want long pants on this hike.

DESCRIPTION

Some trails switchback or wind their way up the side of a mountain to mitigate the steep ascent, but not the Kenny Creek Trail. The miners who worked this area 100 years ago found the most direct means possible to reach their lode, and the Kenny Creek Trail is it. In less than 2.2 miles you gain more than 2,200 feet without ever having to scramble or use your hands.

The Kenny Creek Trail starts on the north side of the road, across from the parking area and restrooms in Bountiful's Mueller Park. While Mueller Park is a popular mountain-biking destination, most mountain bikers find the Kenny Park Trail too steep and narrow for biking pleasure.

From Mueller Park Road, the trail ascends though dense woods along the western bank

Directions

From Salt Lake City, take I-15 north to 2600 South in Bountiful (Exit 315). At the off-ramp, turn right and go east on 2600 South. After a mile, 2600 South curves to the left and becomes Orchard Drive. Continue north on Orchard Drive to 1800 South and turn right (1.7 miles from the I-15 exit). Continue east on 1800 South, which becomes Mueller Park Road, for 2.2 miles to the Mueller Park entrance. Enter the first parking area on the right. You'll find the trailhead across the street.

GPS Trailhead Coordinates

UTM Zone (WGS84) 12T
Easting 0429723
Northing 4523898
Latitude N 40° 51' 47.4"
Longitude W 111° 50' 03.2"

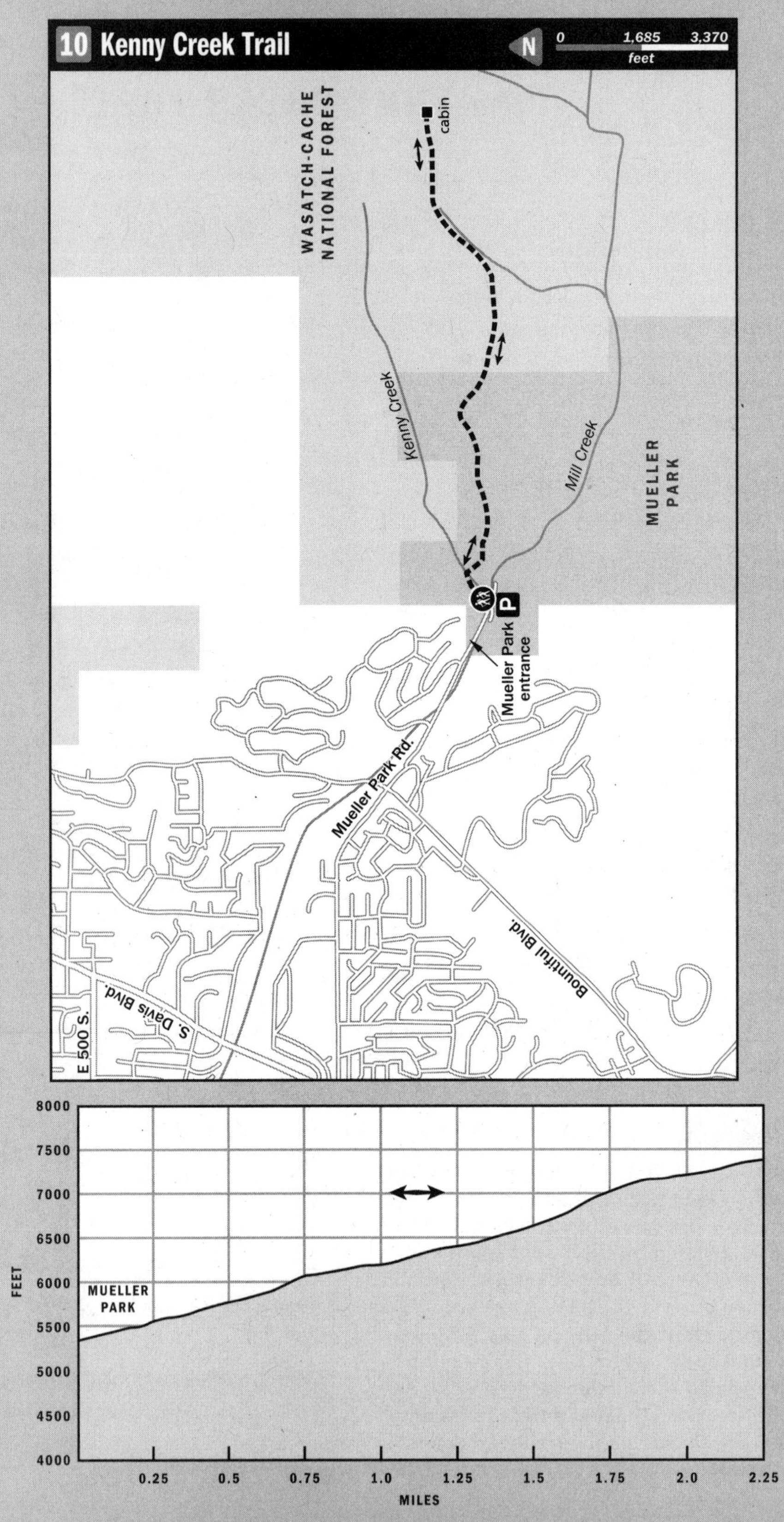
10 Kenny Creek Trail
N
0
1,685
3,370
feet
WASATCH-CACHE NATIONAL FOREST
cabin
Kenny Creek
Mill Creek
MUELLER PARK
Mueller Park entrance
Mueller Park Rd.
Bountiful Blvd.
S. Davis Blvd.
E 500 S.
8000
7500
7000
6500
6000
5500
5000
4500
4000
FEET
MUELLER PARK
0.25
0.5
0.75
1.0
1.25
1.5
1.75
2.0
2.25
MILES

Ruins of miner's cabin on Kenny Creek Trail

of Kenny Creek. Even during spring runoff, Kenny Creek is only a few feet wide and can easily be stepped across without getting your feet wet. After the trail crosses Kenny Creek at 0.2 miles, you won't see it again until your return.

After leaving the creek, the trail ascends quickly through a ground cover of grasses, forbs, and mountain shrubs under the shade of oak and maple. The trail is narrow, and the thick chaparral will scrape unprotected legs to pieces. Wear long pants and save your legs for another hike.

At 0.9 miles, the trail leaves Mueller Park and enters the Wasatch-Cache National Forest. The forest canopy opens briefly to display views of the Great Salt Lake, Antelope Island, and mountains to the west. But even at this overlook, you'll notice hillside homes across the canyon at the same elevation. It will take more climbing to escape encroaching development.

As the trail rises above the meadow, you encounter a large thicket of Gambel oak. You'll swear you're bushwhacking, but a trail really exists under the brush. It's maintained, but intentionally preserved as an unimproved wilderness trail.

The path crosses perennial streams and meadows between stands of oak and maple. At higher elevations, above 7,300 feet, clusters of quaking aspen dot the hillside. Moose and deer inhabit these higher slopes year-round and use the trail regularly. Watch for their tracks on the wet trail, along with those of mountain lions. In the trees, spotted towhees and mountain chickadees make their nests.

After 2.2 miles of heart-pounding ascent, you'll come to an old miner's cabin in a clearing: a great place to take a rest and consider your options. Most hikers make the cabin their destination and turn-around point, but you can also climb the higher ridge in the Sessions Mountains to the northeast and access the Great Western Trail, or head to the southeast along a faint and sometimes nonexistent

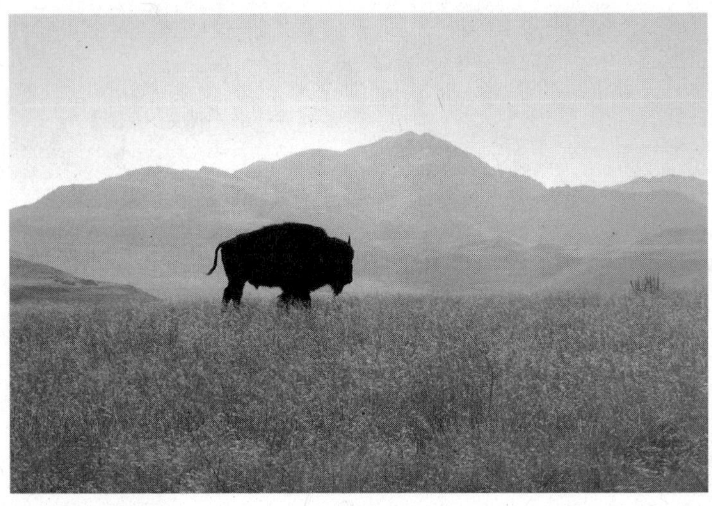

Buffalo on Antelope Island

trail to Willey Hollow. If you choose to turn around at the cabin, you've given your legs and your heart a great workout and you'll enjoy the speedy descent.

NEARBY ACTIVITIES

Mueller Park is within minutes of Bountiful neighborhoods and shopping areas. For mountain bikers, the Mueller Park Trail is a great lower-altitude alpine ride that can be done as a 7-mile route to Big Rock or a 13-mile out-and-back to Rudy's Flat. Restrooms, water, and picnic facilities are available.

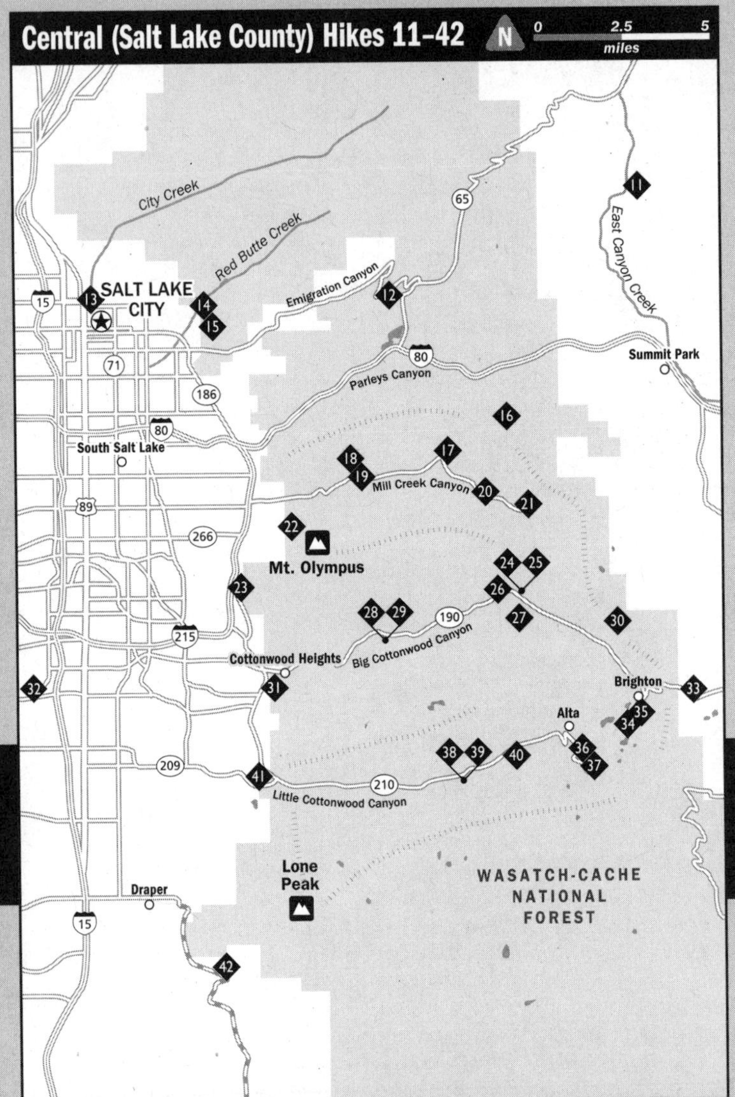
Central (Salt Lake County) Hikes 11–42
N
0
2.5
5
miles
City Creek
Red Butte Creek
Emigration Canyon
SALT LAKE CITY
East Canyon Creek
Summit Park
Parleys Canyon
South Salt Lake
Mill Creek Canyon
Mt. Olympus
Big Cottonwood Canyon
Cottonwood Heights
Brighton
Alta
Little Cottonwood Canyon
Lone Peak
Draper
WASATCH-CACHE NATIONAL FOREST

CENTRAL (SALT LAKE COUNTY)

11 MORMON PIONEER TRAIL

KEY AT-A-GLANCE INFORMATION

LENGTH: 9.1 miles one-way
ELEVATION GAIN: 1,364 feet
ELEVATION AT MORMON FLAT (STARTING TRAILHEAD): 6,039 feet
ELEVATION AT LITTLE DELL RESERVOIR (ENDING TRAILHEAD): 5,796 feet
ELEVATION AT BIG MOUNTAIN PASS (HIGH POINT, MIDPOINT, AND ALTERNATE TRAILHEAD FOR SHORTER HIKE): 7,403 feet
CONFIGURATION: One-way as described, but can be split into sections and done as several one-way or out-and-back hikes.
DIFFICULTY: Moderate
SCENERY: Canyon drainage, mountain views, distant view of Salt Lake Valley
EXPOSURE: Mostly shaded
TRAFFIC: Moderate
TRAIL SURFACE: Dirt, some rocks
HIKING TIME: 4–5 hours
WATER REQUIREMENTS: 2 liters
SEASON: Late spring, summer, early fall
ACCESS: No fees for access or parking at Mormon Flat. Seasonal parking fees charged at Little Dell Reservoir. Gate to Big Mountain and Mormon Flat closes during winter months.

See additional information at end of Description, page 64.

GPS Trailhead Coordinates

UTM Zone (WGS84) 12T

Easting 0450678

Northing 4518440

Latitude–Longitude: See page 64

IN BRIEF

The Donner Party blazed this historic trail in 1846, followed by 70,000 Mormon pioneers from 1847 to 1868. The trail also served as a leg of the Pony Express route. Still, for all its history, this section of the trail remains an inviting, tranquil, and exceptionally beautiful path through the woods of a gentle canyon. It's most alluring in late spring and early fall.

If you can only do a short portion of the hike or a round-trip, choose the quieter, more-remote 4-mile section from Mormon Flat to Big Mountain, where the chances of sharing the trail with wildlife are increased.

DESCRIPTION

As the Mormon Pioneers began their epic 1,300-mile trek from Nauvoo, Illinois, to the Salt Lake Valley, they didn't know that the steepest and longest sustained ascent—and the highest elevation of the entire journey—would occur at the end of the trail, on the day they first caught glimpse of their destination. This historic section of the Mormon Pioneer Trail captures that last full day of the trip and gives modern hikers some sense of what it might have been like to be a pioneer on a westward journey.

The 9.1-mile section of the trail was originally blazed by the ill-fated Donner Party in 1846, a year before the Mormon Pioneers came along. It took the Donner Party's 87 members more than a week to cut a road through the underbrush that you will hike in five hours or less. That delay would prove disastrous, as the party was caught in a winter storm in the Sierra Nevada less than three months later.

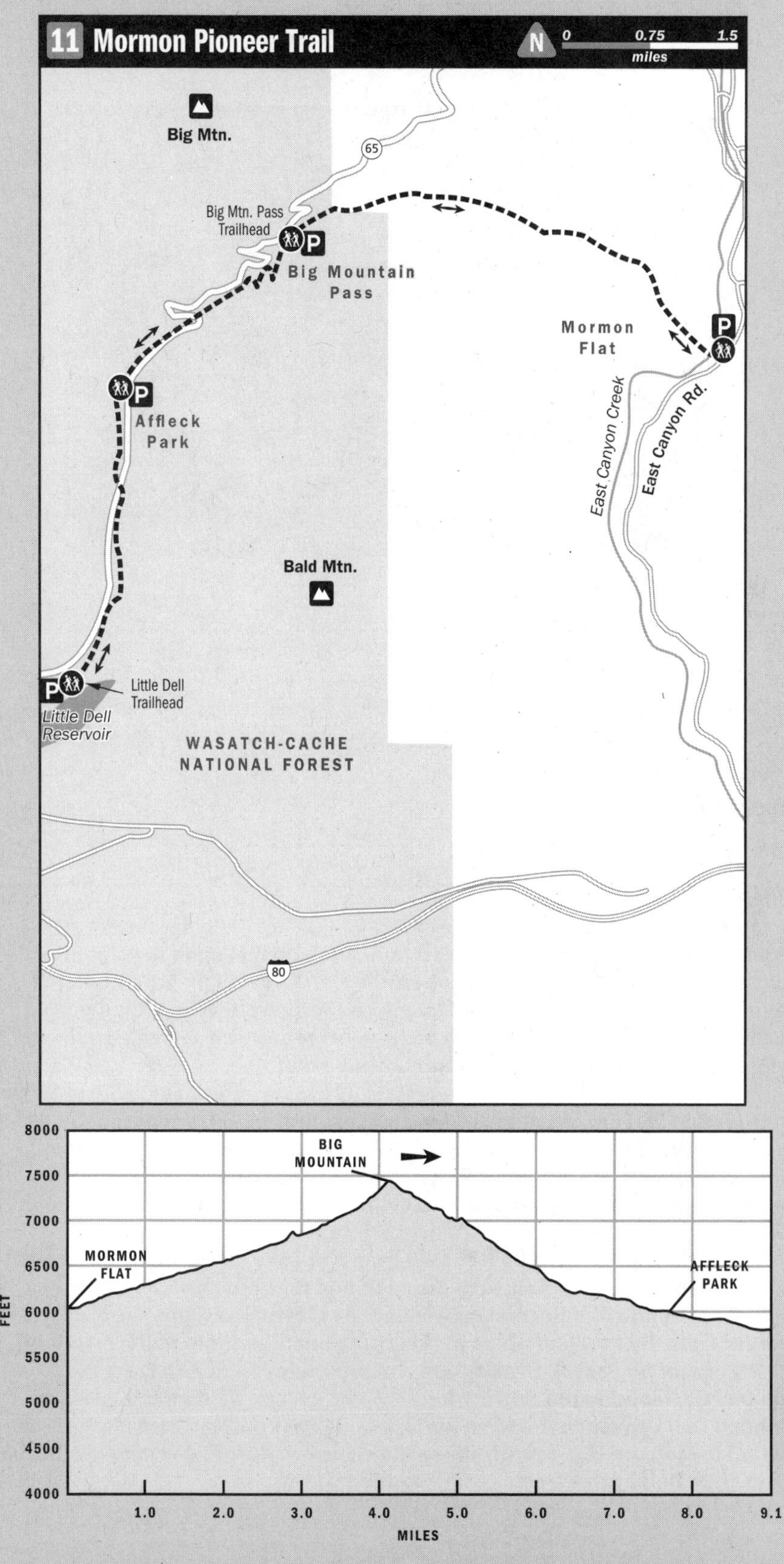
11 Mormon Pioneer Trail
N
0
0.75
1.5
miles
Big Mtn.
65
Big Mtn. Pass
Trailhead
Big Mountain
Pass
Mormon
Flat
Affleck
Park
East Canyon Creek
East Canyon Rd.
Bald Mtn.
Little Dell
Trailhead
Little Dell
Reservoir
WASATCH-CACHE
NATIONAL FOREST
80
8000
7500
7000
6500
6000
5500
5000
4500
4000
FEET
BIG
MOUNTAIN
MORMON
FLAT
AFFLECK
PARK
1.0
2.0
3.0
4.0
5.0
6.0
7.0
8.0
9.1
MILES

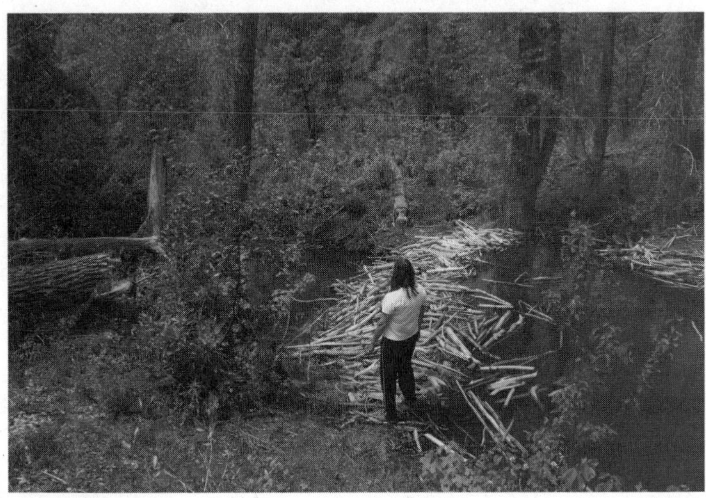

Beaver Dam at Affleck Park

California gold seekers and the Overland Stage used the trail in the 1850s. In 1860 and 1861, the trail served as the Pony Express route through the Wasatch Mountains. Riders would leave Bauchmann's Station (now covered by East Canyon Reservoir) on East Canyon Creek and arrive at the Mountain Dell Station within several hours.

Directions

The Mormon Pioneer Trail is best enjoyed as a one-way hike re-creating the arrival of the pioneers as they traveled from Mormon Flat up to Big Mountain Pass, where they first saw the Salt Lake Valley, and down into Mountain Dell Canyon. The one-way hike requires leaving a shuttle vehicle at Little Dell. The hike can also be done in shorter one-way or round-trip segments using Big Mountain Pass as a stopping or turnaround point.

Mormon Flat trailhead: **Take Interstate 80 east from Salt Lake City to Jeremy Ranch (Exit 143). Turn left at the off-ramp, cross under I-80, and turn left onto Rasmussen Road. Continue for 0.1 mile to Jeremy Ranch Road and turn right. Continue on Jeremy Ranch Road up East Canyon for 4.2 miles to the Mormon Flat parking area on the left. Cross the footbridge over East Canyon Creek to the well-marked trailhead.**

Little Dell trailhead: **Take I-80 east from Salt Lake City to the Emigration and East Canyons (UT 65, Exit 134). Turn left and proceed north on UT 65 for 3 miles to the Little Dell Recreation Area parking lot on the right. The trail can be accessed from the east end of the parking area near the shore of the reservoir.**

Big Mountain Pass (trail midpoint and alternate trailhead): **From the Little Dell Recreation Area parking lot, continue east on UT 65 for 5 miles up Mountain Dell Canyon to the large Big Mountain Pass parking area on the right. The trail to Mormon Flat departs down the slope on the lot's east side, while the trail to Little Dell begins from the lot's southwest side.**

To recapture the lore and scenic appeal of this historic trail, leave a shuttle vehicle waiting at Little Dell Reservoir (the trail's end), then drive on to Mormon Flat on East Canyon Creek. Cross the creek through a meadow of low-lying willow and follow the trail as it enters the mouth of Little Emigration Canyon—immediately you're transported back more than 150 years.

Within 0.5 miles after entering the canyon, the trail joins with a cottonwood-lined creek. The trail gradually ascends the wide canyon floor, which is marked with aspen and spruce. Pioneers would have welcomed the shade of the wooded slopes, having just spent much of their journey on the open plains of Nebraska and Wyoming. Like you, they may have seen their first moose or beaver dam while walking through this lush drainage. They may have spotted a cougar or been lucky enough to augment their diminishing rations with some venison.

At 3.5 miles, the trail steepens as it approaches Big Mountain Pass, gaining about 400 feet of elevation in the final half mile. When you arrive at the pass (now a parking lot with restrooms and a historical marker), take a moment to gaze to the west and imagine what it would have been like to have walked more than 1,300 miles and suddenly see your ultimate destination laid out below. On July 23, 1847, Brigham Young arrived at this pass, gazed out over the Salt Lake Valley, and said, "This is the place. Drive on." Three days earlier, Orson Pratt had arrived at Big Mountain Pass and measured the elevation at 7,245 feet above sea level. Although the actual elevation is 7,403 feet, his calculation was amazingly accurate given the simple handheld instruments of the day.

From Big Mountain Pass, the party locked their wagon wheels with chains, attached a drag shoe, and essentially slid down the slope into Mountain Dell Canyon, arriving near Affleck Park, where they camped for the night. Your Big Mountain descent will be less treacherous on a single-track trail that switchbacks down the head of the canyon through groves of aspen, bigtooth maple, and fir. Within 1.3 miles from the pass, the trail joins Mountain Dell Creek, which continues near the trail until it enters the Little Dell Reservoir. Along the way, the trail crosses the road twice and passes through Affleck Park at 2.5 miles from Big Mountain Pass, with restrooms, campsites, and picnic sites under the shade of towering cottonwoods.

Just down the trail from Affleck Park, you'll notice a small, rounded peak to the west known as Little Mountain. The pioneers camped at the base of Little Mountain before crossing into Emigration Canyon to the west and entering the Salt Lake Valley the next day. While there is a good trail leading over to Emigration Canyon from Affleck Park, the National Historic Trail follows the creek for another 1.6 miles into the Little Dell Recreation Area, where your shuttle vehicle awaits.

ADDITIONAL AT-A-GLANCE INFORMATION

MAPS: USGS Mountain Dell

FACILITIES: Restrooms at both trailheads and at Big Mountain and Affleck Park. No drinking water at trailheads, but nearby creek water can be purified.

DOGS: They are not permitted in Mountain Dell Canyon, a protected watershed, but they're allowed on the section from Mormon Flat to Big Mountain.

SPECIAL COMMENTS: Although road access is closed in winter, this is a popular snowshoeing and backcountry ski destination with a negligible avalanche hazard.

MORMON FLAT LATITUDE–LONGITUDE: N 40° 48' 55.8"; W 111° 35' 05.4"

LITTLE DELL RESERVOIR LATITUDE–LONGITUDE: N 40° 46' 37.2"; W 111° 41' 19.1"

BIG MOUNTAIN PASS LATITUDE–LONGITUDE: N 40° 49' 40.8"; W 111° 39' 13.1"

NEARBY ACTIVITIES

To complete your experience on the Mormon Pioneer Trail, visit This Is The Place Heritage Park, an outdoor living-history attraction that presents the story of everyday life in a typical Utah settlement from 1847 to 1897. The park includes more than 40 re-created and original buildings from settlements throughout Utah. Historically costumed staff demonstrate life as it would have been for 19th-century Utahns. The park is located at the mouth of Emigration Canyon at 2601 East Sunnyside Avenue. Call (801) 582-1847 for information or visit **www.thisistheplace.org.**

EMIGRATION CANYON RIDGELINE 12

IN BRIEF

A Jeep road leads to a dirt trail, then to a game trail, before it disappears completely. Soon you're following nothing more than a ridgeline of rolling foothills overlooking Emigration Canyon to the north and Parley's Canyon to the south. Beginning at Little Mountain, where pioneers began their final descent into the Salt Lake Valley, a walk along the ridgeline recaptures the feeling of crossing the plains on foot.

KEY AT-A-GLANCE INFORMATION

LENGTH: 5.2 miles round-trip
ELEVATION GAIN: 1,139 feet
ELEVATION AT TRAILHEAD: 6,237 feet
CONFIGURATION: Out-and-back
DIFFICULTY: Easy
SCENERY: Rolling hills and views of canyons and Salt Lake Valley
EXPOSURE: No shade
TRAFFIC: Light
TRAIL SURFACE: Dirt and rock
HIKING TIME: 2.5–3 hours
WATER REQUIREMENTS: 1 liter. No water is available at the trailhead or on the trail.
SEASON: Year-round
ACCESS: No fees for access or parking
MAPS: USGS Mountain Dell, Fort Douglas
FACILITIES: Restrooms are available in the trailhead parking lot.
DOGS: Permitted
SPECIAL COMMENTS: Ideal in spring, fall, or as a winter snowshoe hike

DESCRIPTION

Salt Lake City's original hiking destination was Emigration Canyon, though you wouldn't know that today. In 1846 the Donner Party blazed the trail from Little Mountain Summit down to the valley floor. A year later, the first company of Mormon Pioneers, led by Brigham Young, would descend into the Salt Lake Valley through Emigration Canyon. Emigration Canyon was the primary route into the Salt Lake Valley until the road through Parley's Canyon (now the route of Interstate 80) was completed in 1850.

In spite of its proximity to the University of Utah and downtown Salt Lake City, Emigration Canyon has retained its bucolic feel. It's still a popular training ride or day tour for local cyclists. As you drive up the

Directions →

From downtown Salt Lake City, go east on 800 South, crossing 1300 East where it jogs to the right and becomes Sunnyside Avenue. After another 2 miles, pass Hogle Zoo on the right and This Is The Place Heritage Park on the left. Continue for another 8 miles up Emigration Canyon to the Little Mountain Summit parking area on the right.

GPS Trailhead Coordinates

UTM Zone (WGS84) 12T
Easting 0436605
Northing 4511882
Latitude N 40° 46' 28.5"
Longitude W 111° 43' 06.0"

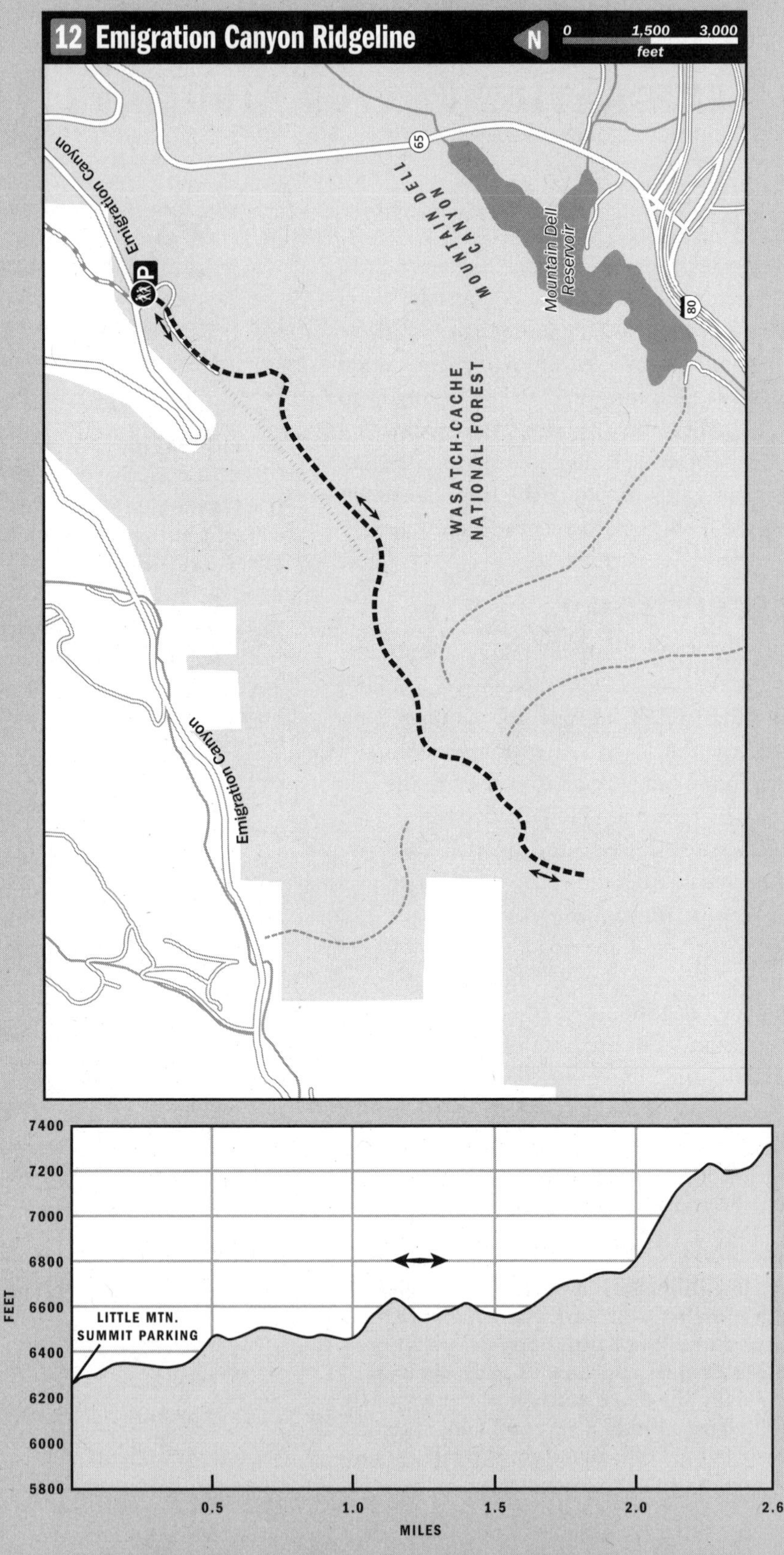
12 Emigration Canyon Ridgeline
N
0
1,500
3,000
feet
65
80
Emigration Canyon
MOUNTAIN DELL CANYON
Mountain Dell Reservoir
WASATCH-CACHE NATIONAL FOREST
7400
7200
7000
6800
6600
6400
6200
6000
5800
FEET
LITTLE MTN. SUMMIT PARKING
0.5
1.0
1.5
2.0
2.6
MILES

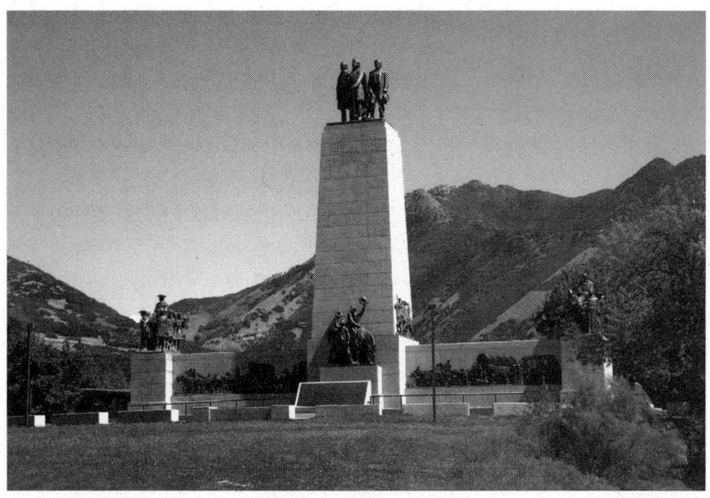

This Is The Place Monument, at the mouth of Emigration Canyon

canyon's gentle grade, be sure to stop at the historical markers along the way, which will give you a glimpse into its early history.

Before taking off on the trail, walk to the east side of the trailhead parking area and look down to Little Dell Reservoir, which fills the mouth of Mountain Dell Canyon. The first wagon trains rolled down this canyon, then climbed the slopes below leading to Little Mountain Summit. From there, they made the crossing and descent into Emigration Canyon. Thirteen years later, a Pony Express station was built near the upper end of Little Dell Reservoir and became the last stop before Salt Lake City.

From the restrooms at the southwest side of the parking area, walk up a faint trail to the west, passing a natural gas utility station on your left and communications towers on your right. Soon you come to a crumbling asphalt road that continues up the ridge for about 100 yards before giving way to an old unmaintained Jeep trail. Before long, even the Jeep trail turns faint and soon becomes a single-track footpath that degrades into a game trail, and then no trail at all. As long as you stick to the ridge, which rolls up and down over six successively higher hills in a southwest direction, you needn't worry about being on a trail.

At some points you'll be walking through sheep grass and sage up to your knees. Scrub oak and curly-leaf mountain mahogany overgrow what little trail there is to be found. In summer, you'll share the route with crickets, lizards, and rattlesnakes. In winter and spring, you're more likely to find deer hiding in the underbrush. Fall brings a blush of color to the patches of scrub oak.

With its low elevations and lack of shade, the ridgeline can be hot and dry in summer. A fresh blanket of snow, though, makes for a rewarding outing on snowshoes. The expanse of hills and low-lying mountains in all directions is particularly scenic in winter.

Even though I-80 lies directly below to the south and luxury homes dot the slopes of Emigration Canyon to the north, a walk along the ridgeline is surprisingly quiet and peaceful. Depending on the season, you're likely to see hummingbirds, raptors, and a variety of field birds along the way. Breezes glide freely over the treeless slopes and easily bend and sway the grasses at your feet.

After 2.6 miles and a little more than an hour of walking, you'll come to an unnamed hilltop, marked on USGS maps as Dale, at an elevation of 7,376 feet. Here you'll find a small, open area ideally suited for a hilltop picnic or snack, where you can enjoy the views into the Salt Lake Valley before returning to the trailhead.

NEARBY ACTIVITIES

Hogle Zoo is located at the mouth of Emigration Canyon across from This Is The Place Heritage Park. The zoo's animals and exhibits, spread over 42 acres, play host to more than 700,000 visitors per year. The zoo is open year-round and closed only on Christmas and New Year's Day. Call (801) 582-1631 or visit **www.hoglezoo.com** to learn about special exhibits and programs.

CITY CREEK CANYON 13

IN BRIEF

With the 26-story LDS Church office building to your back and the Utah State Capitol in front of you, follow a creek through a city park, quickly leaving the city behind. Within 2 miles you'll be walking in a national forest and nature preserve shared with elk, moose, and mountain lions.

DESCRIPTION

City Creek has served as Salt Lake City's primary water source since 1847, when Mormon pioneers first arrived in the valley. No other hike in the United States allows you to be in an urban center, within a block of the state capitol building, then so quickly find yourself following a tumbling creek through the depths of a protected canyon filled with undisturbed wildlife and dense vegetation.

If the hardest part of this hike is finding parking, then the most dangerous part is crossing the pedestrian crosswalk on State Street to access the "trailhead." Starting at the northeast corner of State Street and North Temple, walk one-half block to the east along the decorative sidewalk and continue as the sidewalk curves north onto Canyon Road, away from downtown and into a quiet residential area. Tiles embedded in the concrete identify native animals and birds by their footprint, preparing you for what you're likely to find up-canyon.

On July 21, 1847, near the location of the trailhead, Orson Pratt and Erastus Snow (along with other members of the vanguard party) arrived in the Salt Lake Valley and set up camp. They quickly diverted water from City Creek to soften the soil. By the time Brigham Young arrived three days later, they had already planted five acres of potatoes.

KEY AT-A-GLANCE INFORMATION

LENGTH: 2–9 miles
ELEVATION GAIN: 300–740 feet
ELEVATION AT MAIN TRAILHEAD: 4,370 feet
ELEVATION AT ALTERNATE CANYON TRAILHEAD: 4,705 feet
CONFIGURATION: Out-and-back or one-way
DIFFICULTY: Easy
SCENERY: Riparian canyon with brushy slopes; good bird-watching
EXPOSURE: Partially shaded
TRAFFIC: Moderate to heavy
TRAIL SURFACE: Paved or dirt, depending on options chosen
HIKING TIME: 1–4 hours
WATER REQUIREMENTS: 0.5 liters (water fountains placed along trail)
SEASON: Year-round
ACCESS: Hikable year-round. No fees for access or parking.
MAPS: USGS Fort Douglas
FACILITIES: Restrooms near trailhead and at several places along the parkway
DOGS: Permitted on leash
SPECIAL COMMENTS: City Creek is a multiuse trail, popular with cyclists, joggers, strollers, and hikers. Hikers may choose from dozens of spur trails and dirt trails that parallel the paved parkway.

GPS Trailhead Coordinates

UTM Zone (WGS84) 12T
Easting 0425046; Northing 4513782
Main trailhead:
N 40° 46' 18.0"; W 111° 53' 16.8"
Alternate canyon trailhead:
N 40° 47' 31.0"; W 111° 53' 16.8"

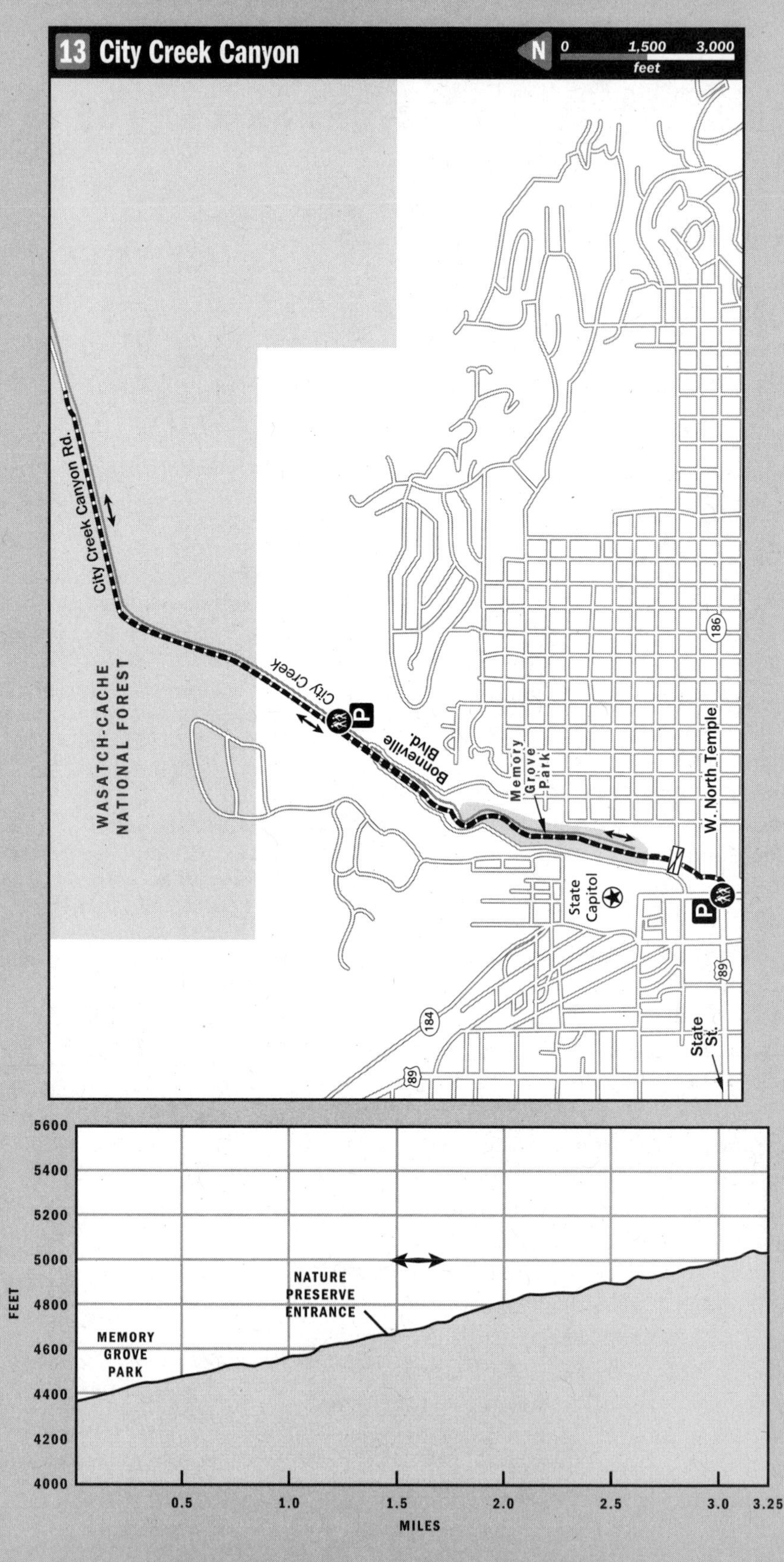

13 City Creek Canyon
N
0
1,500
3,000
feet
City Creek Canyon Rd.
WASATCH-CACHE NATIONAL FOREST
City Creek
P
Bonneville Blvd.
Memory Grove Park
State Capitol
W. North Temple
186
89
184
State St.
5600
5400
5200
5000
4800
4600
4400
4200
4000
FEET
MEMORY GROVE PARK
NATURE PRESERVE ENTRANCE
0.5
1.0
1.5
2.0
2.5
3.0
3.25
MILES

Within a matter of weeks, a grist mill had been built on City Creek. During the early years of Salt Lake City, energy harnessed from City Creek powered many of the essential industries, such as blacksmith shops, furniture makers, and clothing mills. Water from City Creek still supplies drinking water for much of downtown Salt Lake City and the Avenues.

After walking through two residential blocks, pass through the gate at the entrance of Memory Grove Park. As you enter the park, the rising canyon walls have already blocked the view of the city, and it's easy to forget that the State Capitol is just 400 feet to your left but completely out of sight.

Once within the park, you may walk along the main paved road or on any of the pathways that pass the various monuments and benches placed throughout the park. Several footbridges cross the creek and allow you to use the dirt trail on the creek's east side. This trail hugs the creek and provides more shade, solitude, and varied terrain than the paved parkway. It normally delivers a sure footing but can be slick during snowmelt or after a heavy rain.

Follow the creek up Memory Grove Park and through a second gate. After 1.5 miles, the paved parkway curves to the right and crosses over City Creek to join Bonneville Boulevard. Take the narrower paved trail that rises to the left, passing the retention pond on your right (often home to ducks and geese). This area provides a convenient turnaround point for a 3-mile round-trip hike, or you can cross Bonneville Boulevard and enter the City Creek Nature Preserve straight ahead.

After crossing Bonneville Boulevard, walk 0.1 mile to a small parking area with an entrance station, water fountain, and restrooms. You can use this area as an alternate trailhead, allowing you to bypass the hassle of downtown parking and begin your hike in more of a wilderness setting. The road, which continues up the canyon, closes to vehicle traffic from October 30 through May 25, and even when it's open, cars are only allowed on even-numbered days. The city manages the area beyond the entrance station as a protected watershed and wildlife refuge.

Directions

It seems strange to refer to one of the busiest intersections in downtown Salt Lake City as a trailhead. Yet the hike starts at the northeast corner of State Street (US 89) and North Temple, just a block from Temple Square and convenient to downtown hotels and shopping. The most difficult part of getting to the trailhead will be finding a place to park. Use one of the public or commercial lots nearby, since most street parking in the vicinity is limited to two hours.

You can also start the hike farther up the canyon by driving to the City Creek Nature Preserve entrance area. Take North Temple west 0.3 miles to B Street (250 East). Turn left on B Street and continue north through the Avenues for 0.7 miles. At the corner of B Street and 11th Avenue, B Street becomes East Bonneville Boulevard. Continue north on East Bonneville Boulevard for 0.6 miles along the east rim of City Creek Canyon. As East Bonneville Boulevard makes a hairpin turn, go right onto the narrow paved road leading into the City Creek Nature Preserve (marked by a large sign). Drive 0.1 mile to the small parking area at the gateway entrance to City Creek Canyon.

As you walk up the paved parkway, remember that you're sharing the road with cyclists, who often come down the canyon at high speeds. Hikers should stay on the side of the road nearest the creek.

About 800 feet past the entrance station, a trail (marked by a sign) heads up the hillside to the left. This trail parallels the creek and the parkway up the canyon and provides a quieter, more natural alternative to the parkway. The trail follows the gentle slope of the canyon hillside, which is covered by grasses, dense brush, and Gamble oaks. Expect both less shade and less traffic on the trail, which still provides easy access to the frequent restrooms and drinking fountains along the parkway. To the right of the parkway, City Creek descends the canyon in a series of meandering stretches punctuated by dozens of small waterfalls.

The canyon is a year-round home to deer, coyote, and elusive mountain lions. In winter, you may well spot elk and moose, even in the lower elevations below the reservoir. Bird-watchers enjoy the abundant and varied raptor populations throughout the year. Hawks, eagles, falcons, and owls find small rodents on the canyon's grassy slopes to be easy pickings. Grouse, quail, chukar, and pheasants are plentiful in the brush.

Along both the creek and parkway, cottonwoods offer ample shade. About 2 miles from the entrance station, the higher elevation and north-facing slope provide a hospitable environment for stands of balsam and spruce. Scattered along the parkway are convenient rest areas with picnic tables, restrooms, and water fountains, making City Creek Canyon a popular destination for family outings, picnics, and outdoor relaxation.

From the entrance station, City Creek continues up the canyon for 13 miles, and the road is paved for 5.8 miles. The creek is fed by snowmelt, natural springs at the top of the canyon, and many smaller springs along the course of the creek. A reservoir, located 3 miles from the entrance station, makes a convenient turnaround point. Because the area is a protected watershed, no dogs are permitted above the reservoir.

Although most visitors to City Creek Canyon stay close to the parkway, creek, and main trail, dozens of side trails lead up the slopes on either side of the canyon. In less than 15 minutes from a creekside picnic area, you can reach the ridge, which offers commanding views of the Salt Lake Valley to the south.

NEARBY ACTIVITIES

Because the hike originates in downtown Salt Lake City, shopping malls, restaurants, theaters, and hotels are close by. Historic Temple Square is just a block to the west, and the Utah State Capitol is two blocks to the north. Before starting the hike, you may want to walk through the Brigham Young Historic Park on the southeast corner of State Street and North Temple. The park features a waterwheel, mill, and other displays depicting the role of City Creek in Salt Lake City history.

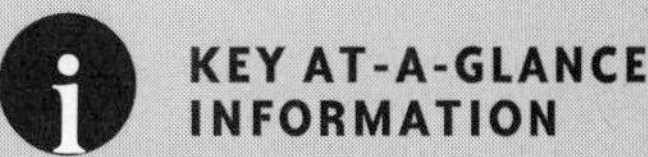

RED BUTTE GARDEN 14

IN BRIEF

Formal gardens give way to natural area trails in a peaceful setting of beauty and historical significance that also provides education and fun. There's something for everyone any time of the year. Located just minutes by foot from the University of Utah campus.

DESCRIPTION

It would be easy to visit Red Butte Garden and spend the better part of a day enjoying the colorful floral gardens, ponds, and waterfalls without ever venturing into the more remote natural trails area. Indeed, most visitors find sufficient variety and entertainment in the 18 acres of landscaped gardens that they never leave the paved trails for the nearly 100 acres of grassy hillsides, wildflower meadows, and rocky outcroppings that lie to the east of the more formal gardens. But those who come prepared with basic trail shoes and water can enjoy a network of more than 4 miles of hill trails offering gentle ascents that lead to sweeping views of the Salt Lake Valley.

Beginning in the late 1800s, the U.S. Army used the strategically important hillside as a camp, firing range, and fort. The red sandstone crags that form the hill's main ridge served as a quarry that was actively

KEY AT-A-GLANCE INFORMATION

LENGTH: 2–4 miles, depending on route and side trails taken
ELEVATION GAIN: 410 feet
ELEVATION AT THE COURTYARD GARDEN, JUST OUTSIDE THE VISITOR CENTER: 5,065 feet
CONFIGURATION: Loop with various side trails and extensions
DIFFICULTY: Easy–moderate
SCENERY: Foothills, outcroppings of red sandstone, riparian corridor, and valley views
EXPOSURE: Full sun, partial shade
TRAFFIC: High in formal gardens; low in natural area
TRAIL SURFACE: Paved in formal gardens; dirt trails in natural area
HIKING TIME: 1–2 hours
WATER REQUIREMENTS: 1 liter
SEASON: The garden is open year-round. Hours vary by season.
ACCESS: Entrance fee paid at visitor center; free admission to garden members. Hours vary by season. Check the schedule online at www.redbuttegarden.org or call (801) 581-IRIS for schedule, events, and guided tours.
MAPS: USGS Sugar House
FACILITIES: Restrooms, water, snacks, phone at visitor center
DOGS: Not permitted

Directions

From Salt Lake City, take either I-80 east to Foothill Drive (Exit 129) or I-215 north to Foothill Drive (Exit 1). Continue north on Foothill Drive (UT 186) for 3.1 miles to Wakara Way. Turn right on Wakara Way and continue 0.6 miles to the Red Butte Garden entrance. Parking is available 0.1 mile ahead on the left. Enter the garden and trail system through the visitor center. Red Butte Garden is located at 300 Wakara Way.

GPS Trailhead Coordinates

(Courtyard Garden)

UTM Zone (WGS84) 12T
Easting 0430485
Northing 4513062
Latitude N 40° 45' 55.75"
Longitude W 111° 49' 25.33"

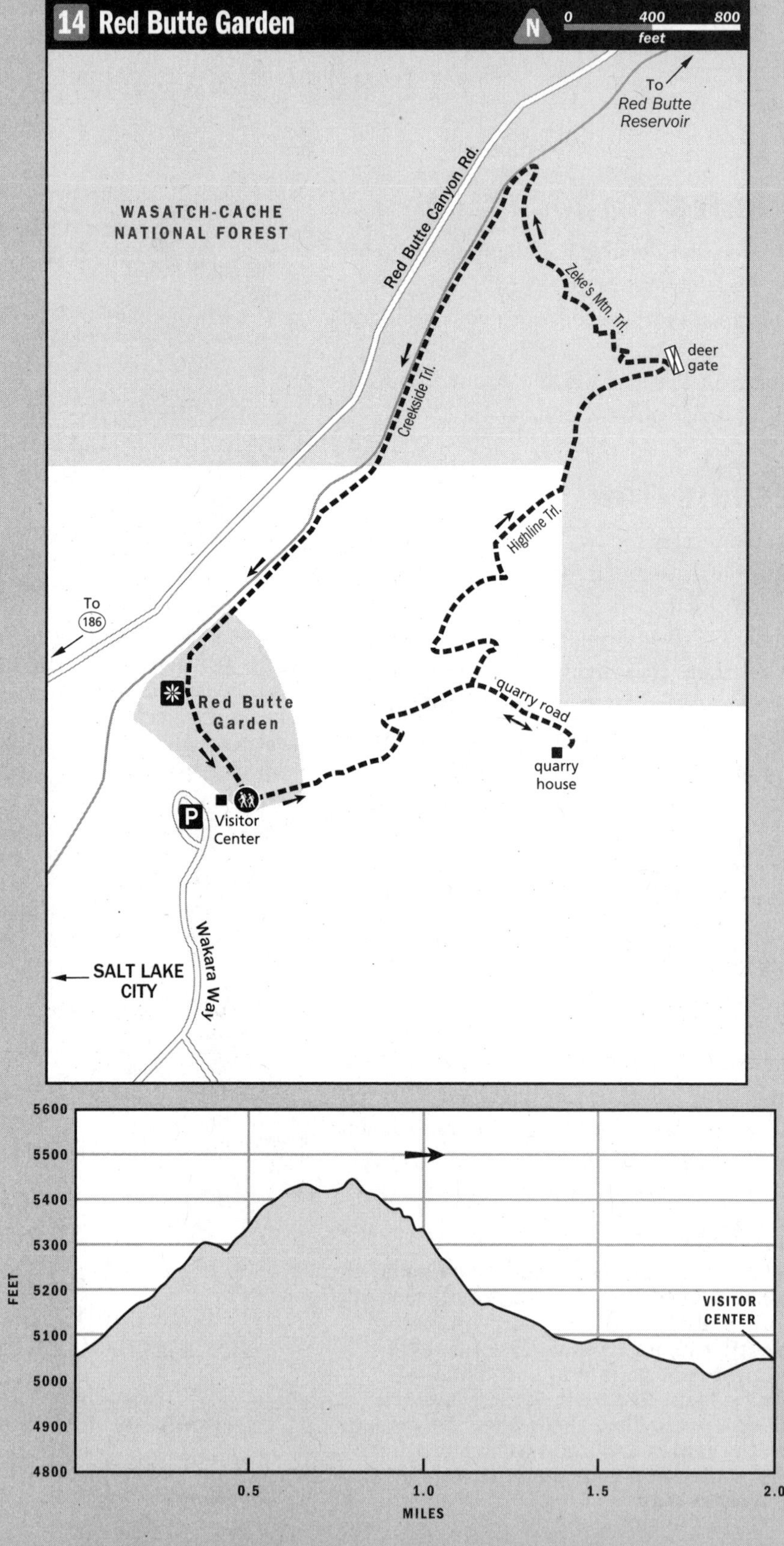

14 Red Butte Garden
N
0
400
800
feet
To
Red Butte
Reservoir
WASATCH-CACHE
NATIONAL FOREST
Red Butte Canyon Rd.
Zeke's Mtn. Trl.
deer
gate
Creekside Trl.
Highline Trl.
To
186
Red Butte
Garden
quarry road
quarry
house
Visitor
Center
P
Wakara Way
SALT LAKE
CITY
5600
5500
5400
5300
5200
5100
5000
4900
4800
FEET
VISITOR
CENTER
0.5
1.0
1.5
2.0
MILES

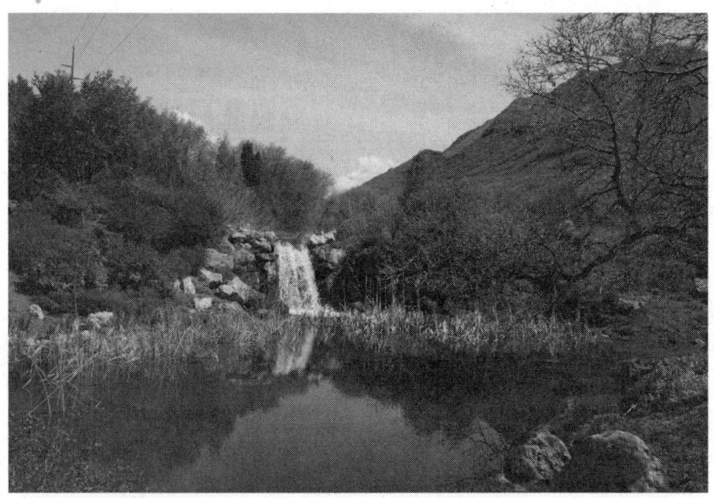

Waterfall and pond at Red Butte Garden

worked until about 1934, producing the redstone blocks still seen in many of the prominent homes and buildings throughout the Salt Lake Valley.

At the visitor center you'll receive a useful guide and map that identify many of the garden highlights, such as the Courtyard Garden, the Herb Garden, the Water Pavilion, and the Children's Garden. The guide also features a map of the natural area trails, showing four different trailheads that access the natural area from the formal gardens.

One popular loop hike follows the perimeter of the Red Butte Garden property and offers a surprising variety of terrain, foliage, and scenery in a 2-mile hike. Beginning at the Courtyard Garden, take the trail for 200 feet along the south side of the Four Seasons Garden. Leaving the formal area, continue to the right along a wide, bark path, cross the Quarry Road, and continue up the Seepy Hollow Trail for 0.2 miles to another Quarry Road crossing. Seepy Hollow follows the course of a natural spring seepage, so in wet conditions you might want to take the longer Quarry Road. A short 0.1-mile walk up Quarry Road brings you to a sign marking the junction of the Zeke's Mountain Trail loop to the left.

From this junction you can take a 0.1-mile spur trail to the end of Quarry Road and visit the historic Quarry House. This fascinating sandstone structure, dating to the late 1800s, was built to store equipment and house the quarry superintendent. Although the roof is gone and some of the walls have been vandalized, the house's stonework shows the masons' enduring craftsmanship. The centerpiece of the Quarry House is a large double-sided fireplace.

Returning to Zeke's Mountain Trail, you'll wind through a thicket of Gambel oak up the craggy hillside to the Bennett Vista Trail, which leads to the hill's crest and offers commanding views of the Salt Lake Valley. From the hilltop, continue east on Zeke's Mountain Trail, generally following the property's fenced perimeter. At the far east side of the property, the trail meets the fence. Here, a one-way gate allows unwelcome deer to leave the property so they can forage on the adjoining National Forest Service land rather than eat the cultivated flowers in Red Butte Garden.

The trail descends along the fence line to the creek, which forms the northern boundary of Red Butte Garden. Along the Creekside Trail you'll enjoy the shade of oaks and bigtooth maples. The Creekside Trail continues for 0.4 miles before returning to the formal garden area.

Throughout the natural area trails, you'll find more than 130 native plants and trees. In spring, when the garden is especially colorful, yellow blooms of arrow-leaf balsam root and speckles of blue Wasatch Penstemon dot the green hillside. You might see a Great Basin rattlesnake sunning itself on the trail, or spot rodents, rabbits, or even evidence of an occasional bobcat.

The natural area trails are well marked with signs at all of the trailheads. While the signs become more scarce in the outlying areas, getting lost is never much of a concern, since the property is fenced on all sides and you can visually orient yourself along most of the trails. If you're ever in doubt, just follow any trail downhill and to the west, and you'll soon find yourself back within the formal gardens.

Red Butte Garden's natural area trails offer plenty of options in the way of short loops, spur trails, and side trails. After exploring the foothills and creekside in the natural area, you can return to the wide, paved trails of the formal gardens and easily spend an additional hour or more enjoying the year-round beauty in this community treasure.

NEARBY ACTIVITIES

Red Butte Garden offers a year-round program of classes, workshops, activities, tours, and community programs. The Outdoor Concert Series features world-renowned performing artists on the garden's amphitheater stage during June, July, and August. Visit **www.redbuttegarden.org** or call (801) 585-0556 for a schedule and tickets. Red Butte Garden lies adjacent to the University of Utah, which provides an abundant offering of concerts, sporting events, and campus activities.

THE LIVING ROOM (with Red Butte Extension) 15

IN BRIEF

The Living Room is the best room in the house for an accessible overview of the Salt Lake Valley. It's furnished with charming sandstone chairs, armrests, and even coffee tables you can put your feet on. The hike leads through foothill vegetation and offers an onward scramble to a higher sandstone outcropping on a ridge above Red Butte Canyon.

KEY AT-A-GLANCE INFORMATION

LENGTH: 2.3 miles round-trip to the Living Room, 2.7 miles round-trip to the Red Butte extension

ELEVATION GAIN: 980 feet to the Living Room, additional 360 feet to Red Butte extension

ELEVATION AT TRAILHEAD: 5,000 feet

CONFIGURATION: Out-and-back

DIFFICULTY: Easy

SCENERY: Foothills and valley views

EXPOSURE: Partial shade to the Living Room, unshaded from the Living Room to Red Butte extension

TRAFFIC: Moderate

TRAIL SURFACE: Dirt and gravel to the Living Room, rock to the Red Butte extension

HIKING TIME: 1.5–2 hours round-trip to the Living Room; 2–3 hours round-trip to Red Butte extension

WATER REQUIREMENTS: 1 liter

SEASON: Spring, summer, fall

ACCESS: No fees for access or parking

MAPS: USGS Fort Douglas

FACILITIES: No restrooms or water at the trailhead

DOGS: Permitted (waste must be bagged and removed)

SPECIAL COMMENTS: A popular sunset hike for locals

DESCRIPTION

Red Butte Canyon is the smallest of seven canyons streaming down the Wasatch ridges east of Salt Lake City. It lies directly east of downtown Salt Lake City and above Fort Douglas and the University of Utah campus. A hike to the popular Living Room overlook will take you through foothill vegetation to Red Butte Ridge, which forms the south side of Red Butte Canyon.

The historical significance of the area was first tied to its use as a sandstone quarry and later to water rights. In 1862, U.S. troops established Fort Douglas and used the spring water of Red Butte Creek for domestic and irrigation purposes, affecting the 3,000 local residents who relied on the creek for their water supply. Today the canyon is managed as a protected Natural Research Area under the

Directions

From Salt Lake City take either I-80 east to Foothill Drive (Exit 129) or I-215 north to Foothill Drive (Exit 1). Continue north on Foothill Drive (UT 186) for 3.1 miles to Wakara Way. Turn right on Wakara Way and continue 0.6 miles to the Red Butte Garden entrance. Turn right on Colorow Drive before entering Red Butte Garden, and continue 0.2 miles to the trailhead on the left side of the street.

GPS Trailhead Coordinates

UTM Zone (WGS84) 12T

Easting 0430675

Northing 4512367

Latitude N 40° 45' 33.4"

Longitude W 111° 49' 16.6"

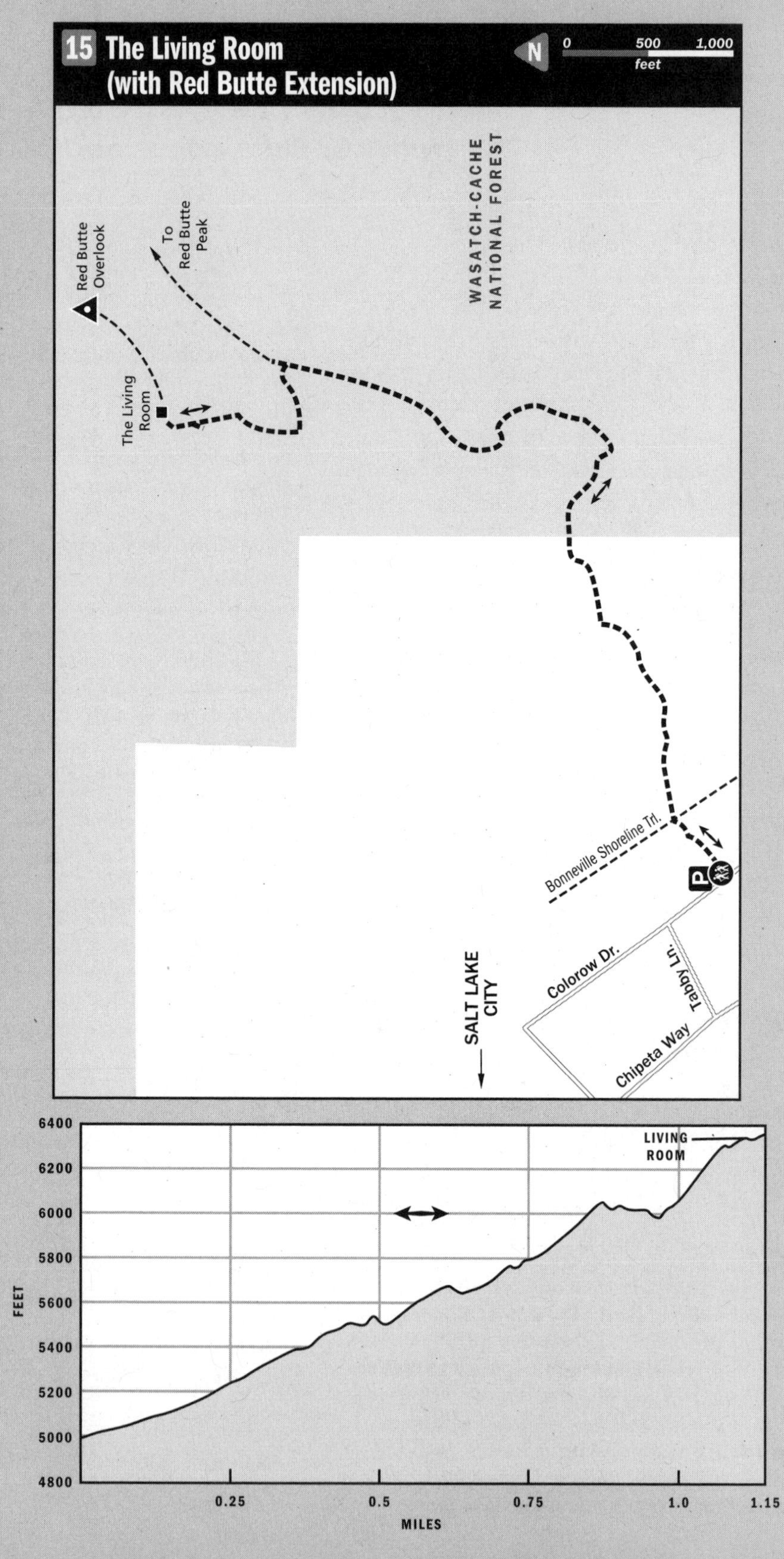
15 The Living Room
(with Red Butte Extension)
N
0
500
1,000
feet
Red Butte Overlook
To Red Butte Peak
WASATCH-CACHE NATIONAL FOREST
The Living Room
Bonneville Shoreline Trl.
P
SALT LAKE CITY
Colorow Dr.
Tabby Ln.
Chipeta Way
6400
6200
6000
5800
5600
5400
5200
5000
4800
FEET
LIVING ROOM
0.25
0.5
0.75
1.0
1.15
MILES

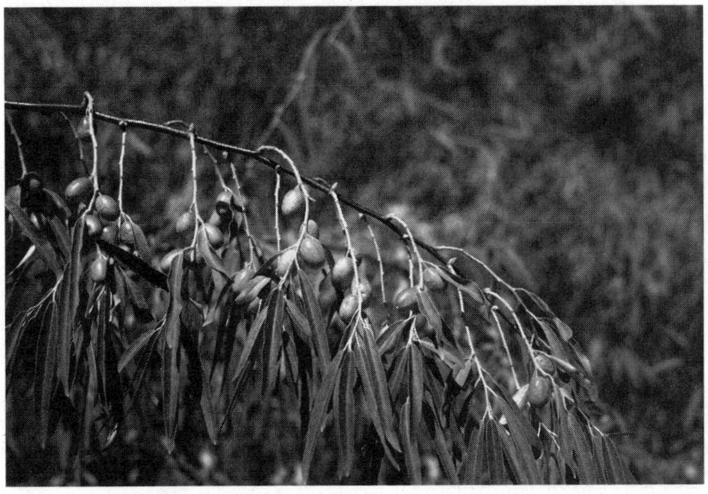

Russian olive tree near trail

control of the U.S. Forest Service and is recognized as the most pristine watershed along the Wasatch Front.

Within 100 yards of the marked trailhead on the east side of Colorow Drive, you come to a small spring-fed creek. The trail crosses the creek at the base of a large, mature Russian olive tree, one of several in the riparian corridor. The path continues up the slope for another 0.1 mile before arriving at the wide Bonneville Shoreline Trail. Here you take a jog to the right for 50 feet before continuing up and to the left along a gravel trail. You'll enter a dense cover of Gambel oak and bigtooth maple near the mouth of a small ravine known as Georges Hollow.

At 0.7 miles from the trailhead, the route breaks out onto a ridgeline that you'll follow up and to the east along the south slope of a ravine. At 1.1 miles, you come to a trail junction at the top of the ravine. Continuing straight ahead leads up to the 6,472-foot Red Butte peak. Instead, take the trail that crosses the ravine and curves to the left. This path to the Living Room now makes a westward ascent along the north side of the ravine. Upon crossing to the north side of the ravine, the rocks change from gray limestone to peach-colored sandstone. After walking just 0.1 mile from the junction along the sandstone-studded slope, you arrive at the Living Room.

The Living Room invites a relaxing stay. A man-made arrangement of angular sandstone slabs provides a comfortable observation point complete with several chairs, armrests, ottomans, and coffee tables. There's no better place to sit and watch a sunset, take in the spring wildflowers or the fall colors, or just relax and enjoy a snack. The Living Room overlooks the University of Utah and Fort Douglas, where athletes were housed during the 2002 Winter Olympics. The extended views stretch from the Great Salt Lake to the north to the Oquirrh Mountains in the west, and down to the southern end of the Salt Lake Valley, clear to the Point of the Mountain.

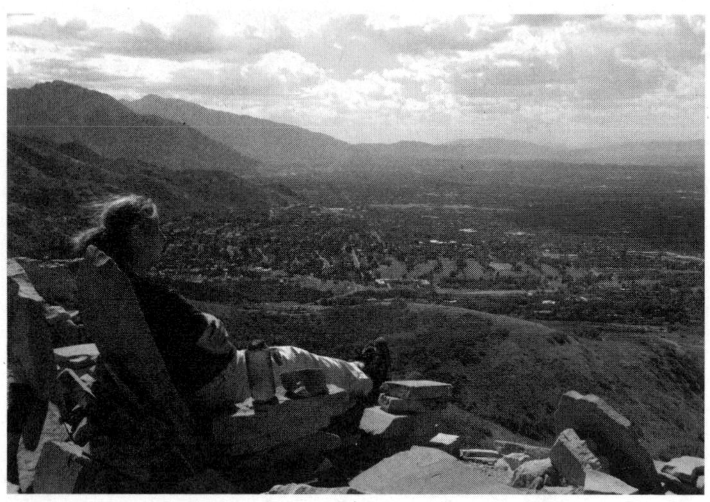

Stone lounge chairs await at the Living Room.

While the Living Room is the final destination for most hikers, there is an easy scramble to a higher overlook if you have a little extra energy. Behind the Living Room, a faint and noticeably steeper trail leads up the sandstone crags to the east along a ridgeline to a clearly visible viewpoint. In about 15 minutes, you'll find yourself on a shelf of large sandstone slabs with views down into Red Butte Canyon and the Red Butte Reservoir to the north. The extension to this overlook adds about 0.4 miles round-trip beyond the Living Room.

NEARBY ACTIVITIES

Ensign Peak is a popular Salt Lake overlook with a well-maintained trail and a round-trip distance of less than 1 mile. From downtown, take State Street to the east of the State Capitol Building on East Capitol Boulevard. Continue up to Edgecombe Drive, turn left, and continue to the trailhead on Churchhill Drive at the Ensign Peak Nature Park.

LAMBS CANYON 16

IN BRIEF

Old-growth forests of spruce and fir, shared with quaking aspen, line a canyon fed by several springs. A steep trail to an 8,100-foot pass offers views into the valley before leading down Elbow Fork and into Mill Creek Canyon. It's a symphony of woods, wildflowers, berries, creeks, and views.

KEY AT-A-GLANCE INFORMATION

LENGTH: 4 miles one-way
ELEVATION GAIN: 1,518 feet
ELEVATION AT LAMBS CANYON: 6,615 feet
ELEVATION AT ELBOW FORK: 6,686 feet
CONFIGURATION: Out-and-back or one-way
DIFFICULTY: Moderate
SCENERY: Abundant plant life in two deep canyons, views of Salt Lake Valley and surrounding peaks from the pass
EXPOSURE: Mostly shaded
TRAFFIC: Light
TRAIL SURFACE: Dirt
HIKING TIME: 2.5–3.5 hours
WATER REQUIREMENTS: 1–2 liters; water in creeks can be purified.
SEASON: Year-round
ACCESS: Mill Creek Canyon is a fee-access area within the Wasatch-Cache National Forest. The gate at Maple Grove is closed November 1–July 1. To hike Lambs Canyon when the gate is closed, park at the Maple Grove picnic area and walk 1.5 miles up the canyon road to the Elbow Fork trailhead.
MAPS: USGS Mount Aire, Trails Illustrated Wasatch Front (709)

See additional info on page 84.

DESCRIPTION

In the 1860s, Abel Lamb recognized the value of the timber in the canyon that now bears his name. He built a cabin in the canyon, and his son, Horace, built a sawmill. To meet the construction demands in the growing Salt Lake Valley, the sawmill hauled lumber down the new Golden Pass Toll Road (now I-80), which was constructed by Parley P. Pratt through Big Canyon (now known as Parley's Canyon). But Lamb's sawmill couldn't make a dent in the thousands of acres of timber that still cover Lambs Canyon today.

Directions

To Lambs Canyon trailhead: From Salt Lake City take I-80 east to Lambs Canyon (Exit 137). Turn right onto Lambs Canyon Road and drive up the canyon 2 miles to the trailhead parking area on the left. The trailhead is across the street on the west side of Lambs Canyon Road.

To Elbow Fork trailhead (Mill Creek Canyon): From I-215 on Salt Lake City's east side, take the 3300 South/3900 South turnoff (Exit 4). Turn left onto Wasatch Boulevard and go north 1 block to 3800 South. Turn right on 3800 South and continue toward the mouth of Mill Creek Canyon. Pass the toll booth at 0.7 miles and continue for another 5.3 miles to the Elbow Fork trailhead, where Mill Creek and the road turn sharply to the right. Roadside parking is available at the trailhead.

GPS Trailhead Coordinates

UTM Zone (WGS84) 12T
Easting 0444525
Northing 4507874
Latitude–Longitude: See page 84

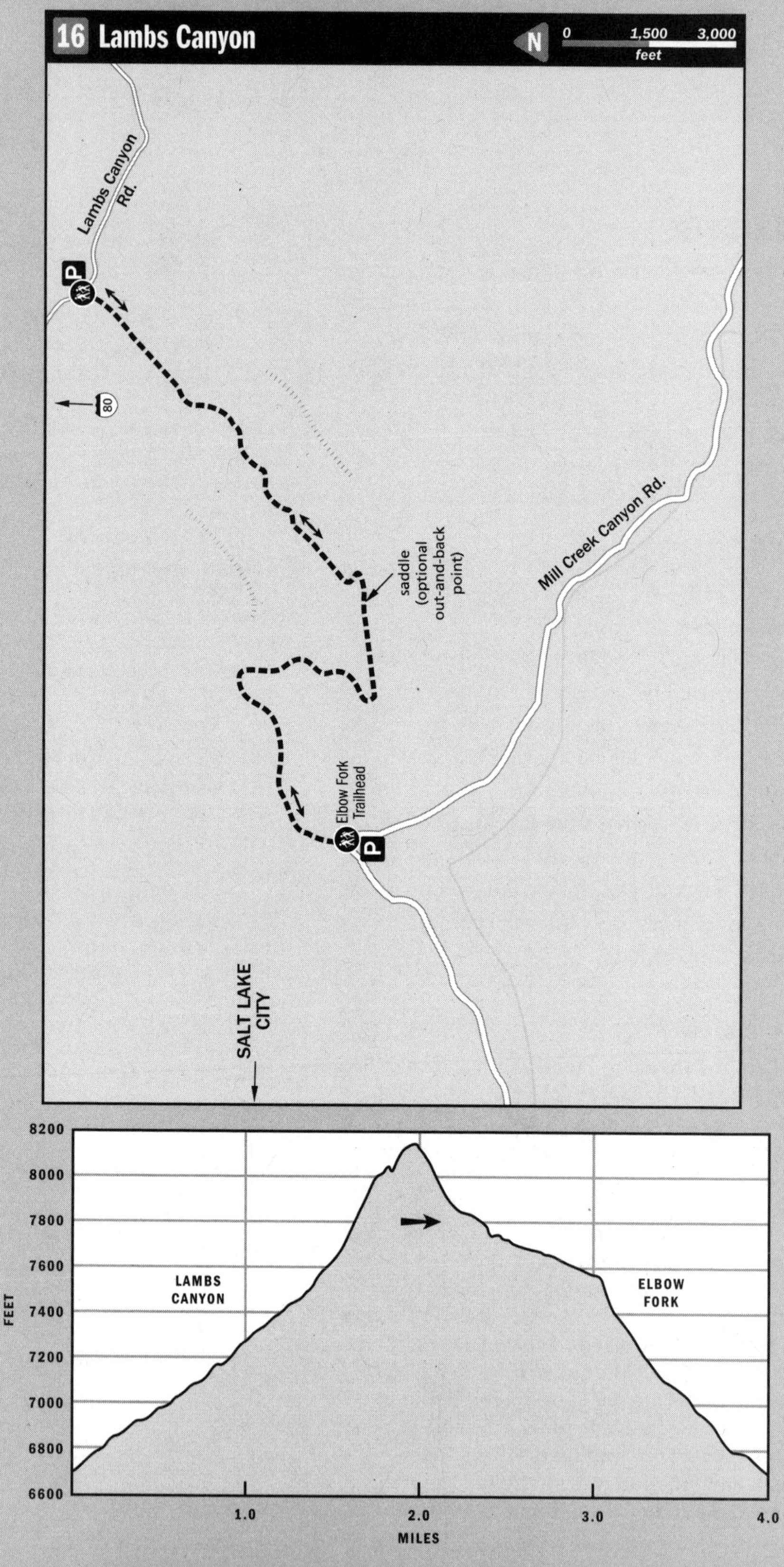

16 Lambs Canyon
N
0
1,500
3,000
feet
Lambs Canyon Rd.
80
saddle (optional out-and-back point)
Mill Creek Canyon Rd.
Elbow Fork Trailhead
SALT LAKE CITY
8200
8000
7800
7600
7400
7200
7000
6800
6600
FEET
LAMBS CANYON
ELBOW FORK
1.0
2.0
3.0
4.0
MILES

Lambs Canyon

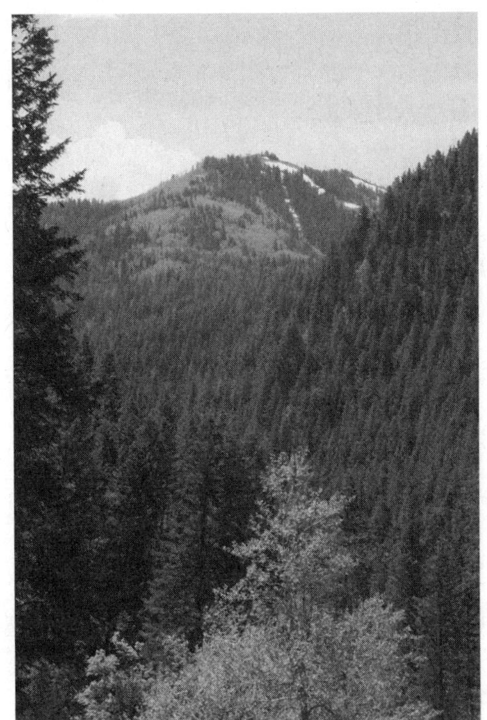

You can explore Lambs Canyon in a variety of ways, and the one-way canyon-to-canyon route described here requires a shuttle vehicle left at either end. It leads from Lambs Canyon to Mill Creek Canyon via the Great Western Trail and Elbow Fork. You can just as easily undertake this hike as a 4-mile out-and-back within Lambs Canyon. Just park at the Lambs Canyon trailhead, hike to the pass for views into the valley, then return back down the trail to your car. This out-and-back Lambs Canyon option also avoids the access fee for Mill Creek Canyon.

The Lambs Canyon Trail also serves as a section of the Great

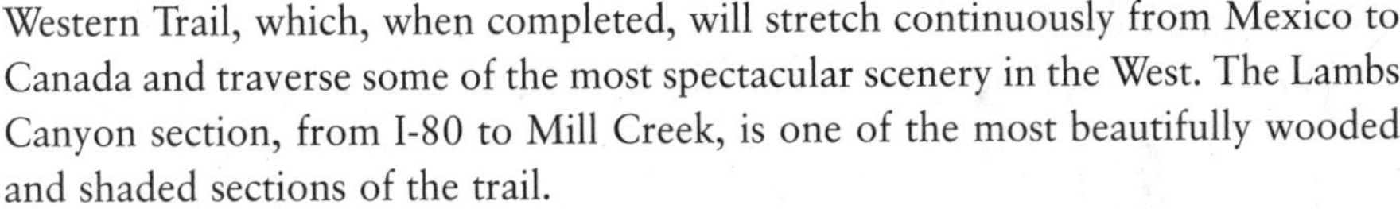

Western Trail, which, when completed, will stretch continuously from Mexico to Canada and traverse some of the most spectacular scenery in the West. The Lambs Canyon section, from I-80 to Mill Creek, is one of the most beautifully wooded and shaded sections of the trail.

From the Lambs Canyon trailhead parking area, cross Lambs Canyon Road and immediately cross a bridge over a stream lined with willows. Immediately, you're engulfed in a forest of aspen, fir, and spruce—but don't ignore the foliage at your feet. Wild strawberries, raspberries, grapes, and mint line the trail. In spring, mulesear, wyethia, larkspur, and harebell brighten the trail—and as long as they're not on your lawn, even dandelions are a welcome wildflower in the woods. Diverse shrubbery also lines the narrow trail and makes long pants preferable. The soil is dark and well packed, sprinkled with fir needles and ribboned with roots of trees.

Moose and deer find Lambs Canyon a welcoming habitat. Watch for the burrows of ground squirrels near the trail, and look out for wrens, varied thrushes, hummingbirds, and sparrows.

At about 1.5 miles up the canyon, the trail departs the spring and enters a series of wide, steep switchbacks through stands of aspen as you approach the pass. At the saddle elevation of 8,133 feet, the woods open up to views of Gobblers Knob and Mount Raymond to the south and Grandeur Peak to the west. To the left of Grandeur Peak, you can also see a slice of the Salt Lake Valley.

From the saddle at the top of the pass, you have a choice based on where your car is waiting. You can return to Lambs Canyon for an out-and-back hike or

Ascending through aspens

continue on down Elbow Fork into Mill Creek Canyon for a one-way hike with all-new territory.

The trail from the pass down to Mill Creek is slightly less shaded than the trail leading up from Lambs Canyon. Still, within minutes you drop into the canyon along a gathering creek and soon find yourself back in the shade. The trail through Elbow Fork lacks the diversity of foliage found in Lambs Canyon but offers some fine views of the surrounding canyon and occasional glimpses of the sandstone crags on Mount Aire to the north.

At 1.8 miles from the pass, and less than 0.2 miles from the Elbow Fork trailhead, you come to a trail junction. The fork to the right leads up the main branch of Elbow Fork on the Mount Aire Trail. Take the fork to the left to return to the Elbow Fork trailhead and Mill Creek Canyon Road. Remember that the gate to the upper canyon, located at Maple Grove, is only open from July 1 to November 1. If you want to access Elbow Fork outside of that season, you'll need to park at Maple Grove and hike an additional 1.5 miles to the trailhead. But a shaded walk on a car-free road with Mill Creek at your side can be enchanting.

ADDITIONAL AT-A-GLANCE INFORMATION

FACILITIES: Vault toilets at both trailheads

DOGS: No dogs are allowed in Lambs Canyon, a protected watershed. In Mill Creek Canyon, dogs must be leashed on even-numbered days and can be unleashed on odd-numbered days.

SPECIAL COMMENTS: This is a great snowshoe trail in the depths of winter, and easily accessed on cross-country skis along Mill Creek Canyon.

LAMBS CANYON LATITUDE–LONGITUDE: N 40° 43' 16.6"; W 111° 39' 29.4"

ELBOW FORK LATITUDE–LONGITUDE: N 40° 42' 23.8"; W 111° 41' 24.5"

NEARBY ACTIVITIES

The Mill Creek Canyon Fishing Dock and Boardwalk is located at the Terraces, just 4.4 miles up the canyon on the right-hand side of the road. A short 0.1-mile walk leads to fishing fun for young and old.

MOUNT AIRE 17

IN BRIEF

Tucked away on the ridge behind Grandeur Peak, Mount Aire is not visible from most of Salt Lake City. Still, it offers excellent views to the east and of surrounding peaks. The Mount Aire Trail connects with many other Mill Creek trails and the Great Western Trail.

KEY AT-A-GLANCE INFORMATION

LENGTH: 3.8 miles round-trip
ELEVATION GAIN: 1,987 feet
ELEVATION AT TRAILHEAD: 6,686 feet
CONFIGURATION: Out-and-back
DIFFICULTY: Moderate
SCENERY: Wooded canyon leading to a summit with panoramic views
EXPOSURE: Mostly shaded the first mile up to ridgeline saddle; partially shaded to summit
TRAFFIC: Light
TRAIL SURFACE: Dirt and rock
HIKING TIME: 2.5–4 hours
WATER REQUIREMENTS: 1–2 liters
SEASON: Year-round
ACCESS: Mill Creek Canyon is a fee-access area within the Wasatch-Cache National Forest. The gate at Maple Grove is closed from November 1 to July 1. To hike Mount Aire when the gate is closed, park at the Maple Grove picnic area and walk 1.5 miles up the canyon road to the Elbow Fork Trailhead.
MAPS: USGS Mount Aire, Trails Illustrated Wasatch Front (709)
FACILITIES: Vault toilet at trailhead. No drinking water at trailhead. Water in creek should be purified.
DOGS: Must be leashed on even-numbered days; can be unleashed on odd-numbered days

DESCRIPTION

Mount Aire is a bite-sized challenge. If you're in great shape, you can drive to the trailhead after work, bag the summit, and be back to your car in 2½ hours. If you're looking to build speed and endurance, Mount Aire offers a steep and steady incline for nearly 2 miles that will let you know if you're ready for a more demanding adventure. It's also an ideal snowshoe ascent in winter that offers a real challenge, rewarding you with great views of snow-covered peaks and hills in all directions.

During the summer you can drive directly to the Elbow Fork Trailhead and go straight to the summit in just 1.9 miles. From November 1 to July 1 (with some variation based on weather) the gate at Maple Grove is closed to motor vehicles, so you'll have to walk or ski the 1.5 miles from Maple Grove up to the Elbow Fork Trailhead. Walking along the shaded road as it

Directions

From I-215 on Salt Lake City's east side, take the 3300 South/3900 South turnoff (Exit 4). Turn left onto Wasatch Boulevard and go north 1 block to 3800 South. Turn right on 3800 South and continue toward the mouth of Mill Creek Canyon. Pass the toll booth at 0.7 miles and continue for another 5.3 miles to the Elbow Fork Trailhead, where Mill Creek and the road turn sharply to the right. Roadside parking is available at the trailhead.

GPS Trailhead Coordinates

UTM Zone (WGS84) 12T
Easting 0441721
Northing 4506431
Latitude N 40° 42' 23.8"
Longitude W 111° 41' 24.5"

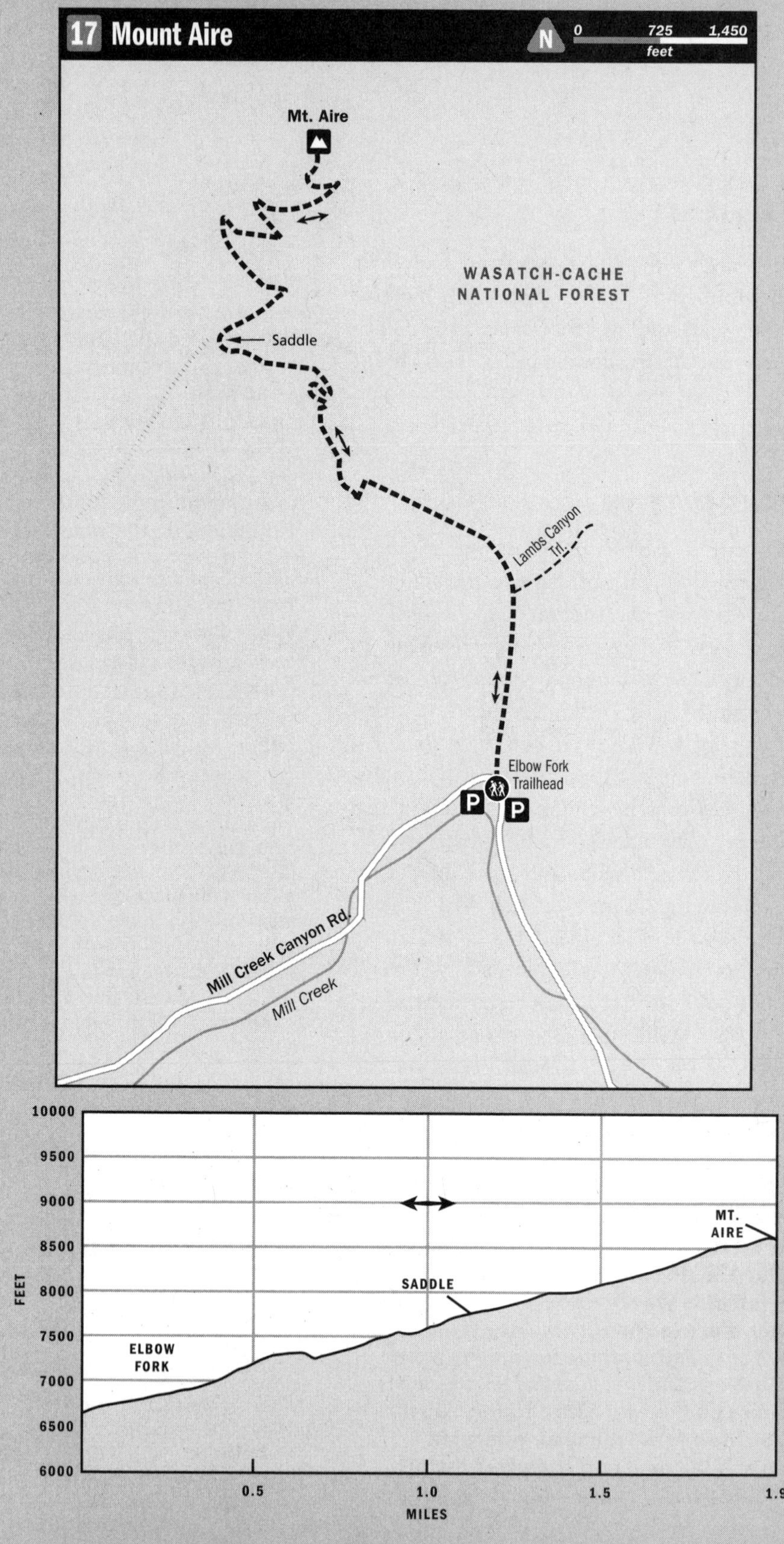
17 Mount Aire
N
0
725
1,450
feet
Mt. Aire
WASATCH-CACHE
NATIONAL FOREST
Saddle
Lambs Canyon Trl.
Elbow Fork Trailhead
P
P
Mill Creek Canyon Rd.
Mill Creek
10000
9500
9000
8500
8000
7500
7000
6500
6000
FEET
MT. AIRE
SADDLE
ELBOW FORK
0.5
1.0
1.5
1.9
MILES

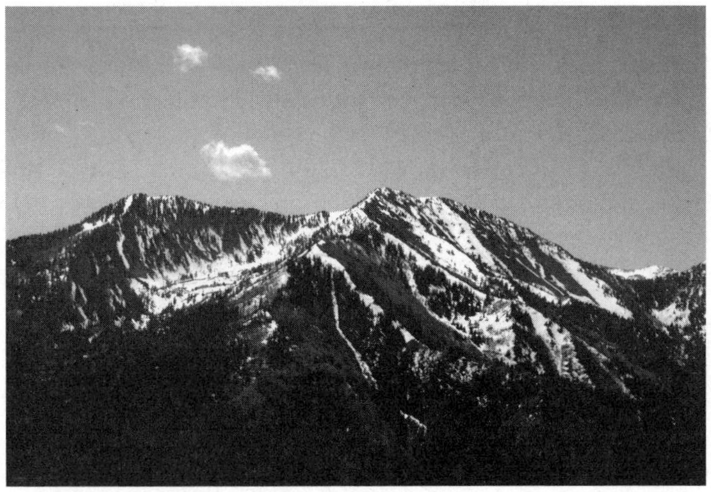

Gobblers Knob from Mount Aire

follows Mill Creek up the canyon is really quite enjoyable, even if it adds 3 miles to the round-trip.

The Elbow Fork trailhead is located at the point where Mill Creek and the road make a sharp 90-degree turn to the south. The trailhead also provides access to the Lambs Canyon Trail, the Pipeline Trail, and the Great Western Trail. Within 0.1 mile of the trailhead, you come to a well-marked fork in the trail, with the Mount Aire Trail taking off to the left. It quickly crosses a footbridge over the small creek and follows the creek up a deep, shaded canyon filled with Douglas-fir, maple, and quaking aspen at the higher elevations.

Continue following the trail along the Elbow Fork tributary for 0.8 miles to the point where the creek is just a trickle. At that point the trail ascends a series of short, steep switchbacks, and within less than a minute you're high above the creek on the east slope of the side canyon. Within another 0.2 miles you emerge from the canyon's shade to arrive at the ridgeline saddle, which offers views down Parley's Canyon to the north. A faint, unmaintained trail follows the ridgeline to the west. With some advance planning you could take this trail to Grandeur Peak and descend to Mill Creek through Church Fork. But for now, keep to the right and set your sights on Mount Aire to the east.

Leaving the saddle, the trail winds through the sandstone along Mount Aire's western and southern slopes. This sandstone formation, while unusual for the Wasatch, is the same formation you see on Grandeur Peak and along the entire ridge. Although the climb along the upper slope is largely shadeless, it is fragranced with sage and arrowleaf balsam root. While the trail is easy to follow during most of the year, adding a foot or more of snow in the winter could pose some routefinding challenges.

Nearing the summit, you come to an overlook with impressive views of the densely wooded slopes of upper Mill Creek Canyon and Gobblers Knob to the south. From this overlook, a sharp turn to the north leads to the summit just 100 yards ahead. Although the summit ridge extends to the north for more than 200 yards, the true summit is the rocky sandstone outcropping first reached from the south. From this spot you can frequently watch eagles soaring high above the canyon. Below and to the east, you'll see I-80 leading toward Park City. The Salt Lake Valley views to the west are limited, but the panoramic views of mountains in all directions go on forever.

NEARBY ACTIVITIES

Most visitors to Mill Creek Canyon find so much to keep them busy—picnicking, hiking, bicycling, mountain biking, snowshoeing, and skiing—that they never seem to have much need for add-ons. But if you have an extra 30 minutes at the end of your hike, consider driving another 3.5 miles up to the top of the canyon to scout your next adventure. When the pavement ends at the Big Water trailhead, you're at an elevation of more than 8,000 feet. From this point you can access the Great Western Trail, or the Desolation Trail into Big Cottonwood Canyon, opening the door to hundreds of miles of hiking and biking trails.

GRANDEUR PEAK 18

IN BRIEF

Grandeur Peak delivers a lot of bang for the buck. One of the most easily accessible peaks along the Wasatch Front, it offers both great trail conditions and commanding views in all directions.

KEY AT-A-GLANCE INFORMATION

LENGTH: 5.4 miles round-trip
ELEVATION GAIN: 2,387 feet
ELEVATION AT TRAILHEAD: 5,912 feet
CONFIGURATION: Out-and-back
DIFFICULTY: Moderate
SCENERY: Canyon, mountain, and city views. Trail follows creek up a wooded side canyon.
EXPOSURE: Mostly shaded for first mile. Mostly exposed for last 1.7 miles to summit.
TRAFFIC: Busy
TRAIL SURFACE: Dirt and rock
HIKING TIME: 2.5–4 hours
WATER REQUIREMENTS: 1–2 liters
SEASON: Spring, summer, fall
ACCESS: Mill Creek Canyon is a fee-access area within the Wasatch-Cache National Forest. From the trailhead to the switchbacks you will be crossing property owned by the Boy Scouts of America.
MAPS: USGS Mt. Aire, Sugar House, Trails Illustrated Wasatch Front (709)
FACILITIES: Restrooms and water at trailhead
DOGS: Must be leashed on even-numbered days; can be unleashed on odd-numbered days

DESCRIPTION

Imagine a warm Saturday in spring. Snow still flanks most of the high peaks surrounding Salt Lake City. You pull out your hiking boots and decide to bag a mountain summit—something impressive; something grand. Grandeur Peak is the perfect pursuit. It lies at the forefront of the ridge just north of Mount Olympus and to the south of Parley's Canyon and I-80. It may not be as high as Timp or Pfeifferhorn, or as instantly recognizable to local residents as Mount Olympus, but from nearly anywhere in Salt Lake City you can be at the trailhead in 20 minutes and on your way to a mountain adventure.

Mill Creek Canyon is Salt Lake City's favorite picnic destination, and Church Fork is the first picnic site you come to driving up the canyon. If you see cars parked along the canyon road, you can safely assume that the

Directions →

From I-215 on Salt Lake City's east side, take the 3300 South/3900 South turnoff (Exit 4). Turn left onto Wasatch Boulevard and go north 1 block to 3800 South. Turn right on 3800 South and continue toward the mouth of Mill Creek Canyon. Pass the toll booth at 0.7 miles and continue for another 2.3 miles to the Church Fork Picnic area on your left. If the gate is open, turn left and drive 0.3 miles up through the picnic area to a small trailhead parking area at the end of the road.

GPS Trailhead Coordinates

UTM Zone (WGS84) 12T
Easting 0437271
Northing 4505790
Latitude N 40° 42' 02.3"
Longitude W 111° 44' 33.1"

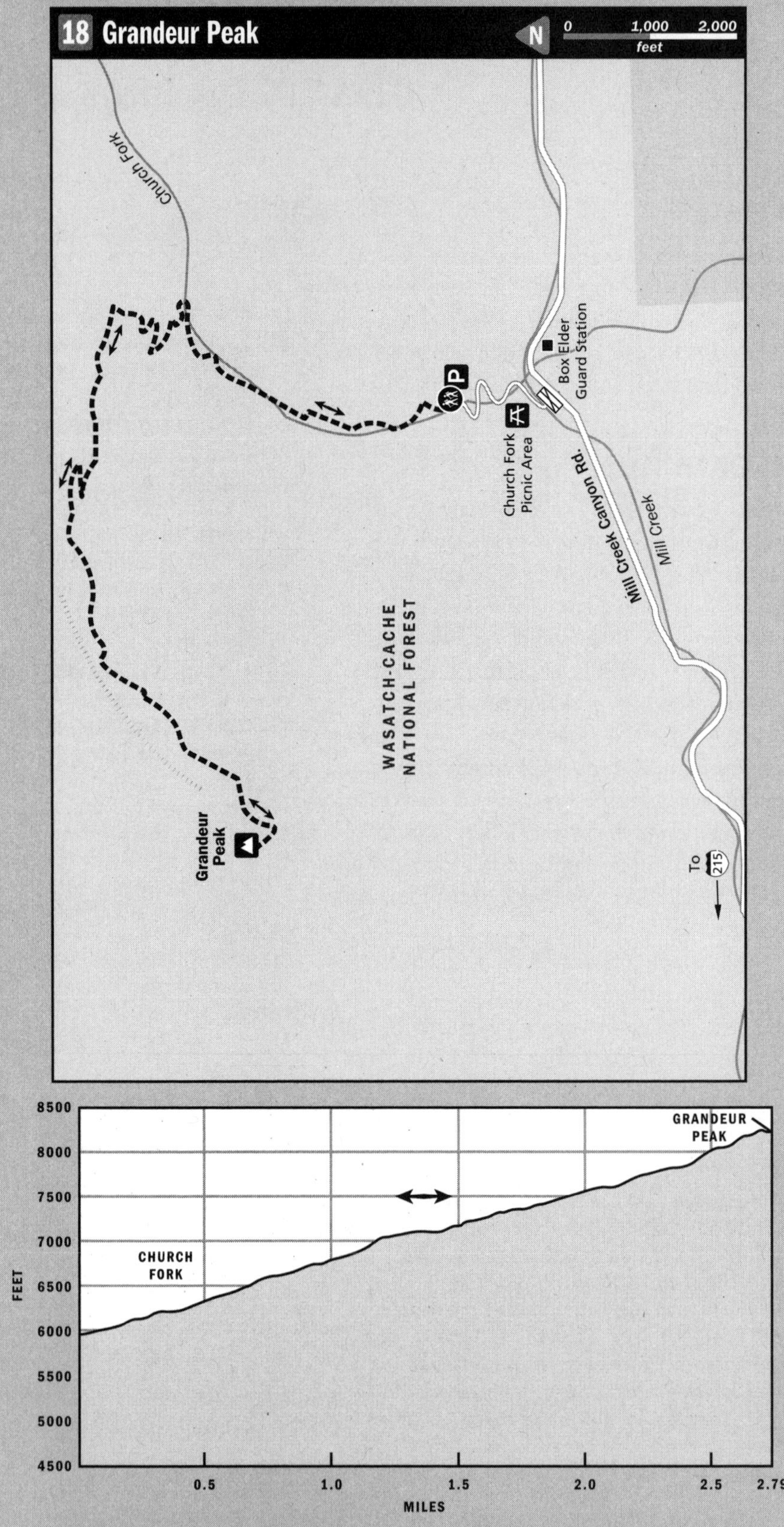

18 Grandeur Peak
N
0
1,000
2,000
feet
Church Fork
Box Elder
Guard Station
P
Church Fork
Picnic Area
Mill Creek Canyon Rd.
Mill Creek
WASATCH-CACHE
NATIONAL FOREST
Grandeur
Peak
To
215
8500
8000
7500
7000
6500
6000
5500
5000
4500
FEET
CHURCH
FORK
GRANDEUR
PEAK
0.5
1.0
1.5
2.0
2.5
2.79
MILES

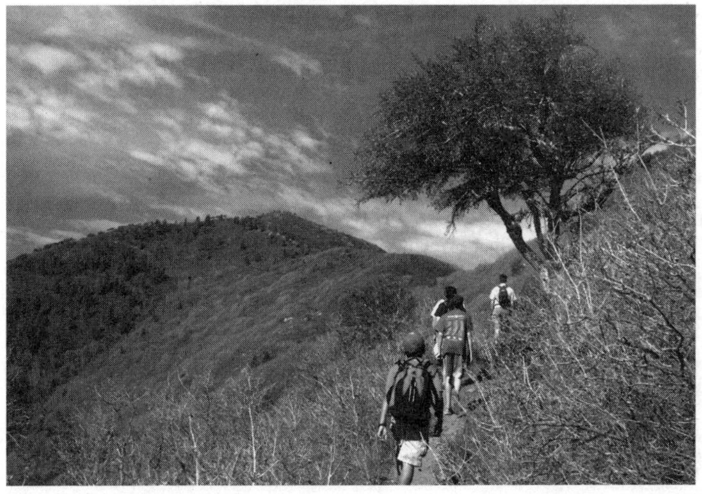

Ridgeline approach to Grandeur Peak

eight parking spaces at the trailhead are already filled. You might as well park on the shoulder of Mill Creek Canyon Road and walk through the Church Fork picnic area to the trailhead, which is marked by a sign pointing to Grandeur Peak.

Church Fork is a small side canyon on the north side of Mill Creek. It was originally a placer mining claim that extended from just above the trailhead to near the ridgeline. This claim was deeded to the Boy Scouts of America in 1918 and remains publicly accessible property owned by the Scouts.

After just 0.1 mile on the trail, you'll cross the Pipeline Trail and take a jog to the left, then continue up the canyon on the Grandeur Peak Trail to the right. The trail leads up a steep canyon shaded by maple conifers and bigtooth maples, with Church Fork Creek descending speedily on your right. Along the creekside, the trail is fragrant with fir, wildflowers, wild mint, and arrowleaf balsam root.

At 0.8 miles, the path begins a series of switchbacks. As you climb the slope, you emerge from the shaded canopy of maple, oak, and fir. From this point on, the trail is largely unshaded. These switchbacks lead toward a sandstone outcropping on the ridge to the north. Below this outcropping, the trail is dotted and bedded with sandstone, uncharacteristic of most Wasatch trails.

As the switchbacks lead up toward the west, you'll have a beautiful straight-on view of Grandeur Peak in front of you, its slopes ribboned with strands of aspen and white fir. At the top of the switchbacks you'll look to the west and see the entire trail as it leads to the summit. From this point on, the ascent is steady but more gradual as it follows a route just below the ridgeline through a low covering of Gambel oak.

On your route to the top, you'll come to a crest dotted with juniper. After passing this false summit, the true summit is just 0.2 miles straight ahead. You may see a few patches of snow through late May and sometimes into June

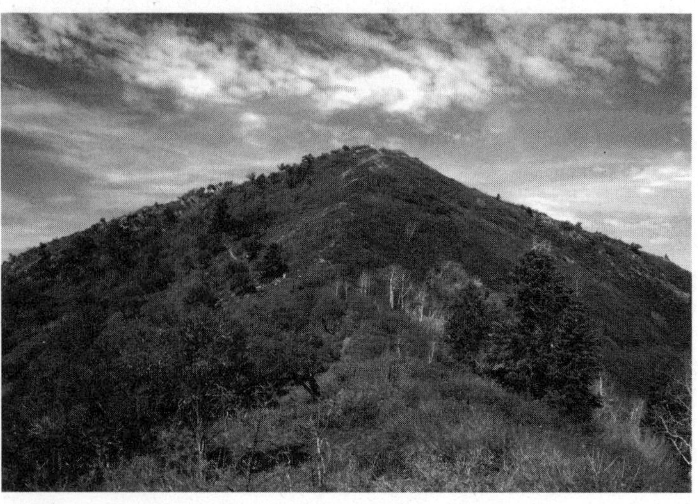

Grandeur Peak viewed from the east

along the higher trail. Because hikers, dogs, and bikers share busy Mill Creek Canyon, wildlife sightings are less likely, but you may see deer grazing near the summit in spring and fall.

At 8,299 feet in elevation, the Grandeur Peak summit offers great views in all directions. The Salt Lake Valley spreads out below to the west, and Mount Olympus lies at the front of the next ridge to the south. Behind you, to the northeast, are Mountain Dell and Little Dell reservoirs. Soak up the panoramic views, then enjoy a carefree and relaxing descent.

NEARBY ACTIVITIES

Just a few blocks from the mouth of Mill Creek Canyon, you'll find REI, the popular outdoor gear store. In addition to outdoor equipment, apparel, and classes, REI is home to the Salt Lake area's Public Lands Information Center, an excellent source of assistance and information about area recreational opportunities. The store is located at 3285 East 3300 South.

DESOLATION TRAIL TO SALT LAKE OVERLOOK 19

IN BRIEF

Hiking through a dense forest scented with spruce and fir is just one of the many delights on the Desolation Trail. Climbing over fallen trees and rocky outcroppings leads to a direct view of Salt Lake with peaks to the north and south.

KEY AT-A-GLANCE INFORMATION

LENGTH: 4.8 miles round-trip

ELEVATION GAIN: 1,239 feet

ELEVATION AT TRAILHEAD: 5,785 feet

CONFIGURATION: Out-and-back

DIFFICULTY: Moderate

SCENERY: Wooded canyon, city overview

EXPOSURE: Mostly shaded

TRAFFIC: Moderate

TRAIL SURFACE: Dirt and rock

HIKING TIME: 1.5–3 hours

WATER REQUIREMENTS: 1–1.5 liters; no water along the trail

SEASON: Spring, summer, fall

ACCESS: Mill Creek Canyon is a fee-access area within the Wasatch-Cache National Forest. From the trailhead to the Salt Lake Overlook, you will be crossing property owned by the Boy Scouts of America. Bicycles are prohibited on the Desolation Trail.

MAPS: USGS Mount Aire, Trails Illustrated Wasatch Front (709)

FACILITIES: Restrooms and water at trailhead

DOGS: On leash on even-numbered days, unleashed on odd-numbered days

DESCRIPTION

Don't let the name *Desolation Trail* conjure up images of a dusty, sun-parched ordeal in the desert. Picture a verdant trail cut along a densely wooded hillside with a bed of needles and cones from the various conifers in the canyon.

You'll find the trailhead at the west end of the small South Box Elder parking area. At 0.1 mile, you come to a fork with the Thayne Canyon Trail leading to the left and the Desolation Trail ascending the hillside to the right. To reach the Salt Lake Overlook, stay to the right, although you also have the extended option of a Thayne Canyon–Desolation Trail loop.

The trail navigates a steady series of masterfully crafted and well-groomed switchbacks that reduce the grade on an otherwise precipitous hillside. These northeast slopes provide a cooler, more moist habitat for

---

Directions

From I-215 on Salt Lake City's east side, take the 3300 South/3900 South turnoff (Exit 4). Turn left onto Wasatch Boulevard and go north 1 block to 3800 South. Turn right on 3800 South and continue toward the mouth of Mill Creek Canyon. Pass the toll booth at 0.7 miles and continue for another 2.5 miles to the South Box Elder trailhead parking area on the right. A road sign also identifies Desolation Trail 019.

GPS Trailhead Coordinates

UTM Zone (WGS84) 12T

Easting 0437484

Northing 4505446

Latitude N 40° 41' 51.0"

Longitude W 111° 44' 24.0"

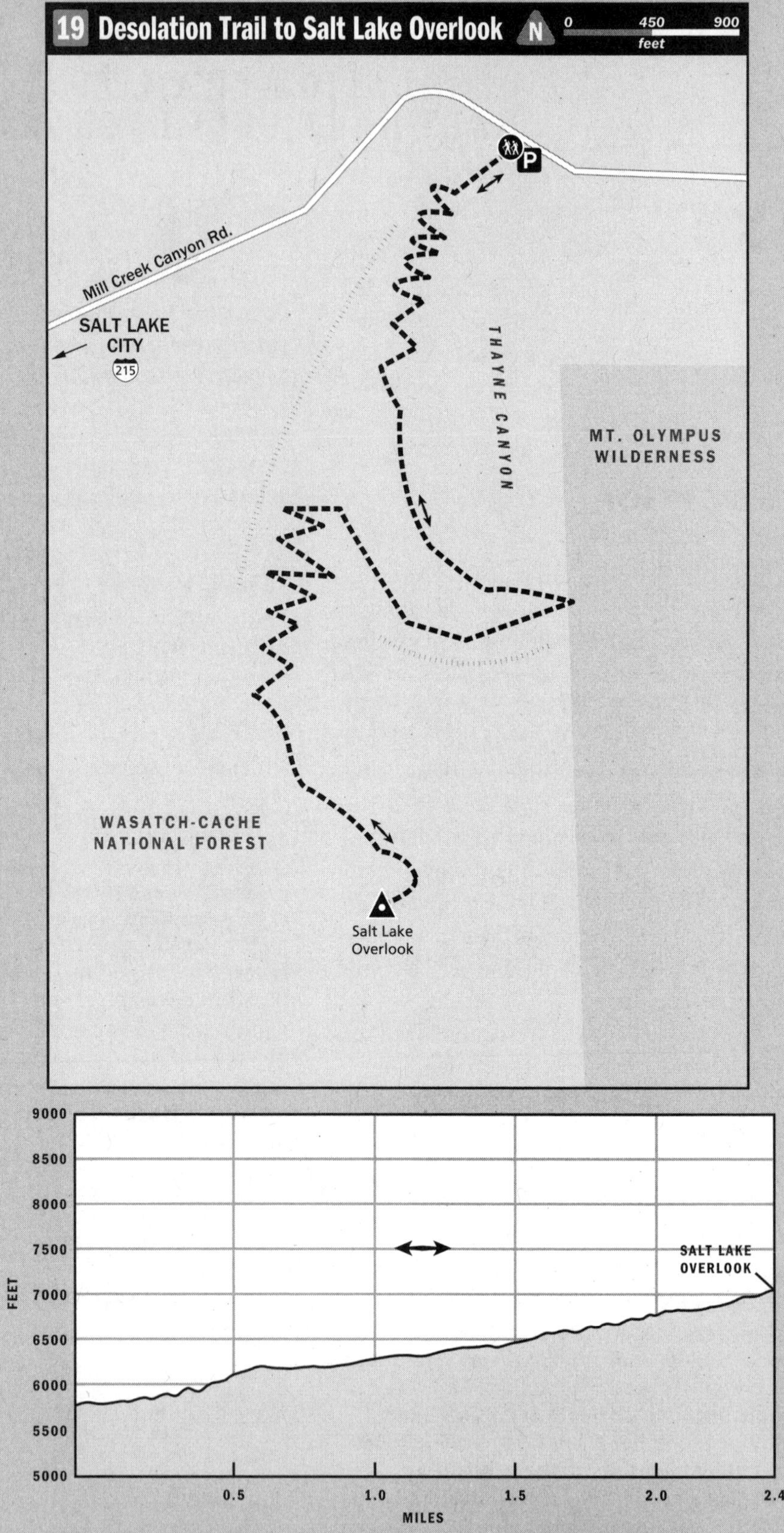
19 Desolation Trail to Salt Lake Overlook
N
0
450
900
feet
Mill Creek Canyon Rd.
SALT LAKE CITY
215
THAYNE CANYON
MT. OLYMPUS WILDERNESS
WASATCH-CACHE NATIONAL FOREST
Salt Lake Overlook
9000
8500
8000
7500
7000
6500
6000
5500
5000
FEET
SALT LAKE OVERLOOK
0.5
1.0
1.5
2.0
2.4
MILES

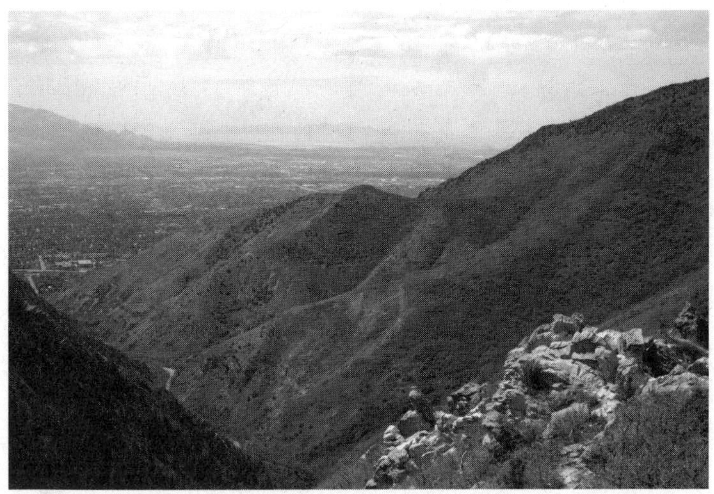

Canyon and valley views from the overlook

mosses and a variety of mountain shrubs. In addition to fir and spruce, you'll see maple, Gamble oaks, and wildflowers along the trail at all elevations. Many fallen trees cross the trail, while others lay parallel to the trail, placed there to fortify the slope against erosion.

At 0.6 miles the trail opens up to sunlight with a patch of Gambel oak, although for most of the hike towering conifers shade hikers. At 0.8 miles the path divides at a rock outcropping. Take the trail on your right, up through the rocky crag.

If you're hiking with young children, be careful of the steep, unprotected drop-offs in many areas where the trail is only a few feet wide. Also, since you're likely to be paying close attention to your feet and the narrow trail, you might well be surprised by a runner or dog coming in the opposite direction. Unleashed dogs appear along the trail frequently on odd-numbered days.

You'll often spot deer and squirrels, and the variety of birds makes Mill Creek Canyon a popular birding destination. Early mornings in summer provide good opportunities to spot blue grouse, Steller's jays, scrub jays, and golden eagles.

At 1.3 miles, a clearing in the woods opens to some beautiful views up Mill Creek Canyon to the east. But the favorite view comes almost by surprise as the trail circles to the west side of the slope. As the trees clear, you'll have a view looking down the canyon with Salt Lake City below. To the north is Grandeur Peak, with Mount Olympus and Hobbs Peak to the south. Several large clusters of jagged rocks offer a place to relax, enjoy the view, and have a snack before heading back down the trail.

Note: This trail, cut along a steep hillside, is particularly susceptible to erosion. Do not shortcut the trails.

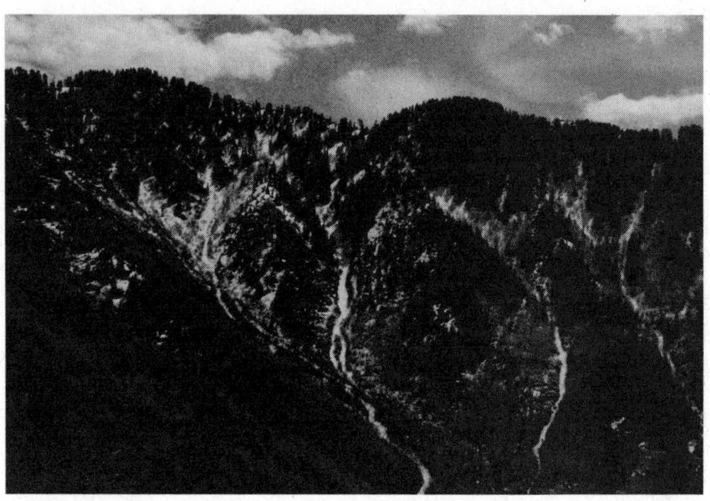

Ridgeline views to the south

NEARBY ACTIVITIES

Mill Creek Canyon is Salt Lake City's favorite summer picnic destination. With nine picnic areas within 3 to 7 miles of the canyon entrance, Mill Creek is the place to go for a weekend brunch or a summer afternoon lunch. Individual sites abound, and group sites accommodate up to 100 people. Many also visit the area for mountain biking, but bikes are allowed on the upper trails only on even-numbered days.

GOBBLERS KNOB (via Alexander Basin) 20

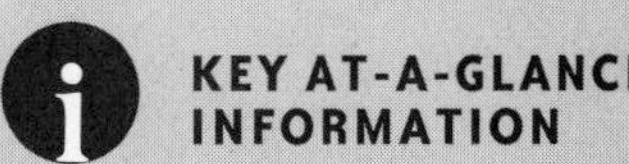

IN BRIEF

This popular summit offers great views in all directions, but the most memorable sight will be of the wildflowers that fill Alexander Basin in spring and summer. The steep hike offers some easy scrambling and route-finding up a glacial cirque to the ridge, followed by a short jaunt to the summit.

KEY AT-A-GLANCE INFORMATION

LENGTH: 4.4 miles round-trip

ELEVATION GAIN: 3,106 feet

ELEVATION AT TRAILHEAD: 7,140 feet

CONFIGURATION: Out-and-back

DIFFICULTY: Moderate

SCENERY: Wildflowers, alpine basin, summit views of Salt Lake and surrounding peaks

EXPOSURE: Mostly shaded

TRAFFIC: Moderate

TRAIL SURFACE: Dirt to the upper bowl, then rocky to the summit

HIKING TIME: 4–5 hours

SEASON: Summer to early fall. Maple Grove gate to upper Mill Creek Canyon is closed from November 1–July 1.

WATER REQUIREMENTS: 2 liters. No perennial water flow near the trail.

ACCESS: Mill Creek Canyon is a fee-access area within the Wasatch-Cache National Forest.

MAPS: USGS Mount Aire, Trails Illustrated Wasatch Front (709)

See additional information at end of Description, page 100.

DESCRIPTION

Although the trail leading to Alexander Basin passes through the Mount Olympus Wilderness, the basin itself is not included in the designated wilderness area. Gobblers Knob is a popular summit climb, and Mill Creek is a busy canyon, but Alexander Basin can feel surprisingly remote, even on a summer weekend.

As you drive up Mill Creek Canyon, and especially past the Elbow Fork area, the road narrows and trees on both sides close in to create a sense of being wrapped up in the woods. From the trailhead parking area, you step onto the trail and within a few seconds the road disappears and you're engulfed in woods of Douglas-fir and white fir.

No one lost any time cutting switchbacks when making this trail. It shoots directly up the center of the basin and follows a steep

Directions

From I-215 on Salt Lake City's east side, take the 3300 South/3900 South turnoff (Exit 4). Turn left onto Wasatch Boulevard and go north 1 block to 3800 South. Turn right on 3800 South and continue toward the mouth of Mill Creek Canyon. Pass the toll booth at 0.7 miles and continue for another 7 miles to the Alexander Basin trailhead (number 010). Parking is available at the trailhead on the south side of the road.

GPS Trailhead Coordinates

UTM Zone (WGS84) 12T

Easting 0443359

Northing 4504763

Latitude N 40° 41' 29.6"

Longitude W 111° 40' 13.3"

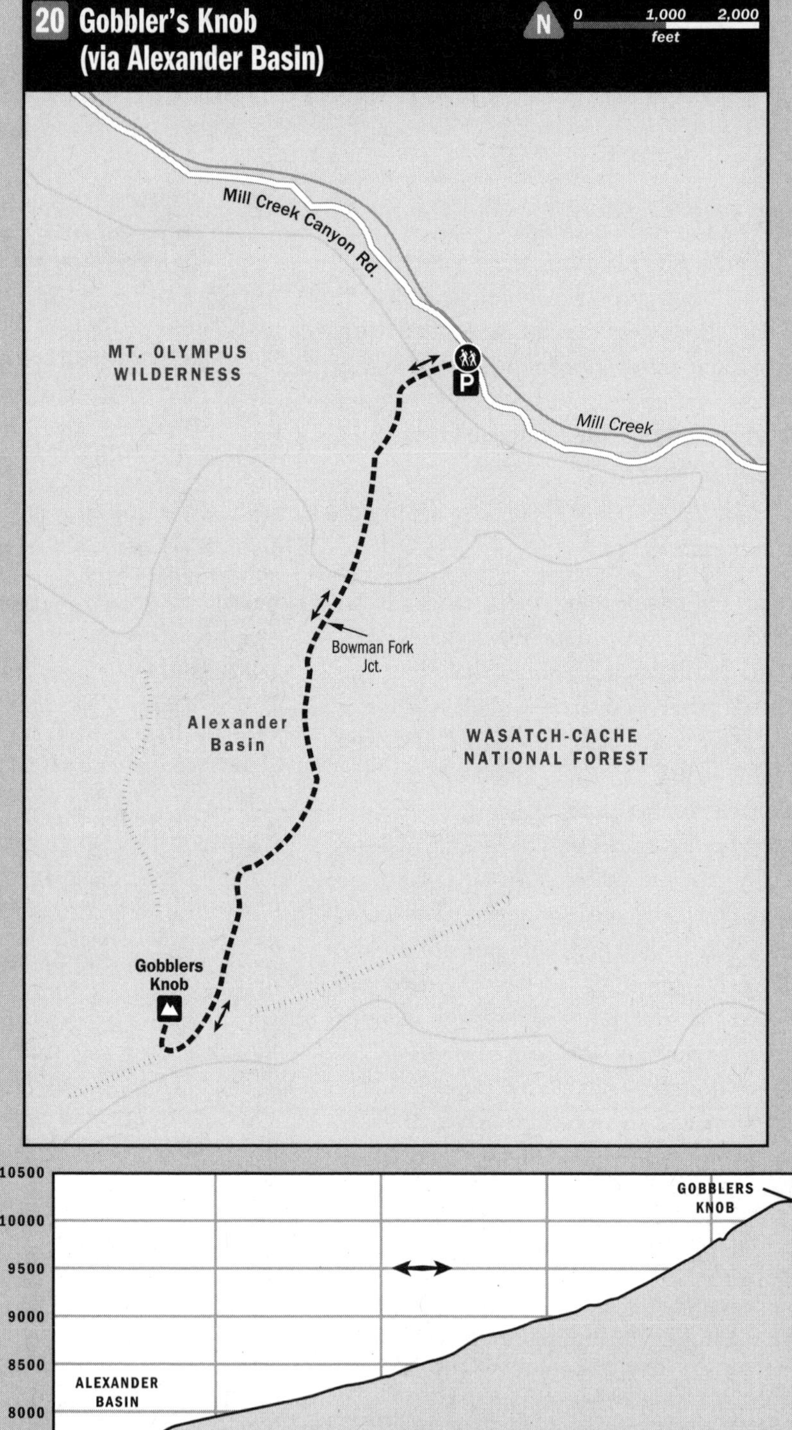
20
Gobbler's Knob
(via Alexander Basin)
N
0
1,000
2,000
feet
Mill Creek Canyon Rd.
MT. OLYMPUS
WILDERNESS
P
Mill Creek
Bowman Fork
Jct.
Alexander
Basin
WASATCH-CACHE
NATIONAL FOREST
Gobblers
Knob
10500
10000
9500
9000
8500
8000
7500
7000
6500
FEET
ALEXANDER
BASIN
GOBBLERS
KNOB
0.5
1.0
1.5
2.0
2.2
MILES

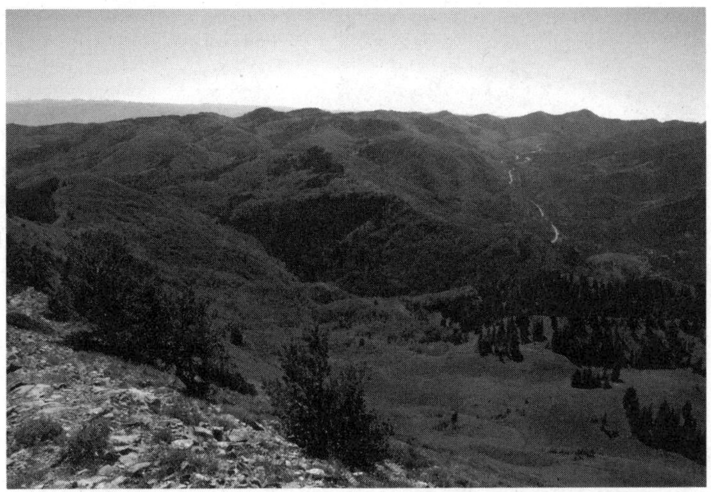

Views into Big Cottonwood Canyon

track throughout. If you keep a steady pace, you should be at the Bowman Fork junction within 30 to 40 minutes. At this point, you've already covered 0.9 miles and gained more than 1,100 feet in elevation. The Bowman Fork Trail drops down and to your right, but you should continue straight ahead. In another 0.2 miles, the woods thin and the trail opens to views leading up the basin.

In late spring and early summer wildflowers line the trail every step of the way—even on the rocky upper slopes—but they're most abundant in the woods and in the open areas of the upper basin. Larkspur, cow parsnip, phlox, and bluebells flourish, and you'll spot the elegant and rare white columbine both in the woods and in the open fields.

Alexander Basin is a stairway of tiered basins leading to an upper bowl. Until you reach the middle of the upper bowl, which is covered with patches of snow into midsummer, the trail proves easy to follow. As you stand in the upper bowl, looking up to the rim, you'll see Gobblers Knob on the right side of the rim. From this point you may have to improvise a bit, but you can usually spot a faint route leading up through the subalpine fir in the bowl's center, or alternatively, another faint cairned route leading up the rocky slope to the right of the trees. If it's at all muddy, choose the rocky slope. Either way, the route will be steep leading to the same destination—the bowl's rim.

Once there, you'll overlook the green expanse of Big Cottonwood Canyon, including many of the prominent peaks along the ridge. From this rim vantage point, look down and make a mental note of your route up the bowl so you'll have a reliable return route.

Now it's just a short climb to the Gobblers Knob summit on a faint but discernible trail leading up to the west and north along craggy slopes. From the rim it's just ten minutes of sustained climbing on the dry south-facing slope to

White columbine

the summit. While you can see large slices of the Salt Lake Valley from the top of Gobblers Knob, many of the peaks at the Wasatch's western front block the view. Instead, focus on the most impressive views: the peaks along the southern ridge of Big Cottonwood Canyon and to the east.

Cliff swallows and mountain bluebirds dart in and out of the fir and limber pine at the summit. As you descend to the ridge, look to the west and you'll see a well-worn path leading along the ridge toward Mount Raymond. From the ridge, this trail leads back down to the Terrace Campground and the Bowman Fork trailhead in Mill Creek Canyon. A wonderful trail, this path is well worth taking if you have a shuttle vehicle waiting or don't mind hiking an additional 3.5 miles up Mill Creek Canyon to your car.

ADDITIONAL AT-A-GLANCE INFORMATION

FACILITIES: No drinking water or restrooms at trailhead. Water in creek should be purified; restrooms are 1.5 miles from trailhead at Elbow Fork or Big Water.

DOGS: Must be leashed on even-numbered days; can be unleashed on odd-numbered days

SPECIAL COMMENTS: Of the four most frequently used trails used to reach the Gobblers Knob summit, Alexander Basin is the shortest and steepest.

NEARBY ACTIVITIES

Big Water is Mill Creek Canyon's Grand Central Station and provides easy access to many of the upper canyon's most popular hikes. The two large Big Water parking areas at the top of the canyon provide easy access to the Great Western Trail, Little Water Trail, and the Lower Big Water Trail. These lots, which often fill on weekends, are also popular with cyclists who find Big Water to be the perfect jumping-off point for the expansive network of trails.

MILL CREEK TO PARK CITY OVERLOOK (including Murdock Peak) 21

IN BRIEF

A gently ascending trail leads along the upper section of Mill Creek to a ridgeline at the top of the canyon. Enjoy the overview at the saddle or continue up to Murdock Peak for the view from the summit.

KEY AT-A-GLANCE INFORMATION

LENGTH: 5.2 miles round-trip to ridgeline saddle, 6.6 miles round-trip to summit of Murdock Peak

ELEVATION GAIN: 1,177 feet to ridgeline saddle, 1,979 to Murdock Peak

ELEVATION AT TRAILHEAD: 7,623 feet

CONFIGURATION: Out-and-back

DIFFICULTY: Moderate

SCENERY: Wooded trail with meadows and rounded peaks; ridgeline and summit views to the east

EXPOSURE: Mostly shaded

TRAFFIC: Moderate

TRAIL SURFACE: Dirt

HIKING TIME: 2–4 hours

WATER REQUIREMENTS: 1–2 liters. Water in creek can be purified.

SEASON: Summer to early fall. Gate to upper Mill Creek Canyon is closed from November 1 to July 1.

ACCESS: Mill Creek Canyon is a fee-access area within the Wasatch-Cache National Forest.

MAPS: USGS Mount Aire, Park City West; Trails Illustrated, Wasatch Front (709)

See additional information at end of Description, page 104.

DESCRIPTION

Mill Creek Canyon is well known and well used by locals. It offers wonderful year-round recreational opportunities for hikers, bicyclists, mountain bikers, cross-country skiers, and snowshoers. Even the farthest reaches of the canyon can get busy on summer weekends. The Upper Big Water trailhead is such a place, with a large parking area that often fills to capacity. But once you get on this trail, the wooded creeksides and the rolling hillsides make the upper canyon a place of serenity.

Big Water Gulch offers plenty of trail options and potential destinations. This less traveled but particularly enjoyable trail heads directly east from the upper parking area and follows Mill Creek to its headwaters, connects to the Great Western Trail, and ascends the ridge overlooking Park City. If a summit destination is what you have in mind, you can climb to a higher overlook or even continue to the summit of Murdock Peak.

Directions →

From I-215 on Salt Lake City's east side, take the 3300 South/3900 South turnoff (Exit 4). Turn left onto Wasatch Boulevard and go north 1 block to 3800 South. Turn right on 3800 South and continue toward the mouth of Mill Creek Canyon. Pass the toll booth at 0.7 miles and continue for another 8.5 miles to the end of Mill Creek Canyon Road. Park in the Upper Big Water trailhead parking area.

GPS Trailhead Coordinates

UTM Zone (WGS84) 12T

Easting 0445355

Northing 4503942

Latitude N 40° 41' 05.0"

Longitude W 111° 38' 48.9"

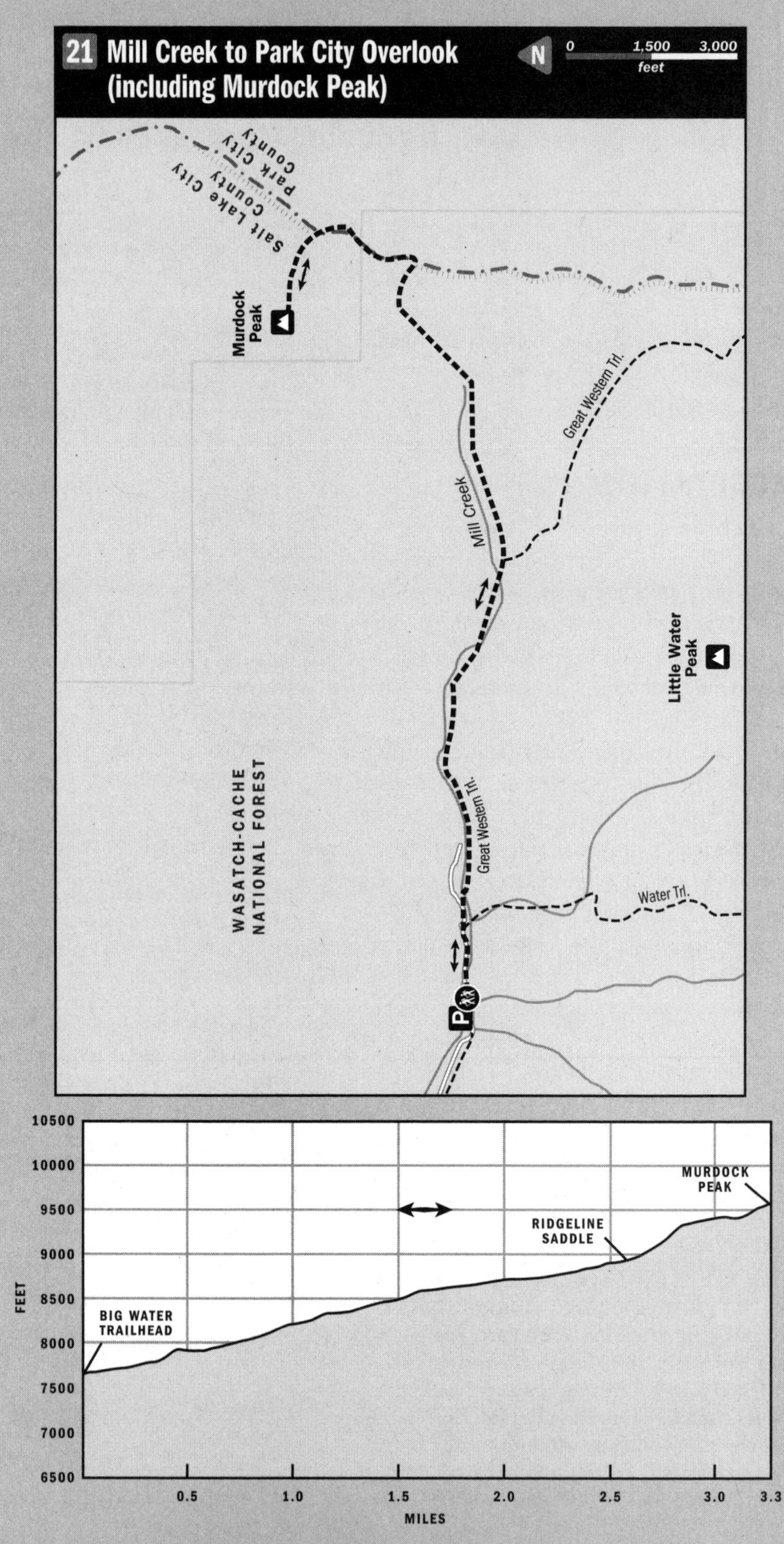
21
Mill Creek to Park City Overlook (including Murdock Peak)
N
0
1,500
3,000
feet
Park City County
Salt Lake City County
Murdock Peak
Great Western Trl.
Mill Creek
Little Water Peak
WASATCH-CACHE NATIONAL FOREST
Great Western Trl.
Water Trl.
P
10500
10000
9500
9000
8500
8000
7500
7000
6500
FEET
MURDOCK PEAK
RIDGELINE SADDLE
BIG WATER TRAILHEAD
0.5
1.0
1.5
2.0
2.5
3.0
3.3
MILES

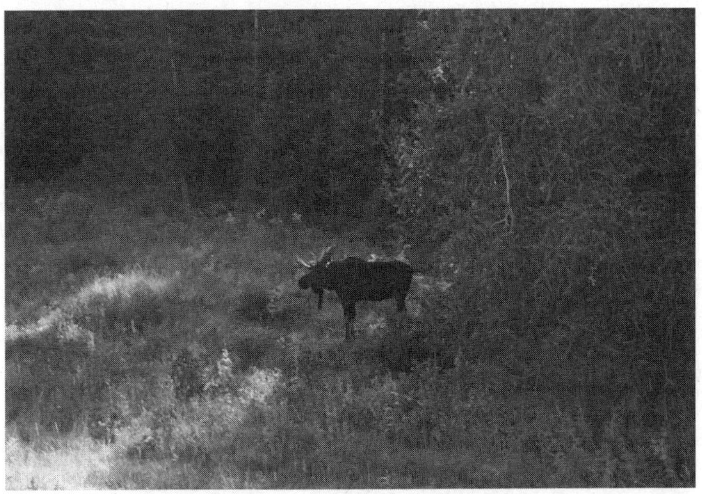

Bull moose on the Great Western Trail

Departing on the main trail to the east, known both as Mill Creek Trail and Red Pine Road, follow the route along the creek to a fork. Even though the sign points to a trail on the right, take the less crowded hiking trail on the left. This will hug the creek bank in a deeply wooded section of the canyon and take you away from the mountain bikers who use the wider trail on the right. This secluded section of trail is soft dirt carpeted with spruce needles, providing a great surface for dogs.

At 0.8 miles, the trail crosses the creek over stepping-stones, then within 0.1 mile crosses again to the south side. At 1.2 miles, the trail crests and drops slightly into a meadow ringed with Douglas-fir and shimmering aspens.

Within a few minutes you'll connect with the Great Western Trail. Although the sign at the junction may seem confusing, go left in the direction of Desolation Lake. This will lead you eastward to the ridge overlooking Park City, at which point the trail eventually turns south toward Desolation Lake.

This section of the Great Western Trail is wide and well traveled, with room for both mountain bikers and hikers. Still, be alert, as mountain bikes can often descend the trail at high speeds and come up on you without warning. Morning hikers may well share the trail with moose and deer, who find a hospitable habitat in these moist meadows.

At 2.2 miles, the landscape opens up to high meadows, grassy aspen-covered slopes, and rounded hilltops—very different from the Wasatch canyons to the south.

As the trail continues its gentle ascent, you arrive almost without warning at the 8,800-foot ridgeline saddle. The Great Western Trail turns south toward Big Cottonwood Canyon and Desolation Lake. Continuing eastward for just another 100 feet gives you a nice view of Park City below. But a quick glance to

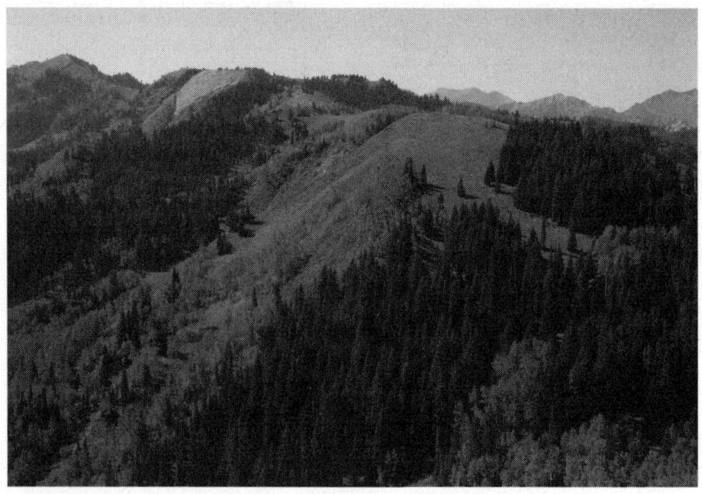

Ridgeline views from Park City overlook

your left reveals the ridgeline leading up to the higher overlook on the way to Murdock Peak.

No real trail takes you to the higher unnamed overlook, or even to Murdock Peak, but the route is clear and the bushwhacking along game trails through low-lying sage and juniper is easy. At a steady pace you'll arrive at the first overlook about 10 minutes after leaving the saddle. From the 9,300-foot overlook you're above the Park City ski lifts and have a sweeping view of the valley below.

Another 10 to 15 minutes and 300 feet of elevation gain will put you on the summit of Murdock Peak, located along the ridge to the west. While the overlook and the summit are both rewarding destinations, the most beautiful parts of the hike can be found in the meadows, gentle slopes, and wooded creeksides of the upper canyon.

ADDITIONAL AT-A-GLANCE INFORMATION

FACILITIES: Restrooms and drinking water at trailhead

DOGS: Must be leashed on even-numbered days; can be unleashed on odd-numbered days

SPECIAL COMMENTS: A popular trail with mountain bikers and dog owners

NEARBY ACTIVITIES

Park City Mountain Resort is a premier summer and winter destination located just 30 minutes east of Salt Lake City. Summer attractions include an alpine slide, the elevated alpine coaster, an exhilarating zipline, and lift-assisted hiking and mountain biking. For information, visit **www.parkcitymountain.com.**

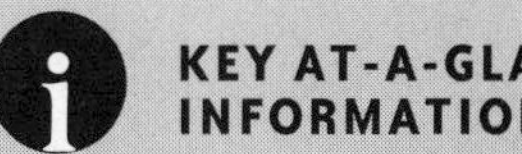

NEFFS CANYON 22

IN BRIEF

This spur canyon just south of Mill Creek Canyon has led its life in the shadows of Mount Olympus, so its beauty and history are often overlooked. The steep trail ascends along one of the many canyon streams to a high, aspen-ringed meadow surrounded by towering peaks.

DESCRIPTION

The canyons that slice through the Wasatch Mountains not only provided water to the Salt Lake Valley but also powered many of its early industries. One 1847 Mormon pioneer, John Neff, brought his milling machinery with him to the Salt Lake Valley. He built the first mill in the valley at the mouth of Mill Creek, and by 1848 he was producing flour. In his lifetime he built 30 mills, including one near the canyon that bears his name.

Today, the Olympus Cove neighborhood has grown up around the access point to Neffs Canyon, and only locals regularly use the trailhead. In all likelihood, fewer people know about Neffs Canyon today than 150 years ago,

Directions →

From I-215 on Salt Lake City's east side, take the 3300 South/3900 South turnoff (Exit 4). Turn left onto Wasatch Boulevard and go north 1 block to 3800 South. Turn right onto Wasatch Boulevard and continue south to Oakview Drive (4275 South), marked by an overhead pedestrian bridge. Turn left on Oakview Drive and continue east for 1.2 miles to Zarahemla Drive. Turn left on Zarahemla Drive and continue north for 0.3 miles to Park Terrace Drive and turn right. Continue for 0.1 mile and turn right onto White Way. Continue for 0.2 miles to the trailhead parking area at the end of White Way.

KEY AT-A-GLANCE INFORMATION

LENGTH: 5.5 miles round-trip
ELEVATION GAIN: 2,445 feet
ELEVATION AT TRAILHEAD: 5,624 feet
CONFIGURATION: Out-and-back
DIFFICULTY: Difficult
SCENERY: Wooded canyon, meadow with surrounding peaks
EXPOSURE: Mostly shaded
TRAFFIC: Light
TRAIL SURFACE: Dirt and rock
HIKING TIME: 4–5 hours
WATER REQUIREMENTS: 1–2 liters. Water from stream can be purified.
SEASON: Year-round
ACCESS: No fees for access or parking. Gate near trailhead parking area closed from 10 p.m. to 6 a.m. Much of the hike is within the Mount Olympus Wilderness Area.
MAPS: USGS Sugar House and Mount Aire, Trails Illustrated Wasatch Front (709)
FACILITIES: No restrooms at trailhead or on trail
DOGS: Permitted (Note that Neffs Canyon is not a city watershed.)
SPECIAL COMMENTS: Neffs Canyon is a great snowshoe destination, but stay in the lower canyon where the routes aren't so steep and rocky.

GPS Trailhead Coordinates

UTM Zone (WGS84) 12T
Easting 0434385
Northing 4503240
Latitude N 40° 40' 37.2"
Longitude W 111° 46' 34.7"

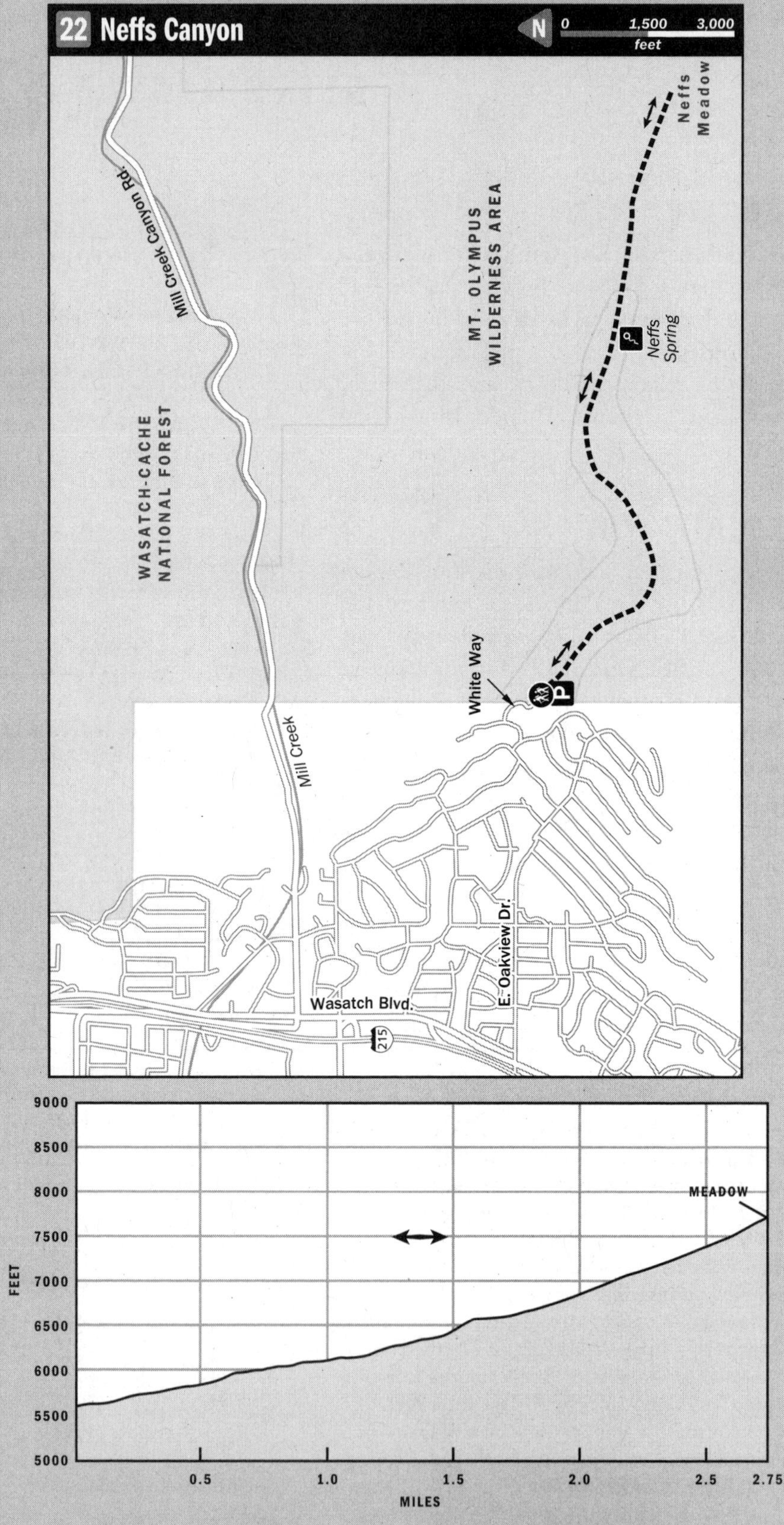

22 Neffs Canyon
N
0
1,500
3,000
feet
Neffs Meadow
Mill Creek Canyon Rd.
MT. OLYMPUS WILDERNESS AREA
Neffs Spring
WASATCH-CACHE NATIONAL FOREST
White Way
Mill Creek
E. Oakview Dr.
Wasatch Blvd.
215
9000
8500
8000
7500
7000
6500
6000
5500
5000
FEET
MEADOW
0.5
1.0
1.5
2.0
2.5
2.75
MILES

Wild roses at the mouth of Neffs Canyon

when it was a hotbed of mining, timber, and grazing activity. The mills, mining, and timber operations have been gone for nearly 100 years, but you can still see one of the old millstones at the Utah State Capitol, along with other pioneer relics.

Standing at the trailhead looking up the canyon, you can tell it's going to be a beautiful setting. What you can't discern is the number of natural springs that dot the canyon, the various routes taken by the streams, and the water flow's steep gradient.

From the large parking area, take the well-marked trail to the east, which rises quickly to a graded service road in just 100 feet. This road continues a gentle incline along the north side of the canyon, passing a water tank on the left at 0.3 miles. At 0.5 miles, the graded road ends as it comes to a wide stream crossing where you can easily step across on rocks without ever getting wet. After the crossing, the trail continues up the canyon on an old roadbed used by wagons more than 100 years ago. At 1.1 miles, the old roadbed ends and the trail continues as a steep single track through Gambel oak and bigtooth maple.

Because of the canyon's long history, dozens of trails follow its springs and streams. Worth exploring, these trails lead through some beautiful conifer wooded areas. If you find yourself on the south side of the canyon, on a faint trail, and up against a rock slab, you're on your own. You'll enjoy nice overlooks and some great rock climbing, but it's not the main trail to the meadow. Although the road may not be the most romantic route, it is reliable and easy to follow. The Neff Canyon Trail doesn't believe in switchbacks, and even if it did, there's not much room for them in this narrow canyon.

At 1.5 miles, the trail enters the Mount Olympus Wilderness Area. The trail, by now a well-worn dirt track, steepens considerably. After climbing steadily through spruce and fir, the trail crosses the stream over a log bridge at 1.8 miles. As the trail gains elevation, you enter large stands of quaking aspens blended with conifers and maples.

Eventually, the steep ascent lets up just a bit as the trail reaches the crest and enters the meadow at 2.5 miles. Another 0.2 miles and you're at the upper, eastern end of the meadow. Bounded by a dense aspen forest on the south, you have perfect views of Mount Raymond and Hobbs Peak above the aspens.

Another little-known feature on one of the slabs to the south of the meadow is Neffs Canyon Cave, a National Natural Landmark. At 1,165 feet, it's one of the deepest caves in the United States. An extremely dangerous cave with most passages dipping steeply at a 45- to 60-degree slope, it has been locked by the U.S. Forest Service. The service grants admission only to experienced cavers.

The meadow is a great place for a snack or to sit quietly and watch for wildlife—especially deer, moose, and elk—as it comes to the stream at the south side of the meadow. The return to the trailhead takes about 1.5 hours. From the meadow you can also follow the trail as it curves to the north. Within a mile it intersects with the Thayne Canyon Trail, which descends into Mill Creek.

NEARBY ACTIVITIES

On the northeast side of the trailhead parking area is a well and pumping station for Mount Olympus Spring Water. The water, which was originally bottled in 1899, is low in dissolved solids and high in oxygen, with a slightly sweet taste. Stainless steel tankers transport the water from Neffs Canyon to a bottling plant in Salt Lake City. From there, it's distributed to offices, homes, and retail outlets throughout the Mountain West.

MOUNT OLYMPUS 23

IN BRIEF

Mount Olympus is the best-known and most recognizable peak on Salt Lake City's eastern skyline. Geologically, it's a mammoth anticline of purple quartzite slabs jutting out nearly a mile above the valley floor. Physically, it's a steep, demanding trail capped by a Class 3 scramble to the rocky summit, where exceptional views await.

DESCRIPTION

Many locals assign mythic proportions to a Mount Olympus climb. Its foreboding, craggy summit appears to be unclimbable from the valley floor. Typically, it's not the final rock scramble, but the steep trail to the saddle that eliminates unconditioned and unprepared hikers. How you handle the trail's first 100 yards best predicts whether you'll make it to the summit. Those first 100 yards accurately represent the entire trail in terms of steepness. If you need to stop for a rest after 100 yards, multiply that by 60 and you'll have some sense of what the hike entails. As the trail ascends the canyon and leads toward the summit, it becomes more wild and beautiful, but its steep angle doesn't ease up one bit. The trail's lower portions consist of Bonneville Shoreline alluvium studded with quartzite talus and boulders from above.

KEY AT-A-GLANCE INFORMATION

LENGTH: 7 miles round-trip

ELEVATION GAIN: 4,060 feet

ELEVATION AT TRAILHEAD: 4,966 feet

CONFIGURATION: Out-and-back

DIFFICULTY: Difficult

SCENERY: Exceptional views of the valley with Big Cottonwood Canyon peaks to the south and east

EXPOSURE: Largely exposed to sun for the first mile. Mostly shaded in canyon for the next 2 miles, then mostly exposed on the scramble to the summit.

TRAFFIC: Busy

TRAIL SURFACE: Rock and dirt

HIKING TIME: 5–7 hours

WATER REQUIREMENTS: 1–2 liters

SEASON: Late spring, summer, early fall

ACCESS: No fees required for access or parking. Hike is located within the Mount Olympus Wilderness Area.

MAPS: USGS Sugar House, Trails Illustrated Wasatch Front (709)

FACILITIES: No water or toilets at trailhead. Water at creek can be purified.

DOGS: Permitted (Note that Tolcats Canyon is not a city watershed.)

Directions →

From I-215 on Salt Lake City's east side, go south to 4500 South (Exit 5). Turn left on 4500 South (UT 266), cross over the freeway, and turn right onto Wasatch Boulevard. Drive south for 1.6 miles and turn left onto an unmarked paved road leading up the hillside to a small parking area.

GPS Trailhead Coordinates

UTM Zone (WGS84) 12T

Easting 0431840

Northing 4500408

Latitude N 40° 39' 06.9"

Longitude W 111° 48' 22.4"

23 Mt. Olympus

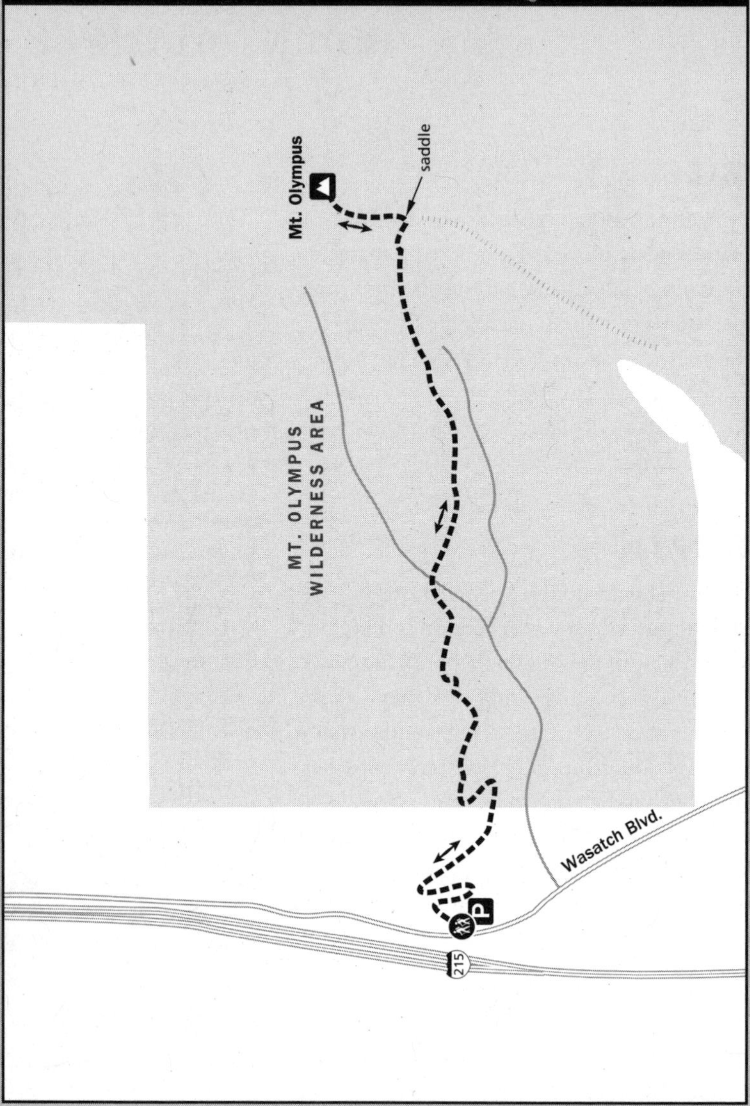

N

0 1,300 2,600
feet

Mt. Olympus
saddle
MT. OLYMPUS WILDERNESS AREA
Wasatch Blvd.
215

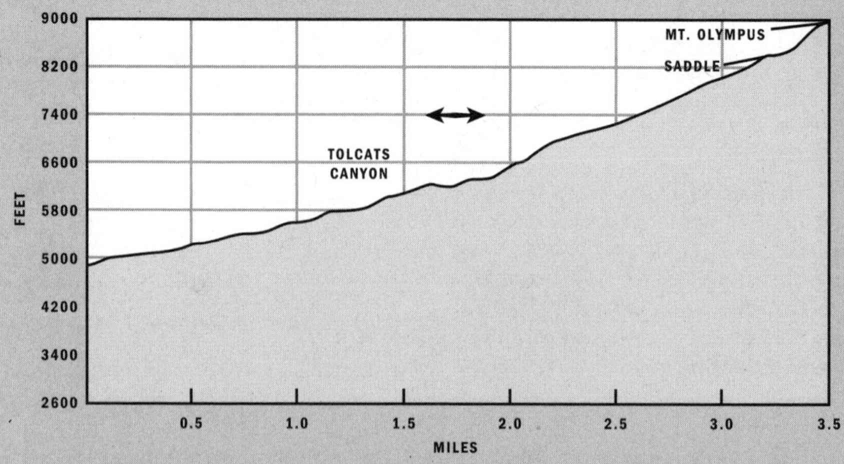

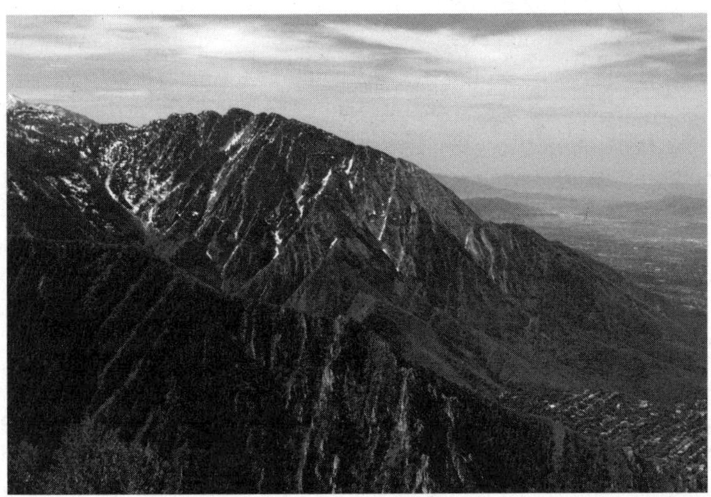

Mount Olympus viewed from the north

Because the Mount Olympus Trail begins just a stone's throw from I-215, you may find it disturbing to hear the roar of freeway traffic in a federally protected wildnerness area. But that disturbance lasts for only the first mile or so.

At 0.5 miles the trail curves to the left around a quartzite outcropping, then proceeds up Tolcats Canyon to the east. At 0.7 miles the path enters the Mount Olympus Wilderness Area, marked by a sign. Eventually, at a point fairly deep in the canyon and 1.7 miles from the trailhead, you'll cross a small creek. The crossing's elevation is 6,256 feet, a 1,290-foot gain from the trailhead. The shade and boulders surrounding the creek make it a popular rest stop.

Beyond the creek crossing, the trail continues its steep ascent to the head of the canyon, aided by several series of switchbacks. Deep in the canyon, at 2.4 miles from the trailhead, conifers begin to appear, and at higher elevations, stands of aspen line the trail. This section of trail is particularly beautiful, rocky, and steep.

Soon you approach the saddle, at an elevation of 8,400 feet. The trail levels and turns to the north through a peaceful grove of Douglas-fir. Take a minute and walk 20 feet or so over to the eastern side of the saddle. The view to the east, a maze of rocky crags, looks absolutely inaccessible and deserving of the wilderness designation.

Because of the trail's popularity and its proximity to the city, wildlife sightings are rare—but rattlesnakes appear fairly often, both on the trail and on the lower sections of the summit scramble. As you're climbing through this area, use caution when placing your hand on rocky ledges so as not to surprise a rattler.

From the saddle, follow the trail to the north toward the summit. Within 100 yards of traversing the saddle, the grove of Douglas-fir gives way to rocky slopes, and soon you'll be climbing hand over hand. The trail becomes faint, but with some careful scouting, it's generally discernible. No exceptionally difficult or technical movements are required, so if you come to an insurmountable point, retrace your steps and relocate the trail. The route from the saddle to the summit entails 15 to 20 minutes of sustained scrambling. This section is prone to rockfall, so be careful not to dislodge rocks onto climbers below.

The summit of Mount Olympus consists of an enormous rockpile of angular quartzite boulders. As you'd expect, spectacular views of the Salt Lake Valley await. On a clear day, they extend far up the Great Salt Lake to the northwest and to Deseret Peak in the distant west. The views of the Twin Peaks Wilderness to the south are equally striking.

Mount Olympus's summit is the last place you want to be if the weather forecast calls for lightning. Do not attempt the summit if there is any chance of lightning or rain. Remember that descending from the rocky summit is generally more dangerous and more time-consuming than the climb up. Take your time and save your strength for the jarring downhill return.

Note: No motorized vehicles or bicycles are permitted within the Mount Olympus Wilderness Area. The trailhead parking area accommodates just 18 cars. On busy summer weekends, overflow parking is available on Wasatch Boulevard.

NEARBY ACTIVITIES

Just 5 miles from the Mount Olympus trailhead, Wheeler Historic Farm offers tours, tractor rides, wagon rides, and demonstrations of agriculture and Salt Lake County's rural lifestyle from 1890 to 1920. Open year-round, Wheeler Historic Farm is located at 6351 South 900 East in Salt Lake City. Visit the farm online at **www.wheelerfarm.com.**

DOG LAKE 24

IN BRIEF

Dog Lake, a small, peaceful lake ringed by quaking aspens, lies at the junction of several trails leading to other peaks and canyons. A well-used mountain-biking trail, the Dog Lake Trail is wide and easy to follow.

KEY AT-A-GLANCE INFORMATION

LENGTH: 4.6 miles round-trip
ELEVATION GAIN: 1,452 feet
ELEVATION AT TRAILHEAD: 7,295 feet
CONFIGURATION: Out-and-back or one-way connecting to other area trails
DIFFICULTY: Easy
SCENERY: Wooded canyon and lake
EXPOSURE: Mostly shaded
TRAFFIC: Moderate
TRAIL SURFACE: Dirt
HIKING TIME: 2–3 hours
WATER REQUIREMENTS: 1 liter; water from stream and lake may be purified.
SEASON: Late spring, summer, early fall
ACCESS: No fees for access or parking
MAPS: USGS Mount Aire, Trails Illustrated Wasatch Front (709)
FACILITIES: Restrooms are located across the street from the trailhead.
DOGS: Prohibited in Big Cottonwood Canyon, a protected watershed
SPECIAL COMMENTS: You'll be sharing the trail with cyclists, as this is a popular mountain-biking trail.

DESCRIPTION

Dog Lake is both remote and accessible; out of the way, yet easy to find. Located in Big Cottonwood Canyon, it can easily be accessed from Mill D North Fork (as described here) or Butler Fork in the Mount Olympus Wilderness Area. It is also frequently accessed from Mill Creek Canyon. Armed with a good trail map of the area, it's easy to plan a canyon-to-canyon hike with Dog Lake as the centerpiece.

A hike to Dog Lake from Big Cottonwood's Mill D North Fork is one of the few trails in the Wasatch without a single switchback. In a little more than 2 miles, the trail ascends steadily but never too steeply. Because of the gradual incline, the trail is popular with mountain bikers. Hikers also love the wide, easily followed trail, which readily accommodates those who want to chat and walk side by side. Since it cuts through aspen and meadows, visibility is good, allowing hikers and bikers to see one another on its long, straight stretches.

Directions

From Salt Lake City's east side, take I-215 south to 6200 South (Exit 6). At the off-ramp turn left and proceed south for 1.7 miles, as 6200 South changes to Wasatch Boulevard (UT 190). Turn left at the signal, staying on UT 190, and continue up Big Cottonwood Canyon for 9.1 miles to the Mill D North Fork trailhead and parking area on the left side of the road.

GPS Trailhead Coordinates

UTM Zone (WGS84) 12T
Easting 0445151
Northing 4500103
Latitude N 40° 38' 58.7"
Longitude W 111° 38' 53.6"

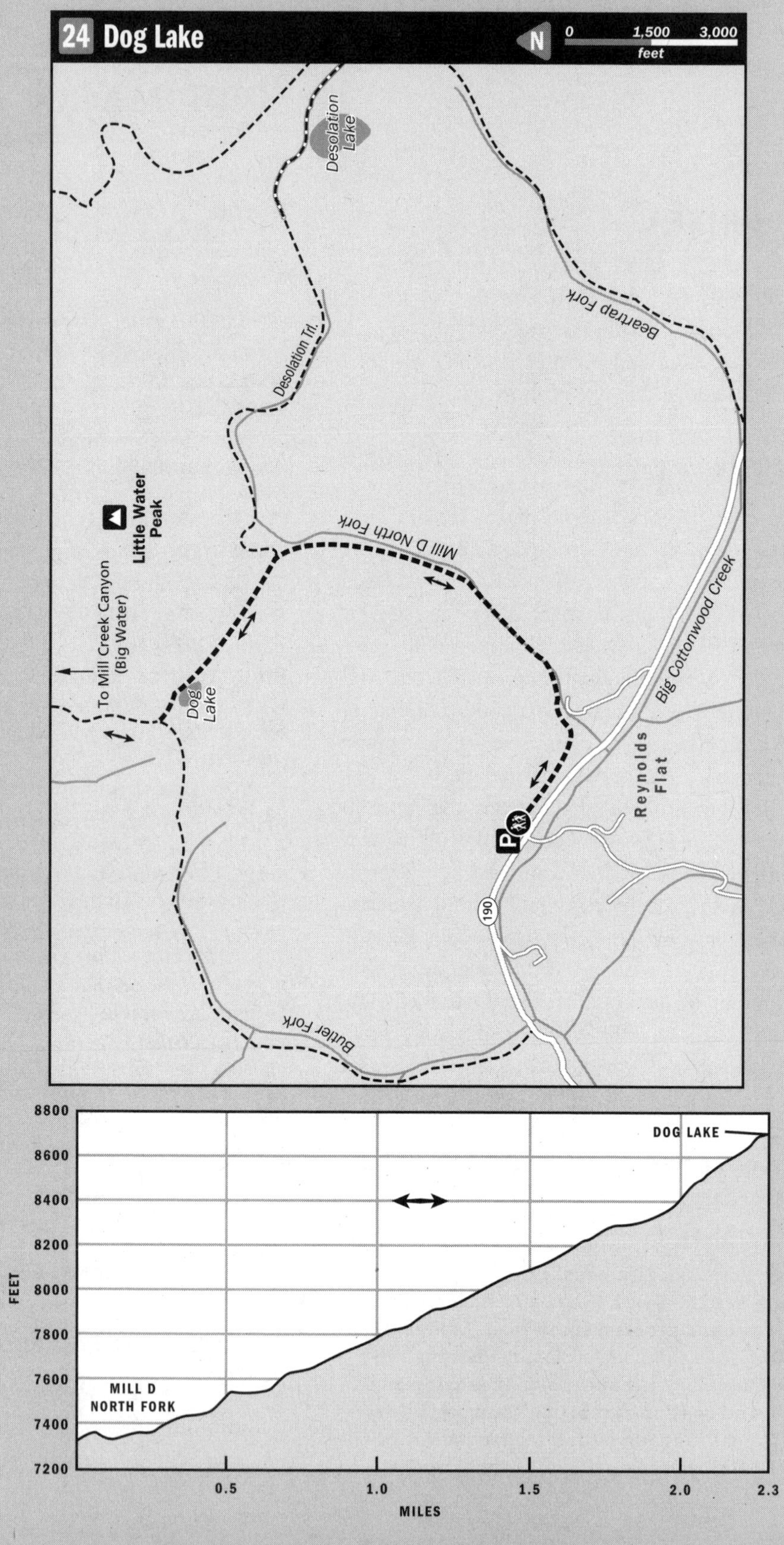

24 Dog Lake
N
0
1,500
3,000
feet
Desolation Lake
Beartrap Fork
Desolation Trl.
Little Water Peak
Mill D North Fork
To Mill Creek Canyon (Big Water)
Dog Lake
Big Cottonwood Creek
Reynolds Flat
P
190
Butler Fork
8800
8600
8400
8200
8000
7800
7600
7400
7200
FEET
DOG LAKE
MILL D
NORTH FORK
0.5
1.0
1.5
2.0
2.3
MILES

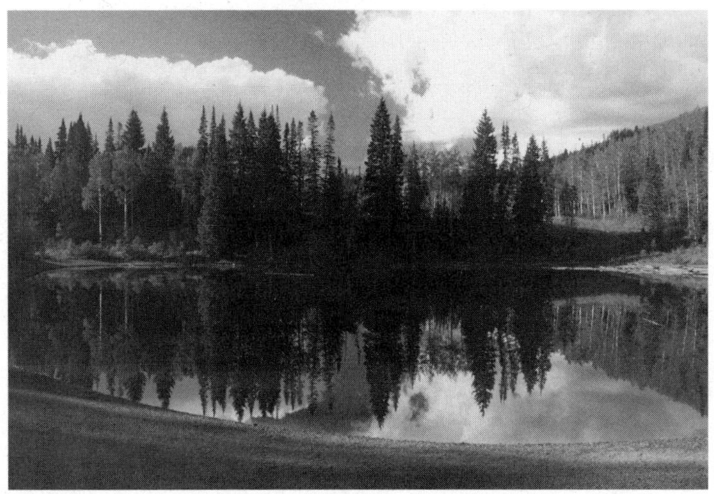

Dog Lake

From the Mill D North Fork trailhead, the trail quickly ascends to the north, then immediately turns right to rise parallel to the canyon road on your right. The trail parallels the road for 0.4 miles before curving to the left and entering Mill D North Fork. At this point the trail is already far above the canyon floor, and it maintains a gentle ascent for another 0.8 miles until it joins with Mill D Creek.

Mill D has more-moderate and less-rugged slopes than other Big Cottonwood side canyons. While it's not as dramatic or rocky, it is beautiful, especially in fall as the aspens turn bright yellow. In the summer, daisies and alpine asters line the path.

At 1.7 miles from the trailhead, you arrive at a signed junction and the Desolation Trail. The path to the right leads to Desolation Lake. Take the route to the left, which takes you directly to Dog Lake, just 0.6 miles farther. This trail leads through more aspens sprinkled with Douglas-fir. As you near the lake, the gradient increases a bit, but never long enough to become tiring. With a steady pace you should arrive at Dog Lake, which lies at an elevation of 8,544 feet, about an hour after you leave the trailhead.

Dog Lake may be too small to be called a lake and too large to be called a pond. It's a still, shallow, circular basin ringed by aspen and conifers. Because it's shielded from wind, the lake typically has a glassy surface that reflects the surrounding trees like a flawless mirror. Bring your camera, walk around the lake, and enjoy the peaceful setting.

At the north end of the lake is a marked junction on the Desolation Trail. Continuing to the west for 2.8 miles will lead down Butler Fork and back to Big Cottonwood Canyon. From the Butler Fork trailhead, it's just 0.8 miles up the canyon road back to the Mill D North Fork trailhead. If you're adventurous and energetic, take the Big Water Trail over the ridge into Mill Creek Canyon.

It's a scenic route, but unless you have a shuttle vehicle awaiting you, it could be a long walk back to your car.

NEARBY ACTIVITIES

Storm Mountain is the imposing barrier that sits 2.5 miles up Big Cottonwood Canyon and made access to the canyon so difficult for early pioneers. Stairs Gulch is a short, half-mile hike up a rocky couloir at the base of Storm Mountain. To access the trail, park near the geology sign on the right side of the road 100 yards beyond the Storm Mountain Picnic Area. Follow the trail up and to the west before turning south into Stairs Gulch.

DESOLATION LAKE 25

IN BRIEF

A gentle canyon trail ascends to a high alpine lake, then leads to a ridge overlooking Park City and Big Cottonwood Canyon. A steep descent of a little-known canyon returns you to the Big Cottonwood Canyon floor.

DESCRIPTION

The 17-mile Desolation Trail stretches from the mouth of Mill Creek Canyon to the top of Big Cottonwood Canyon—from canyon floor to ridgeline. While few hikers ever follow the complete trail from end to end, sections of this scenic trail are popular as a means of connecting various canyons, lakes, and trailheads.

A hike to Desolation Lake—also labeled as Lake Desolation on USGS maps—is an excellent orientation hike to Big Cottonwood Canyon because it leads hikers through two side canyons (Mill D North Fork and Beartrap Fork), ascends a panoramic ridgeline, and affords a stop at Desolation Lake. Dog Lake can also be included in the hike by means of a short side trip.

From the Mill D North Fork trailhead, you'll ascend quickly to the north, then immediately turn right to rise parallel to the canyon road on your right. The trail parallels the road for 0.4 miles before curving to the left and

KEY AT-A-GLANCE INFORMATION

LENGTH: 6.6 miles, plus 1.6 miles by shuttle vehicle or on foot
ELEVATION GAIN: 2,465 feet
ELEVATION AT TRAILHEAD: 7,295 feet
CONFIGURATION: One-way or loop
DIFFICULTY: Moderate
SCENERY: Canyons, alpine lake, ridgeline views
EXPOSURE: Mostly shaded
TRAFFIC: Moderate
TRAIL SURFACE: Dirt and rock
HIKING TIME: 3–4 hours
WATER REQUIREMENTS: 1–2 liters. Water in lake and streams may be purified.
SEASON: Spring, summer, fall
ACCESS: No fees for access or parking
MAPS: USGS Mount Aire, Park City West, Trails Illustrated Wasatch Front (709)
FACILITIES: Restrooms are located across the street from the trailhead.
DOGS: Prohibited in Big Cottonwood Canyon, a protected watershed.
SPECIAL COMMENTS: You'll be sharing the trail with cyclists, as Mill D North Fork and the Desolation Trail are popular mountain-biking trails. The descent down Beartrap Fork is more secluded.

Directions

From Salt Lake City's east side take I-215 south to 6200 South (Exit 6). At the off-ramp, turn left and proceed south for 1.7 miles, as 6200 South changes to Wasatch Boulevard (UT 190). Turn left at the signal, staying on UT 190, and continue up Big Cottonwood Canyon for 9.1 miles to the Mill D North Fork trailhead and parking area on the left side of the road.

GPS Trailhead Coordinates

UTM Zone (WGS84) 12T
Easting 0445158
Northing 4500090
Latitude N 40° 38' 58.7"
Longitude W 111° 38' 53.6"

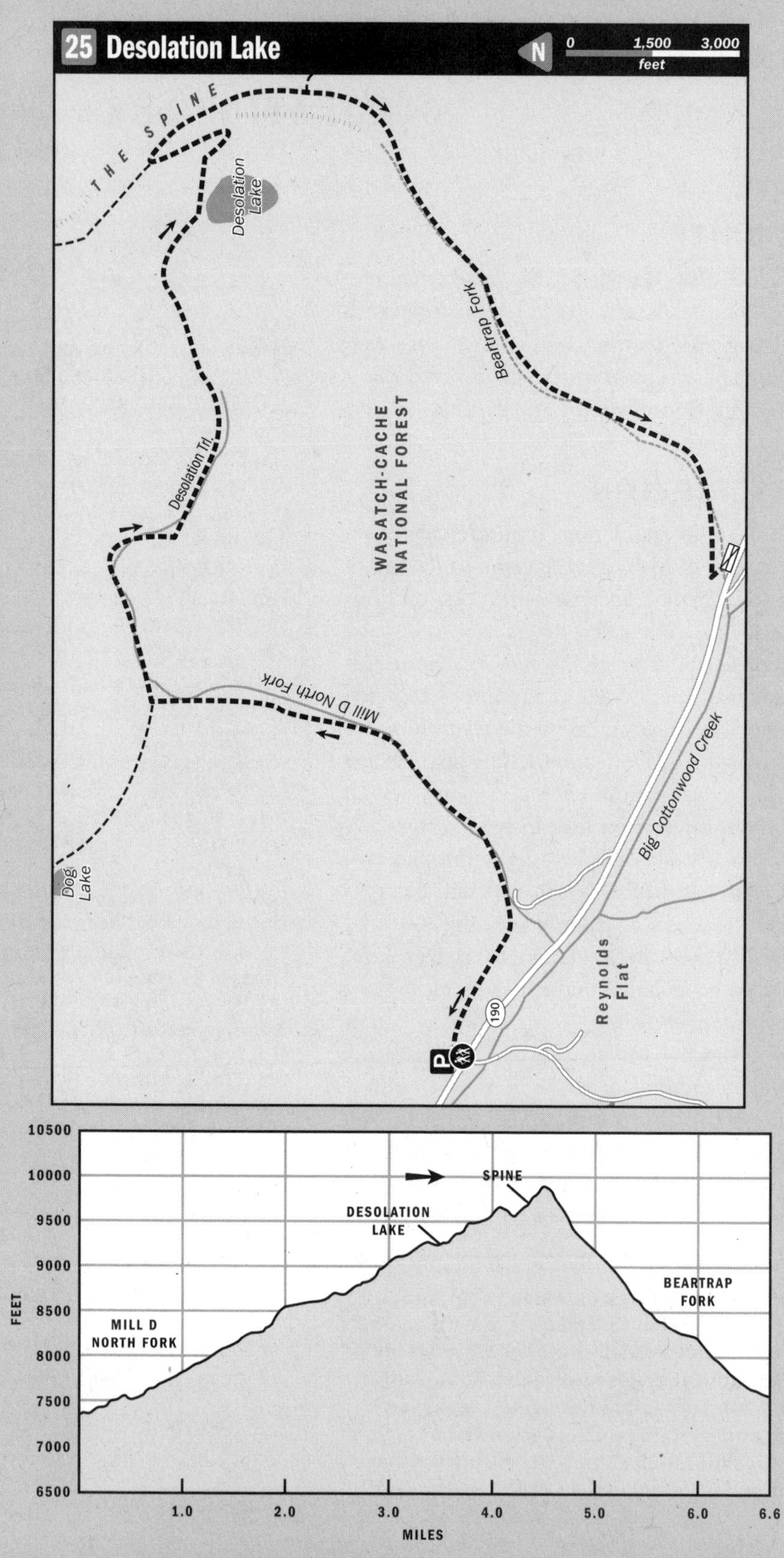
25 Desolation Lake
N
0
1,500
3,000
feet
THE SPINE
Desolation Lake
Beartrap Fork
WASATCH-CACHE NATIONAL FOREST
Desolation Trl.
Mill D North Fork
Big Cottonwood Creek
190
Dog Lake
Reynolds Flat
P
10500
10000
9500
9000
8500
8000
7500
7000
6500
FEET
SPINE
DESOLATION LAKE
MILL D NORTH FORK
BEARTRAP FORK
1.0
2.0
3.0
4.0
5.0
6.0
6.6
MILES

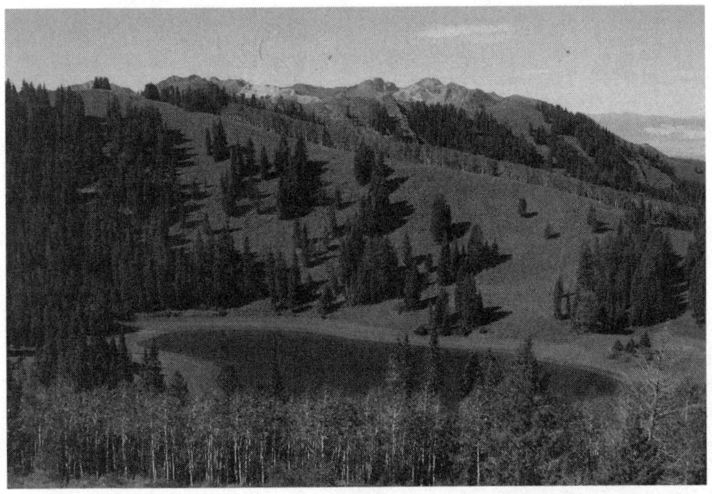

Desolation Lake viewed from ridgeline to the east

entering Mill D North Fork. At this point the trail is already far above the canyon floor, and it maintains a gentle ascent for another 0.8 miles until it joins with Mill D Creek.

As you ascend Mill D, you'll notice that the slopes on both sides of the canyon are more moderate and less rugged than slopes in other Big Cottonwood side canyons. While Mill D is not as dramatic or rocky, it is beautiful, especially in fall as the aspens turn bright yellow. In the summer, daisies and alpine asters line the path.

At 1.7 miles from the trailhead, you arrive at a signed junction and the Desolation Trail. Before continuing on the path to the right, which leads to Desolation Lake, consider a side trip to Dog Lake, just 0.6 miles farther along the path to your left. The Dog Lake option will add another 30 minutes and 1.2 miles to your trip.

From the junction, continue another 1.9 miles along the north slope of a small canyon as it leads through aspens in its ascent to Desolation Lake. Desolation Lake lies at an elevation of 9,232 feet in a broad, shallow bowl ringed by a treeless shoreline—hence the *desolation* moniker. In actuality, the meadow to the north and the trees on the upper slopes create a peaceful openness that is anything but desolate. It's not uncommon to see deer and elk feeding near Desolation Lake.

A trail rings the lake and makes a pleasant extension if you want to visit the woods at the south side of the lake. From the north side, you can turn around and retrace your ascent route to return to the Mill D North Fork trailhead, or you can continue up to the ridge on the east for an interesting variation leading back to Big Cottonwood Canyon.

From Desolation Lake, take the trail from the northeast shore of the lake as it leads up to the ridgeline along an extended switchback. Within a few minutes you'll

Trail through aspens from Mill D to Desolation Lake

be at the top of the ridge on the Great Western Trail leading toward Guardsman Pass and approaching a jagged section popularly known among mountain bikers as "the spine." Along this ridge you'll have fine views down into Park City to the east. Passing the spine, the trail leads south to the right of a knoll and continues along a level contour. As the Great Western Trail begins to curve to the left, you'll notice a faint, unmarked trail that leads to the southwest, down a grassy slope into a canyon. This is Beartrap Fork, a quiet side canyon on the north side of Big Cottonwood.

Continuing down the trail, you will soon connect with a seasonal creekbed at the bottom of Beartrap Canyon. Follow this creek as it leads toward the floor of Big Cottonwood Canyon. The total distance from the Great Western Trail junction through Beartrap Fork down to Big Cottonwood Canyon is 2.2 miles. Once you arrive at the canyon floor and near the road, you'll pass through a metal gate, but no signs indicate that you've just descended Beartrap Fork. Unless you've left a shuttle vehicle at the Beartrap Fork gate, you'll need to walk 1.6 miles down the canyon road back to the Mill D North Fork trailhead.

NEARBY ACTIVITIES

Solitude Mountain Resort, well known for its winter skiing, also offers a varied summer program. Featured activities include lift-served hiking, mountain biking, mountain scooters, disc golf, and casual dining. For information on Solitude's summer offerings, call (801) 534-1400 or visit **www.skisolitude.com.**

MOUNT RAYMOND (via Butler Fork) 26

IN BRIEF

Admittedly, neighboring Gobblers Knob is five feet higher in elevation and has a more interesting name, but Mount Raymond is the more interesting hike. Groves of aspen blanket the lower trail, and a variety of conifers clings to a rocky knife-ridge leading to the summit. You'll have great views in all directions.

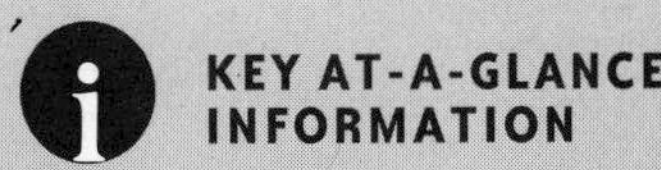

LENGTH: 8 miles round-trip
ELEVATION GAIN: 3,071 feet
ELEVATION AT TRAILHEAD: 7,170 feet
CONFIGURATION: Out-and-back as described here, with many one-way, spur-trail, and loop options
DIFFICULTY: Difficult
SCENERY: Wooded drainage, aspen slopes, high ridgeline ascent to a 10,241-foot peak with great views
EXPOSURE: Mostly shaded for first 2 miles. Partially shaded to the summit.
TRAFFIC: Moderate
TRAIL SURFACE: Dirt and rock
HIKING TIME: 4.5–5.5 hours
WATER REQUIREMENTS: 1–2 liters. For the first mile you'll have access to Butler Fork water, which can be purified.
SEASON: Late spring, summer, to midfall
ACCESS: No parking or access fees
MAPS: USGS Mount Aire, Trails Illustrated Wasatch Front (709)
FACILITIES: No restrooms or water at trailhead
DOGS: Prohibited in Big Cottonwood Canyon, a protected watershed

DESCRIPTION

A hike to the summit of Mount Raymond supplies a great example of the interconnection of many Wasatch trails. As you browse the summit log, you may find that most of the other hikers arrived by some other route. The path described here departs from the Butler Fork Trailhead in Big Cottonwood Canyon, but you could just as easily use the Mill B North Fork trailhead, or one of several Mill Creek Canyon trailheads. The Butler Fork route attains the summit with the least vertical ascent, though, and still offers an appealing approach. Along the route to the summit, you'll come to five trail junctions, and while you'll want to explore them all, you may have to save some for another day.

From the small roadside parking area, follow the trail leading north along the west side of a small stream. The trail immediately

---

Directions ⟶

From Salt Lake City's east side, take I-215 south to 6200 South (Exit 6). At the off-ramp, turn left and proceed south for 1.7 miles, as 6200 South changes to Wasatch Boulevard (UT 190). Turn left at the signal, staying on UT 190, and continue up Big Cottonwood Canyon for 4.3 miles. As the road makes a hairpin turn to the left, enter the Mill B South Trailhead parking area on the right.

GPS Trailhead Coordinates

UTM Zone (WGS84) 12T
Easting 0444071
Northing 4500055
Latitude N 40° 38' 58.0"
Longitude W 111° 39' 43.0"

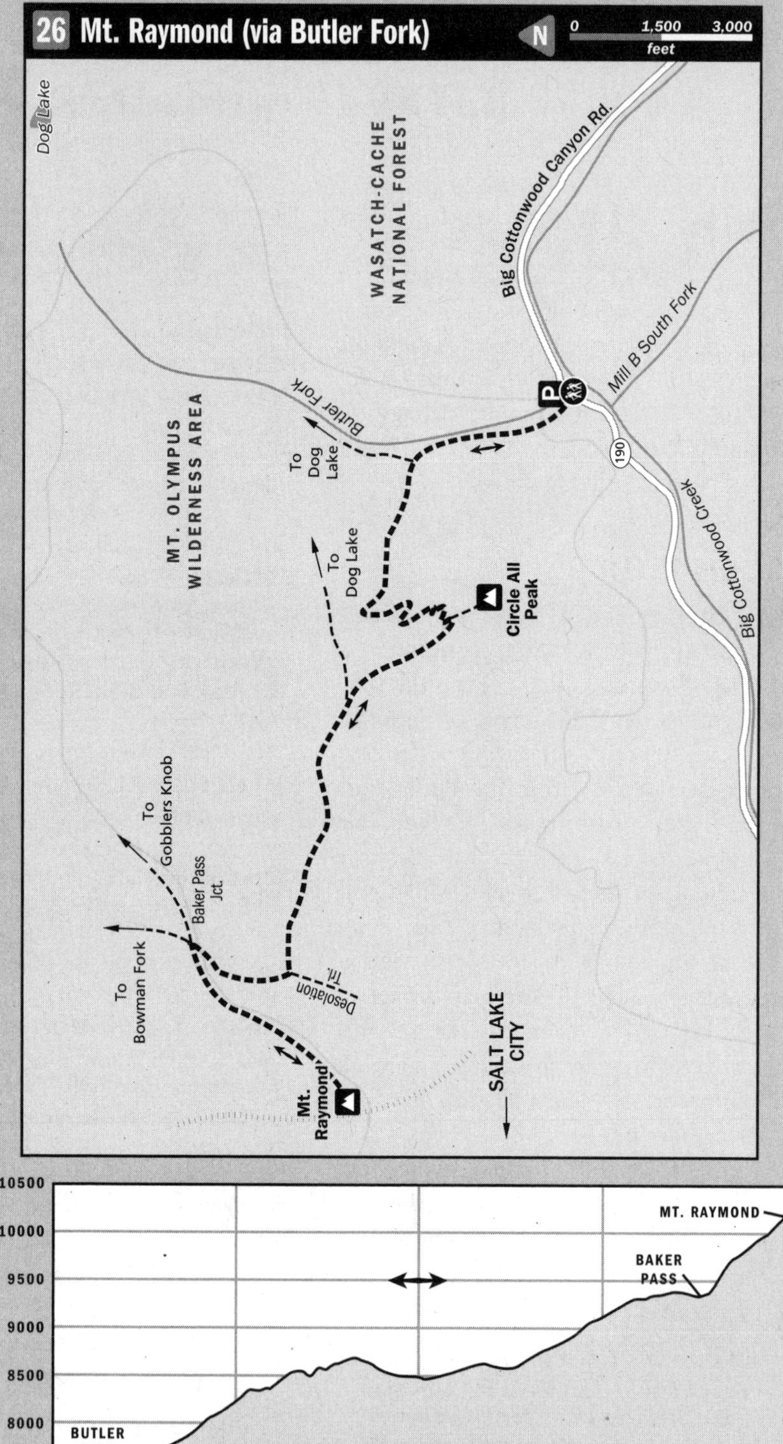
26 Mt. Raymond (via Butler Fork)
N
0 1,500 3,000
feet
Dog Lake
WASATCH-CACHE NATIONAL FOREST
Big Cottonwood Canyon Rd.
Mill B South Fork
Butler Fork
190
Big Cottonwood Creek
MT. OLYMPUS WILDERNESS AREA
To Dog Lake
To Dog Lake
Circle All Peak
To Gobblers Knob
Baker Pass Jct.
To Bowman Fork
Desolation Trl.
Mt. Raymond
SALT LAKE CITY
10500
10000
9500
9000
8500
8000
7500
7000
6500
FEET
MT. RAYMOND
BAKER PASS
BUTLER FORK
1.0
2.0
3.0
4.0
MILES

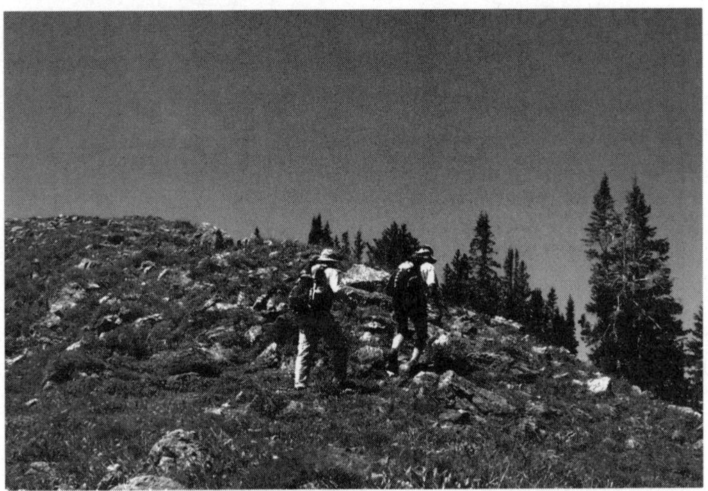

Hikers make their final ascent to Mount Raymond's summit.

crosses to the east side of the stream and enters the Mount Olympus Wilderness Area, marked by a large Forest Service sign. At 0.5 miles from the trailhead you'll come to a junction marked by a small Forest Service sign indicating a trail to Dog Lake on the right and Mill A Basin on the left. Go to the left up into the aspen-lined drainage.

Within a hundred yards, the aspens give way to a clearing about the size of a football field. This area will be your best chance to see a moose, especially in the early-morning hours. Do not approach a moose, but try to work your way around it or wait for the moose to move. Never come between a moose cow and a calf, or between a moose and the water.

From the clearing, the trail continues up the slope through a series of switchbacks. At 1.6 miles from the trailhead, you arrive at a saddle. A faint trail, normally blocked by fallen limbs to steer hikers along the main trail, takes off to the left. It leads to Circle All Peak, an 8,707-foot outcropping overlooking Big Cottonwood Canyon and also Mount Raymond. It's just 0.2 miles to the viewpoint and an elevation gain of 150 feet from the junction. It's certainly worth ten minutes of your time, and if you're rushed for time it could be a suitable alternate destination for a hike of less than two hours.

Back on the main trail, continue along a gently ascending slope to another sign pointing to Dog Lake on the right and Mill A on the left. Follow the trail to the left as it sweeps along the upper slope of the Mill A Basin. This is a particularly enjoyable section of the hike with excellent views of Mount Raymond directly to the west. These slopes also provide abundant habitat for many birds, including American redstarts and yellow warblers, which you should be able to hear, even if you can't see them.

As you near the top of the Mill A Basin, there is a faint trail, normally unmarked, that takes off along a level contour to the west and leads down to the

Mill B North Fork Trailhead. Stay to the right as the trail continues another 0.2 miles up to the saddle of Baker Pass.

From Baker Pass (elevation 9,340) you have your first views into Mill Creek Canyon and west to the Great Salt Lake. Four separate trails meet at this pass. If you turn to the right, a fairly straightforward walk ascends 900 feet in 0.8 miles to the summit of Gobblers Knob. To the left, a more rigorous climb ascends 900 feet in 0.6 miles to the summit of Mount Raymond. Many hikers do both on the same hike, and that's certainly an option you can consider. You can bag two summits in one afternoon.

Departing Baker Pass and walking toward Mount Raymond to the west, you pass an amazing variety of conifers, including Douglas-fir, limber pine, bristlecone pine, and subalpine fir. Some are firmly planted in soil, and others cling tenaciously with exposed roots hugging the rocks. The first 0.3 miles from the pass offer some beautiful steep ascents along a grassy alpine ridge trail. Then the trail ends and you're face to face with a fractured ridge of angular limestone and quartzite. It's a good scramble with some exposure but not anything that would demand protective equipment or technical climbing experience. There's just enough maneuvering to make it fun.

As you might expect, the summit offers excellent views in all directions. You'll enjoy seeing Mount Olympus from the less familiar back side, and Twin Peaks and Dromedary Peak to the south. At the summit you'll find a USGS marker and a summit log. You'll probably share the views with a handful of other hikers and a few interested chipmunks.

Note: The trail lies within the federally protected Mount Olympus Wilderness Area. Domestic animals, horses, bicycles, motorized vehicles, and open campfires are not permitted.

NEARBY ACTIVITIES

Big Cottonwood Canyon trails are known for their steep ascents to towering peaks and shimmering lakes. An enjoyable introduction to the canyon is the Mill B South Interpretive Trail, which follows the rushing Big Cottonwood Creek for a 0.7-mile round-trip out-and-back. The trail is paved and handicap accessible, and there are restrooms at the trailhead. The trail starts at the Mill B South Fork Trailhead parking lot, just 4.3 miles up the canyon as you enter the **S**-curves.

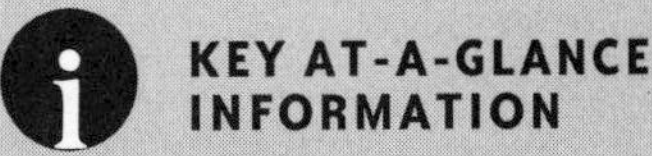

DOUGHNUT FALLS 27

IN BRIEF

Doughnut Falls is unique—a waterfall that plunges through a hole in the rock and into a grotto before cascading down the rocky drainage below. It's a short hike, popular with families and youth groups. If you want to climb to the top of the falls, you'll face a challenging but rewarding scramble.

KEY AT-A-GLANCE INFORMATION

LENGTH: 1.4 miles round-trip
ELEVATION GAIN: 337 feet
ELEVATION AT TRAILHEAD: 7,493 feet
CONFIGURATION: Out-and-back
DIFFICULTY: Easy
SCENERY: Spruce forest, stream, and waterfall
EXPOSURE: Mostly shaded
TRAFFIC: Busy
TRAIL SURFACE: Dirt and rock
HIKING TIME: 1–2 hours
WATER REQUIREMENTS: 1 liter
SEASON: Late spring, summer, early fall
ACCESS: No fees to access canyon or parking. Gate to trailhead parking closed in winter and early spring.
MAPS: USGS Mount Aire
FACILITIES: Vault toilet at trailhead. No drinking water, but water from stream may be purified.
DOGS: Pets and horses are prohibited in Big Cottonwood Canyon, a protected watershed.
SPECIAL COMMENTS: The road to the trailhead passes through private property with NO TRESPASSING signs posted. However, public access to the falls has been maintained.

DESCRIPTION

Doughnut Falls is irresistible. In less than a mile of easy walking, you come to a rocky chasm with a waterfall that drops through a hole in the rock. The sight is so intriguing that you are compelled to climb as close as possible to see where all that water goes.

As you drive up Big Cottonwood Canyon you'll notice signs referring to Mill B, Mill C, and so on. This naming system dates back to the 1850s, when the side canyons in Big Cottonwood Canyon were named alphabetically, A through F, with a lumber mill placed at the mouth of each canyon. Doughnut Falls is located on the Mill D South Fork. As you drive up the canyon to the trailhead, the canyon widens into a large, open meadow called Reynolds Flat, site of the Jordan Pines picnic area.

Some disputes with private-land holders in the area resulted in a number of PRIVATE

Directions

From Salt Lake City's east side, take I-215 south to 6200 South (Exit 6). At the off-ramp, turn left and proceed south for 1.7 miles, as 6200 South changes to Wasatch Boulevard (UT 190). Turn left at the signal, staying on UT 190, and continue up Big Cottonwood Canyon for 9 miles. Turn right at the Jordan Pines picnic area and continue for 0.8 miles to the trailhead parking area on the left.

GPS Trailhead Coordinates

UTM Zone (WGS84) 12T
Easting 0444919
Northing 4498924
Latitude N 40° 38' 22.5"
Longitude W 111° 39' 05.2"

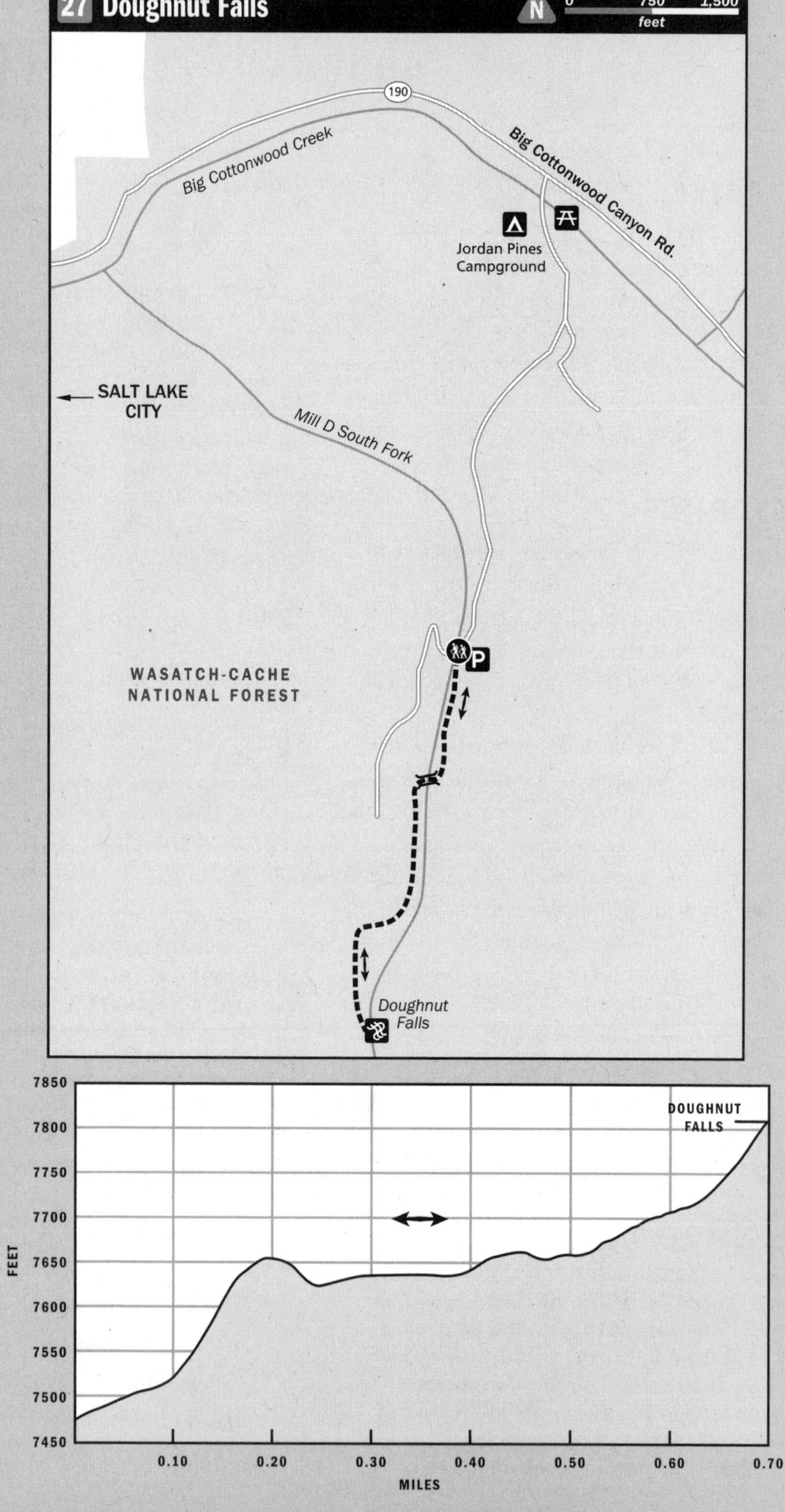
27 Doughnut Falls
N
0
750
1,500
feet
190
Big Cottonwood Creek
Big Cottonwood Canyon Rd.
Jordan Pines
Campground
SALT LAKE
CITY
Mill D South Fork
WASATCH-CACHE
NATIONAL FOREST
P
Doughnut
Falls
7850
7800
7750
7700
7650
7600
7550
7500
7450
FEET
DOUGHNUT
FALLS
0.10
0.20
0.30
0.40
0.50
0.60
0.70
MILES

Hidden Falls (see Nearby Activities on following page for more information)

PROPERTY and NO TRESPASSING signs being put up, giving some visitors the impression that Doughnut Falls is closed to the public. After a visitor fell through the falls to his death in 1990, signs directing people to Doughnut Falls were removed, which led some to believe that the falls were off-limits. In 2007, Salt Lake City purchased the falls and about 144 surrounding acres as a watershed. The U.S. Forest Service's management of the area preserves public access to the falls.

From the trailhead parking area, the wide trail leads up the canyon through a forest of white, blue, and yellow spruce, dotted with limber pine and an occasional Douglas-fir. Stands of quaking aspen also brighten the trail, especially in the fall as they turn lemon yellow. At 0.2 miles the wide trail constricts and veers off to the right. At 0.4 miles the trail enters an open area shaded by large conifers. From here, cross the bridge over Mill D South Fork to your right, then immediately turn left onto the old mining road and continue up the canyon with the stream at your left. At 0.1 mile past the bridge, you'll arrive at a fork in the mining road, where you'll stay to the left, following the stream up the canyon.

Almost instantly, the canyon becomes a rocky chasm. By staying close to the stream, you'll be drawn into the boulder-filled drainage below the falls. In the spring, the snow-fed stream spans the chasm, and continuing up toward the falls will require some boulder-hopping and scrambling up steep rock ledges. Getting wet is almost inevitable. In the summer, as the stream flow is reduced, some scrambling will be required, but it's easier to avoid getting wet. Even though Doughnut Falls is a popular family hike, climbing up to the falls may be too hazardous for children younger than age 6.

As you weave through the large boulders below the falls and scale the rocky ledges leading up to them, be sure to stay on the west side of the stream, to the right of the falls. This will give you the safest access and put you face-to-face with the falls' intriguing layout.

Doughnut Falls plunges through a hole about 6 feet in diameter and drops into a grotto about 20 feet long and 10 feet wide. You'll want to get close—and most get within a few feet of the grotto—but be careful. It's easy to spend an hour or more playing around the falls.

On your way there and back, be on the lookout for moose, who find a luxurious habitat in this drainage. Beaver still appear in the stream, and foxes occasionally dart behind trees. But the most likely sightings will be ground squirrels and chipmunks in a lush home of spruce and aspen.

NEARBY ACTIVITIES

As long as you're visiting Doughnut Falls, don't miss Hidden Falls on your way up the canyon. It's only 100 yards from the road and takes just a few minutes to visit. As you come to the **S**-curve, 4.3 miles up the canyon, enter the Mill B North Fork parking area 100 yards past the Mill B South Fork parking area. Take the trailhead at the north side of the parking area, and cross the road. Rather than following the Mill B North Fork Trail, follow the creek to your left, and within a few seconds, Hidden Falls magically appears.

LAKE BLANCHE 28

IN BRIEF

Lake Blanche is a classic glacial tarn at the base of a cirque. The hike to Lake Blanche begins at the Big Cottonwood Canyon floor and follows the dramatically glaciated side canyon to an exceptionally scenic and remote alpine setting. It's one of the most popular hikes in the Salt Lake area—and justifiably so.

DESCRIPTION

It's entirely possible to walk out of a meeting in the Fort Union business and financial district and within 15 minutes be following a roaring stream up a glacial canyon in a federally designated wilderness area. And that's only the beginning. The highlight, Lake Blanche, awaits under a glacial cirque at the top of the canyon. No wonder this is such a popular hike.

The parking area at the Mill B South Fork trailhead holds 24 cars, but you can also park along the road. The parking lot serves both the Broads Fork trailhead at the west end of the lot and the Mill B South Fork (Lake Blanche) trailhead at the east side of the lot, to the left of the vault toilet. Take this paved trail as it parallels Big Cottonwood Creek to your left. Within about 0.2 miles and just before the paved trail crosses a bridge, the Lake Blanche

KEY AT-A-GLANCE INFORMATION

LENGTH: 5.8 miles round-trip

ELEVATION GAIN: 2,670 feet

ELEVATION AT TRAILHEAD: 6,240 feet

CONFIGURATION: Out-and-back

DIFFICULTY: Moderate

SCENERY: Canyon with glacial geology, stream, glacial lakes, surrounding peaks

EXPOSURE: Mostly shaded up to lake, then partially shaded

TRAFFIC: Busy

TRAIL SURFACE: Dirt and rock

HIKING TIME: 3.5–5 hours

WATER REQUIREMENTS: 1–2 liters

SEASON: Late spring, summer, early fall. Avalanche hazard in winter and early spring.

ACCESS: No fees for canyon access or parking

MAPS: USGS Mount Aire, Dromedary Peak; Trails Illustrated Wasatch Front (709)

FACILITIES: Vault toilet at trailhead. No drinking water, but water from stream and lake may be purified.

DOGS: Prohibited in Big Cottonwood Canyon, a protected watershed

Directions

From Salt Lake City's east side take I-215 south to 6200 South (Exit 6). At the off-ramp, turn left and proceed south for 1.7 miles, as 6200 South changes to Wasatch Boulevard (UT 190). Turn left at the signal, staying on UT 190, and continue up Big Cottonwood Canyon for 4.3 miles. As the road makes a hairpin turn to the left, enter the Mill B South trailhead parking area on the right.

GPS Trailhead Coordinates

UTM Zone (WGS84) 12T

Easting 0438816

Northing 4498331

Latitude N 40° 37' 58.1"

Longitude W 111° 43' 24.9"

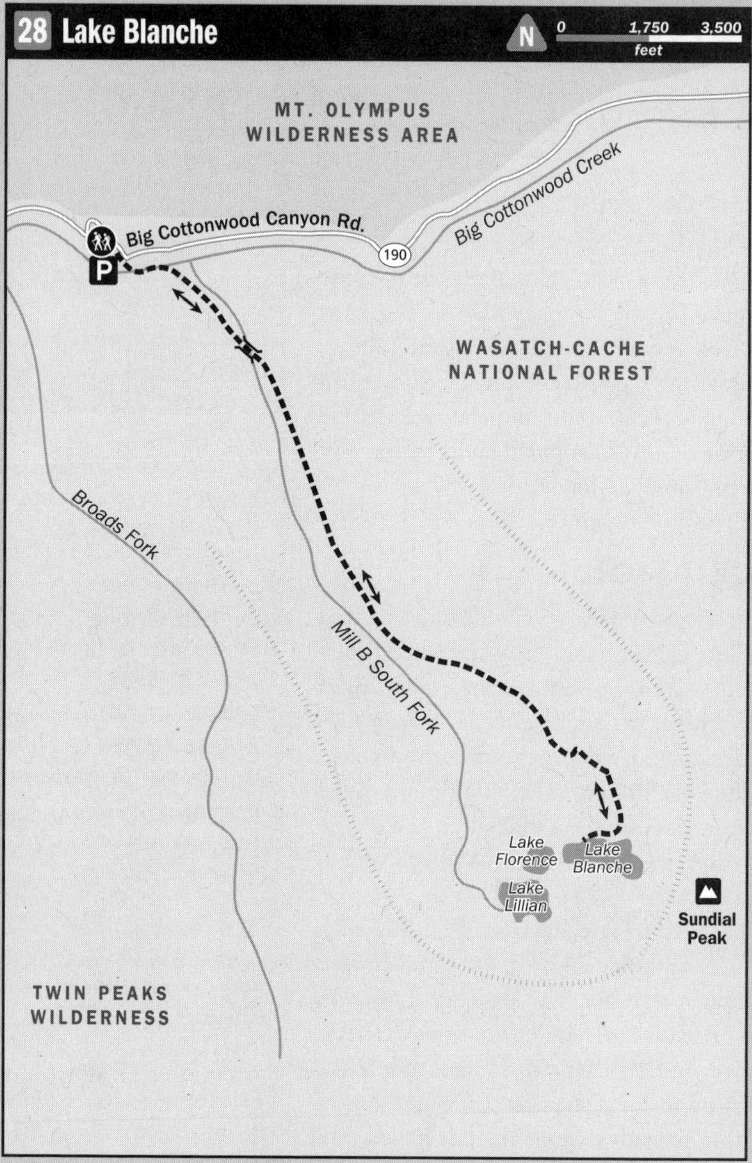

28 Lake Blanche
N
0
1,750
3,500
feet
MT. OLYMPUS
WILDERNESS AREA
Big Cottonwood Canyon Rd.
190
Big Cottonwood Creek
P
WASATCH-CACHE
NATIONAL FOREST
Broads Fork
Mill B South Fork
Lake
Florence
Lake
Blanche
Lake
Lillian
Sundial
Peak
TWIN PEAKS
WILDERNESS

10000
9500
9000
8500
8000
7500
7000
6500
6000
FEET
LAKE
BLANCHE
MILL B
SOUTH FORK
0.5
1.0
1.5
2.0
2.5
2.9
MILES

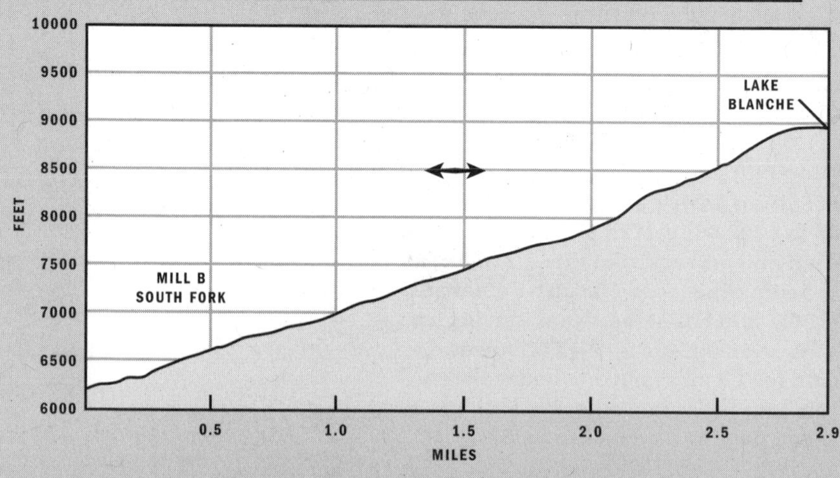

Lake Florence

Trail departs the paved trail, bearing to the right and becoming a rocky path.

After 0.1 mile on the Lake Blanche dirt trail, you'll cross a bridge to the east side of the Mill B South Fork and continue up a switchback to the north. Within another 0.2 miles, you'll enter the Twin Peaks Wilderness Area with the stream at your right as you head up the canyon.

The trail steadily ascends the canyon in a shaded forest. Soon, within the upper area of the canyon, you'll pass through several acres of avalanche damage, where hundreds of trees have been toppled like so many toothpicks. Follow the course of destruction by looking at the release area on the denuded avalanche-prone slope to the west. Observe how the avalanche crossed the stream and took out trees on the opposite slope from where you stand. Above and below the avalanche zone, the trail is largely shaded by a blanket of aspen and dotted with Douglas-fir.

Near the top of Mill B South Fork, you ascend the slope above the aspen to the eastern side of the canyon. Along the high switchbacks you can catch a narrow glimpse of the Salt Lake Valley through the canyon's mouth. At 2.4 miles from the trailhead, you come to a talus slope composed of quartzite boulders. The trail skirts the large rock pile and continues up to the south. Within 100 yards of the first talus field, the trail crosses another quartzite field.

As you approach the large quartzite formation at the top of the canyon, you'll begin to notice evidence of glacial activity. As glaciers transported rocks and debris over the surface of the formation, they left striations on the quartzite's surface that are still clearly visible.

As you crest the formation, Lake Blanche comes into full view. As you look across the lake, Sundial Peak stands at the center of the cirque. While the quartzite formation forms the northern shore of the lake, the remains of a concrete reinforced rock dam are visible on both sides of the quartzite dome. This dam was built in the 1930s to contain a much larger reservoir. Many of the upper Wasatch lakes were controlled and maintained as reservoirs to ensure a consistent supply

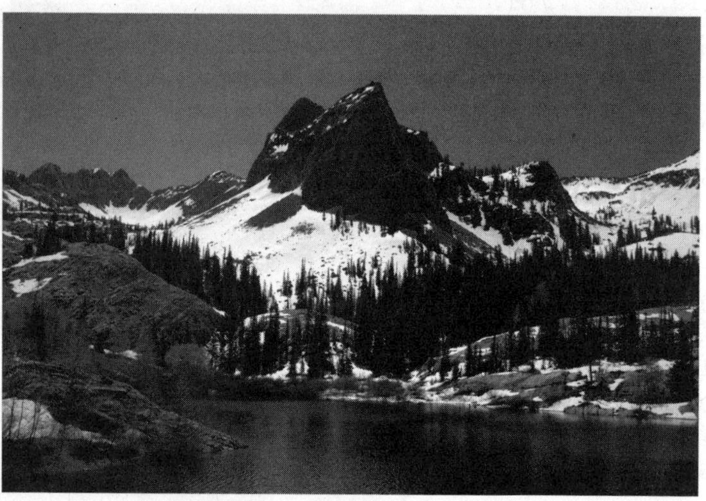

Lake Blanche at the base of Sundial Peak

of water throughout the summer. The Lake Blanche dam broke along the western rim in 1983, leaving the lake at its present size. If you're tempted to take a dip in the icy waters, remember that swimming is not permitted in watershed lakes.

Lake Blanche is a destination resort in the wilderness. Take your time, walk around, study the geology, count the wildflowers, look for waterfalls, and explore the woods at the far end of the lake. Allow at least an hour at and around the lake. As you walk to the western side of Lake Blanche, you'll discover two smaller tarns—Lake Florence and Lake Lillian—in a lower glacial bowl. These more-remote lakes get less traffic, provide a quiet place to rest, and offer better chances for wildlife viewing.

Note: The Lake Blanche Trail lies within the federally protected Twin Peaks Wilderness Area. Domestic animals, horses, bicycles, motorized vehicles, and open campfires are not permitted.

NEARBY ACTIVITIES

As you drive back down Big Cottonwood Canyon following your hike, you may want to stop at the Storm Mountain Picnic Area. Near the picnic sites is the Storm Mountain Amphitheater, which can be reserved for private programs and concerts. The amphitheater holds up to 200 people and offers a dramatic setting for a business or organization event. For reservations, call (877) 444-6777.

BROADS FORK TWIN PEAKS 29

IN BRIEF

Broads Fork would be a spectacular destination even without summiting Twin Peaks. The steep hike leads from an expansive drainage to an upper bowl where the scrambling begins. This is a challenging Wasatch summit, entirely within federally protected wilderness.

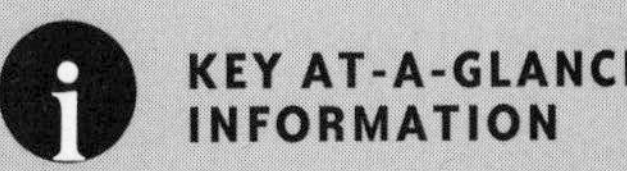

KEY AT-A-GLANCE INFORMATION

LENGTH: 9.8 miles round-trip
ELEVATION GAIN: 5,090 feet
ELEVATION AT TRAILHEAD: 6,240 feet
CONFIGURATION: Out-and-back
DIFFICULTY: Difficult
SCENERY: Wooded canyon, upper drainage with stream and ponds, glacial bowl, great summit views
EXPOSURE: Mostly shaded to 8,200 feet and partially shaded to 9,200 feet. Fully exposed to sun above 9,000 feet.
TRAFFIC: Light
TRAIL SURFACE: Dirt to 9,000 feet, rock to the summit
HIKING TIME: 8–10 hours
WATER REQUIREMENTS: 2 liters
SEASON: Late spring, summer, early fall. Avalanche hazard in winter and early spring.
ACCESS: No fees for canyon access or parking
MAPS: USGS Mount Aire, Dromedary Peak; Trails Illustrated Wasatch Front (709)
FACILITIES: Restrooms at trailhead. No drinking water, but water from stream and lake may be purified.
DOGS: Prohibited in Big Cottonwood Canyon, a protected watershed

DESCRIPTION

Twin Peaks is the most commanding peak on the Wasatch Front as viewed from the Salt Lake Valley. Its position at the west end of the ridge between Big Cottonwood and Little Cottonwood canyons makes it easy to spot and identify from nearly anywhere in the valley. With so many peaks in the Wasatch, you can forgive the early pioneers for running out of inventive names, but how did we get three Twin Peaks in Salt Lake County, and two—both more than 11,000 feet elevation—within just 5 miles of each other?

The smallest of the three Twin Peaks is located two miles north of the University of Utah. To distinguish the two larger Twin Peaks, the summit described in this chapter is often referred to as Broads Fork Twin Peaks, or sometimes as Salt Lake Twin Peaks. The highest of the three is located on the ridge

Directions →

From Salt Lake City's east side, take I-215 south to 6200 South (Exit 6). At the off-ramp, turn left and proceed south for 1.7 miles, as 6200 South changes to Wasatch Boulevard (UT 190). Turn left at the signal, staying on UT 190, and continue up Big Cottonwood Canyon for 4.3 miles. As the road makes a hairpin turn to the left, enter the Mill B South Trailhead parking area on the right.

GPS Trailhead Coordinates

UTM Zone (WGS84) 12T
Easting 0438786
Northing 4498322
Latitude N 40° 37' 58.1"
Longitude W 111° 43' 24.9"

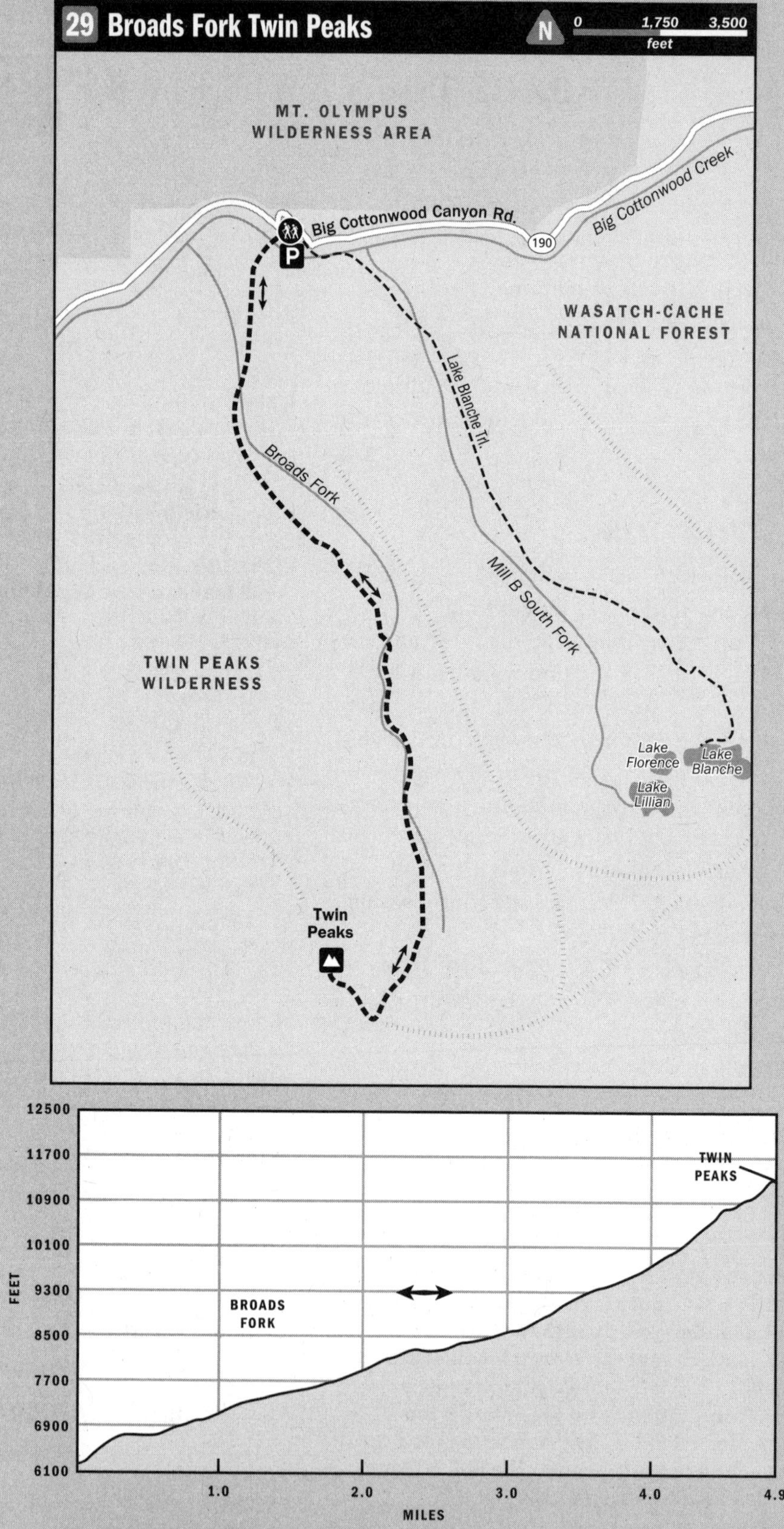
29 Broads Fork Twin Peaks
N
0
1,750
3,500
feet
MT. OLYMPUS
WILDERNESS AREA
Big Cottonwood Canyon Rd.
190
Big Cottonwood Creek
P
WASATCH-CACHE
NATIONAL FOREST
Lake Blanche Trl.
Broads Fork
Mill B South Fork
TWIN PEAKS
WILDERNESS
Lake
Florence
Lake
Blanche
Lake
Lillian
Twin
Peaks
12500
11700
10900
10100
9300
8500
7700
6900
6100
FEET
BROADS
FORK
TWIN
PEAKS
1.0
2.0
3.0
4.0
4.9
MILES

Beaver pond in upper Broads Fork

between Little Cottonwood and American Fork canyons, and is referred to as American Fork Twin Peaks. (See Hike 42, page 183.)

The trailhead for Broads Fork is located at the southwest end of the Mill B South Fork parking area, which also serves the Lake Blanche Trail. On any given weekend in summer you may find 50 to 100 people visiting Lake Blanche, while only five or ten will find their way up Broads Fork. To be sure, it's a much more challenging hike, but the rewards are worth the effort.

Without switchbacks to ease the incline, the trail starts steep from the moment you leave the parking lot. It saves its most punishing elevation gain for a summit scramble. Beyond the trailhead, the path ascends in a southwest direction through a conifer forest. After you climb 1,000 feet of elevation in a mile, you'll find a wooden bridge that crosses to the west side of Broads Fork. From there the trail takes you to the south as it moves up Broads Fork. About 0.3 miles after the bridge, the deep woods open up to views of the lower drainage at an elevation of 7,500 feet. Here you'll have first views of Dromedary Peak to the south with the higher Sunrise Peak to the right. Sunrise Peak is also called O'Sullivan Peak on USGS maps.

From the lower drainage, the trail ascends through a beautiful stand of aspen. Near the top of this section, you'll pass a large, red slab. Shortly beyond the top of the slab, at an elevation of 8,100 feet, you arrive at a knoll that overlooks the large upper drainage. From here several faint trails diverge in different directions. To the right, a route known as Robinsons Variation climbs a steep rock gully to a saddle on the north side of Twin Peaks. The standard route, described here, dips to the left toward a beaver pond. Cross over the crude bridge made of tree branches just below the beaver dam. A faint trail continues up the drainage below the ledges on the east side. With snow often covering this section of trail into midsummer, you may find yourself scrambling up the streambed. Once you arrive at the upper bowl, the trail ends and the scramble up the slope

The Uinta ground squirrel spends about eight months of the year in hibernation.

to the west begins. At an elevation of about 9,400 feet, you'll see a saddle to the south of Twin Peaks. Make your way up this rocky slope to the saddle. Patches of subalpine fir dot much of the upper bowl.

Marmots are abundant in this area, and moose are often sighted in the ponds below. Wild Rose is the signature wildflower of Broads Fork, accompanied by arrowleaf balsam root, larkspur, and a dash of magenta with Parry's primrose.

From the saddle, several trail variations lead to the summit. The most common leads to the base of a 20-foot cliff. By following the ledges along the south side of the ridge for about 100 feet, you skirt the cliffs and come to a chimney that will take you back to the main ridge. A faint trail in the scree zigzags up the summit cone to the 11,330-foot eastern summit. The eastern summit is only two feet higher than the western summit. Your return will be slow as you descend the unstable rocky slopes down to the 9,000-foot level, but once back at the knoll and on the reliable lower trail, you'll make good time back to the trailhead.

Note: Broads Fork and Twin Peaks lie within the federally protected Twin Peaks Wilderness Area. Domestic animals, horses, bicycles, motorized vehicles, and open campfires are not permitted.

NEARBY ACTIVITIES

After climbing Twin Peaks you may be too tired for anything else. But as you leave the canyon, take note of the Stairs Hydroelectric Power Plant, about 2 miles from the mouth of the canyon. Built 1894–96 and ideally situated along the Stairs cascade on Big Cottonwood Creek, the project constructed the first hydroelectric plant to provide power to Salt Lake City. It was also one of the first plants in Utah to transmit power long distances using alternating current rather than direct current. You'll find a historical marker and picnic tables near the plant, which is still in use today.

WILLOW HEIGHTS 30

IN BRIEF

A short, little-known hike to a high meadow and lake. Located at the top of Big Cottonwood Canyon, Willow Heights is filled with wildflowers and wildlife, and attracts few people.

DESCRIPTION

You'll find most hikes that lead to lakes in Big Cottonwood Canyon well marked, with ample trailhead parking, and often crowded. Willow Lake has none of these features. With no marked trailhead, you'll need to park on the south side of the road (UT 190), cross to a residential drive leading 0.1 mile to the west, then switch back for another 0.1 mile to the east. As the pavement ends, the trail begins.

The wide path leads through a hillside of aspen, sprinkled with just a few young fir. Occasionally, the trail steepens, but it's never too strenuous. At 0.8 miles you come to Willow Creek, which can be crossed by the crude bridge of fallen branches or by the steppingstones several feet upstream.

Within 0.1 mile, the aspen grove opens to a large meadow and views of the upper canyon and ridgeline to the east. As you follow the trail to the upper end of the meadow, you come to

Directions

From Salt Lake City's east side take I-215 south to 6200 South (Exit 6). At the off-ramp, turn left and proceed south for 1.7 miles, as 6200 South changes to Wasatch Boulevard (UT 190). Turn left at the signal, staying on UT 190, and continue up Big Cottonwood Canyon for 11.1 miles to the Silver Fork Lodge on the right. Continue another 0.2 miles up the canyon and park on the right side of the road. The trail begins across the street on a narrow, paved road leading to a residential area.

KEY AT-A-GLANCE INFORMATION

LENGTH: 2 miles round-trip

ELEVATION GAIN: 675 feet

ELEVATION AT TRAILHEAD: 7,815 feet

CONFIGURATION: Out-and-back

DIFFICULTY: Easy

SCENERY: Aspen forest, meadows, and a quiet lake

EXPOSURE: Mostly shaded

TRAFFIC: Moderate

TRAIL SURFACE: Paved for first 0.2 miles, then dirt to the meadow and lake

HIKING TIME: 1–1.5 hours

WATER REQUIREMENTS: 1 liter. Water at stream and in lake may be purified.

SEASON: Year-round

ACCESS: No fees for access or parking

MAPS: USGS Park City West

FACILITIES: No restrooms or water at the trailhead

DOGS: Prohibited in Big Cottonwood Canyon, a protected watershed

SPECIAL COMMENTS: Willow Heights is a great snowshoe hike or backcountry ski tour in winter.

GPS Trailhead Coordinates

UTM Zone (WGS84) 12T

Easting 0449450

Northing 4498611

Latitude N 40° 37' 55.7"

Longitude W 111° 36' 31.1"

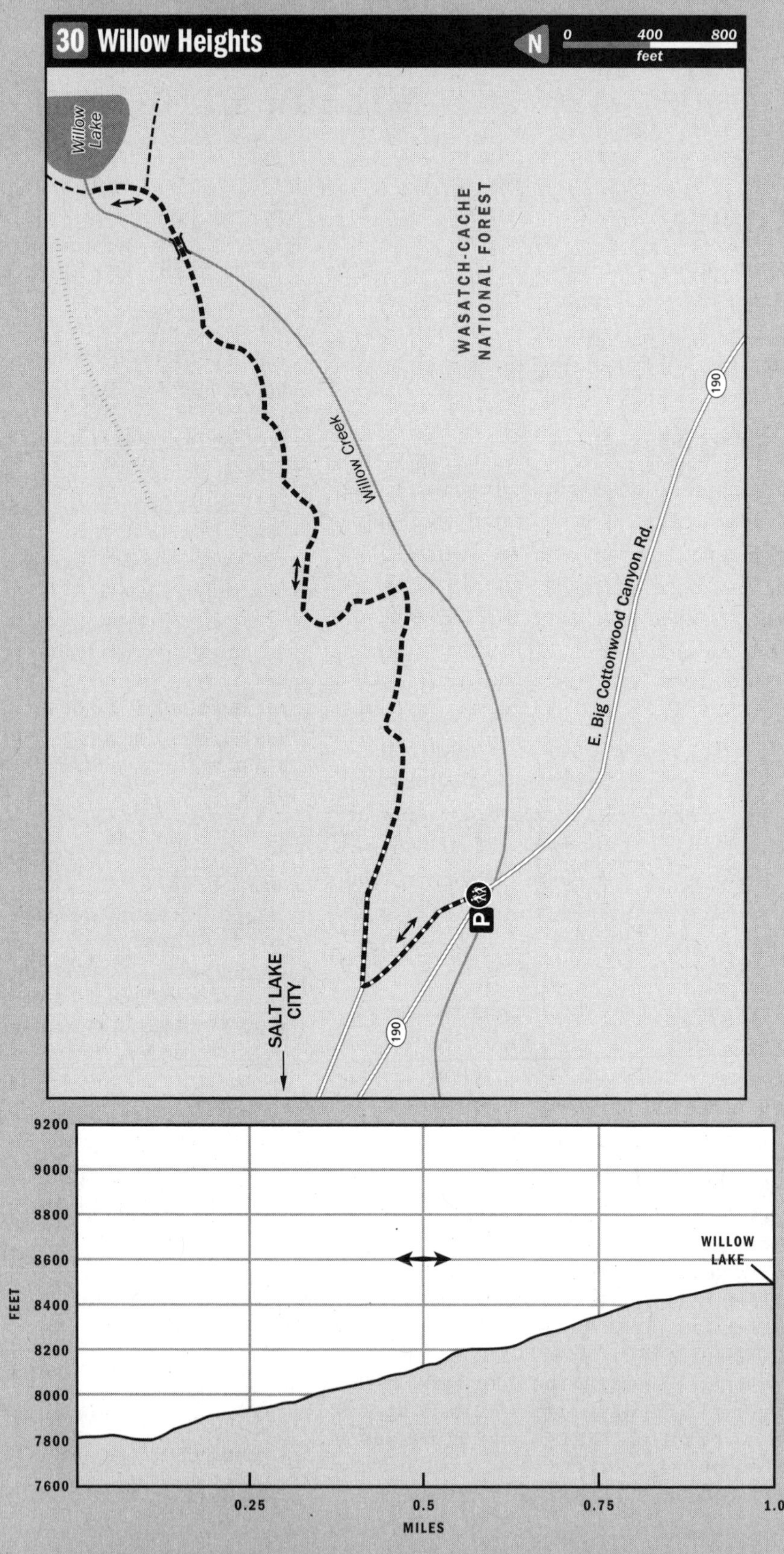

30 Willow Heights
N
0
400
800
feet
Willow Lake
WASATCH-CACHE NATIONAL FOREST
Willow Creek
190
E. Big Cottonwood Canyon Rd.
P
SALT LAKE CITY
9200
9000
8800
8600
8400
8200
8000
7800
7600
FEET
WILLOW LAKE
0.25
0.5
0.75
1.0
MILES

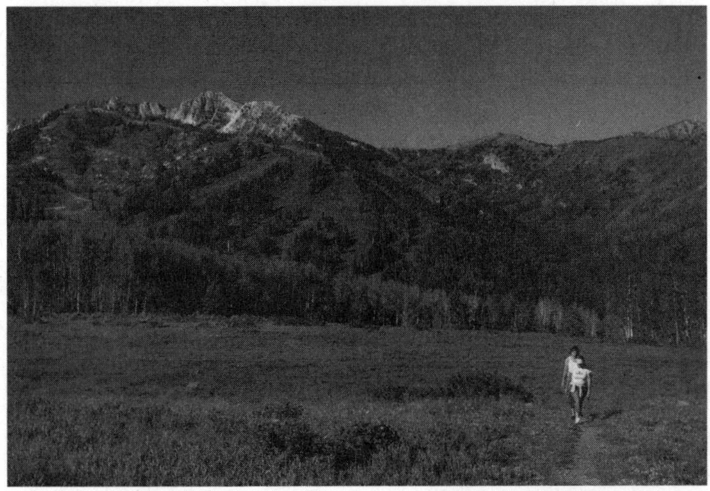

The meadow south of Willow Lake

a fork. Turning left will lead you to Willow Lake in less than 100 yards. Continuing straight will lead to aptly named Dry Lake, about 0.5 miles to the northeast.

While Willow Lake may be a short hike, don't make it a fast one. Take your time as you approach the lake: explore, walk around the shore, and watch for wildlife. It's the perfect place to spot moose and deer, especially in the early morning and at dusk. A large beaver lodge rises from the middle of the shallow lake, and ducks nest and live near the water in spring and summer. Cliff swallows skim the surface of the lake, and raptors circle high overhead.

Several primitive campsites await on the north side of the lake for those wanting a short hike to a setting of solitude and natural beauty. Willow Lake and the meadow can be buggy in summer, so come prepared with insect repellent.

The meadow and the flatlands around the lake are alive with wildflowers in spring and summer. Phlox is the most abundant, while larkspur and penstemon are also common.

Willow Heights, the open area encompassing both the meadow and the lake, makes a wonderful short morning hike. You can be up to the lake before the sun rises over the ridge, watch the wildlife awaken, and still be back to your nearby lodge or cabin before breakfast. In winter or early spring, a midday snowshoe hike exposes the wildlife as the sun beams through leafless aspen.

NEARBY ACTIVITIES

Silver Fork Lodge is a great choice for lunch or an extended stay. The lodge offers nearby access to skiing, hiking, fishing, and mountain biking. It has a patio and indoor casual dining that you can enjoy without having to get dressed up—even if you've just come off the trail or the ski slopes. Silver Fork Lodge has seven rustic rooms without phones and television, plus an outdoor hot tub. Call (888) 649-9551 for reservations or go to **www.silverforklodge.com.**

31 FERGUSON CANYON

KEY AT-A-GLANCE INFORMATION

LENGTH: 3.4 miles round-trip
ELEVATION GAIN: 1,650 feet
ELEVATION AT TRAILHEAD: 5,247 feet
CONFIGURATION: Out-and-back
DIFFICULTY: Easy
SCENERY: Deep canyon with stream and rock walls
EXPOSURE: Mostly shaded
TRAFFIC: Light
TRAIL SURFACE: Dirt and rock
HIKING TIME: 1–2 hours
WATER REQUIREMENTS: 1 liter
SEASON: Spring, summer, fall
ACCESS: No fees for access or parking
MAPS: USGS Draper, Dromedary Peak
FACILITIES: No facilities at the trailhead
DOGS: Permitted
SPECIAL COMMENTS: Ferguson Canyon is located in the Twin Peaks Wilderness Area.

GPS Trailhead Coordinates

UTM Zone (WGS84) 12T
Easting 0433300
Northing 4495773
Latitude N 40° 36' 37.4"
Longitude W 111° 47' 17.6"

IN BRIEF

Ferguson Canyon is a little-known retreat near residential areas where you can find yourself in a secluded wilderness setting just minutes from the city. Ideal for a peaceful getaway, a walk with the dog, or a chance to see fall colors.

DESCRIPTION

It's easy to overlook Ferguson Canyon. It may be the most frequently seen, yet unknown, canyon along the Wasatch Front. Located directly south of the mouth of Big Cottonwood Canyon, it's easily visible when looking east from the valley floor. Yet most hikers bypass Ferguson Canyon in favor of the forks that lead to well-known lakes, waterfalls, and summits. Ferguson Canyon is one destination that you hike for its own sake—to discover the simple beauties and unique features of a deep canyon world.

Ferguson Canyon also shows how close Salt Lake City and its surrounding communities are to the wilderness. In this case, the Cottonwood Heights neighborhood street

Directions

From Salt Lake City's east side, take I-215 south to 6200 South (Exit 6). At the off-ramp, turn left and proceed south for 1.7 miles, as 6200 South changes to Wasatch Boulevard (UT 190). Pass the mouth of Big Cottonwood Canyon and continue south on Wasatch Boulevard (now UT 210) for 0.3 miles to Prospector Drive (7780 South). Turn left onto the Prospector Drive access street, make an immediate right, and head south on Prospector Drive for 0.3 miles. Turn left onto Timberline Drive, continue north for about 100 yards, and park on the right side of the street near the trailhead sign. Observe neighborhood parking signs. No parking from 10 p.m. to 8 a.m.

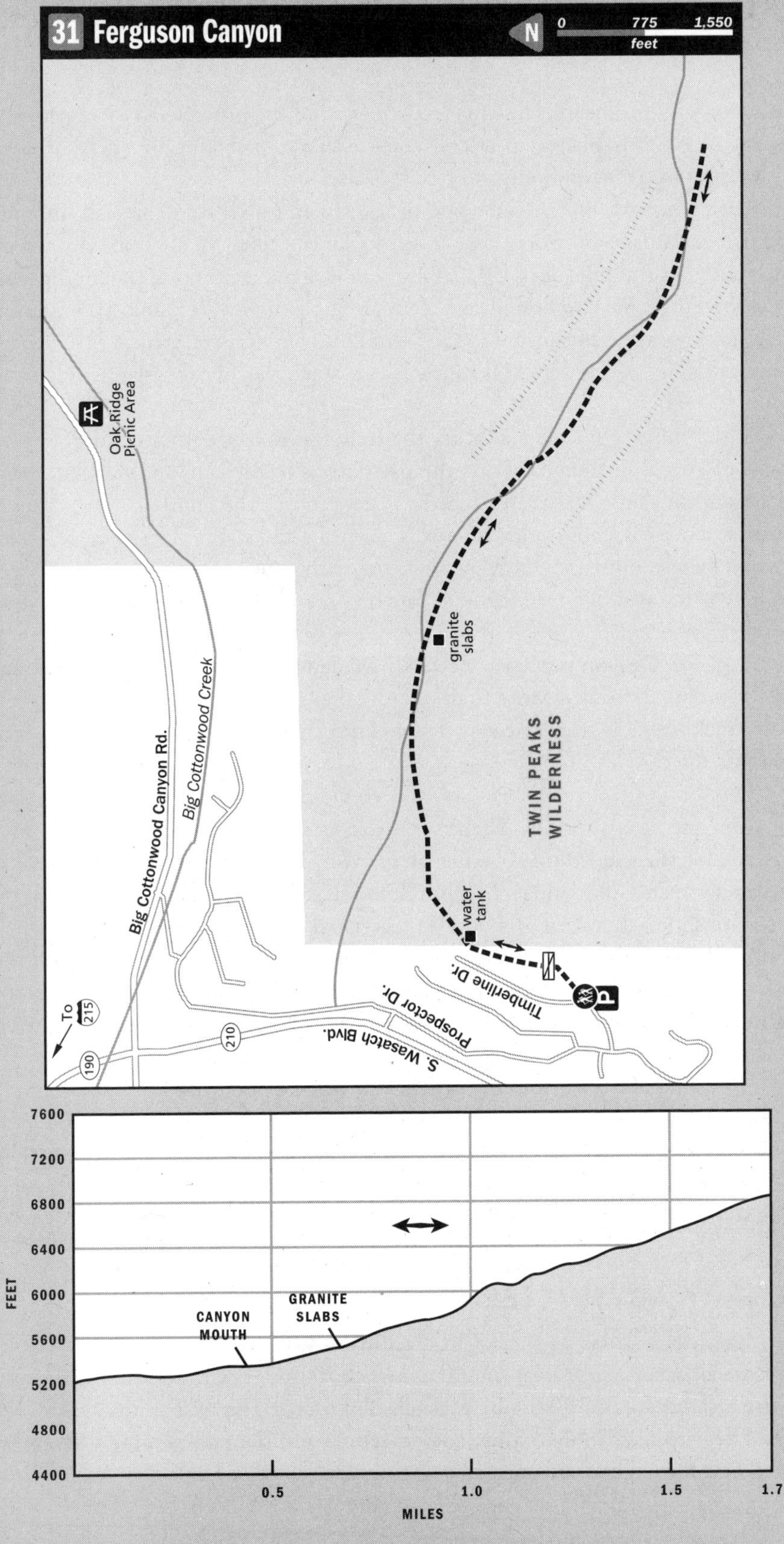
31 Ferguson Canyon
N
0
775
1,550
feet
Oak Ridge Picnic Area
granite slabs
TWIN PEAKS WILDERNESS
Big Cottonwood Canyon Rd.
Big Cottonwood Creek
water tank
Timberline Dr.
Prospector Dr.
S. Wasatch Blvd.
To 215
210
190
7600
7200
6800
6400
6000
5600
5200
4800
4400
FEET
CANYON MOUTH
GRANITE SLABS
0.5
1.0
1.5
1.7
MILES

that serves as a trailhead is less than 200 feet from the protected Twin Peaks Wilderness Area. This places an added responsibility on hikers to obey the local ordinances governing parking and hours of use.

After you park on the right side of the street, you'll start the trail on a dirt road that ascends to the northeast. Pass through the gate and continue toward the water tank on the hillside. At 0.2 miles you'll arrive at the water tank, located inside the Forest Service boundary. Continuing past the water tank, you arrive at a sign marking your entrance into the Twin Peaks Wilderness Area. A trail departs from both sides of the sign. Take either one, since they merge into a single trail within 50 feet.

At 0.5 miles from the trailhead, the trail curves to the south and enters the mouth of Ferguson Canyon. Soon the path drops to the canyon floor and meets the stream on the left. The dry hillside vegetation of the approach gives way to lush riparian ferns, moss, and willows. The spring-fed stream has small perennial flow but swells immensely in May and June with snowmelt. In those months, as you follow the winding trail through canyon narrows, keeping your feet dry isn't always possible.

Ferguson Canyon is deep and heavily shaded with maples, cottonwoods, and oaks crowding its banks. More than in any other local canyon, the roots of these trees are exposed as they finger their way into the creek. Many fallen trees also crisscross the canyon floor.

At 0.7 miles from the trailhead, you come to the first of many granite slabs that form the canyon walls. These walls are especially popular with local rock climbers, whom you'll find working on canyon climbing routes with names like the Watchtower, Goldenfingers Wall, Cathedral, or Bat Guano Wall. Most of the routes are short—between 50 and 100 feet—and require placing protection.

At about 1 mile up the canyon, a trail ascends a slope on the left side of the creek to an overlook. This route isn't necessarily easy to find, and plenty of better overlooks and viewpoints exist in the Wasatch, so it isn't an essential destination. On this hike, the canyon itself is its own reward.

Ferguson Canyon is a living canyon—a work in progress and a museum of the erosion that's been at work for thousands of years. It's also a vibrant habitat filled with birds, ducks, and small mammals such as foxes, raccoons, squirrels, and chipmunks. Although it teems with life, humans are a minority species, making it easy to enjoy the canyon's cozy solitude.

NEARBY ACTIVITIES

Rocky Mouth is a half-mile hike to a dramatic waterfall through a narrow slot canyon—all accessible from a suburban neighborhood. Use the small parking area on the east side of 11300 South Wasatch Boulevard. The trail to the falls makes a great year-round family outing, and travel beyond the falls is a high-adventure experience for expert canyoneers.

JORDAN RIVER PARKWAY 32

IN BRIEF

The Jordan River Parkway stays close to the river, passing along and through a riparian habitat and floodplain. You can easily reach the trail at dozens of points at parks, street crossings, and residential neighborhoods.

DESCRIPTION

The Jordan River, Utah Lake's outlet, is one of the three major rivers that empty into the Great Salt Lake. Originally named the Utah River, Mormon pioneer Heber C. Kimball renamed it, likening the river to its Holy Land namesake, which also flows from a freshwater lake into an inland salt sea.

The Jordan River Parkway is an ambitious urban trail project that will eventually follow the river throughout Salt Lake County. Presently, the longest completed section of the trail passes through the municipalities of West Jordan, Taylorsville, Murray, West Valley City, and finally into Salt Lake City. This section can easily be accessed at Gardner Village at the south, at Redwood Trailhead Park at the north, and dozens of points in between.

The trail snakes its way around the various inlets and marshes that dress the banks of the river, making the trail even more circuitous than the river itself. As the crow flies, this section measures only 7.7 miles in length, but as the trail follows the meandering river, it covers a distance of more than 11 miles. While the Jordan River does wind and meander, dropping only about five feet per mile, it still flows at a surprisingly fast clip.

Leaving Gardner Village (7800 South), the trail stays on the west bank of the Jordan until 6300 South. As the river flows north, the trail makes several river crossings and also

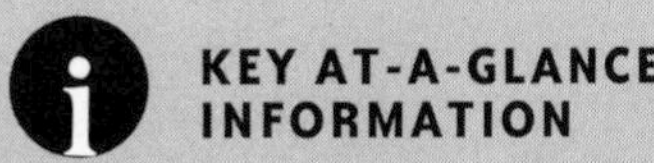

KEY AT-A-GLANCE INFORMATION

LENGTH: 11 miles

ELEVATION GAIN: –58 feet (from beginning to end)

ELEVATION AT TRAILHEAD: 4,290 feet (Gardner Village); 4,232 feet (Redwood)

CONFIGURATION: One-way or out-and-back

DIFFICULTY: Easy

SCENERY: Jordan River and surrounding wetlands

EXPOSURE: Partial shade

TRAFFIC: Busy

TRAIL SURFACE: Completely paved and striped

HIKING TIME: Varies greatly based on distance selected

WATER REQUIREMENTS: 0.5 liters–1 liter. You'll find drinking fountains along the trail in most of the parks, as well as restaurants and convenience stores at some nearby street crossings.

SEASON: Year-round

ACCESS: Hikable year-round. No access fees or permits required.

MAPS: None

See additional information at end of Description, page 146.

GPS Trailhead Coordinates

UTM Zone (WGS84) 12T

Easting 0422235

Northing 4508096

Latitude–Longitude: See page 146

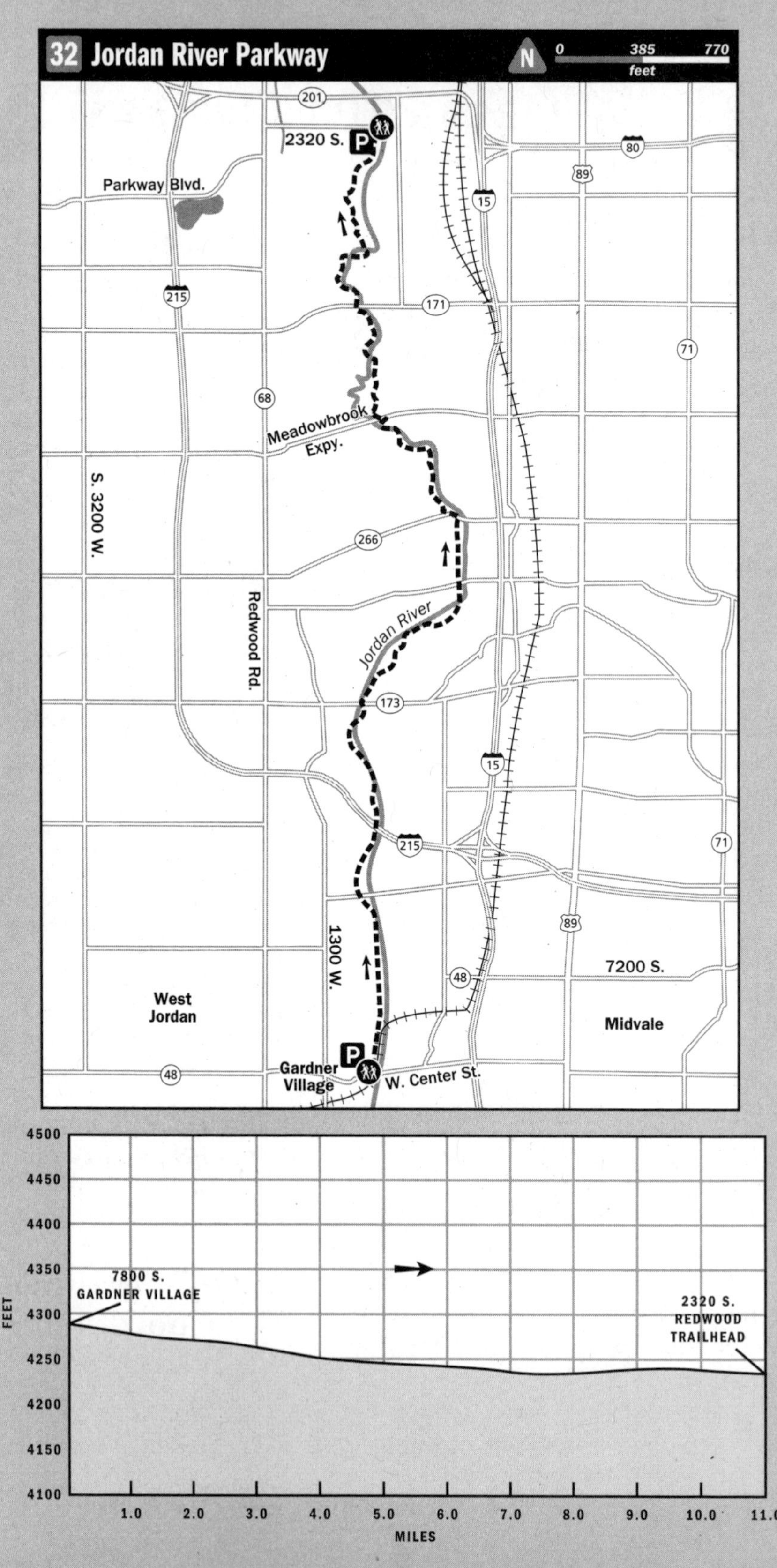

32 Jordan River Parkway
N
0
385
770
feet
201
2320 S.
P
80
89
Parkway Blvd.
15
215
171
71
68
Meadowbrook
Expy.
S. 3200 W.
266
Redwood Rd.
Jordan River
173
15
215
71
89
1300 W.
7200 S.
48
West
Jordan
Midvale
P
Gardner
Village
W. Center St.
48
4500
4450
4400
4350
4300
4250
4200
4150
4100
FEET
7800 S.
GARDNER VILLAGE
2320 S.
REDWOOD
TRAILHEAD
1.0
2.0
3.0
4.0
5.0
6.0
7.0
8.0
9.0
10.0
11.0
MILES

manages to adeptly avoid most major thoroughfares and two freeways with some well-placed underpasses. For the most part, road noise is easy to escape along the trail.

When early pioneers arrived in the Salt Lake Valley, they noted that the cottonwood- and willow-lined river corridor stood in sharp contrast to the treeless, sage-covered plains on either side. They soon built settlements along the river and shared the land with wolves and coyotes, while beavers built dams along the river. All are gone today, but foxes, skunks, raccoons, and muskrats still live in the wooded areas near the river.

More than any other species, you'll see waterfowl. Mallards, grebes, coots, Canada geese, and great blue herons make the parkway marshlands their permanent home. Ring-necked pheasants, chukars, and quail can also be spotted year-round.

As late as 1910, the riverbanks provided seasonal camping for Ute, Paiute, and Shoshone tribes. Native Americans traded tanned skins and dried meat for supplies. Trailhead markers provide interpretive background on the natural history of the area as well as insights into pioneer homesteads and early settlements along the river.

The growth of the Salt Lake Valley, industrialization, dredging, and channeling has not always been kind to the Jordan River. Many of the rich riparian and wetland areas have been lost over the last 100 years. Today, natural resource damage settlement funds from the Sharon Steel Superfund Site are being used to restore more than 270 acres of river corridor and floodplain by removing invasive plants, establishing native plants, and contouring some sections of the riverbank.

A number of spur trails and oxbow divisions mark the trail. At some points, the trail divides into a pedestrian portion, while bicycles stay on the paved route. The West Valley City Cross Towne Trail and other spurs connect the main trail

---

Directions

Gardner Village Trailhead (south end of trail): From Salt Lake City take I-15 south to 7200 South (Exit 297). Turn right onto 7200 South (UT 48) toward Midvale. Take the first left onto 700 West. Continue south on 700 West (Holden Street) for 0.7 miles. Turn right (west) on Center Street and continue 0.5 miles to the Gardner Village entrance on the right. Access the trail from the Gardner Village parking lot's southeast corner.

Redwood Trailhead (north end of trail): From downtown Salt Lake City, take I-15 south to UT 201 (Exit 305A). Continue westbound on UT 201 for 1.7 miles and take the Redwood Road exit. At the off-ramp, turn left (south) onto Redwood Road (UT 68). Continue south for 0.2 miles and turn left at West 2320 South. Continue east on West 2320 South for 0.9 miles. Turn right into the Redwood Trailhead parking area.

In addition to these starting and ending trailheads, more than a dozen official trailheads supply public parking and easy trail access along the way.

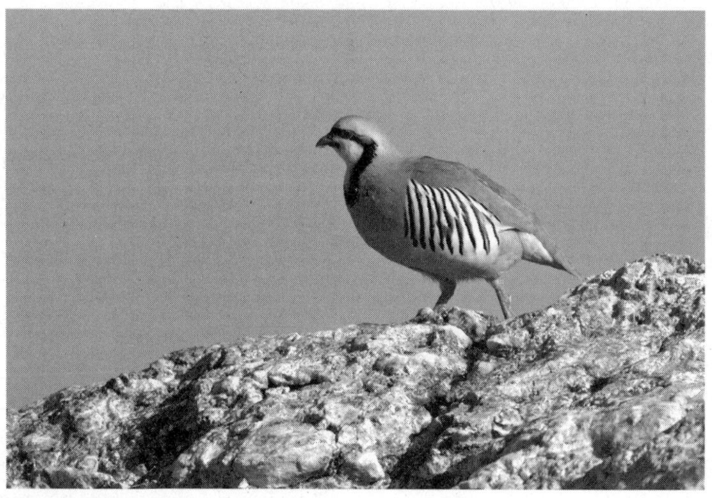

In addition to waterfowl, chukars can be seen along the parkway.

to nearby neighborhoods. These poorly marked spurs typically follow a diversion canal or side channel. When in doubt, stay on the trail nearest the river.

North of the Redwood Park Trailhead, the parkway continues unobstructed for another 2 miles, but the surrounding area loses much of its natural beauty and scenic appeal. The setting becomes more industrial with less shade—and for cyclists, more thorns to flatten your tires.

ADDITIONAL AT-A-GLANCE INFORMATION

FACILITIES: Restrooms, water, telephones, and other services are available at the trailhead and throughout the hike.

DOGS: Permitted on leash

SPECIAL COMMENTS: When completed, the Jordan River Parkway will extend from the Utah County line on the south to the Davis County line on the north. The section of the parkway featured here is the longest continuous completed portion and features some of the path's most accessible and enjoyable scenery.

GARDNER VILLAGE LATITUDE–LONGITUDE (SOUTH END OF TRAIL):
N 40° 36' 34"; W 111° 55' 20"

REDWOOD LATITUDE–LONGITUDE (NORTH END OF TRAIL):
N 40° 43' 12"; W 111° 55' 14"

NEARBY ACTIVITIES

Gardner Village, an early-Utah-themed shopping village, had its start in 1853, when the first flour mill in the South Salt Lake Valley was built on the site. Today, specialty shops, a restaurant, bakery, and day spa cluster in a historic setting, linked by brick paths, gardens, and a covered bridge. Gardner Village is located at 1100 West 7800 South.

GREAT WESTERN TRAIL (Guardsman Pass to Clayton Peak) 33

IN BRIEF

The Great Western Trail is a corridor of trails traversing 4,455 miles through Arizona, Utah, Idaho, Wyoming, and Montana. Within Utah, the Great Western Trail roughly follows the Wasatch ridge running north and south. A short hike from Guardsman Pass to Clayton Peak follows a section of the trail along a scenic ridgeline.

DESCRIPTION

Ridgeline hikes have the benefit of delivering panoramic views and enabling you to put surrounding peaks and canyons in perspective. This small section of the Great Western Trail demonstrates how interconnected Wasatch canyons are and how easy it is to connect to trails in Park City and Heber Valley to the east. With most of the hike above 10,000 feet in elevation, there's not much to block the view.

Guardsman Pass offers a high-elevation start for the hike. From the trailhead parking area, take a look around in all directions. Summit County and Park City lie to the north and east, Wasatch County and Heber Valley lie to the south and east, and Big Cottonwood canyon lies directly below to the west. The trail leading to Clayton Peak stretches in front of you to the south.

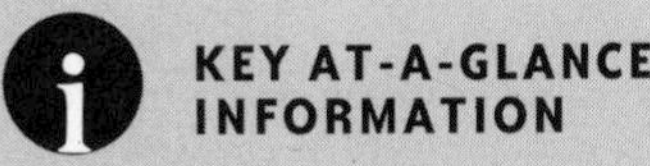

LENGTH: 2.2 miles round-trip
ELEVATION GAIN: 1,015 feet
ELEVATION AT TRAILHEAD: 9,706 feet
CONFIGURATION: Out-and-back
DIFFICULTY: Moderate
SCENERY: Mountain scenery, panoramic views
EXPOSURE: Partially shaded
TRAFFIC: Light
TRAIL SURFACE: Dirt and rock
HIKING TIME: 2–2.5 hours
WATER REQUIREMENTS: 1 liter. No water on the trail.
SEASON: Late spring to early fall
ACCESS: No access fees or permits required
MAPS: USGS Brighton
FACILITIES: No restrooms or water at the trailhead
DOGS: Permitted on trail from pass eastward
SPECIAL COMMENTS: This is a great hike for dogs, especially when it includes a loop down into the lakes in the basin to the east. No dogs are allowed in Big Cottonwood Canyon on the west, a protected watershed.

Directions

From Salt Lake City's east side take I-215 south to 6200 South (Exit 6). At the off-ramp, turn left and proceed south for 1.7 miles, as 6200 South changes to Wasatch Boulevard (UT 190). Turn left at the signal, staying on UT 190, and continue up Big Cottonwood Canyon for 13.8 miles to the Guardsman Pass Road turnoff on the left. Turn left and continue up the Guardsman Pass Road for 3.1 miles to the Guardsman Pass parking area on the right.

GPS Trailhead Coordinates

UTM Zone (WGS84) 12T
Easting 0453027
Northing 4495262
Latitude N 40° 36' 24.1"
Longitude W 111° 33' 17.8"

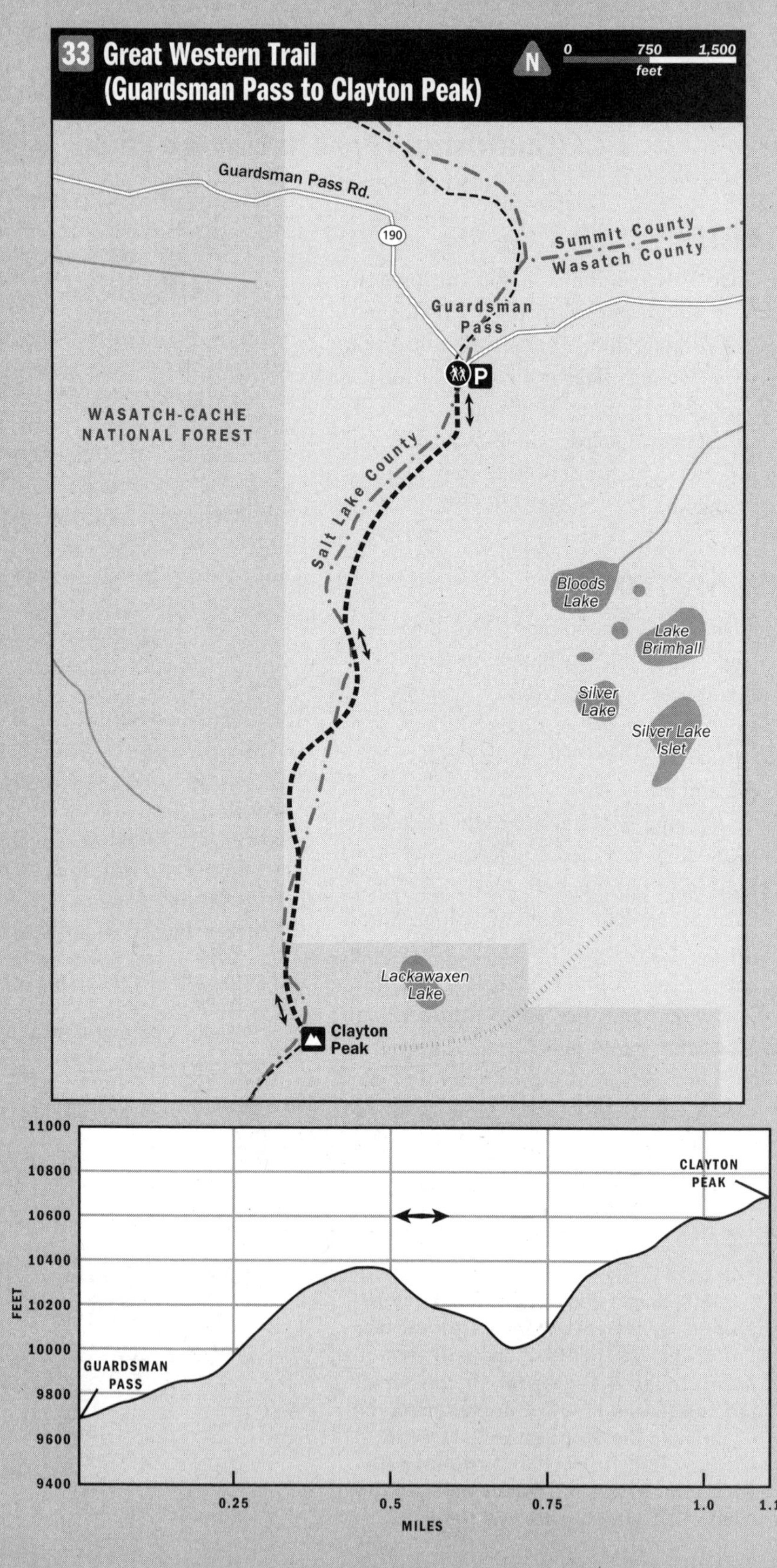

33 Great Western Trail (Guardsman Pass to Clayton Peak)
N
0
750
1,500
feet
Guardsman Pass Rd.
190
Summit County
Wasatch County
Guardsman Pass
P
WASATCH-CACHE NATIONAL FOREST
Salt Lake County
Bloods Lake
Lake Brimhall
Silver Lake
Silver Lake Islet
Lackawaxen Lake
Clayton Peak
11000
10800
10600
10400
10200
10000
9800
9600
9400
FEET
GUARDSMAN PASS
CLAYTON PEAK
0.25
0.5
0.75
1.0
1.1
MILES

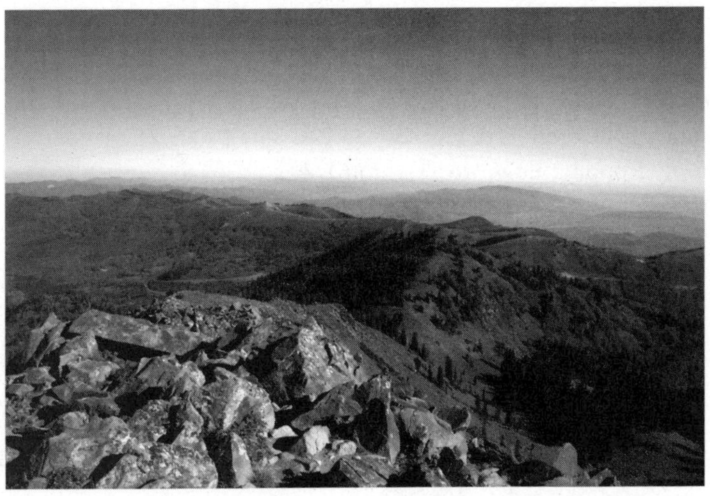

A mountainous panorama from Clayton Peak

Like most Wasatch trails, it rises quickly from the trailhead. After less than 30 minutes of hiking at a steady pace, you've already covered 0.6 miles and gained more than 700 feet of elevation. You'll find yourself on top of an unnamed knoll along the ridgeline at an elevation of 10,420 feet. The views are great, but Clayton Peak still looms in the distance to the south. Descend the slope on a faint trail and continue along the ridge, dropping more than 300 feet of hard-earned elevation gain.

Along the way, you can't help but notice the many lakes in the basin to the east. They're not well known by most Wasatch hikers, and include Bloods Lake, Lake Brimhall, Silver Lake, Silver Lake Islet, and Lackawaxen Lake. You can reach them by trails leading down from the ridgeline, in particular as part of a loop hike returning to Guardsman Pass.

As you work your way up the ridge, a quick glance to the right will surprise you with a view of the Brighton ski lift just 50 feet below, but this is only a brief distraction and doesn't significantly impact the feeling of remoteness. About halfway up the northern slope of Clayton Peak, the trail turns from a rocky path to a ridge made entirely of rock. For the final stretch leading to the summit, you'll be navigating boulders at a slow pace.

Most Wasatch hikes focus on westward views to the Salt Lake Valley. Clayton Peak offers panoramic views, but the most interesting are those to the east, with Heber Valley in the forefront and the Uintas in the distance.

Even near the summit, there are aspens and firs near the trail. At this elevation, snow can cover the ridge into mid-June, and the aspens often change colors in the first week of September. During summer, you may spot deer and coyotes near the ridge, and you'll see chipmunks along the entire trail. Clark's nutcrackers favor the high slopes in the summer, and raptors often circle nearby.

The Great Western Trail is a hike for aspiring peak baggers and a good way to train and acclimatize above 10,000 feet. The trail follows the ridgeline, so even when it becomes faint, it's unlikely you'll get too far off track. From the Clayton Peak summit you can return to Guardsman Pass along your ascent route, or extend your hike by dropping down to Brighton Lakes or on to Sunrise Peak along the ridge to the southwest.

NEARBY ACTIVITIES

Wasatch Mountain State Park in Midway is just 10 miles down the Guardsman Pass Road to the east. The 22,000-acre park is a year-round mountain retreat with a USGA-sanctioned 27-hole golf course, camping, hiking, and nature trails, and an interpretive center. In winter, snowshoeing and cross-country skiing are popular activities. For reservations or information, call (435) 654-1791 or visit **www.utah.com/stateparks.**

LAKE SOLITUDE (via the Silver Lake Interpretive Trail)

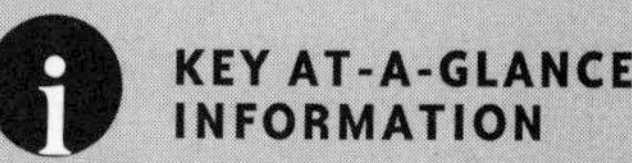

IN BRIEF

Two hikes for the price of one—the Silver Lake Interpretive Trail circles the alpine marsh around Silver Lake, and the connected Lake Solitude Trail leads through a forest of fir and aspen to a small glacial tarn. You'll get a hands-on education in alpine ecosystems in a scenic mountain setting.

KEY AT-A-GLANCE INFORMATION

LENGTH: 3.5 miles round-trip (consists of 1 mile on the Silver Lake Interpretive Trail and 2.5 miles on the Lake Solitude Trail)

ELEVATION GAIN: 500 feet

ELEVATION AT TRAILHEAD: 8,720 feet

CONFIGURATION: Loop with out-and-back extension

DIFFICULTY: Easy

SCENERY: Alpine lake with surrounding mountains

EXPOSURE: Partially shaded on Silver Lake Interpretive Trail; mostly shaded on Lake Solitude Trail

TRAFFIC: Busy

TRAIL SURFACE: Boardwalk and dirt

HIKING TIME: 1.5–2 hours

WATER REQUIREMENTS: 1 liter

SEASON: Summer

ACCESS: No fees for access or parking. Bicycles are not permitted on the Silver Lake boardwalk. The Silver Lake Interpretive Trail is wheelchair accessible.

MAPS: USGS Brighton

See additional information at end of Description, page 154.

DESCRIPTION

Silver Lake has been one of Salt Lake City's most popular summer recreation areas since July 23, 1849, when more than 2,000 residents escaped the valley's summer heat to hold their first Pioneer Day celebration here. Brighton remains a great summer getaway, and Silver Lake is the ideal short family hike.

Silver Lake, a shallow alpine lake surrounded by wetlands, teems with life during its short season. A brilliantly conceived trail, the Silver Lake Interpretive Trail allows visitors to explore the fragile wetlands ecosystem without ever getting wet or damaging the marshy areas. In the wooded areas along the lake's southern shore, the trail leaves the boardwalk and enters moist woods of fir and aspen along a dirt path.

Start your adventure at the Silver Lake Visitor Center, staffed in summer by the U.S. Forest Service. From the visitor center you

---

Directions

From Salt Lake City's east side, take I-215 south to 6200 South (Exit 6). At the off-ramp, turn left and proceed south for 1.7 miles, as 6200 South changes to Wasatch Boulevard (UT 190). Turn left at the signal, staying on UT 190, and continue up Big Cottonwood Canyon for 14.5 miles. The Silver Lake Recreation Area and parking are on your right as you enter the Brighton Loop.

GPS Trailhead Coordinates

UTM Zone (WGS84) 12T

Easting 0422235

Northing 4508096

Latitude N 40° 36' 12.8"

Longitude W 111° 35' 05.0"

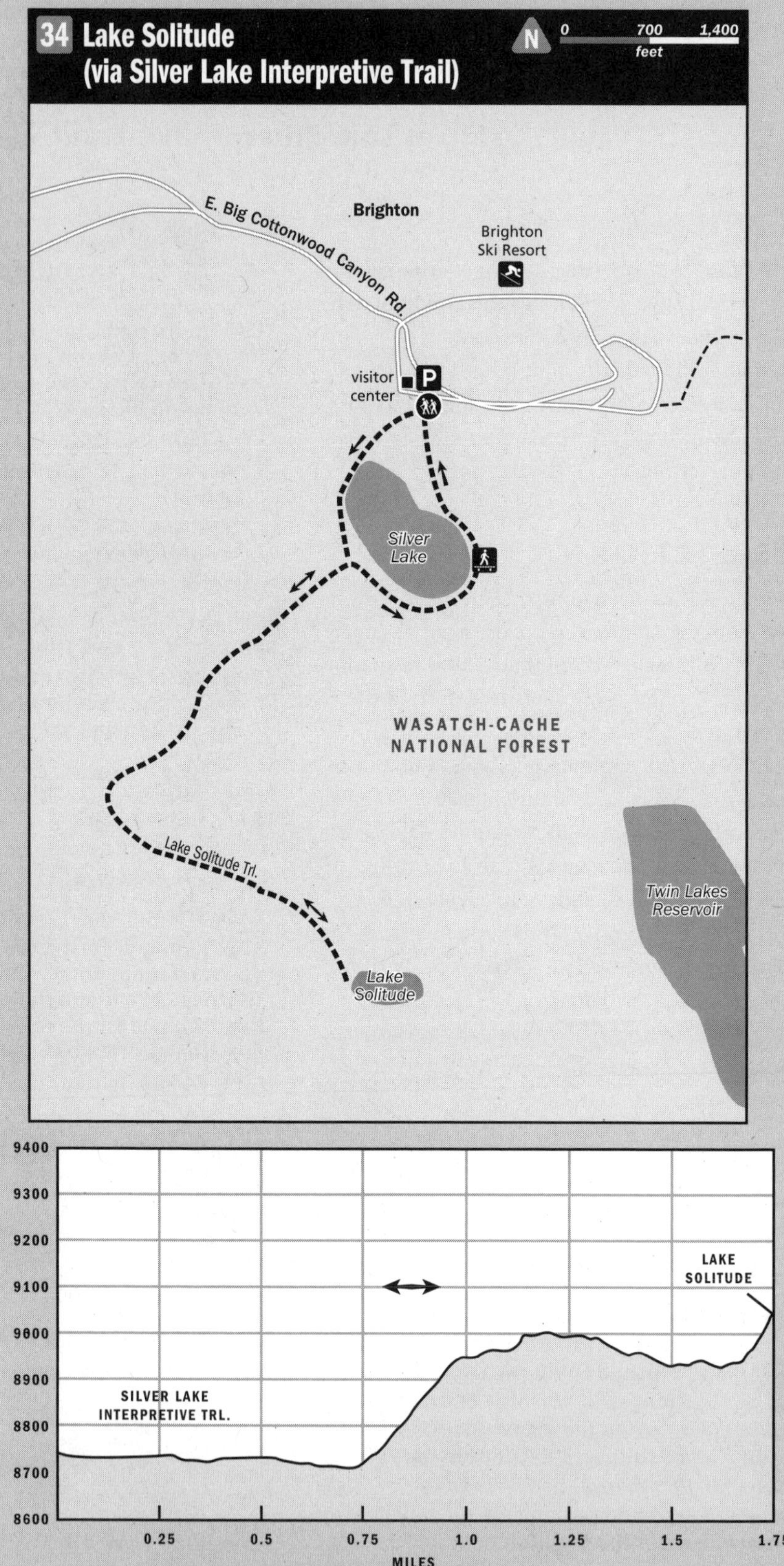
34 Lake Solitude
(via Silver Lake Interpretive Trail)
N
0
700
1,400
feet
E. Big Cottonwood Canyon Rd.
Brighton
Brighton
Ski Resort
visitor
center
P
Silver
Lake
WASATCH-CACHE
NATIONAL FOREST
Lake Solitude Trl.
Twin Lakes
Reservoir
Lake
Solitude
9400
9300
9200
9100
9000
8900
8800
8700
8600
FEET
LAKE
SOLITUDE
SILVER LAKE
INTERPRETIVE TRL.
0.25
0.5
0.75
1.0
1.25
1.5
1.75
MILES

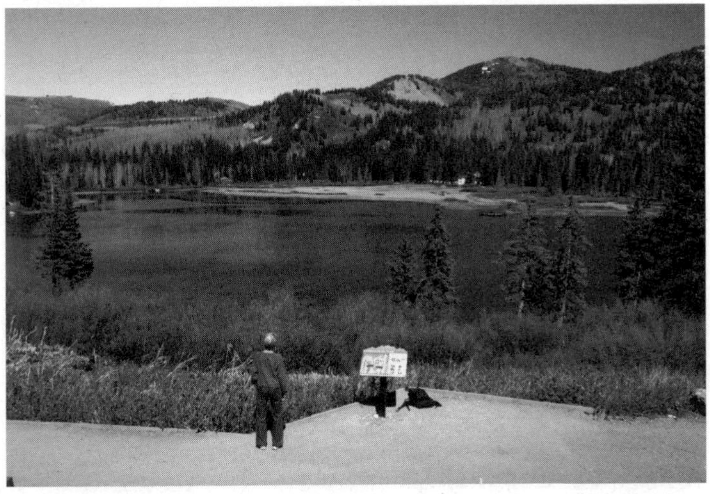

Sliver Lake from the interpretive trail

can follow the circular path in either direction, although most traffic seems to flow counterclockwise. Along the way, signs and displays describe the area's flora, fauna, and ecosystems, as well as watershed and drinking-water concerns. Rainbow trout and small brook trout stock the lake, making it an ideal destination for young anglers going after their first catch.

Winters are long and life is hard in this alpine environment. With an average of 33 feet of snow each winter, plants and animals have adapted to survive. The quaking aspen photosynthesizes through its bark and doesn't leaf out until mid-June in order to conserve energy. Snowshoe hares turn snow-white in winter and float over the snow with their giant feet. The Uinta ground squirrels, whose burrows line the path, hibernate for eight months of the year.

Wildlife flourishes around the lake and in the wetlands during the summer. Ducks find welcome habitat in the willows, sparrows nest in the nearby trees, and raptors soar overhead. Early-morning visitors may find moose munching on wetland vegetation, while those who arrive later in the day will certainly see their tracks in the boggy marsh. Squirrels start bulking up with seeds and vegetation early in the spring, before returning to their sleep cycle in mid-July.

On the west side of Silver Lake, a wide, well-marked trail leads into woods toward Twin Lakes Reservoir and Lake Solitude. Soon, after crossing a Forest Service road, the trail forks, with the Lake Solitude Trail taking off to the right.

Mature spruce, subalpine fir, and aspen shade the fragrant trail, which is lined with fir needles. Columbine, mountain bluebell, shooting star, monkshood, and other flowers dot the slopes. Patches of snow often cover the trail into late June.

While bikes aren't allowed on the boardwalk, you can expect to see mountain bikers on the Lake Solitude Trail and connecting roads and trails. You'll also pass signs for ski trails, cross ski-resort service roads, and even pass directly under a Solitude ski-resort lift.

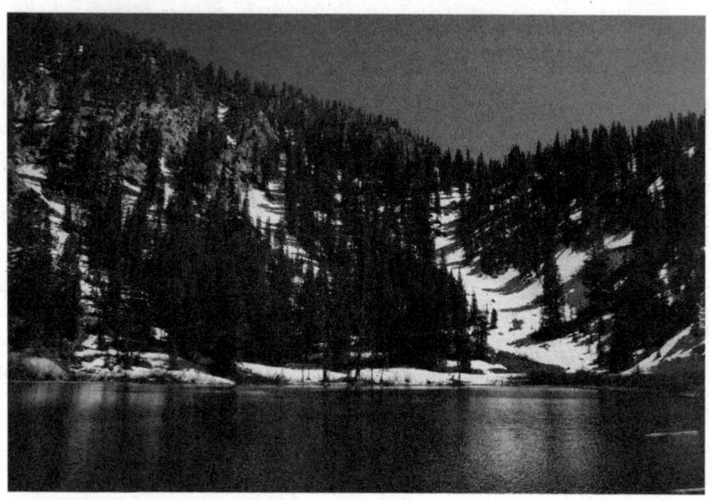

Lake Solitude

Nearing the lake, the trail steepens somewhat but never becomes punishing. Occasionally you'll have to surmount fallen trees, but this only makes the trail more appealing to youngsters. Arriving at the lake, you'll want to explore at least some of the shoreline to the west. Lake Solitude lies at the head of the Mill F South Fork, and you'll cross the stream outlet on the tarn's northwest rim. Mount Evergreen rises above to the south.

As you return to the Silver Lake Interpretive Trail, you'll want to complete the loop and continue your education in alpine ecology. The south shore is more wooded and has several landings that extend into the lake. They are ideal for fishing, but remember that this is a protected watershed, and swimming—or even dangling your feet in the water—is not allowed. From Silver Lake's south side, you can literally watch snowmelt flow into trickles, then into small streams that enter the lake. Within days, you'll be drinking this water at home or in restaurants throughout the valley.

ADDITIONAL AT-A-GLANCE INFORMATION

FACILITIES: Restrooms and water at the trailhead. A store and restaurant are located across the street. The visitor center is open on summer weekends and holidays only from 11 a.m. to 5 p.m.

DOGS: Prohibited in Big Cottonwood Canyon, a protected watershed

SPECIAL COMMENTS: In the winter, the Silver Lake Visitor Center becomes the Solitude Nordic Center, where cross-country skiers can access 20 kilometers (12 miles) of trails.

NEARBY ACTIVITIES

The Brighton Store and Cafe, across the street from the Silver Lake Visitor Center, provides a convenient stop for a drink, snack, or lunch after your hike. You can relax at the outdoor eating area and take in the views.

BRIGHTON LAKES (Lake Mary, Lake Martha, Lake Catherine, and Dog Lake) 35

IN BRIEF

Explore a chain of pristine alpine lakes at the top of Big Cottonwood Canyon. It's a favorite hike for families and couples in search of remote mountain scenery, fir-scented woods, and photogenic lakes—all within 30 minutes of your car. The section from just below Lake Mary to Lake Catherine is part of the Great Western Trail.

DESCRIPTION

Silver mining brought William Stuart Brighton to the upper bowl of Big Cottonwood Canyon in the 1870s. But he soon realized that a better living could be made feeding and housing miners than in actually mining silver.

After spending three summers in a tent, he built a hotel in 1874 near the shores of Silver Lake and soon developed the area into a popular mountain resort. His wife, Catherine, would serve the trout she had caught in Silver Lake with hot buttermilk biscuits.

In winter, Brighton's sons, Will and Dan, made crude skis out of wood just to get around in the deep snow. But skiers would have to wait until 1936 before a towrope was installed to create Brighton, Utah's first ski resort.

Your hike to the beautiful chain of glacial lakes that dot the southern side of Big

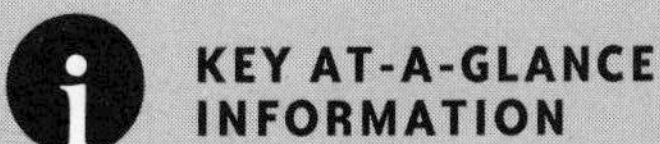

LENGTH: 2.2 miles round-trip to Lake Mary. Additional 2 miles round-trip to Lake Catherine. Additional 0.3 miles round-trip to Dog Lake. Total mileage to visit all four lakes is 4.5 miles round-trip.

ELEVATION GAIN: To Lake Mary, 760 feet; to Lake Catherine, 1,200 feet

ELEVATION AT TRAILHEAD: 8,762 feet

CONFIGURATION: Out-and-back

DIFFICULTY: Moderate

SCENERY: Conifer woods, alpine lakes, glacial cirque

EXPOSURE: Partially shaded

TRAFFIC: Busy

TRAIL SURFACE: Dirt and rock

HIKING TIME: 2.5–3.5 hours

WATER REQUIREMENTS: 1–1.5 liters. Water from lakes and streams may be purified.

SEASON: Late spring, summer, early fall

ACCESS: No fees for access or parking

MAPS: USGS Brighton

FACILITIES: Restrooms, water, and public telephone available at the Silver Lake Visitor Center

See additional information at end of Description, page 158.

Directions →

From Salt Lake City's east side, take I-215 south to 6200 South (Exit 6). At the off-ramp, turn left and proceed south for 1.7 miles, as 6200 South changes to Wasatch Boulevard (UT 190). Turn left at the signal, staying on UT 190, and continue up Big Cottonwood Canyon for 14.5 miles. The trailhead is located on south-east side of the Brighton Loop at the base of the Majestic lift at the Brighton Ski Resort.

GPS Trailhead Coordinates

UTM Zone (WGS84) 12T

Easting 0450509

Northing 4494288

Latitude N 40° 35' 53.6"

Longitude W 111° 35' 04.1"

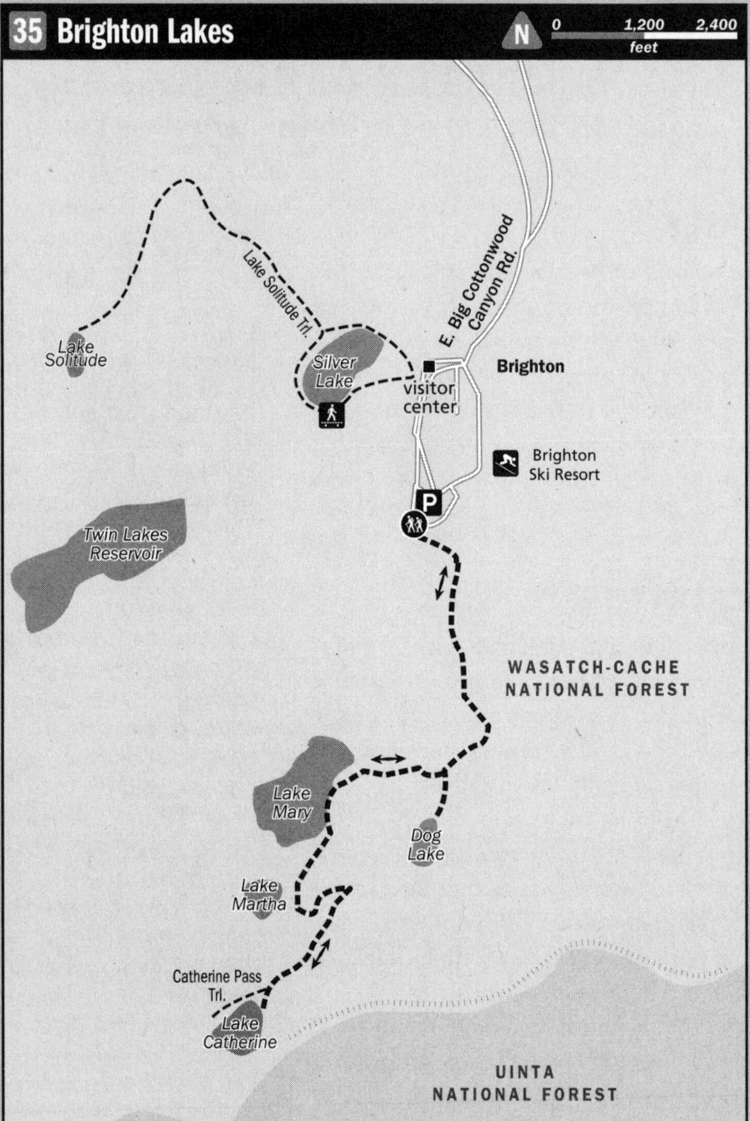

35 Brighton Lakes
N
0
1,200
2,400
feet
Lake Solitude Trl.
E. Big Cottonwood Canyon Rd.
Lake Solitude
Silver Lake
visitor center
Brighton
Brighton Ski Resort
P
Twin Lakes Reservoir
WASATCH-CACHE NATIONAL FOREST
Lake Mary
Dog Lake
Lake Martha
Catherine Pass Trl.
Lake Catherine
UINTA NATIONAL FOREST

FEET
10000
9800
9600
9400
9200
9000
8800
8600
8400
BRIGHTON
LAKE MARY
LAKE MARTHA
LAKE CATHERINE
0.5
1.0
1.5
2.0
2.2
MILES

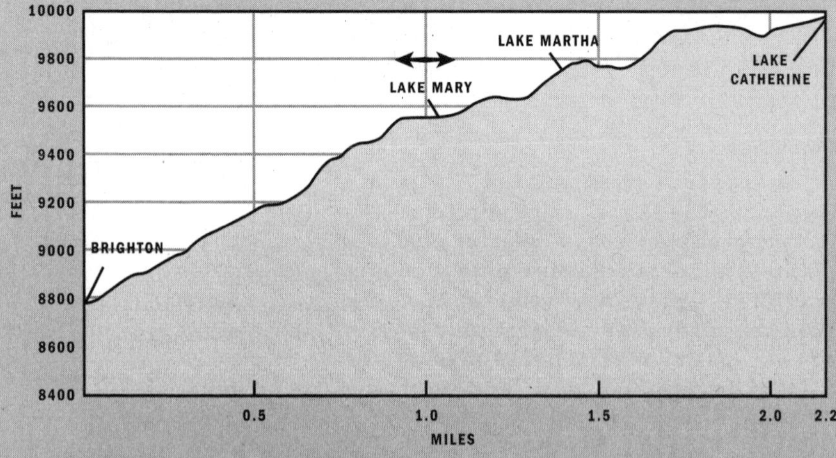

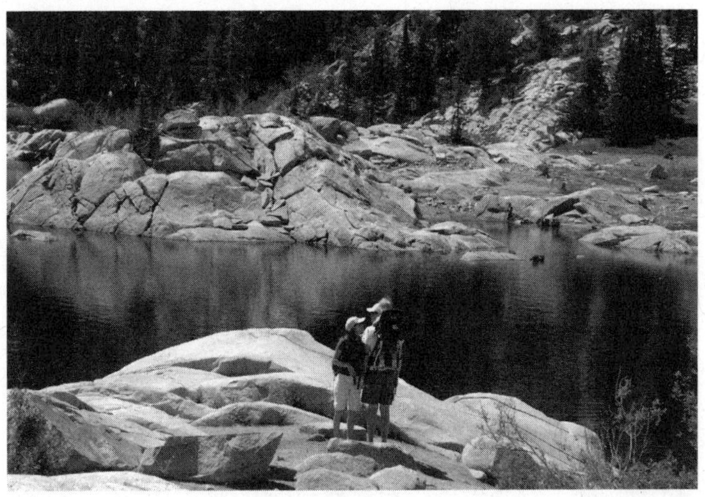

Lake Mary, with its granite shore, is a popular family hike.

Cottonwood's upper bowl departs from the base of Brighton Resort's Majestic chairlift. A large sign in front of the lift (at the parking lot's southeast edge) displays the route, marked as the Lake Mary–Catherine Pass Trail.

The trail is steep as it crosses under two chairlifts and ascends some of Brighton's ski slopes. At 0.6 miles, the trail leaves the slopes and enters a wooded area, offering a more wilderness feel. At 0.9 miles you come to a gateway of gray granite that forms the bowl of Lake Mary. A large sign at a trail junction marks the spur that leads to Dog Lake. Within moments, a concrete dam—which enlarges and regulates Lake Mary—appears in front of you on the trail. At this point, note an unmarked trail leading off to the right about 30 feet before the dam. It accesses Lake Mary's western side and also leads to Twin Lakes.

The trail ascends to the left of the dam, and within minutes you'll find yourself in the exquisite granite basin that contains Lake Mary. The one-way distance from the trailhead to the Lake Mary shore is 1.1 miles. Even if your ultimate destination is Lake Catherine, you'll want to stop to enjoy the beauty of Lake Mary's granite shoreline. It offers lots of coves, nooks, and smooth granite outcroppings where you can pause for a snack and to enjoy the view.

The trail continues along Lake Mary's eastern shore for 0.3 miles before arriving at Lake Martha, at an elevation just 38 feet higher than Lake Mary. Lake Martha lacks Lake Mary's granite lining but is perfectly charming and provides more solitude.

At this point, Lake Catherine is just 0.7 miles up the trail, so it would be a shame to miss it. Departing Lake Martha, the crowds thin considerably and the trail, now part of the Great Western Trail, becomes more moist and wooded. Your chances of seeing wildlife—especially moose, deer, and porcupine—increase.

Continuing upward, the trail ascends to the east of Lake Martha, then switches back to the north and comes to a ridgeline promontory overlooking the

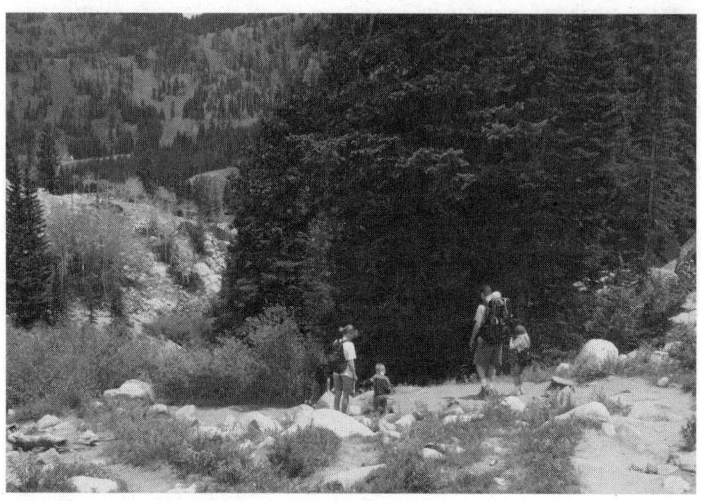

Descending the trail from Lake Mary

upper bowl of Big Cottonwood Canyon. The trail continues for 0.6 miles past Lake Martha through alpine forests of spruce and fir before coming to a crest and a fork in the trail. To the right is the Catherine Pass Trail, which leads over the rim of the cirque into Little Cottonwood Canyon. To the left, the trail arrives at the shore of Lake Catherine in less than 0.1 mile.

In a fitting tribute, William Brighton named the jewel of the upper Big Cottonwood Canyon after his wife. Lake Catherine is a perfectly inviting place for a picnic, a rest, or a relaxing afternoon of fishing. Be sure to walk to the top of the granite formation at the north end of the lake, where you'll find the ideal overview of Lake Martha and Lake Mary. On your return trip, Dog Lake is just 700 feet off the main trail below Lake Mary. Although less scenic than the other lakes, it is a great place to watch for moose, particularly in the early-morning hours.

ADDITIONAL AT-A-GLANCE INFORMATION

DOGS: Prohibited in Big Cottonwood Canyon, a protected watershed

SPECIAL COMMENTS: Lake Mary may be the most popular alpine hike in the Salt Lake area, with hundreds of hikers enjoying its beauty on any given summer Saturday. But only a small percentage of those hikers go on to Lake Martha or Lake Catherine, where you can often find yourself completely alone.

NEARBY ACTIVITIES

Big Cottonwood Canyon provides a field course in Wasatch geology. As you drive up Big Cottonwood Canyon, a series of large blue-and-brown signs at roadside turnouts provides interpretive information about the canyon. Explaining specific features like folding, faulting, and glaciation, these signs will enrich your hiking experience and give you a better appreciation for the canyon.

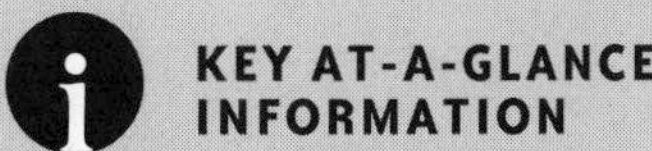

SUNSET PEAK 36

IN BRIEF

Sunset Peak is one of the most popular summit trails in the Wasatch. It's a great jaunt, suitable for hikers of all skill levels. Wildlife, wildflowers, and rewarding views along the trail and at the summit justify its popularity.

DESCRIPTION

With a high-elevation trailhead at the top of Little Cottonwood Canyon, a hike from Albion Basin to Catherine Pass offers a chance for nearly any hiker, regardless of skill level or conditioning, to ascend to a high-mountain ridge near the tree line and gaze down at alpine lakes and off to distant ranges. From the Catherine Pass ridgeline, a short climb on to 10,648-foot Sunset Peak delivers even more expansive views stretching east to the Uintas.

The large trailhead parking area fills quickly on weekends, so either come early or plan to take the free shuttle from the Albion Basin entrance station above Alta. An early arrival will also give you the best chance to spot the moose that browse the verdant meadows.

Directions →

From Salt Lake City, go south on I-15 to 9000 South (Exit 295). Turn left onto 9000 South (UT 209) and proceed east toward the mouth of Little Cottonwood Canyon for 7.2 miles. Along the way, UT 209 changes names from 9000 South to 9400 South and eventually becomes Little Cottonwood Road. At the mouth of Little Cottonwood Canyon, UT 209 comes to a junction with UT 210. Turn right onto UT 210 and continue up Little Cottonwood Canyon for 10 miles to the Albion Basin entrance booth and gate above Alta. Continue on the dirt road for 2 miles to the Catherine Pass trailhead parking area on the right.

KEY AT-A-GLANCE INFORMATION

LENGTH: 4.2 miles round-trip

ELEVATION GAIN: 1,269 feet

ELEVATION AT TRAILHEAD: 9,379 feet

CONFIGURATION: Out-and-back

DIFFICULTY: Easy

SCENERY: Wildflowers, alpine scenery, and panoramic views from the summit

EXPOSURE: Partially shaded

TRAFFIC: Busy

TRAIL SURFACE: Dirt and rock

HIKING TIME: 2–3 hours

WATER REQUIREMENTS: 1 liter. No water is available at the trailhead or on the trail.

SEASON: Summer

ACCESS: No fees for access or parking

MAPS: USGS Brighton, Trails Illustrated Wasatch Front (709)

FACILITIES: Restrooms are available in the trailhead parking lot.

DOGS: Pets and horses are prohibited in Little Cottonwood Canyon, a protected watershed.

SPECIAL COMMENTS: The Albion Basin gate above Alta is generally open July 1–November 1.

GPS Trailhead Coordinates

UTM Zone (WGS84) 12T

Easting 0447659

Northing 4492647

Latitude N 40° 34' 58.0"

Longitude W 111° 37' 06.4"

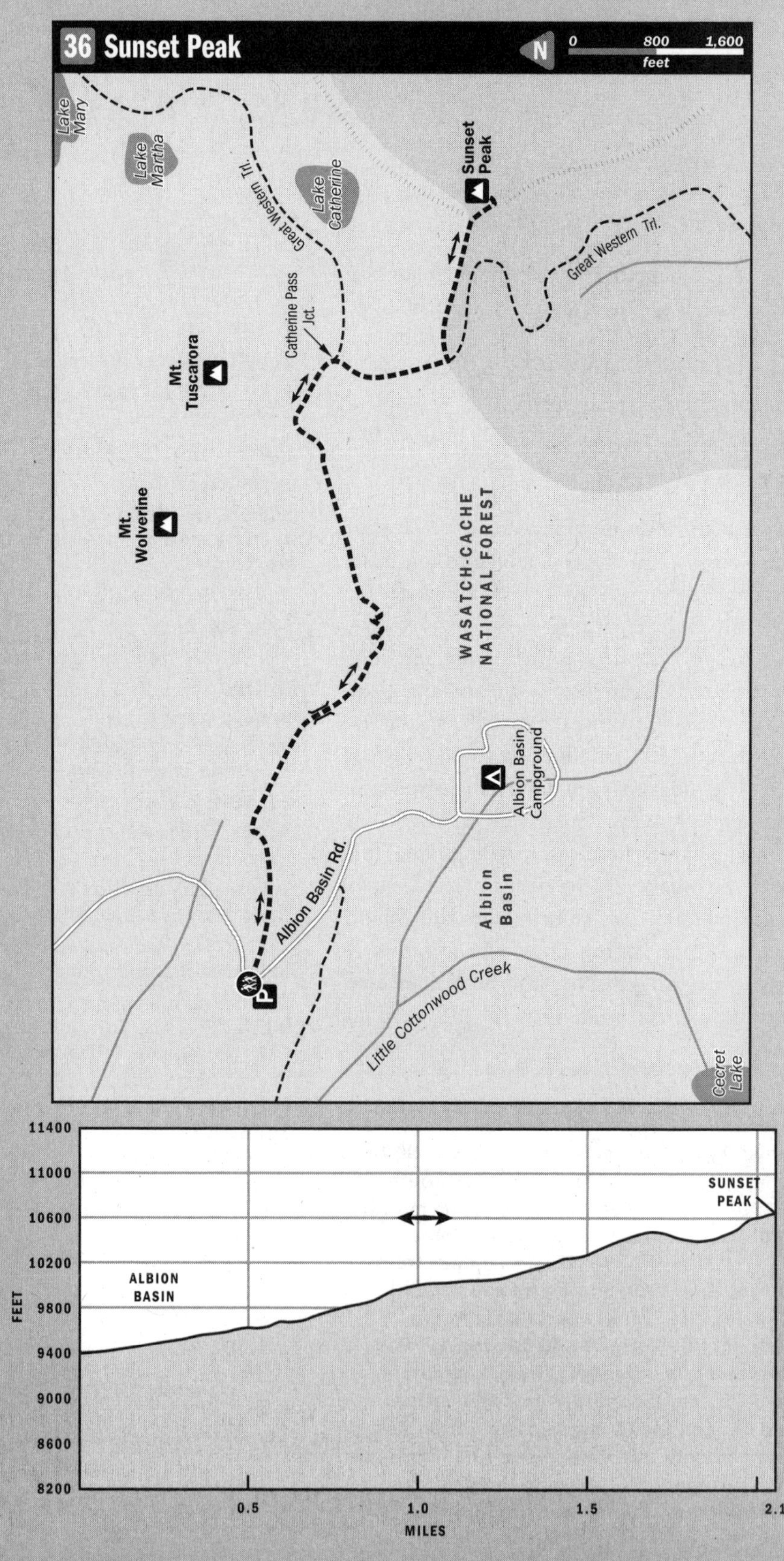

36 Sunset Peak
N
0
800
1,600
feet
Lake Mary
Lake Martha
Lake Catherine
Great Western Trl.
Sunset Peak
Great Western Trl.
Catherine Pass Jct.
Mt. Tuscarora
Mt. Wolverine
WASATCH-CACHE NATIONAL FOREST
Albion Basin Campground
Albion Basin Rd.
Albion Basin
Little Cottonwood Creek
Cecret Lake
11400
11000
10600
10200
9800
9400
9000
8600
8200
FEET
ALBION BASIN
SUNSET PEAK
0.5
1.0
1.5
2.1
MILES

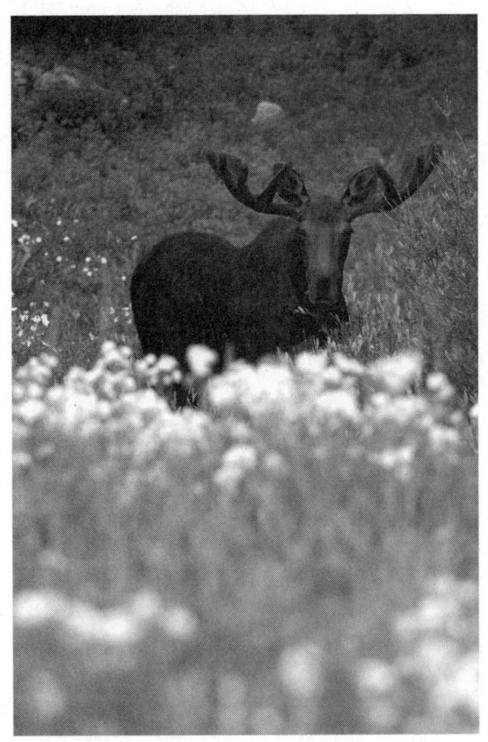

Bull moose in Albion Basin

From the trailhead parking area just south of an Alta chairlift, cross the Forest Service road and follow the marked trail leading up to Catherine Pass. At 0.2 miles the trail comes to a ski-resort utility road. Turn left onto the road and follow it up and to the left. Leaving the road, the trail soon crosses a granite outcropping and ascends to the right.

At 0.5 miles, the trail crosses a small wooden bridge, then narrows. It quickly crests at an outcropping, then dips a bit before continuing its ascent. At 0.7 miles, a spur trail leads off to the right to give hikers a nice overview of the Albion Basin, with views of Baldy, Sugarloaf, and Devil's Castle to the left.

Albion Basin is famous for its variety and density of wildflowers. With more than 50 feet of snow per year and a short growing season, the basin is home to dwarf species that have adapted to the harsh environment. An example is alpine asters, with blooms about half the size of the normal species. Both golden and bald eagles can be seen riding the updrafts that rise from the basin to the ridgeline.

At 0.9 miles the trail ascends into a draw with gentle slopes on both sides before entering a small basin meadow. At the upper or east end of the meadow, the trail climbs a few switchbacks dotted with granite boulders as it makes its way up to Catherine Pass. At Catherine Pass the trail merges with the Great Western Trail and ascends to the right along a fine, sandy surface leading to Sunset Pass to the south. Here the Great Western Trail continues along the ridge to the south, while the trail to Sunset Peak turns left and to the east. This ridge forms the boundary of Salt Lake and Utah counties.

The trail maintains a steady ascent along a timberline route dotted with subalpine fir. Soon it curves to the left and arrives at the summit. Sunset Peak is the only point in the area to form the boundary of three counties; Salt Lake County to the north and west, Utah County to the south, and Wasatch County to the east. On a clear day you can enjoy excellent views of Mount Timpanogos to the south and Heber Valley to the east. In the distant east, the flat-topped Uintas appear on

Brighton Lakes (with Lake Catherine in the foreground), viewed from Sunset Peak

the horizon. To the north, Lake Catherine is cradled by Mount Tuscarora on the left and Pioneer Peak on the right. Lake Catherine, Lake Martha, and Lake Mary glisten below and almost appear to be adjoining lakes on the same plane.

You can return to the trailhead parking area along your ascent route, or at Sunset Pass take a trail that descends to the west, leading into Albion Basin Campground. From there it's an easy half-mile stroll along the Forest Service road back to the Catherine Pass parking area.

NEARBY ACTIVITIES

The Albion Basin entrance station is a good source of information on hikes and trail conditions in the area. The Albion Basin Shuttle operates on summer weekends and holidays from 10 a.m. to 4:30 p.m. The service is free and offers pickup and drop-off at the entrance station. It makes stops at the Catherine Pass trailhead and the Albion Basin Campground.

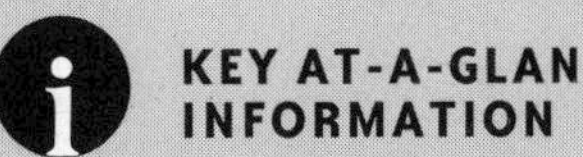

CECRET LAKE 37

IN BRIEF

Albion Basin is ablaze with wildflowers and wildlife in summer. This popular and easy hike travels along a well-marked interpretive trail through flowered meadows to a rock-rimmed alpine lake at the head of Little Cottonwood Canyon.

DESCRIPTION

In its heyday, Alta was a hotbed of silver mining activity. In the 1870s, thirsty miners had 26 saloons to choose from. Many of those miners came from Great Britain and named the area at the head of Little Cottonwood Canyon Albion Basin, evoking an ancient poetic name for their native England.

Today the most valued natural resource in the area is water. The Albion Basin receives more than 50 feet of snow per year and provides 15 percent of Salt Lake City's drinking water. Cecret Lake, the small glacial tarn above Albion Basin to the south, serves as the headwaters of Little Cottonwood Creek.

The other treasured natural resource in the Albion Basin is wildflowers. More than

KEY AT-A-GLANCE INFORMATION

LENGTH: 1.6 miles round-trip
ELEVATION GAIN: 458 feet
ELEVATION AT TRAILHEAD: 9,874 feet
CONFIGURATION: Out-and-back
DIFFICULTY: Easy
SCENERY: Wildflowers, alpine lake, and mountain scenery
EXPOSURE: Partially shaded
TRAFFIC: Busy
TRAIL SURFACE: Dirt and rock
HIKING TIME: 1–2 hours
WATER REQUIREMENTS: 1 liter
SEASON: Summer
ACCESS: No fees for access or parking
MAPS: USGS Brighton, Trails Illustrated Wasatch Front (709)
FACILITIES: You'll find water and restrooms in the campground near the trailhead.
DOGS: Pets and horses are prohibited in Little Cottonwood Canyon, a protected watershed.
SPECIAL COMMENTS: The gate above Alta is generally open July 1–November 1.

Directions

From Salt Lake City, go south on I-15 to 9000 South (Exit 295). Turn left onto 9000 South (UT 209) and proceed east toward the mouth of Little Cottonwood Canyon for 7.2 miles. Along the way, UT 209 changes names from 9000 South to 9400 South and eventually becomes Little Cottonwood Road. At the mouth of Little Cottonwood Canyon, UT 209 comes to a junction with UT 210. Turn right onto UT 210 and continue up Little Cottonwood Canyon for 10 miles to the Albion Basin entrance booth and gate above Alta. Continue on the dirt road for 2.5 miles to the Cecret Lake Trailhead parking area on the left.

GPS Trailhead Coordinates

UTM Zone (WGS84) 12T
Easting 0448129
Northing 4492077
Latitude N 40° 34' 40.4"
Longitude W 111° 36' 46.9"

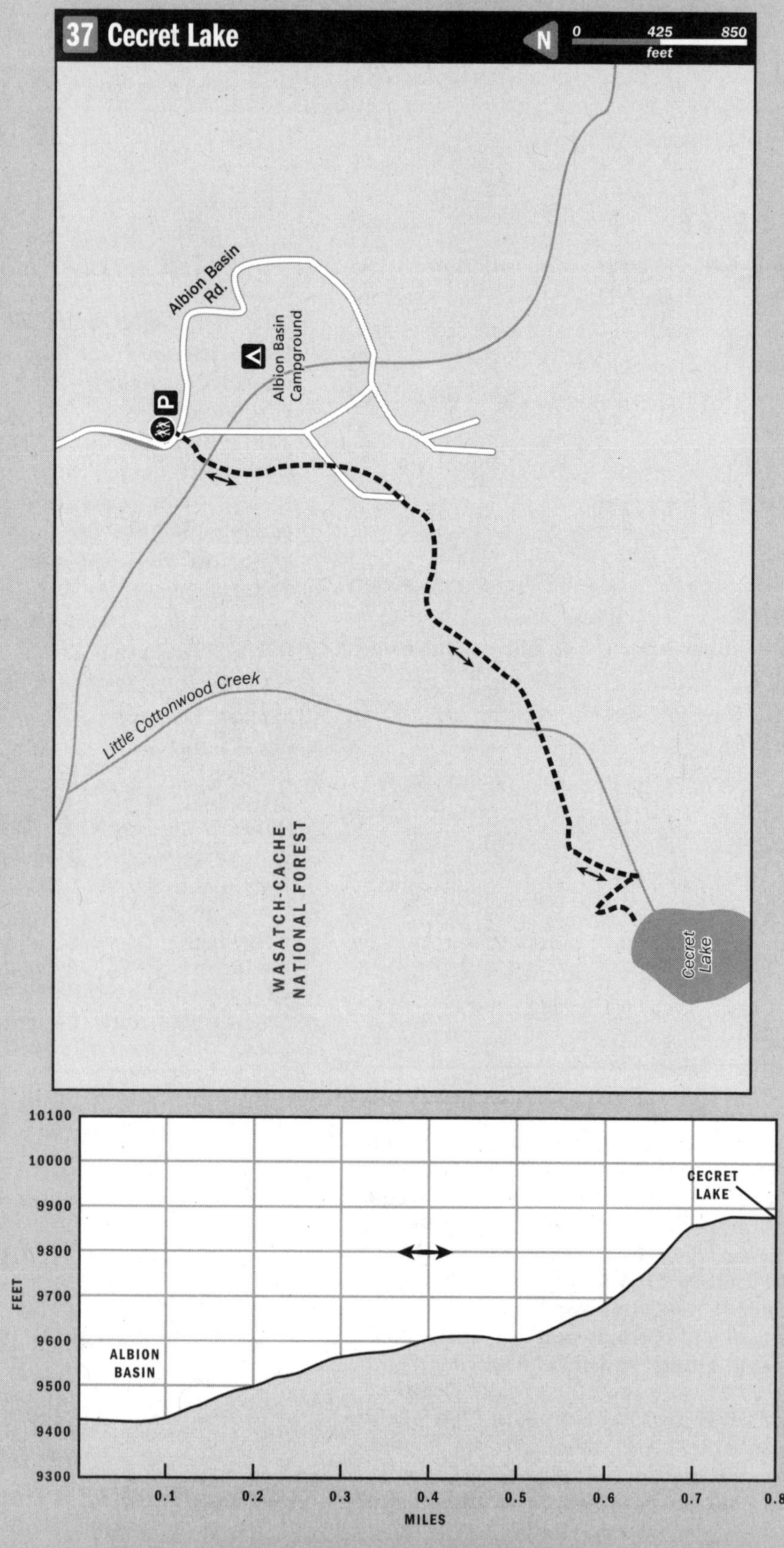

37 Cecret Lake
N
0
425
850
feet
Albion Basin Rd.
Albion Basin Campground
Little Cottonwood Creek
WASATCH-CACHE NATIONAL FOREST
Cecret Lake
10100
10000
9900
9800
9700
9600
9500
9400
9300
FEET
ALBION BASIN
CECRET LAKE
0.1
0.2
0.3
0.4
0.5
0.6
0.7
0.8
MILES

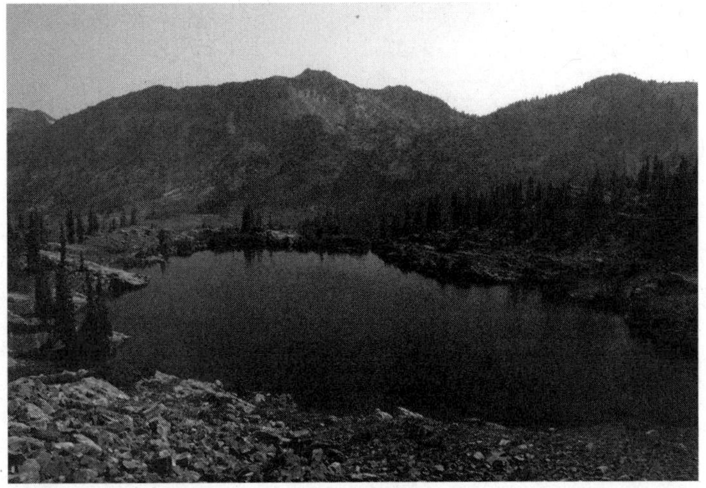

Cecret Lake

120 species of wildflowers bloom in the basin during the short summer season. They start to appear as soon as the snow begins to melt and reach a climax in August. More than 20,000 visitors come to Albion Basin every summer, so it becomes each visitor's responsibility to tread lightly, stay on the trail, and protect this fragile natural environment.

From the large Cecret Lake parking area, just north of the Albion Basin Campground, take the trail that leads south. It quickly crosses a small brook fed by seasonal runoff from the snow patches that remain well into summer. At 0.1 mile, you'll cross under an Alta ski-resort chairlift before the trail turns onto a dirt road. At 0.2 miles, you'll pass beneath a second Alta chairlift.

At 0.4 miles, the trail leaves the service road and veers to the left. Along the way you'll see several interpretive signs describing the alpine environment and the delicate balance of life that exists in the area. As you pass through this meadow you'll likely see moose grazing on the plant life, especially in the early-morning hours.

At an elevation of 9,500 feet, winters are long and the growing season is short. Wildflowers bloom in a rapid and predictable sequence with sprays of yellow, red, blue, purple, and white. Each color of flower attracts different birds and insects, which then pollinate the flower, enabling it to seed and return the following year. Flies and beetles are drawn to green and brown foliage and flowers, hummingbirds prefer red, and bees will go to any color. As you walk along the main trail, you'll see many side trails leading into the meadow. Most of these work their way back to the campground or the main trail and are always worth exploring.

At 0.6 miles, the trail leaves the flowered basin and crosses a rocky field before ascending a steep slope along a switchback into the upper basin, home

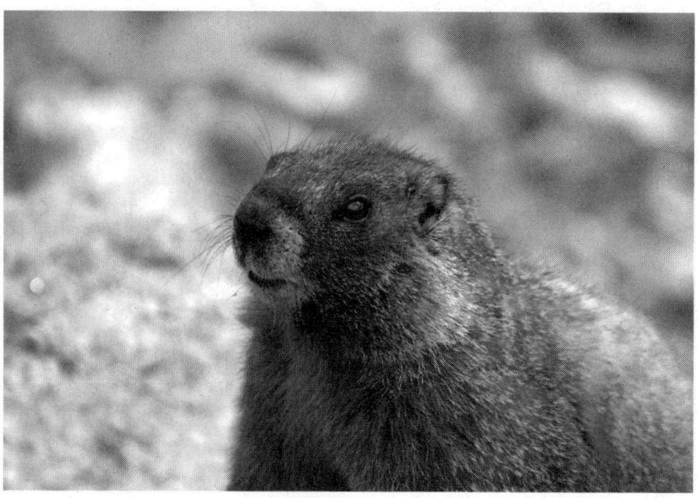

Marmots, which emit a loud warning whistle, are often seen on the slopes of Wasatch peaks.

to Cecret Lake. Near the northeast side of the lake is a small outlet that allows the water to cascade down the slope and through the meadow below. The headwaters of Little Cottonwood Creek, this outlet continues to be fed by many forks and creeks along the way as it swells to become a raging torrent just 10 miles downstream.

Once you arrive at the lake, you'll see a faint track that circles the shore, crossing boulder fields and talus slopes. Sugarloaf Peak, at 11,051 feet in elevation, lies to the south and can be climbed by scrambling up the slope to the left of the summit.

Moose rarely approach the shores of Cecret Lake, since they find most of their food in the lush lower meadows. But ground squirrels and marmots love the rocky regions near the lake. Because of the lake's popularity, they have become accustomed to humans and are quite fearless. If you leave a pack on the rocks near the lake, you can expect a squirrel to come nosing around looking for a bag of trail mix or crackers.

NEARBY ACTIVITIES

Use the Albion Basin Campground as a perfectly situated base for exploring the upper reaches of Little Cottonwood Canyon. In addition to overnight camping, it's also available for day use, making it an ideal meeting place for families and groups who want to escape the heat in the valley below and spend a day hiking, picnicking, and enjoying the beauty of Albion Basin. Each campsite has a fire grill, parking spur, and picnic table. The campground is open for day use from 7 a.m. to 10 p.m. For reservations, call the National Reservation Service at (877) 444-6777 or visit **www.reserveusa.com.**

WHITE PINE LAKE 38

IN BRIEF

Surprise—a glacial lake in Little Cottonwood Canyon that can be reached along a gently ascending trail. The open trail leads to wonderful canyon views, a glacial cirque dotted with alpine vegetation, and one of the prettiest lakes in Utah.

DESCRIPTION

The loggers and miners who worked Big Cottonwood and Little Cottonwood canyons in the late 1800s and early 1900s were an ambitious lot. They built the first two timber slides in White Pine Canyon and adjoining Red Pine Canyon. Loggers cut Engelmann spruce, which they called white pine, and Douglas-fir, which they called red pine.

After the loggers came miners in search of silver, lead, and zinc. They never made much money, but the miners left their mark in the canyons by building many of the roads to access the mines. The White Pine Trail follows the route of a mining road built in the early 1900s. Don't worry about hiking on Jeep trails, though: the Forest Service closed the road more than 50 years ago, and now it's

Directions

From Salt Lake City, go south on I-15 to 9000 South (Exit 295). Turn left onto 9000 South (UT 209) and proceed east toward the mouth of Little Cottonwood Canyon for 7.2 miles. Along the way, UT 209 changes names from 9000 South to 9400 South and eventually becomes Little Cottonwood Road. At the mouth of Little Cottonwood Canyon, UT 209 comes to a junction with UT 210. Turn right onto UT 210 and continue up Little Cottonwood Canyon for 5.2 miles to the White Pine Trailhead parking lot on your right.

KEY AT-A-GLANCE INFORMATION

LENGTH: 9.8 miles round-trip

ELEVATION GAIN: 2,452 feet

ELEVATION AT TRAILHEAD: 7,698 feet

CONFIGURATION: Out-and-back

DIFFICULTY: Moderate

SCENERY: Deep glacial valley rising to high glacial lake

EXPOSURE: Mostly shaded to 9,700 feet; partially shaded above 9,700 feet and at lake

TRAFFIC: Moderate

TRAIL SURFACE: Dirt and rocks. Mostly rock above 9,800 feet.

HIKING TIME: 5–7 hours

WATER REQUIREMENTS: 1.5–2 liters. Springs, streams, and lake provide ample opportunities to purify water.

SEASON: Spring, summer, fall. Ideal snowshoeing or cross-country ski trail when snow has stabilized and avalanche risk is minimal.

ACCESS: No fees for access or parking

MAPS: USGS Dromedary Peak; Trails Illustrated, Uinta National Forest (701), Wasatch Front (709)

FACILITIES: Restrooms at trailhead

DOGS: Little Cottonwood Canyon, a protected watershed, prohibits dogs, horses, and pets.

GPS Trailhead Coordinates

UTM Zone (WGS84) 12T

Easting 0442345

Northing 4491898

Latitude N 40° 34' 32.2"

Longitude W 111° 40' 52.1"

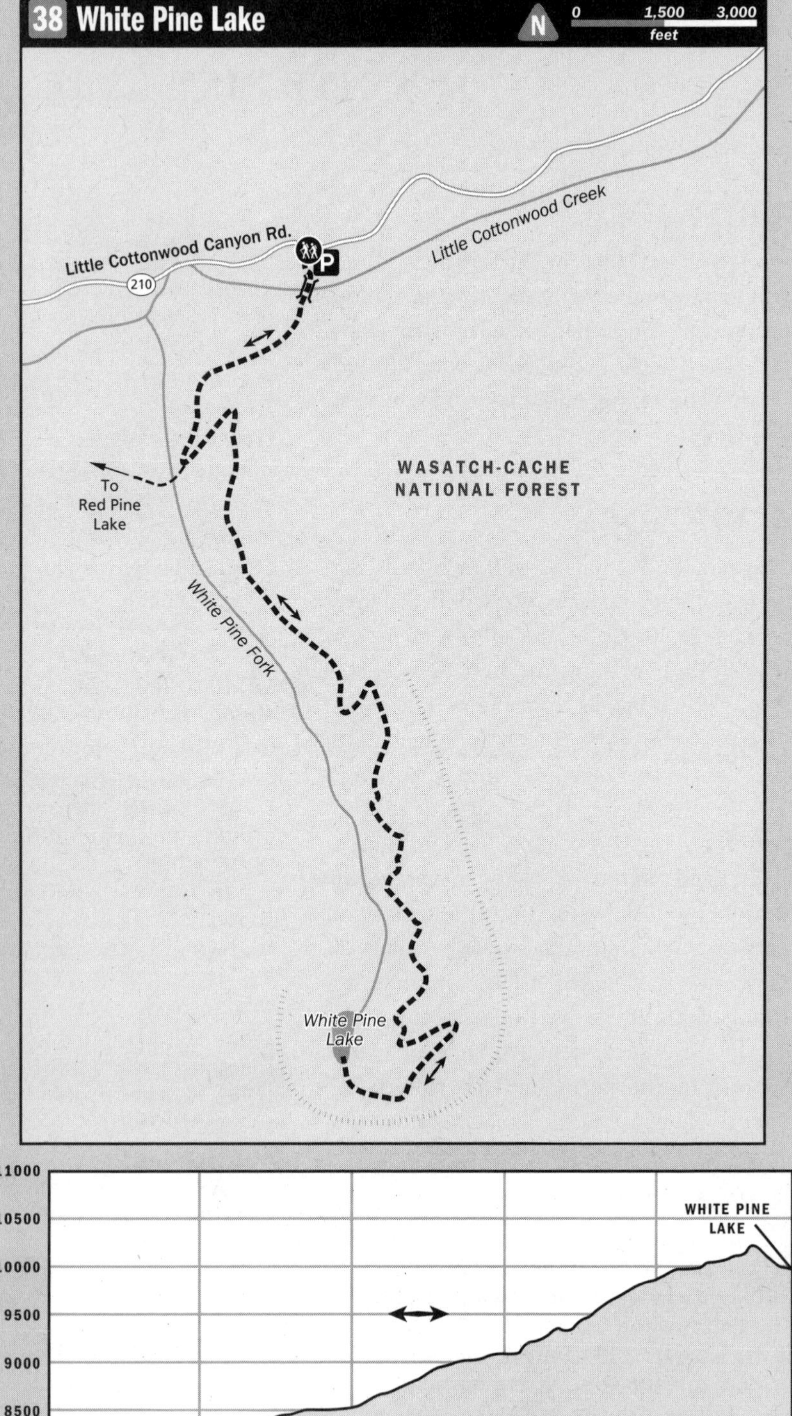

38 White Pine Lake
N
0 1,500 3,000
feet
Little Cottonwood Canyon Rd.
210
Little Cottonwood Creek
WASATCH-CACHE
NATIONAL FOREST
To
Red Pine
Lake
White Pine Fork
White Pine
Lake
11000
10500
10000
9500
9000
8500
8000
7500
7000
FEET
WHITE PINE
FORK
WHITE PINE
LAKE
1.0
2.0
3.0
4.0
4.9
MILES

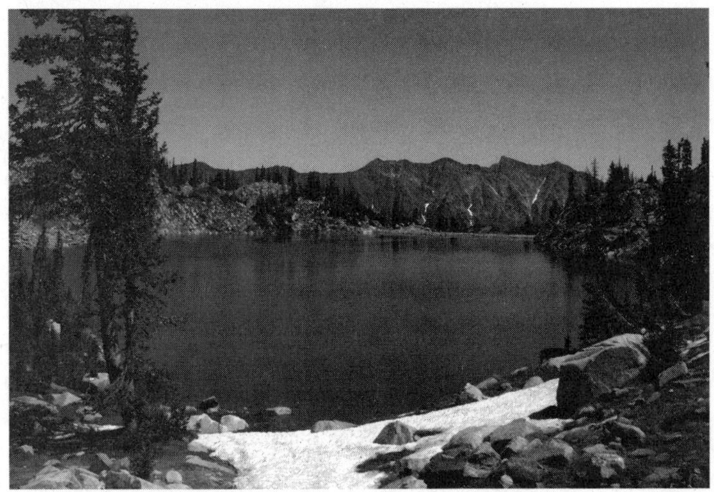

White Pine Lake

almost completely reclaimed. It looks and feels like a wide trail, not a rutted Jeep trail, allowing you to walk side by side with your hiking companion. Its openness reduces the chances of getting lost, so the hike is well suited and safe for inexperienced hikers and children who are capable of the distance. Because the trail began as a road, the gradient is not as steep as most trails', but the route is longer and more circuitous.

The trail departs from the south side of the large White Pine Trailhead parking lot. Even though the parking lot accommodates 35 cars, it often fills on summer weekends, and latecomers may find themselves parking along Little Cottonwood Canyon Road. From the parking area the trail dips, and within 100 yards you cross Little Cottonwood Creek and begin your ascent.

Immediately after crossing the bridge, the trail passes through an area damaged by avalanche. Looking at some of the leveled aspens with trunk diameters in excess of a foot, you get a sense of the power and force of snow thundering down the mountain. The White Pine Trail is a popular snowshoe- and cross-country-skiing area, but only after the avalanche danger has passed.

At 0.9 miles you arrive at a junction with the Red Pine Trail. With the White Pine Fork at your right, continue along the wide trail as it makes a sharp turn to the left and ascends along a straight course. At the top of this stretch you arrive at a canyon overlook at 8,200 feet in elevation before making a hairpin turn and continuing through forests of conifer and aspen.

By now the trail is high above the canyon floor, following a well-crafted path along the eastern side of White Pine Fork. Along the way, numerous springs and creeks cross the trail. Wildflowers, including white columbine and buttercups, dot the side of the trail.

At 3.4 miles the trail enters a large open meadow, and the upper reaches of the glacial bowl become more apparent. Soon the terrain changes from dense spruce and fir forests to a rocky glacial terrain. Near the top of the canyon, the trail crosses a wide talus slope, often covered by a snowfield into early summer. Once you cross the slope, the trail remains on glacial moraine to the rim above the lake. As the trail nears the lake, at an elevation just under 10,000 feet, the trail sweeps widely to the east, then turns west as it rounds the bowl and heads toward the lake. You might think it faster to scramble the slope to the west and drop down directly into White Pine Lake, but even though the trail looks long, you can move quickly along its gradual ascent.

Within minutes you'll be at the rim overlooking White Pine Lake, the high elevation for the hike. From there, a downhill stroll of 0.2 miles will put you at the water's edge. If you're an early riser, you can sit on one of the smooth granite boulders and watch trout jump from the lake to snag live flies. If you look up the drainage to the south, you may see deer grazing on the sparse high grasses. Marmot and pica also find a welcoming habitat in the surrounding boulder fields.

White Pine Lake provides a beautiful setting for a relaxing lunch before you return. By crossing the boulder fields and ridge directly to the west, you can also drop into the Red Pine Lake basin and return to the trailhead from there. This traverse involves some scrambling and navigating your way along an unmarked route before arriving at Red Pine Lake, about 360 feet below White Pine Lake's elevation. This makes for an enjoyable loop hike, but come prepared with a detailed topo map and solid route-finding skills before attempting the traverse.

Note: White Pine Lake is adjacent to but not located in the Lone Peak Wilderness Area. Bicycles are permitted on the trail all the way to the lake, although you can expect some rocky terrain.

NEARBY ACTIVITIES

The White Pine Trail offers some spectacular scenery and a beautiful lake, but no major waterfalls. If you yearn to see a canyon stream spraying and cascading over granite cliffs, try Lisa Falls, just 2.5 miles down the canyon from the White Pine Trailhead. The Lisa Falls trailhead is located on the north side of the road. The path climbs along the stream for 0.1 mile before arriving at the falls.

PFEIFFERHORN (via Red Pine Lake) 39

IN BRIEF

Pfeifferhorn is one of the best summit hikes in the Wasatch. A scenic canyon trail leads to a glistening alpine lake. A challenging traverse over a saddle of large boulders and a steep scramble to the 11,326-foot summit offer wonderful views.

DESCRIPTION

The Pfeifferhorn (identified as Little Matterhorn Peak on USGS maps) is recognizable from the floor of both Salt Lake Valley and Utah Valley by its distinctive pyramid shape and its location behind Lone Peak on Little Cottonwood's southern ridge. Lying within the rugged Lone Peak Wilderness Area, the mountain was named in honor of Chuck Pfeiffer, an early leader of the Wasatch Mountain Club.

A climb of the Pfeifferhorn offers hikers an excellent variety of trail scenery, alpine lakes, boulder-hopping, and a challenging scramble to the top. In spite of the challenges, the Pfeifferhorn remains one of the most popular summit climbs in the Wasatch.

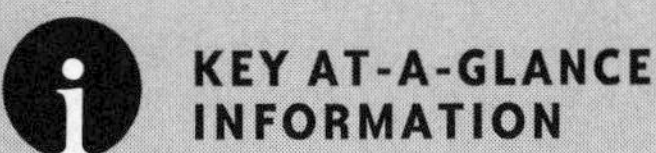

KEY AT-A-GLANCE INFORMATION

LENGTH: 7 miles round-trip to Red Pine Lake; 10 miles round-trip to Pfeifferhorn summit

ELEVATION GAIN: 3,628 feet

ELEVATION AT TRAILHEAD: 7,698 feet

CONFIGURATION: Out-and-back

DIFFICULTY: Difficult

SCENERY: Wooded canyon, alpine lakes, summit views

EXPOSURE: Mostly shaded to Red Pine Lake; partially shaded to saddle; no shade from saddle to summit

TRAFFIC: Moderate

TRAIL SURFACE: Dirt and rock to lake; mostly rock from lake to summit

HIKING TIME: 7–9 hours

WATER REQUIREMENTS: 2–3 liters. Water in nearby streams and lakes may be purified.

SEASON: Late spring–early fall

ACCESS: No fees for access or parking

MAPS: USGS Dromedary Peak

FACILITIES: Restrooms and water at trailhead

DOGS: Pets and horses are prohibited in Little Cottonwood Canyon, a protected watershed.

Directions →

From Salt Lake City, go south on I-15 to 9000 South (Exit 295). Turn left onto 9000 South (UT 209) and proceed east toward the mouth of Little Cottonwood Canyon for 7.2 miles. Along the way, UT 209 changes names from 9000 South to 9400 South and eventually becomes Little Cottonwood Road. At the mouth of Little Cottonwood Canyon, UT 209 comes to a junction with UT 210. Turn right onto UT 210 and continue up Little Cottonwood Canyon for 5.2 miles to the White Pine trailhead parking lot on your right.

GPS Trailhead Coordinates

UTM Zone (WGS84) 12T

Easting 0442326

Northing 4491888

Latitude N 40° 34' 32.2"

Longitude W 111° 40' 52.1"

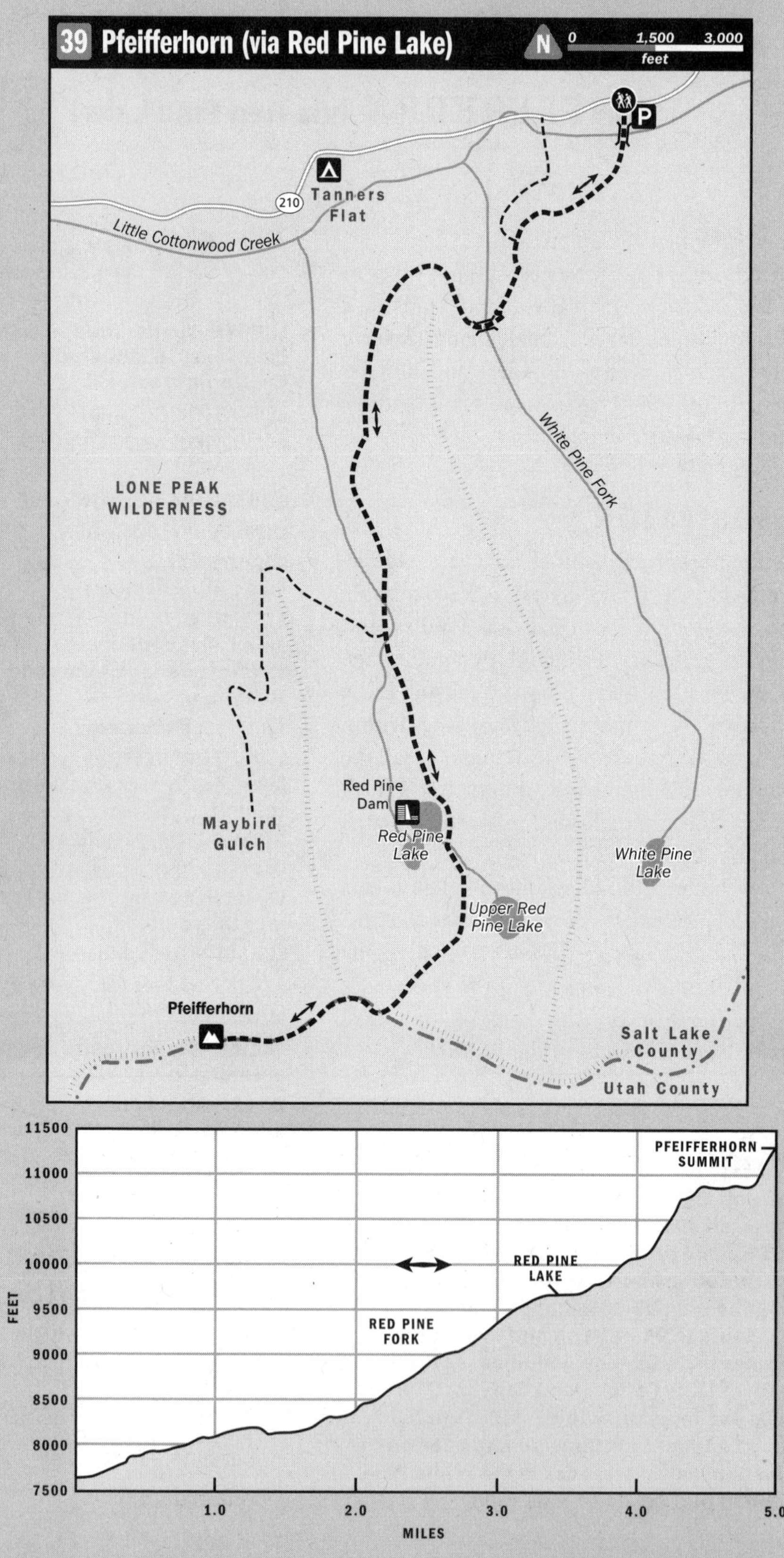
39 Pfeifferhorn (via Red Pine Lake)
N
0
1,500
3,000
feet
P
210
Tanners Flat
Little Cottonwood Creek
White Pine Fork
LONE PEAK WILDERNESS
Red Pine Dam
Red Pine Lake
Maybird Gulch
White Pine Lake
Upper Red Pine Lake
Pfeifferhorn
Salt Lake County
Utah County
11500
11000
10500
10000
9500
9000
8500
8000
7500
FEET
PFEIFFERHORN SUMMIT
RED PINE LAKE
RED PINE FORK
1.0
2.0
3.0
4.0
5.0
MILES

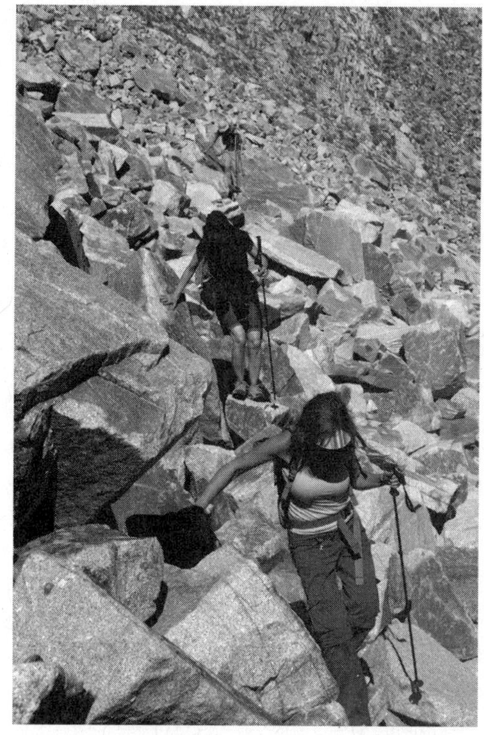

Boulder-hopping on the way to the summit

From the White Pine trailhead parking lot, the trail descends to the south to cross Little Cottonwood Creek over a wooden bridge. The trail then begins with a steady ascent along an old mining road into the mouth of White Pine Canyon. An early start will give you the best opportunity to spot deer and moose on the trail below Red Pine Lake, and will give you plenty of time to reach the summit.

At 0.8 miles, you arrive at a junction where the mining road ascends to the left on its way to White Pine Lake. Avoid this route by continuing straight ahead for another 20 feet. Here the trail climbs to the left before immediately turning right and crossing a bridge over White Pine Fork. After the bridge crossing, the trail ascends to the northwest as it makes its way around the canyon wall to enter Red Pine Canyon. As the trail moves up into the canyon, you'll have a fleeting glimpse of the Pfeifferhorn to the south.

At 2.1 miles from the trailhead, you'll arrive at a steep stretch littered with boulders and marked by avalanche scarring. Soon the trail unites with Red Pine Creek and levels out a bit. At 2.5 miles you'll pass the cutoff and bridge to Maybird Gulch on your right. Immediately after the cutoff, the trail passes through a boggy meadow where the stream spills onto the trail and passes mine tailings on the left. A steep, rocky section of trail brings you to the shores of Red Pine Lake. With a steady pace, the hike from the trailhead to Red Pine Lake can be accomplished in just under two hours.

Sitting on the north shore of Red Pine Lake, take a moment to enjoy the view and plan your route to the summit. The Pfeifferhorn is not visible from Red Pine Lake, but it lies to the southwest, obscured by the rocky slopes to the west of the lake. The easiest, most reliable route to the summit starts by following the trail along the east side of the lake. Although it may look more direct and very appealing, avoid the talus boulder field to the west of the lake.

Arriving at the south end of the lake, pass a large rock slab the size of a school bus on your right. Cross over the creek that descends from Upper Red Pine Lake and climb a beautiful section of steep trail leading through fragrant stands of spruce. This trail winds its way up and to the southwest, eventually rising above the wooded area onto a steep, rocky slope leading toward the saddle.

The most impressive feature of the climb from Red Pine Lake to the Pfeifferhorn summit is the quality of the rock. Often mistaken for granite, the talus slopes, saddle, and summit of the Pfeifferhorn are composed almost entirely of quartz monzonite, an intrusive igneous rock. Quartz monzonite provides an excellent climbing and nonskid hiking surface, making boulder-hopping on the route a true delight.

Once at the saddle, you'll have a clear view of the Pfeifferhorn down the ridgeline to the west. But before ascending the final 500 feet to the summit, you need to traverse a 100-yard-long, knife-edged, boulder-capped saddle. Although no technical climbing equipment is necessary, it does require moving carefully over and around large boulders with some exposure. You'll want to stow your trekking poles in your pack and consider bringing along a pair of gloves to protect your hands. Most hikers pick a route that stays primarily to the right or north side of the ridge.

Once off the boulders, the trail resumes its steep climb up a chute to the left of the peak's southeast ridge. From the massive slabs that form the small summit platform, you'll have great views into the populated valleys. The most intriguing views, though, are those directly below as you survey the wild, rocky, and rugged terrain of the Lone Peak Wilderness. From the Pfeifferhorn summit, you'll find some challenging descent routes into Maybird Gulch and Bells Canyon to the north and west, but most day hikers are content with a return to Red Pine Lake and back to Little Cottonwood Canyon.

Note: Red Pine Lake and the Pfeifferhorn are located in the Lone Peak Wilderness Area. Little Cottonwood Canyon may have avalanche closures from November 1 to May 15.

NEARBY ACTIVITIES

The brilliant quartz monzonite that graces the summit of both Pfeifferhorn and Lone Peak was also admired by early Mormon pioneers, who quarried the stone for the building of the Salt Lake Temple. The Temple Quarry Trail is a 0.3-mile, wheelchair-accessible interpretive loop trail that will give you a greater appreciation for the monumental effort involved in quarrying stone. The trailhead is located at the mouth of Little Cottonwood Canyon on UT 209 just south of its intersection with UT 210, the main canyon road.

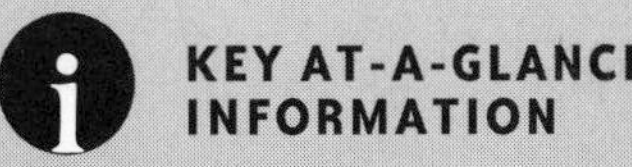

AMERICAN FORK TWIN PEAKS 40

IN BRIEF

This challenging route along a knife ridge and up a steep rocky slope leads to the dual summit that forms the highest peak in Salt Lake County. In just over a mile one-way, you'll achieve a first-class mountaineering scramble capped by commanding views in all directions.

DESCRIPTION

Let's begin with a pop quiz: What is the most frequently summited 11,000-plus-foot peak in Utah?

If you guessed Mount Timpanogos or even Kings Peak, you're thinking clearly; but neither of those peaks come close to the hundreds of skiers and summer visitors who reach the summit of 11,000-foot Hidden Peak at the top of Snowbird's Aerial Tram. The highest lift-accessed peak in the Wasatch, Hidden Peak is also a convenient trailhead for climbing American Fork Twin Peaks along the ridge to the southwest. In spite of the crowds that ride the tram to the top of Hidden Peak, very few ever make the traverse to the summit of

KEY AT-A-GLANCE INFORMATION

LENGTH: 2.2 miles round-trip
ELEVATION GAIN: 660 feet (from top of tram)
ELEVATION AT TRAILHEAD (SUMMIT OF HIDDEN PEAK, AT THE TOP OF THE SNOWBIRD AERIAL TRAM): 11,000 feet
CONFIGURATION: Out-and-back
DIFFICULTY: Moderate
SCENERY: High-alpine rock slopes and spectacular views
EXPOSURE: No shade on trail
TRAFFIC: Light
TRAIL SURFACE: Rock and dirt
HIKING TIME: 2.5–3 hours
WATER REQUIREMENTS: 1–1.5 liters
SEASON: Late spring, summer, early fall
ACCESS: Hike lies on US Forest Service land accessed through the Snowbird Resort. You must purchase a ticket to ride the aerial tram to the Hidden Peak summit.
MAPS: USGS Dromedary Peak, Trails Illustrated Wasatch Front (709)
FACILITIES: Restrooms and water available at the Hidden Peak trailhead
DOGS: Pets and horses are prohibited in Little Cottonwood Canyon, a protected watershed.

Directions

From Salt Lake City, go south on I-15 to 9000 South (Exit 295). Turn left onto 9000 South (UT 209) and proceed east toward the mouth of Little Cottonwood Canyon for 7.2 miles. Along the way, UT 209 changes names from 9000 South to 9400 South and eventually becomes Little Cottonwood Road. At the mouth of Little Cottonwood Canyon, UT 209 comes to a junction with UT 210. Turn right onto UT 210 and continue up Little Cottonwood Canyon for 8 miles to the Snowbird parking area on your right. The tram base is located in the Snowbird Center on the Plaza Deck.

GPS Trailhead Coordinates

UTM Zone (WGS84) 12T
Easting 0444584
Northing 4492605
Latitude N 40° 33' 38.4"
Longitude W 111° 38' 43.6"

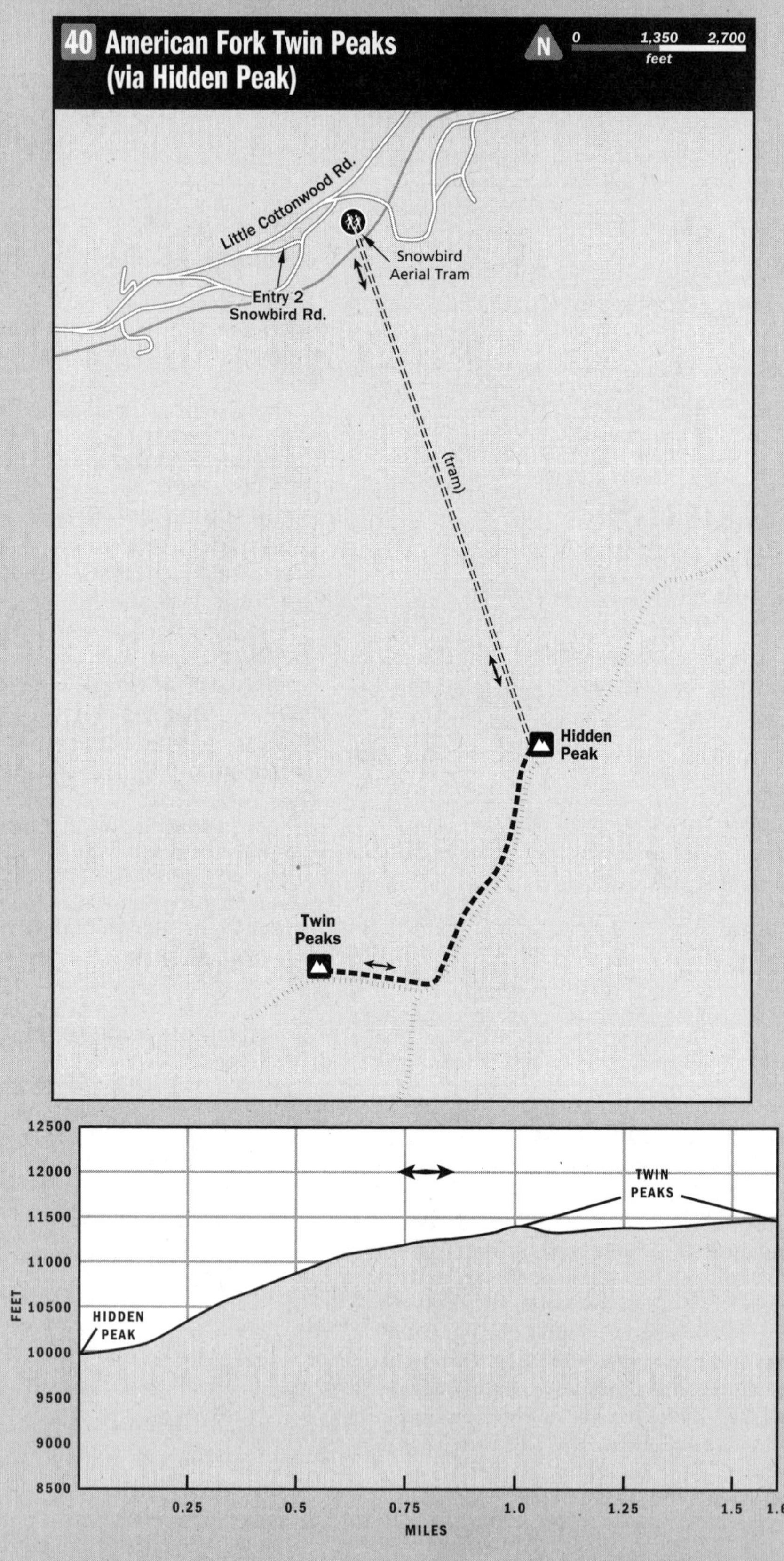
40 American Fork Twin Peaks (via Hidden Peak)
N
0
1,350
2,700
feet
Little Cottonwood Rd.
Snowbird Aerial Tram
Entry 2 Snowbird Rd.
(tram)
Hidden Peak
Twin Peaks
12500
12000
11500
11000
10500
10000
9500
9000
8500
FEET
HIDDEN PEAK
TWIN PEAKS
0.25
0.5
0.75
1.0
1.25
1.5
1.6
MILES

Twin Peaks. You might enjoy the entire route to yourself, even on a summer weekend.

American Fork Twin Peaks lies across the canyon and to the east of Broads Fork (or Salt Lake) Twin Peaks. The East Twin is 11,433 feet and the West Twin is 11,489 feet, making the West Twin the highest peak in Salt Lake County. The ridgeline constitutes the county line, with Utah County lying to the south. The scramble from Hidden Peak to Twin Peaks is one of the more challenging sections of a longer hike from Albion Basin to Red Pine Lake known as the Bullion Divide.

From the top of the tram, walk down the road to the southwest that leads into Mineral Basin. About 0.1 mile down the road, the rocky thumb of a ridge forms to the west. Ascend the ridge along a faint trail as it becomes rockier and more jagged. An occasional subalpine fir or limber pine will dot the ridgeline's rocks, but for the most part the route is treeless, even as it dips below the 11,000-foot tree line.

As the knife ridge dips down to an elevation of about 10,800 feet, you'll encounter the most challenging sections of the trail, with some exposure and long sections that require the use of both hands and some basic climbing moves. Along the way you may be tempted to take a lower route, but you'll find that the ridgeline rocks are large and stable, while the rocks just 8 to 10 feet below the ridge are small and loose.

As you near the end of the ridgeline scramble, a formation of black rock leads up toward the eastern slope of East Twin. Follow this dike while still staying close to the top of the ridge. Use extreme caution: the black rock has particularly sharp edges. Even the slightest fall could result in severe injury.

The 100-yard ascent from the knife ridge to the summit of East Twin follows a faint but discernible trail that zigzags up the steep, rocky slope. You'll often spot mountain goats that graze on these slopes. From the bald, rounded summit of East Twin, it's a leisurely 10-minute stroll along rocky tundra to the West Twin summit. Another route from East Twin leads to a little-known and rarely visited South Twin, at the end of a gentle tundra ridge 0.3 miles to the south. Most summer days will be clear and refreshing at the summit, but don't come if storm clouds form: with any chance of lightning, Twin Peaks' exposed ridge and expansive summit is the last place you want to be.

You'll find exceptional views in all directions. Some of the highlights include the back side of Mount Timpanogos, Heber Valley to the east, and the many peaks along the Little Cottonwood and Big Cottonwood ridgelines. From the summit, descend one of the steep couloirs to the north into Gad Valley or return along the ridge back to the tram at Hidden Peak.

Note: Snowbird's Aerial Tram achieves 2,900 feet of vertical lift in about 1.6 miles and offers a convenient 11,000 foot starting point. You can also climb Twin Peaks unassisted from Snowbird's Gad Valley.

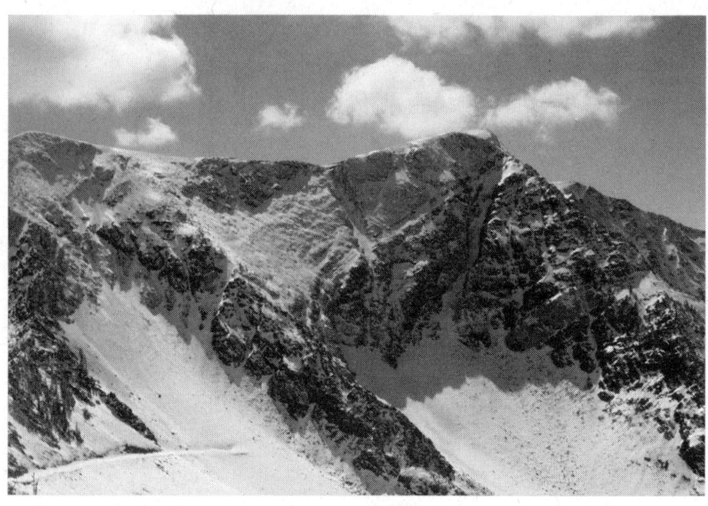

East and West Twin Peaks, viewed from Snowbird's Hidden Peak

NEARBY ACTIVITIES

Snowbird offers a varied selection of summer activities for all ages and interests. Whether you rent bikes and mountain scooters or bring your own, you can ride on easier trails near the base or on the expert trails that descend from the top of the tram. ATV and horseback riding tours are available in Mineral Basin. Other choices: spend the day riding the alpine slide, zipline, and mechanical bull or doing acrobatics on the bungee trampoline, then visit the Cliff Spa to recover. You'll also find restaurants, shopping, and accommodations on-site. For a schedule of events, concerts, classes, and activities, visit **www.snowbird.com.**

BELLS CANYON 41

IN BRIEF

Bells Canyon is a long, deep, beautiful canyon with cascading falls, lush vegetation, and a rocky cirque. The trail is steep and challenging, but the varied views and granite setting are spectacular.

DESCRIPTION

Rising from the valley floor to a high glacial bowl below the summit of Lone Peak, Bells Canyon is as appealing to geologists as it is to hikers. Because the glacier that formed this canyon reached the foot of the mountains and the elevation of Lake Bonneville, Bells Canyon is geologically unique. This allows geologists to study glacial advance and the lake's rising elevation. Equally fascinating are the exposed Precambrian rocks at the mouth of Bells Canyon, some of the oldest rocks on earth.

Located immediately south of Little Cottonwood Canyon, Bells Canyon is easily accessible from a low-elevation suburban trailhead. From the parking area, the trail makes a steep switchback ascent onto the moraine of the glacier that once filled the canyon.

After 0.7 miles of sage-and-oak-covered foothills, you come to a dirt utility road leading up toward the mouth of the canyon.

KEY AT-A-GLANCE INFORMATION

LENGTH: 5.6 miles round-trip to upper waterfall; 8.4 miles to Upper Bells Canyon Reservoir

ELEVATION GAIN: 2,361 feet to upper waterfall; 4,149 feet to Upper Bells Canyon Reservoir

ELEVATION AT TRAILHEAD: 5,239 feet

CONFIGURATION: Out-and-back

DIFFICULTY: Difficult

SCENERY: Deep wooded canyon, waterfalls, towering canyon walls, and some valley views

EXPOSURE: Mostly shaded

TRAFFIC: Light

TRAIL SURFACE: Dirt and rock

HIKING TIME: 2.5–3 hours to upper waterfall; 6–8 hours to Upper Bells Canyon Reservoir

WATER REQUIREMENTS: 2–3 liters. Water in stream and reservoir can be purified.

SEASON: Spring, summer, fall

ACCESS: No access fees or permits

MAPS: USGS Draper; Trails Illustrated Wasatch Front (709), Uinta National Forest (701)

FACILITIES: Restrooms and water at trailhead

DOGS: Prohibited in Bells Canyon, a protected watershed

Directions

From Salt Lake City, go south on I-15 to 9000 South (Exit 295). Turn left onto 9000 South (UT 209) and proceed east toward the mouth of Little Cottonwood Canyon for 6.1 miles. Along the way, UT 209 changes names from 9000 South to 9400 South and eventually becomes East Little Cottonwood Road. The Granite trailhead, which provides access to Bells Canyon and other local trails is located at 3470 East Little Cottonwood Road.

GPS Trailhead Coordinates

UTM Zone (WGS84) 12T

Easting 0432573

Northing 4491532

Latitude N 40° 34' 18.3"

Longitude W 111° 47' 48.8"

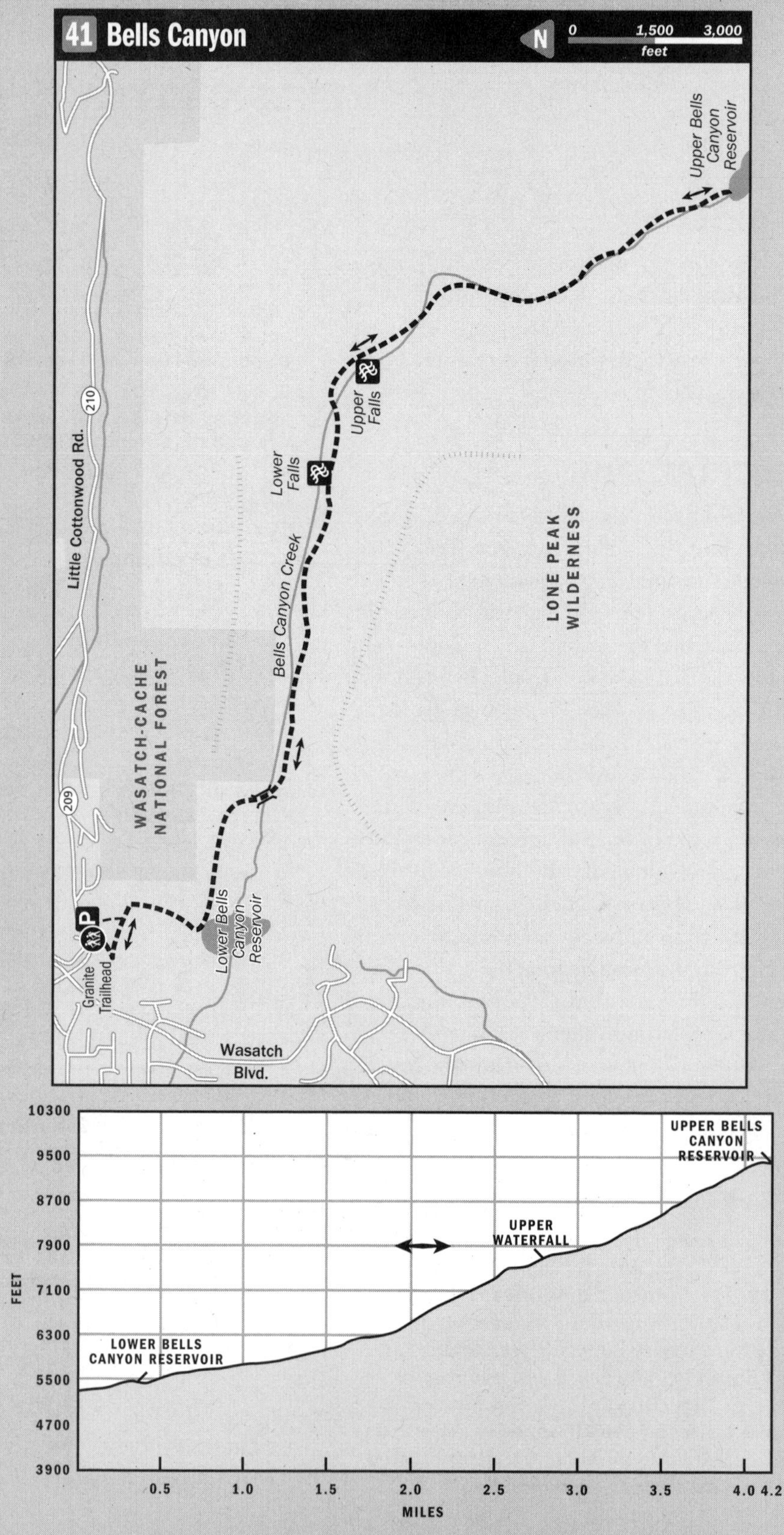
41 Bells Canyon
N
0
1,500
3,000
feet
Upper Bells Canyon Reservoir
Upper Falls
Lower Falls
Bells Canyon Creek
Little Cottonwood Rd.
210
209
LONE PEAK WILDERNESS
WASATCH-CACHE NATIONAL FOREST
P
Lower Bells Canyon Reservoir
Granite Trailhead
Wasatch Blvd.
10300
9500
8700
7900
7100
6300
5500
4700
3900
FEET
UPPER BELLS CANYON RESERVOIR
UPPER WATERFALL
LOWER BELLS CANYON RESERVOIR
0.5
1.0
1.5
2.0
2.5
3.0
3.5
4.0
4.2
MILES

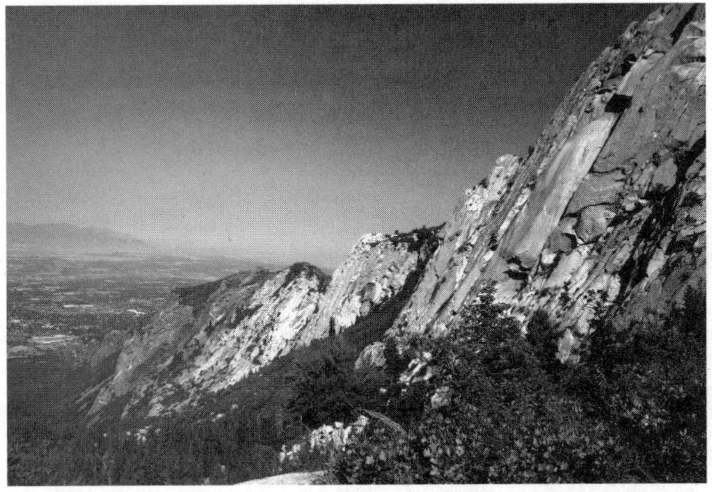

Steep canyon walls and valley views from the Bells Canyon Trail

The shallow waters of the drained Lower Bells Canyon Reservoir are on the right. You can frequently see such migrating waterfowl as ducks and Canada geese around the pondlike remains of the reservoir, and deer on the slopes above it.

After 100 yards on the utility road, take an unmarked trail that leads off to the left. This trail ascends gently at first through bigtooth maple and curly-leaf mountain mahogany. At 1.3 miles from the trailhead, the path crosses a sturdy wooden footbridge to the south side of a stream.

The trail enters the mouth of Bells Canyon along a granite-strewn pathway that is sometimes overgrown but easy to follow. As you ascend the canyon, conifers become more predominant and aspens begin to appear. Along the way, several spur trails depart from the main trail, but stay on the main trail, defined by the granite boulders. At about 1.7 miles from the trailhead, you'll come to a junction with a spur trail leading off to the left. A steep descent on this spur takes you to the base of the lower falls. You may want to make this the destination for a short day hike.

From the lower falls, the main trail continues its vertical ascent along a staircase of granite boulders. After 2.2 miles from the trailhead, the steps ease up a bit, but the dirt trail is still punctuated with plenty of granite.

At 2.6 miles, the trail meets with the stream on the left and a large granite slab on the right. Follow the trail across the slab, and within a few minutes you'll arrive at the smaller upper falls. This is a great destination in its own right and certainly worth a rest stop and trail snack. At this elevation the forest is dense and moist; ferns and moss line the trail, and spruce and aspen provide the canopy.

To continue upward, look for a crude log bridge 100 feet below the waterfall. The bridge crosses the stream to the north side of the creek. This trail leads initially through a dense passage of fern before ascending a granite slope.

Bells Canyon waterfall

The trail passes through a meadow and crosses the creek over another log bridge on its way to the Upper Bells Canyon Reservoir.

Set within a rocky cirque, the upper reservoir is a remote, pristine glacial lake at an elevation of 9,388 feet. The reservoir is surrounded by Lone Peak, Bearstooth, and Thunder Mountain. Any routes leading beyond the reservoir in the direction of those peaks require difficult scrambling and technical climbing expertise. The most reliable way out of the canyon is to retrace your route and descend the steep granite stairs back to the trailhead.

Note: Bells Canyon lies within the federally protected Lone Peak Wilderness Area.

NEARBY ACTIVITIES

The Rocky Mouth Canyon Trail is a short scenic hike through a slot canyon to a beautiful waterfall. The trailhead is located at 11300 South Wasatch Boulevard in Sandy. Be sure to park at the trailhead and not in the neighborhood. The first quarter mile follows a sidewalk to a dirt trail, which continues another quarter mile to the waterfall.

LONE PEAK (via Jacobs Ladder) 42

IN BRIEF

The toughest, and perhaps the most rewarding, of these 60 hikes. A Lone Peak ascent demands a long, dry, steep approach into a beautiful rock bowl surrounded by towering cliffs. The final climb to the summit over massive rock slabs offers spectacular views.

KEY AT-A-GLANCE INFORMATION

LENGTH: 12 miles round-trip
ELEVATION GAIN: 5,460 feet
ELEVATION AT TRAILHEAD: 5,793 feet
CONFIGURATION: Out-and-back
DIFFICULTY: Difficult
SCENERY: Rocky high-alpine basins, rock cliffs, exceptional summit views
EXPOSURE: Partial shade in lower bowl between 9,200 and 10,000 feet elevation. Remainder of trail is fully exposed to the sun. Dry, exposed, south-facing slopes can be particularly hot in the summer.
TRAFFIC: Moderate
TRAIL SURFACE: Dirt and rock
HIKING TIME: 8–11 hours
WATER REQUIREMENTS: 3–4 liters. No water on trail after spring snowmelt.
SEASON: Late spring, summer, and early fall
ACCESS: No fees for parking or access. Corner Canyon Road is open from 6 a.m. to 10 p.m. up to the Ghost Falls trailhead.
MAPS: USGS Draper; Trails Illustrated Uinta National Forest (701)
FACILITIES: No restrooms or water at the trailhead

DESCRIPTION

Lone Peak is the prominent summit that dominates both the south end of the Salt Lake Valley and the north end of Utah Valley. Its west-lying ridge trails off into the valley at Point of the Mountain. The jagged spires and sheer rock face of the 11,253-foot summit are identifiable from miles around. But only those who hike into the Lone Peak Wilderness Area and approach the mountain's higher reaches can appreciate the impressive and inspiring qualities of Lone Peak.

While many routes lead to the summit of Lone Peak, all are difficult and require 5,000 to 6,000 feet of vertical elevation gain.

Directions

From Salt Lake City, go south on I-15 to 12300 South (Exit 291). Turn left and proceed east on 12300 South (UT 71) for 1.9 miles to 1300 East. Turn right and drive south on 1300 East for 0.2 miles to the traffic circle. Enter the traffic circle and make a three-quarter loop, exiting eastbound onto Pioneer Road. Continue east on Pioneer Road for 1 mile to 2000 East. Turn right on 2000 East and continue south for 0.2 miles to the Orson Smith trailhead located at 12601 South 2000 East. From the Orson Smith trailhead parking area, turn right on Upper Corner Canyon Road, a dirt road that leads south. Continue on Upper Corner Canyon Road for 2.6 miles to the Ghost Falls trailhead parking area.

GPS Trailhead Coordinates

UTM Zone (WGS84) 12T
Easting 0430757
Northing 4482985
Latitude N 40° 29' 39.3"
Longitude W 111° 49' 00.1"

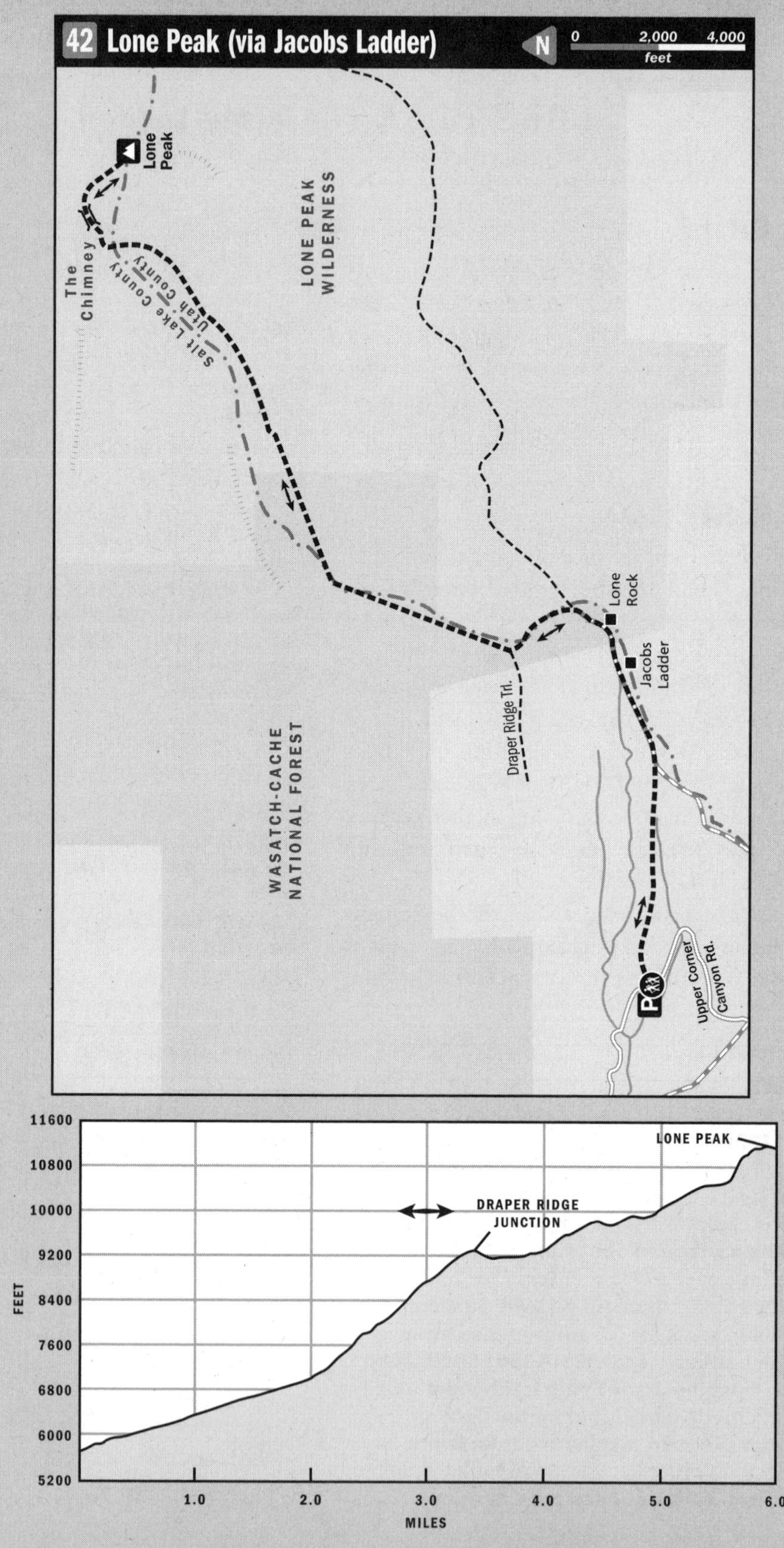

42 Lone Peak (via Jacobs Ladder)
N
0
2,000
4,000
feet
Lone Peak
LONE PEAK WILDERNESS
The Chimney
Utah County
Salt Lake County
Lone Rock
Jacobs Ladder
Draper Ridge Trl.
WASATCH-CACHE NATIONAL FOREST
Upper Corner Canyon Rd.
11600
10800
10000
9200
8400
7600
6800
6000
5200
FEET
LONE PEAK
DRAPER RIDGE JUNCTION
1.0
2.0
3.0
4.0
5.0
6.0
MILES

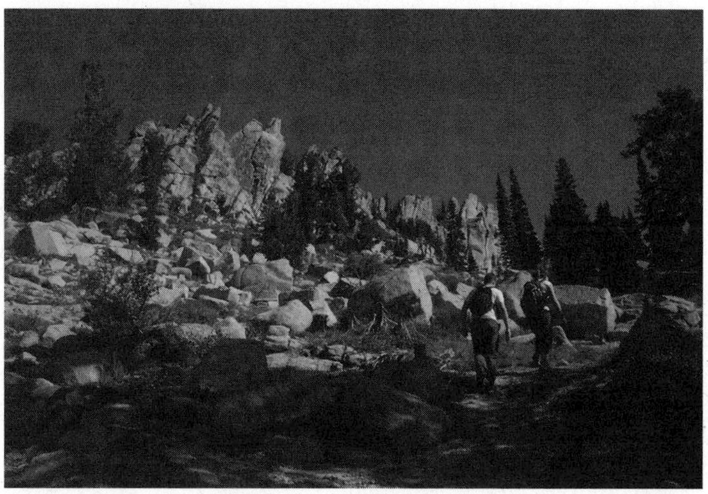

Ascending through boulders to the Lone Peak cirque

Population growth in Draper, where residential subdivisions abut national forest, has diminished access to some trails. The Jacobs Ladder Trail, starting at the Ghost Falls trailhead (commonly referred to as the Jacobs Ladder trailhead), has emerged in recent years as one of the more popular and accessible summit routes. Like other Lone Peak trails, Jacobs Ladder, leading to the Draper Ridge, is long, dry, and steep.

From the trailhead parking area, the trail makes a quick rise to the north and east before topping out on a scrubby ridge with Corner Canyon on the right. The unmarked trail follows this ridge in an easterly direction as it parallels, merges, and diverges from various Jeep roads and ATV tracks. At 1.3 miles, the trail approaches a limestone outcropping known as Lone Rock and curves north along a much narrower trail to begin the Jacobs Ladder climb. It's a steep ascent through Gambel oak, sage, and curly-leaf mountain mahogany, leading up to Draper Ridge.

At 3.3 miles, the Jacobs Ladder Trail meets the Draper Ridge Trail on a dry slope at an elevation of 9,120 feet. At this point you've been climbing for about two hours and you've gained more than 3,300 feet, or about two-thirds of your overall vertical ascent for the hike. Take a short rest on the nearby log and know that the toughest part of the trail is behind you—and the most beautiful section is right in front of you.

From the Draper Ridge junction, the trail descends slightly into a meadow dotted with quartz monzonite and lined with conifers. As it rises above the meadow, the trail crosses giant slabs of rock, appropriately marked by cairns. From the meadow to the summit, the trail surface is predominately rock, dotted with spruce and fir, then alpine tundra nearing the tree line. Crossing exposed slabs before entering a narrow, boulder-strewn draw, the trail leads to the upper cirque. Along this rock route it's easy to lose the trail, but as long as you maintain an ascent

The summit spires of Lone Peak from the cirque

in a northeasterly direction toward the upper cirque, you're on track.

Arriving at the cirque, you'll be awestruck by the full view of Lone Peak's summit cliffs on the right. As you stand in the cirque facing due north, the cliffs will be at the three o'clock position. Either follow the cairns or walk up toward the boxy chute at one o'clock known as "the Chimney." Some easy Class 3 scrambling will lead you up the Chimney.

As you emerge from the Chimney on the west side of the ridge, the trail crosses over the ridge and follows a faint route up a rocky slope to the large boulders that comprise the summit formation. As you make your final approach to the summit, cautiously weaving your way through the massive angular slabs, it's hard to ignore the stunning majesty of the peak and cliffs in front of you. Lone Peak is one of the most breathtakingly beautiful summits in the United States.

The summit block of Lone Peak has enough space for just a few climbers to sit and enjoy the views. Lone Peak is not the highest peak in the Wasatch—it's not even the highest peak in the Lone Peak Wilderness Area—but it does have the most commanding views. Because of its forefront position, Lone Peak is one summit from which you have unobstructed views of every other major peak in the Wasatch, as well as extended views to the north and south. Take time to enjoy these views before beginning your long, dry descent back to the trailhead.

Note: The long distance, lack of water, and exposed rock scrambling to the summit make this trail unsuitable for dogs. Lone Peak lies within the federally protected Lone Peak Wilderness Area. Horses, bicycles, motorized vehicles, and open campfires are not permitted.

NEARBY ACTIVITIES

The Orson Smith trailhead, located at 12601 South 2000 East, provides a convenient, well-maintained starting point for many area hikes. The park has restrooms, water, picnic tables, and signs showing the area's trail system. From the trailhead you can access the Bonneville Shoreline Trail, the Aqueduct Trail, the Orson Smith Trail, and other connector trails. You can also reach two Lone Peak trails—Little Willow Trail and Cherry Canyon Trail—from the Orson Smith trailhead.

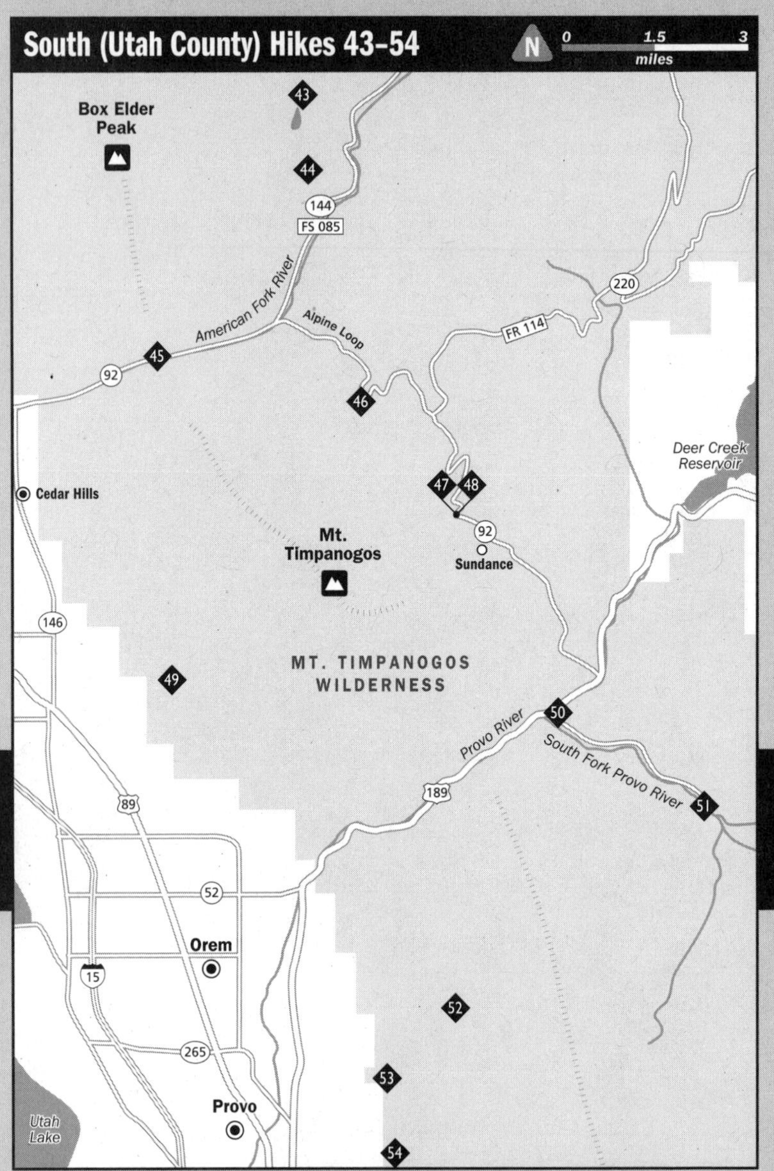
South (Utah County) Hikes 43–54
N
0
1.5
3
miles
Box Elder Peak
Mt. Timpanogos
MT. TIMPANOGOS WILDERNESS
American Fork River
Alpine Loop
FR 114
FS 085
144
220
92
146
89
189
52
15
265
Cedar Hills
Sundance
Deer Creek Reservoir
Provo River
South Fork Provo River
Orem
Provo
Utah Lake
43
44
45
46
47
48
49
50
51
52
53
54

SOUTH (UTAH COUNTY)

43 SILVER LAKE

KEY AT-A-GLANCE INFORMATION

LENGTH: 4.4 miles round-trip
ELEVATION GAIN: 1,449 feet
ELEVATION AT TRAILHEAD: 7,536 feet
CONFIGURATION: Out-and-back
DIFFICULTY: Moderate
SCENERY: Alpine lake, granite ridgeline, canyon views, woodlands
EXPOSURE: Mostly shaded for first mile; partially shaded for the second.
TRAFFIC: Moderate
TRAIL SURFACE: Dirt
HIKING TIME: 2.5–3.5 hours
WATER REQUIREMENTS: 1–2 liters. Water from stream and lake can be purified.
SEASON: Spring, summer, fall
ACCESS: You reach the hike, which is located in the Lone Peak Wilderness Area, through American Fork Canyon, a fee access area. There are no parking fees.
MAPS: USGS Dromedary Peak, Trails Illustrated Uinta National Forest (701)
FACILITIES: Restrooms at trailhead
DOGS: Permitted on leash in the Lone Peak Wilderness Area
SPECIAL COMMENTS: No mechanized vehicles, bikes, or horses are permitted on the trail.

GPS Trailhead Coordinates

UTM Zone (WGS84) 12T
Easting 0444389
Northing 4484231
Latitude N 40° 30' 25.2"
Longitude W 111° 39' 22.8"

IN BRIEF

Breathtaking alpine scenery, abundant wildlife, and a well-designed new trail to a blue lake nestled in a glacial bowl make Silver Lake one of the most perfect hikes in Utah County. It's a great day hike, but you'll want to stay longer.

DESCRIPTION

What begins as a pleasant and shaded uphill stroll concludes with one of the most dramatic wilderness settings in Utah. You'll think you've been transported to Yosemite in the Sierra Nevada. It has all the iconic elements of the far-more-famous national park: towering gray granite walls, blue glacial lakes, spruce and fir trees, cascading waterfalls, glistening streams, and moose—lots of moose.

The 3 miles of dirt road leading to the trailhead and its location within the Lone Peak Wilderness Area discourage many less-serious hikers from visiting Silver Lake. As a result, the hike is not as crowded as one might expect for a jewel of this magnitude. The dirt road from Granite Flat to the trailhead at Silver Lake Flat

Directions

From Salt Lake City, take Interstate 15 south to Highland/Alpine (Exit 284). At the bottom of the off-ramp, turn left on UT 92 and continue east for 12.4 miles to the junction of UT 92 and UT 144 (FS 085). Turn left onto UT 144 toward Tibble Fork. Continue on UT 144 for 2.5 miles, to the east end of Tibble Fork Reservoir. Turn left onto the paved road going up to Granite Flat Campground. After 0.7 miles, turn right onto Forest Service Road 008 toward Silver Lake Flat, immediately before entering the Granite Flat Campground. Continue on this dirt road for 3.2 miles to Silver Lake Flat, where you'll find trailhead parking on your left at the north end of the lake.

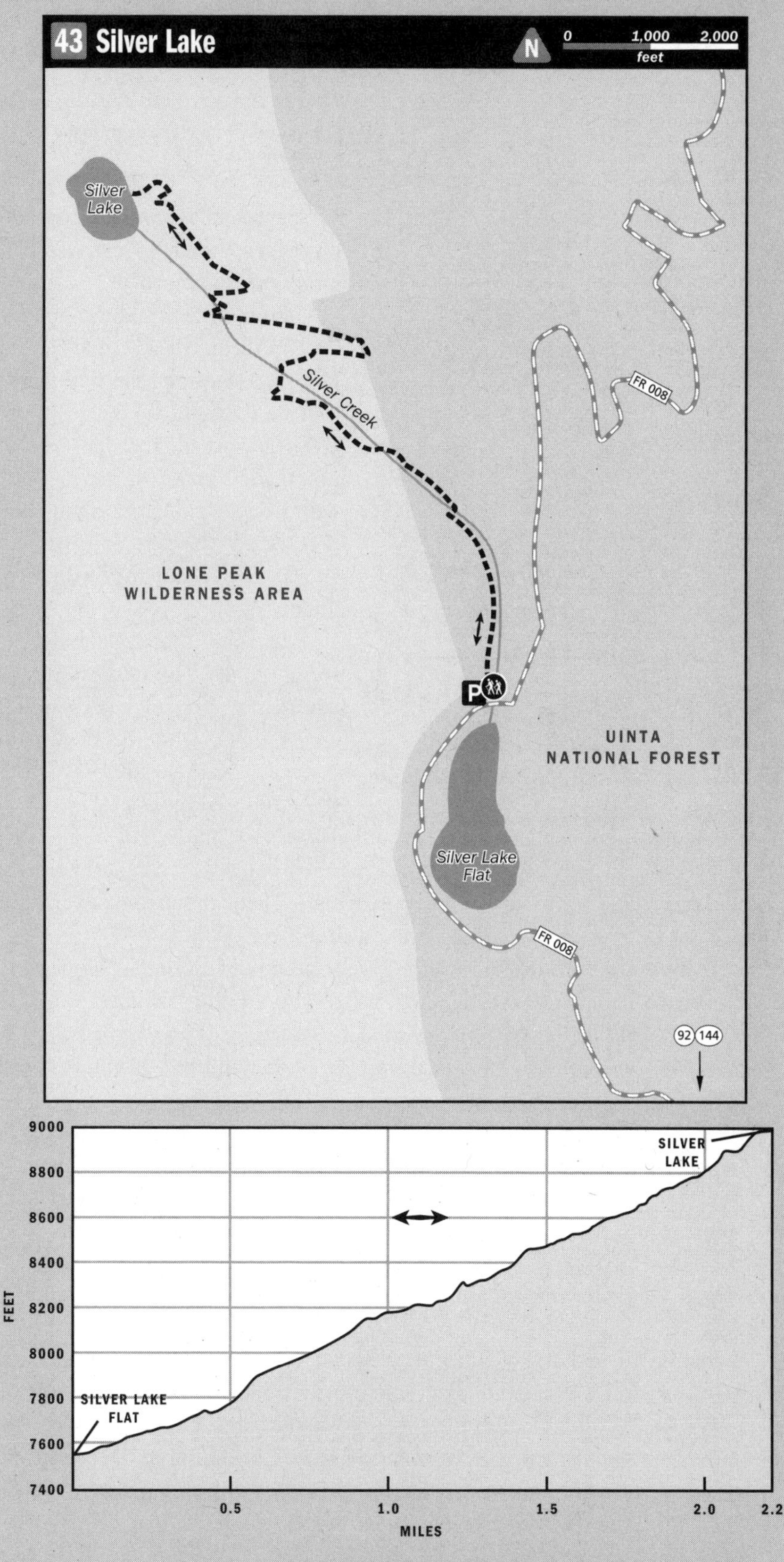
43 Silver Lake
N
0
1,000
2,000
feet
Silver Lake
Silver Creek
FR 008
LONE PEAK
WILDERNESS AREA
P
UINTA
NATIONAL FOREST
Silver Lake Flat
FR 008
92
144
9000
8800
8600
8400
8200
8000
7800
7600
7400
FEET
SILVER LAKE
SILVER LAKE FLAT
0.5
1.0
1.5
2.0
2.2
MILES

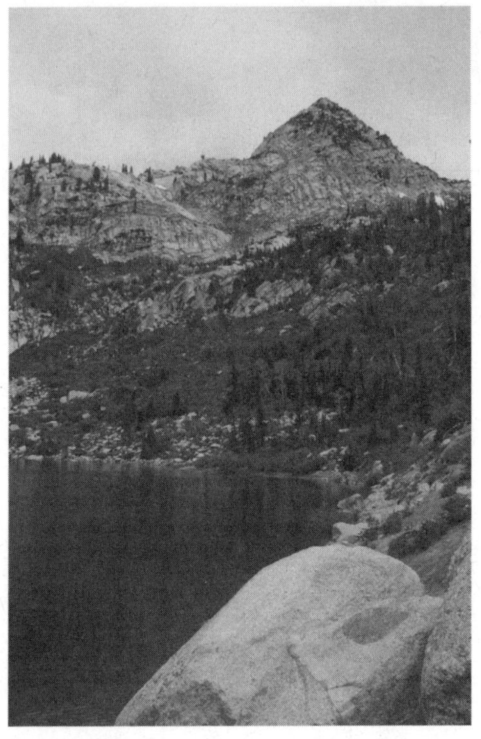

Silver Lake with White Baldy in the background

is rugged but passable for most passenger vehicles—just watch for large, protruding rocks.

From the trailhead parking area on the north side of Silver Lake Flat reservoir, take the well-marked trail to the right of the restrooms. The trail ascends through a beautiful, shaded grove of aspen dotted with Douglas-fir. Large granite boulders, many the size of a car, also appear throughout the Silver Creek drainage.

Birds fill the woodland in the spring and summer. Red-tailed hawks and golden eagles nest in the conifers, while American robins and black-headed grosbeaks share the deciduous groves.

At 0.4 miles from the trailhead, you'll pass a clearing on the right where beavers have leveled an acre or so of aspen for their dams. At 0.5 miles, you enter the Lone Peak Wilderness Area, marked by a sign. Throughout this lower drainage, you can often see deer feeding on the lush undergrowth.

At 1.1 miles the trail rises above the creek and moves up the dry slope to the east. As you emerge from the shade of the aspens, you'll find striking views of the canyons and ridgeline to the south. Along this section of the trail, watch for chokecherry bushes with their white flowers in spring and red-purple berries in summer.

When you reach the upper drainage, below the granite bowl that cradles Silver Lake, you may well spot both mountain goats and moose. Remember that a large bull moose can weigh 1,200 pounds and stand more than seven feet tall at the shoulder. Since they can be temperamental and aggressive—and will charge at high speeds if provoked—you should avoid approaching a moose and keep a safe distance. Don't come between a moose cow and its calf or between a moose and the water.

Just below Silver Lake, you'll pass a cascading waterfall along Silver Creek to the left as it drains from the lake. Subalpine fir makes its appearance at this higher elevation. Within five minutes you crest the large granite boulders that form the rim of the lake, and you've instantly arrived at the shore. Depending on the amount of snowfall and the spring temperatures, Silver Lake may well be frozen into May, and occasionally into June.

By quickly scanning the shore, you'll often spot moose grazing on the aquatic plant life in the lake. Also, keep your eyes peeled for mountain goats on the rocky slopes above the lake. The Yosemite-quality granite cathedral towering over the northeast side of the lake is White Baldy. At 11,321 feet, it is one of the higher, but least-visited peaks on the ridge. A good scramble typically approached from Red Pine Lake in Little Cottonwood Canyon, the White Baldy hike can also be approached from Silver Lake.

Once you've hiked the 2.2 miles from the trailhead to the shores of Silver Lake, circle the lake through the maze of granite boulders at its rim. You can also ascend another 0.7 miles and 900 vertical feet to the northeast and discover the smaller Silver Glance Lake with an even rockier, more rugged setting. But most visitors are content to find a natural granite countertop on which to enjoy a snack and take in the mesmerizing beauty of this alpine treasure.

NEARBY ACTIVITIES

American Fork Canyon is a year-round scenic wonder and recreational playground that's popular with all types and all ages of outdoor enthusiasts. You'll find a wide range of camping options, with wilderness and improved campgrounds, as well as many picnic and day-use facilities. Hiking, rock climbing, fishing, ATV riding, snowmobiling, cross-country skiing, horseback riding, and mountain biking are all popular pursuits in American Fork Canyon.

44 BOX ELDER PEAK

KEY AT-A-GLANCE INFORMATION

LENGTH: 9.8 miles round-trip to the summit

ELEVATION GAIN: 4,323 feet

ELEVATION AT TRAILHEAD: 6,778 feet

CONFIGURATION: Out-and-back with loop options

DIFFICULTY: Difficult

SCENERY: Mountain wilderness, glacial terrain, excellent views from summit

EXPOSURE: Mostly shaded below 8,700 feet; partially shaded to ridgeline. Fully exposed to sun above 9,700 feet

TRAFFIC: Light

TRAIL SURFACE: Dirt, becoming rockier toward summit

HIKING TIME: 6.5–8 hours

WATER REQUIREMENTS: 2–3 liters. Water in streams and at springs may be purified.

SEASON: Late spring, summer, fall

MAPS: USGS Timpanogos Cave, Trails Illustrated Uinta National Forest (701)

FACILITIES: Restrooms at trailhead. Water available at nearby campsites.

See additional information at end of Description, page 197.

GPS Trailhead Coordinates

UTM Zone (WGS84) 12T

Easting 0444382

Northing 4482347

Latitude N 40° 29' 23.9"

Longitude W 111° 39' 23.4"

IN BRIEF

One of the lesser-known big peaks of the Wasatch, Box Elder Peak offers exceptional mountain wilderness scenery and wildlife viewing. Most fit hikers can achieve the adventurous off-trail scramble to the summit.

DESCRIPTION

Tucked in the midst of slightly larger and more frequently climbed peaks, including Lone Peak, Pfeifferhorn, and Mount Timpanogos, Box Elder Peak is easily overlooked—even with its 11,101-foot triangular summit. Although marked trails ring the peak, no maintained trail leads to the summit. As a result, Box Elder gives hikers the opportunity to enjoy a stunning alpine wilderness setting at the lower elevations and then experience the challenge of a summit quest involving some scrambling and routefinding on rarely used routes.

You can access the trails around Box Elder Peak from Alpine to the west and from American Fork Canyon to the east. Most people who set out to climb the peak use the Deer Creek/Dry Creek Trail (number 043)

Directions

From Salt Lake City, take I-15 south to Highland/Alpine (Exit 284). At the bottom of the off-ramp, turn left then turn east on UT 92 and proceed 12.4 miles to the junction of UT 92 and UT 144 (FS 085). Turn left onto UT 144 toward Tibble Fork. Continue on UT 144 for 2.5 miles, to the east end of Tibble Fork Reservoir. Turn left onto the paved road going up to Granite Flat and enter the campground at 0.7 miles. You'll find trailhead parking to the right of the road at the Sandwagon Group Site, and the trailhead at the north end of the parking lot.

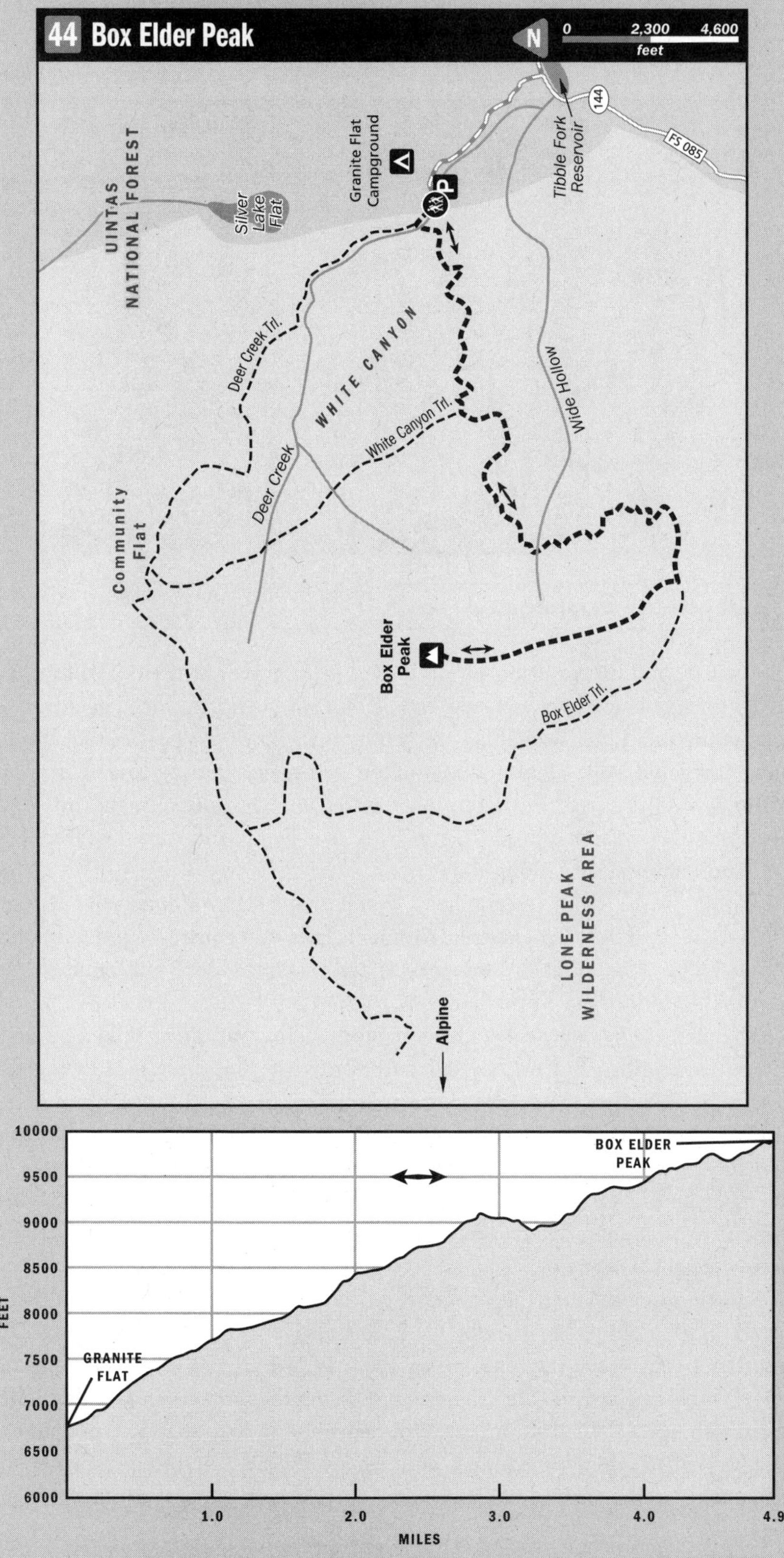
44 Box Elder Peak
N
0
2,300
4,600
feet
144
FS 085
Tibble Fork Reservoir
Granite Flat Campground
UINTAS NATIONAL FOREST
Silver Lake Flat
WHITE CANYON
Deer Creek Trl.
White Canyon Trl.
Wide Hollow
Deer Creek
Community Flat
Box Elder Peak
Box Elder Trl.
LONE PEAK WILDERNESS AREA
Alpine
BOX ELDER PEAK
GRANITE FLAT
FEET
MILES
10000
9500
9000
8500
8000
7500
7000
6500
6000
1.0
2.0
3.0
4.0
4.9

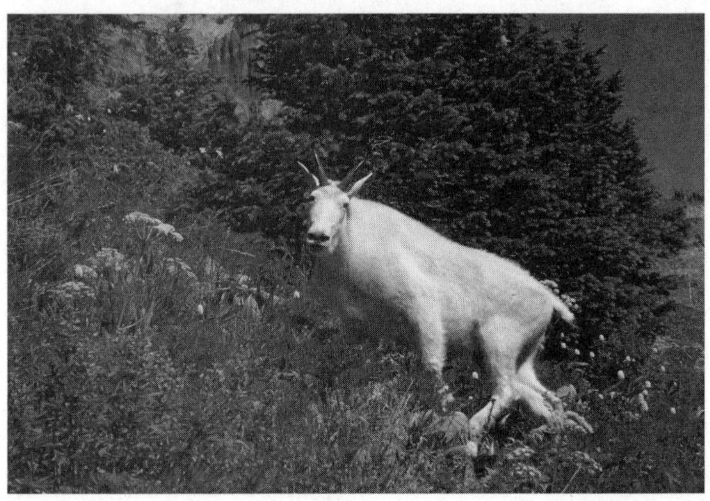

Mountain goat in American Fork Canyon

and either start at an elevation of 5,600 feet in Alpine or at the 6,778-foot level at Granite Flat. They then approach the peak from the north side. The advantage of taking the Box Elder trail along the southern flanks of the peak is that it offers a more favorable ridge route to the summit and makes getting lost or dropping into the wrong drainage less likely on the descent. Additionally, the Box Elder Peak Trail offers greater solitude, better wildlife viewing, and some less frequently visited mountain scenery along the way.

Within 100 yards of the trailhead, you'll pass a sign marking your entrance into the Lone Peak Wilderness Area. Moments later you come to a junction of the Deer Creek/Dry Creek Trail (number 043) and the Box Elder Trail (number 044). Take the Box Elder Trail to the left.

The path rises steeply through successively higher meadows linked by stands of aspen and conifer, but no box elder trees. By entering these meadows slowly and quietly, visually scanning the rim, you'll have a good chance of spotting deer and occasionally moose. At 1.8 miles, you'll come to a natural spring trickling down the side of a rock to the right of the trail. At 2.3 miles, you'll see the remains of an old cabin on the left side of the trail. This cabin must have been "property with a view," as it is perched near a ledge overlooking Wide Hollow, a deep, glacial side canyon.

Shortly after passing the cabin, you'll come to a sign marking the White Canyon Trail (number 188), which heads north and connects with the Deer Creek/Dry Creek Trail. Stay on the Box Elder Peak Trail to the left as it dips into Wide Hollow and crosses the seasonal runoff. As the trail crosses Wide Hollow and rises above the 8,700-foot level, you leave the mostly shaded woodland for partially shaded alpine meadows and ridges. Snowpack often remains into midsummer in the bowls and on the north-facing slopes at these higher elevations. You're in wilderness, and along the trail you're just as likely to see bear tracks as boot tracks. It's important to trust the trail, since the route is not intuitive and the summit never comes into sight until you cross the upper ridge.

When you arrive at the saddle, views to Utah Valley open up to the west. The trail continues to the northwest along a level contour near 9,700 feet. Here you'll see the summit, and you must determine the best place to depart the trail and head for it. One good choice appears after crossing a steep shale slope. A faint ridgeline leads up to the northwest, and while it's a steep ascent, it provides better footing than some of the scree slopes.

On the way to the summit, and often once you're there, you can see a herd of mountain goats that find safety from predators in this high, rocky terrain. From the summit, you have good views of Utah Valley but excellent ones of Mount Timpanogos to the south and Lone Peak and Pfeifferhorn ridge to the north.

If the summit isn't your ultimate destination, you can also continue circling Box Elder Peak in a clockwise direction, eventually connecting with the Deer Creek/Dry Creek Trail and returning to the Granite Flat trailhead. After all, Box Elder Peak isn't just about the summit; it's a wilderness experience and an adventure in mountain solitude.

ADDITIONAL AT-A-GLANCE INFORMATION

ACCESS: Located in The Lone Peak Wilderness Area, the trail can be reached through American Fork Canyon, as described in this chapter, or from the city of Alpine via the Dry Creek or Phelps Canyon trails. The American Fork Canyon access requires an entrance fee; the Alpine access does not. There are no parking fees.

DOGS: Permitted on leash

SPECIAL COMMENTS: Box Elder Peak is located in the Lone Peak Wilderness Area. No mechanized vehicles or bikes are permitted.

NEARBY ACTIVITIES

The city of Alpine, settled in 1850 by Mormon pioneers under the name of Mountainville, lies at the base of Box Elder Peak. Today, Alpine is a growing residential community proud of its rural roots. The Petersen Arboretum, in Petersen Park on Alpine's East Ridge Drive, features hundreds of trees of both native and nonnative species.

45 TIMPANOGOS CAVE NATIONAL MONUMENT

KEY AT-A-GLANCE INFORMATION

LENGTH: 3 miles round-trip
ELEVATION GAIN: 1,092 feet
ELEVATION AT TRAILHEAD: 5,638 feet
CONFIGURATION: Out-and-back
DIFFICULTY: Moderate
SCENERY: Riparian canyon with rock cliffs and subalpine slopes leading to the cave
EXPOSURE: Mostly shaded to 8,000 feet elevation, partially shaded to 9,000 feet elevation, and no shade above 9,000 feet
TRAFFIC: Busy
TRAIL SURFACE: Paved
HIKING TIME: 1–2.5 hours on trail, plus 1 additional hour for cave tour
WATER REQUIREMENTS: 1 liter. No water is available on the trail.
SEASON: Early May–early October
ACCESS: The hike is located within Timpanogos Cave National Monument in American Fork Canyon, a fee-access area. There is no charge to hike the cave trail. Tickets for cave tours are sold at the visitor center. The cave trail and caves are closed from early October through early May.

See additional information at end of Description, page 201.

IN BRIEF

A spectacular trail carved into and through rocky cliffs rising high above American Fork Canyon. The trail ascends 1,000 feet of canyon wall to arrive at the entrance of Timpanogos Cave. The trail alone is worth the admission price to the cave.

DESCRIPTION

Even if this weren't a national monument with a fascinating cave system awaiting at the end of the short paved trail, this would still be an exceptional hike. It takes you from the American Fork River on the canyon floor, up sheer rock cliffs exposing millions of years of geology, and through a subalpine forest of fir and pine, with breathtaking canyon views all along the way.

In 1887, long before anyone thought of building a trail up the canyon cliffs, settler Martin Hansen was cutting timber high on the slopes of American Fork Canyon. He noticed mountain lion tracks leading up the hillside and followed them to a high ledge where he found an opening in the limestone cliff to a small cave. This cave was the first of three linked caverns that contain about 2 miles of underground passages filled with colorful limestone deposits and clear-water pools.

GPS Trailhead Coordinates

UTM Zone (WGS84) 12T
Easting 0440209
Northing 4477258
Latitude N 40° 26' 36.4"
Longitude W 111° 42' 17.9"

Directions

From Salt Lake City, take I-15 south to Highland/Alpine (Exit 284). At the end of the off-ramp, turn left and continue east on UT 92 for 10 miles to the Timpanogos Cave National Monument parking area and visitor center on the right. The trailhead is on the east side of the visitor center.

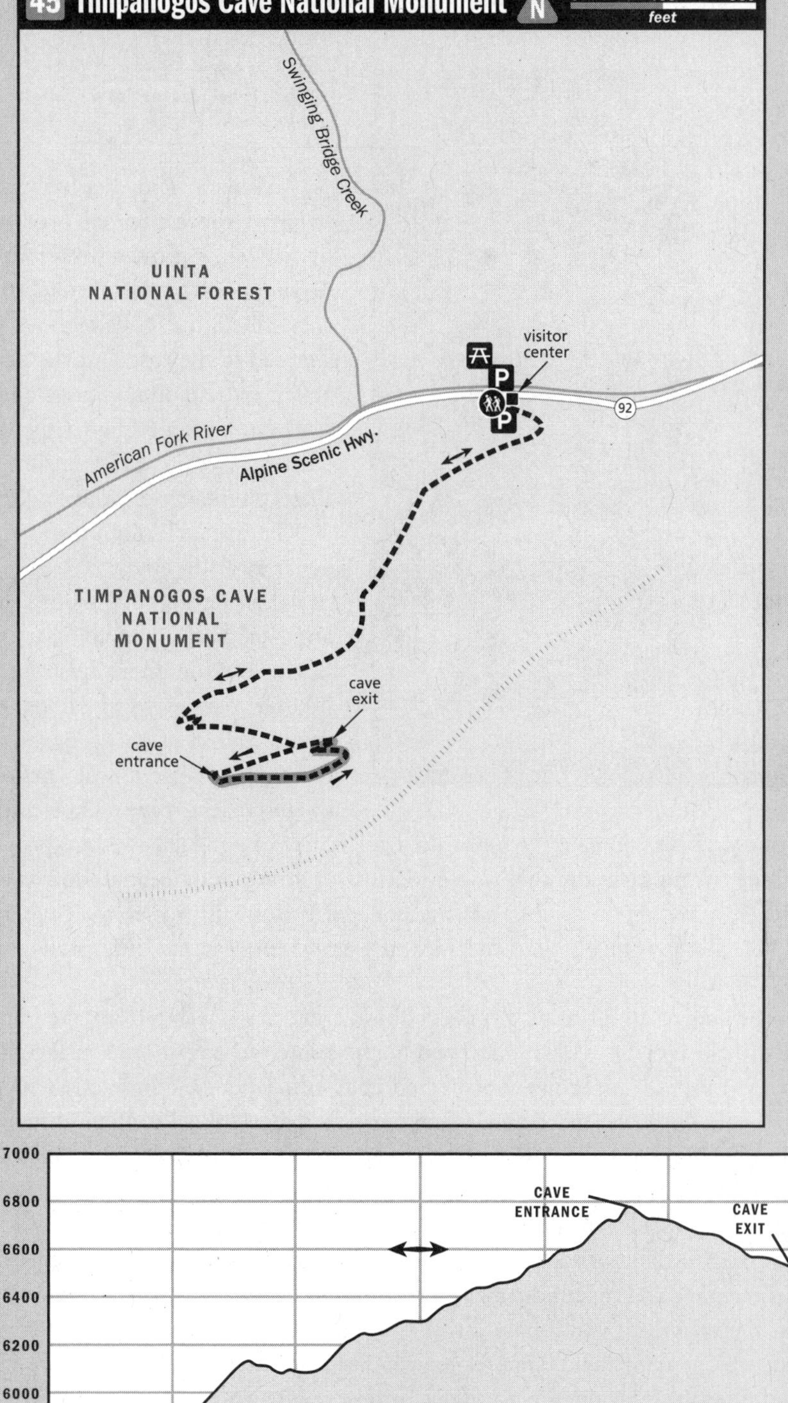
45 Timpanogos Cave National Monument
N
0
450
900
feet
Swinging Bridge Creek
UINTA
NATIONAL FOREST
visitor
center
92
American Fork River
Alpine Scenic Hwy.
TIMPANOGOS CAVE
NATIONAL
MONUMENT
cave
exit
cave
entrance
7000
6800
6600
6400
6200
6000
5800
5600
5400
FEET
CAVE
ENTRANCE
CAVE
EXIT
VISITOR
CENTER
0.25
0.5
0.75
1.0
1.25
1.5
MILES

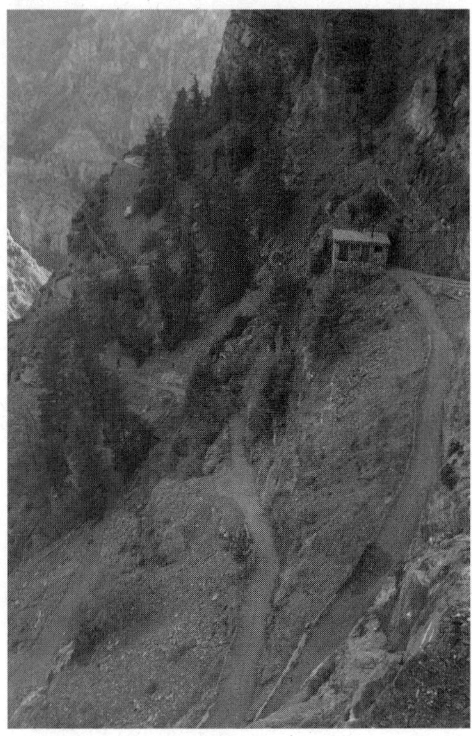

The trail includes several well-designed switchbacks.

Miners and early visitors stripped the center cave of many of its slow-growing formations. At one point, two railroad freight cars filled with flowstone were shipped to the east. But the discovery of two adjoining caves and the protection granted by the National Park Service in 1934 ensure that these fragile underground wonders will be available for us and future generations to enjoy.

During its five-month operating season, Timpanogos Cave National Monument hosts around 70,000 visitors from all over the world. Most of those guests hike the trail because it's the only way to get to the cave. Thousands of additional visitors come just to hike the trail as part of a regular exercise program. The hike to the cave entrance is a good test of your conditioning and readiness for other, more strenuous hikes. If the point of your visit is to see the cave, make sure you allow yourself time to enjoy the trail and read the interpretive signs along the way.

The fact that the trail is paved doesn't detract one bit from the pristine beauty of the canyon wall. In fact, you'll appreciate the sure-footed surface, especially as you pass numerous unprotected drop-offs where a simple misstep could prove fatal. The caves are closed when weather makes hiking to them difficult or dangerous. No strollers or wheelchairs are allowed on the trail. Some sections of the trail are particularly susceptible to rockfall and are marked by a red stripe. No stopping or standing is allowed in these areas.

A hike to the caves is a field course in Wasatch geology, with an open display of sedimentary and metamorphic layers, uplifted layers, and an active fault. Starting at the trailhead, you'll pass through an initial layer of quartzite, followed by distinctive layers of shale, limestone, dolomite, and finally two layers of beautiful black limestone embedded with fossils of sea creatures and other remains of plant and animal life.

The canyon cliffs support an amazing range of conifers, many of which cling to the rocky ledges with twisted and gnarled exposed roots. Douglas-fir, white fir, and limber pine line the trail; scrub oak and bigtooth maple fill in the gaps.

A steep cliffside trail leads to the cave.

Wildlife sightings on the trail are uncommon, but don't be surprised by chipmunks and squirrels along the way, or even an occasional rattlesnake on the rocky ledges. Looking across the canyon, you can often see red-tailed hawks and golden eagles soaring above. Birdwatchers may find their best opportunities on the Swinging Bridge Nature Trail across the road from the visitor center. The riverside vegetation is home to brightly colored western tanagers, Steller's jays, canyon wrens, and American dippers.

Allow 1.5 to 2 hours on the trail, plus an additional hour for the ranger-guided cave tour. Even when canyon temperatures hover in the 90s, the temperature in the cave remains a constant 45°F. Since you'll be in the cave for about an hour, make sure you come prepared with warm clothing for the tour. After completing the cave tour, you will exit at the east end of the cave and follow a short loop back to the main trail for your descent.

ADDITIONAL AT-A-GLANCE INFORMATION

MAPS: USGS Timpanogos Cave, Trails Illustrated Uinta National Forest (701)

FACILITIES: Restrooms, phones, water, snack stand, gift shop, and visitor center at trailhead. A vault toilet is located along the trail near the cave entrance.

DOGS: No dogs permitted on the trail; temporary kennel facilities available for cave visitors with dogs

SPECIAL COMMENTS: A perfect summer outing and must-see destination

NEARBY ACTIVITIES

A visit to Timpanogos Cave National Monument is typically centered around a cave tour. In summer, all tours usually sell out by early afternoon. Buy tickets in advance at the visitor center, or arrive early in the day to avoid long delays or disappointment. While waiting for your tour to depart, you can watch the introductory video at the visitor center, enjoy the picnic areas across the street, or explore the 0.25-mile nature trail. For reservations and information, call the park at (801) 756-5238 or visit **www.nps.gov/tica.**

46 MOUNT TIMPANOGOS (via the Timpooneke Trail)

KEY AT-A-GLANCE INFORMATION

LENGTH: 14.8 miles round-trip to summit; 13 miles round-trip to saddle

ELEVATION GAIN: 4,389 feet to summit

ELEVATION AT TRAILHEAD: 7,360 feet

CONFIGURATION: Out-and-back

DIFFICULTY: Difficult

SCENERY: Mountain scenery, glacial basins, flowered meadows, lakes, and valley views

EXPOSURE: Mostly shaded below 8,000 feet, partially shaded to 9,500 feet, and fully exposed to sun above 9,500 feet

TRAFFIC: Busy

TRAIL SURFACE: Dirt and rock to saddle. Exclusively rock from the saddle to the summit.

HIKING TIME: 6–11 hours

WATER REQUIREMENTS: 2–3 liters. Water from lake, streams, springs, and snowmelt may be purified.

SEASON: Late spring, summer, early fall

ACCESS: The trail is accessed from American Fork Canyon, a fee access area. There are no parking fees.

DOGS: Permitted

See additional information at end of Description, page 205.

IN BRIEF

The Timpanogos massif dominates the skyline of Utah County. At 11,749 feet, this majestic peak is the second highest in the Wasatch (just below Mount Nebo to the south at 11,928 feet). But looking at the steep, barren, western slope of Mount Timpanogos, it's hard to imagine the spectacular beauty to be found on the expansive, wooded eastern slopes, where trails lead past glistening lakes, flowered meadows, cascading waterfalls, and on to the summit.

DESCRIPTION

Mount Timpanogos, or "Timp" as it is known informally, is the most popular mountain hiking destination in Utah. On any given summer Saturday, between 700 and 1,000 hikers depart from the two trailheads leading to the summit. Many have a summit destination in mind, and typically about 200 to 300 of those hikers make it to the top of the 11,749-foot peak. Some hikers make their ultimate destination one of the many waterfalls, meadows, or lakes, while others go as far as the saddle, less than a mile from the summit, and consider the view from the saddle as a worthy reward for their effort.

A frequent topic of discussion among Timp hikers is, "Which is the best trail to the summit: Aspen Grove or Timpooneke?" Truth

---

GPS Trailhead Coordinates

UTM Zone (WGS84) 12T

Easting 0445830

Northing 4475886

Latitude N 40° 25' 52.7"

Longitude W 111° 38' 19.7"

Directions

From Salt Lake City, go south on I-15 to Highland/Alpine (Exit 284). At the bottom of the off-ramp, turn left on UT 92 and proceed 18 miles to the Timpooneke Campground. Turn right into the campground and continue 0.3 miles to the trailhead parking lot on the left.

46 Mt. Timpanogos (via Timpooneke Trail)

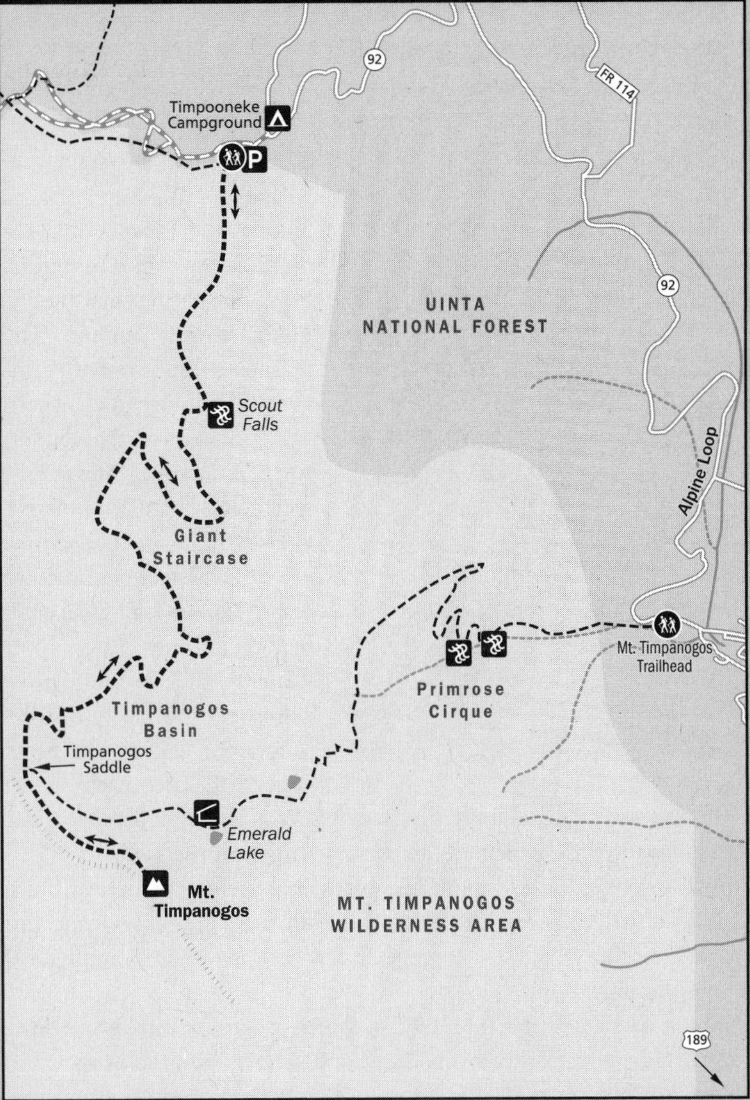

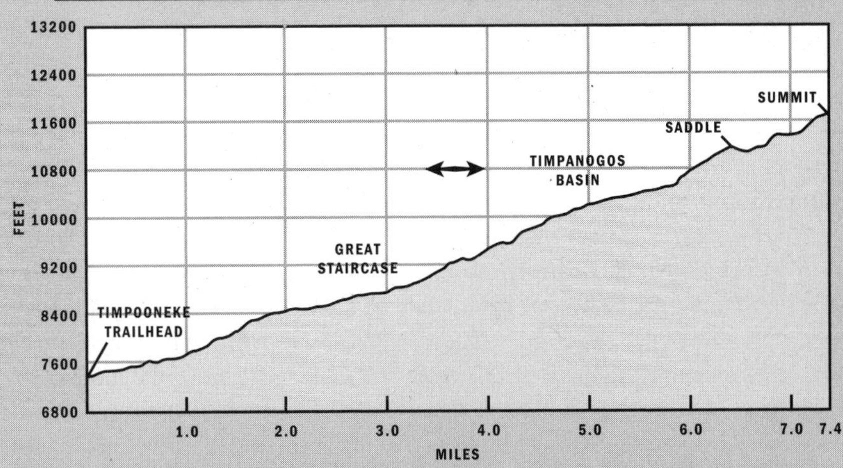

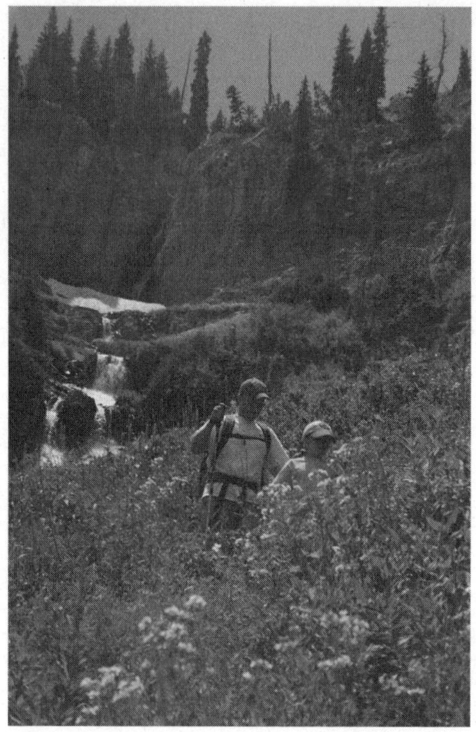

Hikers descend brush-covered slopes.

is, the routes are equally popular, with about as many starting on one as the other. Each route arrives at the saddle from a different direction, but they share the final 0.9 miles to the summit. The Timpooneke Trail is only 0.6 miles longer than the Aspen Grove Trail, but Timpooneke has the gentler grade, since its starting elevation is 471 feet higher than that of the Aspen Grove Trail. The Timpooneke Trail ascends 593 feet per mile, while the Aspen Grove Trail ascends 714 feet per mile. Both offer comparable scenery—the Aspen Grove Trail climbs the gaping Primrose Cirque to Emerald Lake, while the Timpooneke Trail ascends the Giant Staircase to Timpanogos Basin. Admittedly, Aspen Grove has more accessible waterfalls and lakes along the trail, which add to the enjoyment of the hike.

For most hikers, it's a toss-up, and many experience the best of both routes by leaving a car at each trailhead and hiking up the Timpooneke and down the Aspen Grove. Either way, it's a great hike and the quintessential climb to a Wasatch mountain summit.

Climbing Timp can be a long day, so an early start—even before dawn—can work to your advantage. This is especially important if you're not acclimatized to the high elevations and you're forced to move a little more slowly. In summer, an early start enables you to gain most of your elevation in the shade, before the sun comes over the mountain and casts its direct rays. Also, on weekends and holidays the Timpooneke trailhead parking lot can fill by 7 a.m. and you may be forced to park a mile or more away at an additional cost. As you might imagine, the Timpooneke Trail can be a bustling thoroughfare on weekends, so if you want a bit of mountain solitude, plan a midweek hike.

From the trailhead parking area, sign the register and begin your climb on trail 053 through woods of Douglas-fir. The trail ascends a tiered drainage along a series of five benches known as the Giant Staircase. The Timpanogos massif is composed almost entirely of gray Oquirrh limestone, with alternating layers of limestone, sandstone, and shale exposed in the upper reaches of the mountain.

Each of the benches along the Giant Staircase becomes more open and is accompanied by a meadow of wildflowers. Finally at the upper basin, known as the

Timpanogos Basin, hikers are exposed to a riot of wildflowers, with alpine aster, white columbine, Parry's primrose, and larkspur providing a colorful foreground to views of the summit directly to the south. At this point, the elevation is 10,200 feet and the remaining hike to the summit is above tree line along rocky slopes.

On the north side of the basin, you'll come to a trail marker pointing to a backcountry toilet to the right, while the main trail continues straight ahead. Following the spur to the toilet also leads you to the wreckage of a B-25 airplane that crashed in the basin in 1955. The two engines and some sections of the fuselage remain. Continuing up a switchback on this slope, you'll come to a small cascade descending from snowmelt on an upper bowl. This is your last access to water before heading on to the summit.

As you ascend the rocky slope to the saddle, notice a steep trail descending on the left and to the south. This trail leads across a boulder field, often covered with snow, to Emerald Lake and the Aspen Grove Trail. Hikers coming up the Aspen Grove Trail to the summit typically use this steep trail to reach the saddle. A few minutes after passing this junction, you'll arrive at the saddle.

The Timpanogos saddle, at an elevation of 11,050 feet, offers excellent views of Utah Valley to the west. It's a popular gathering place and comfortable rest stop—so comfortable that many hikers make it their final destination without going to the summit. Continuing on to the summit is another 0.9 miles of steady and sometimes steep ascents along a well-crafted rocky trail. A steady pace should take you from the saddle to the summit in 35 minutes, but most hikers frequently stop to catch their breath, and the trip takes between 45 minutes and one hour to gain 700 vertical feet to the metal summit hut.

You can expect your return trip to be faster than your ascent, but be particularly careful descending the loose scree below the summit. Once below the saddle you'll find the trail provides a surefooted gradual descent, but with afternoon sun beaming down on exposed slopes, you'll want plenty of sunscreen and water.

ADDITIONAL AT-A-GLANCE INFORMATION

MAPS: USGS Timpanogos Cave, Trails Illustrated Uinta National Forest (701)

FACILITIES: Restrooms and water at trailhead. Toilet located near trail at Timpanogos Basin.

SPECIAL COMMENTS: The Timpooneke Trail to the summit of Mount Timpanogos lies within the Mount Timpanogos Wilderness Area.

NEARBY ACTIVITIES

The Alpine Loop (UT 92) is a 20-mile scenic byway winding through canyons and forests of aspen and Douglas-fir. It goes up American Fork Canyon and continues through the Uinta National Forest to Provo Canyon. The road is open late May to late October, and offers wonderful fall colors. When snow closes part of the road in winter, it becomes a favorite snowmobiling and cross-country-skiing trail. The narrow, winding road is not recommended for vehicles more than 30 feet long.

47 EMERALD LAKE AND MOUNT TIMPANOGOS (via Aspen Grove Trail)

KEY AT-A-GLANCE INFORMATION

LENGTH: To Emerald Lake, 9.6 miles round-trip; to Mt. Timpanogos summit, 13.6 miles round-trip

ELEVATION GAIN: To Emerald Lake, 3,491 feet; to Mt. Timpanogos summit, 4,860 feet

ELEVATION AT TRAILHEAD: 6,889 feet

CONFIGURATION: Out-and-back

DIFFICULTY: Difficult

SCENERY: Mountain scenery, glacial basins, flowered meadows, lakes, and valley views

EXPOSURE: Partially shaded to 9,500 feet, fully exposed to sun above 9,500 feet

TRAFFIC: Busy

TRAIL SURFACE: Asphalt for first mile; dirt and rock to Emerald Lake; mostly rock to summit

HIKING TIME: 4.5–7 hours to Emerald Lake; 7–11 hours to summit

WATER REQUIREMENTS: 2–3 liters. Water in streams, springs, lakes, and snowfields along trail may be purified.

SEASON: Summer to early fall

ACCESS: The trail is accessed from the Aspen Grove trailhead on the Alpine Loop, a fee access area.

See additional information at end of Description, page 209.

GPS Trailhead Coordinates

UTM Zone (WGS84) 12T

Easting 0448605

Northing 4472875

Latitude N 40° 24' 15.8"

Longitude W 111° 36' 19.4"

IN BRIEF

The Mount Timpanogos Wilderness Area is full of superlatives. Whether you're hiking to a waterfall in Primrose Cirque, an alpine meadow, Emerald Lake, the Timpanogos snowfield, or on to the summit, you'll find plenty to grab your attention and make you want to go higher and farther.

DESCRIPTION

The Aspen Grove Trail, like its sister, the Timpooneke Trail, leads up an immense drainage to a glacial bowl, then on to the saddle and summit of Mount Timpanogos. While both are great trails and offer a challenging, spectacular, and often-overcrowded wilderness experience, the Aspen Grove Trail provides more access to water (in the form of waterfalls, streams, lakes, and snowfields) than the Timpooneke Trail. The Aspen Grove Trail also has more vertical elevation gain and is slightly shorter and steeper than the Timpooneke Trail. Finally, it offers a better chance of seeing the herd of mountain goats that call "Timp" home.

The name Timpanogos (timp-ah-NO-gus) comes from the Paiute name for the Provo River, meaning "rock and running water," and

Directions

From Salt Lake City, go south on I-15 to Orem 800 North (Exit 272). At the bottom of the off-ramp, turn left and proceed east on 800 North (UT 52) toward the mouth of Provo Canyon for 3.7 miles. Take the left ramp onto East Provo Canyon Road (US 189). Continue up the canyon for 7 miles to UT 92, the first left after the tunnel. Continue up UT 92, passing Sundance and the Aspen Grove Family Camp on the left. Pass the Forest Service fee booth at 4.6 miles and enter the trailhead parking lot immediately on the left.

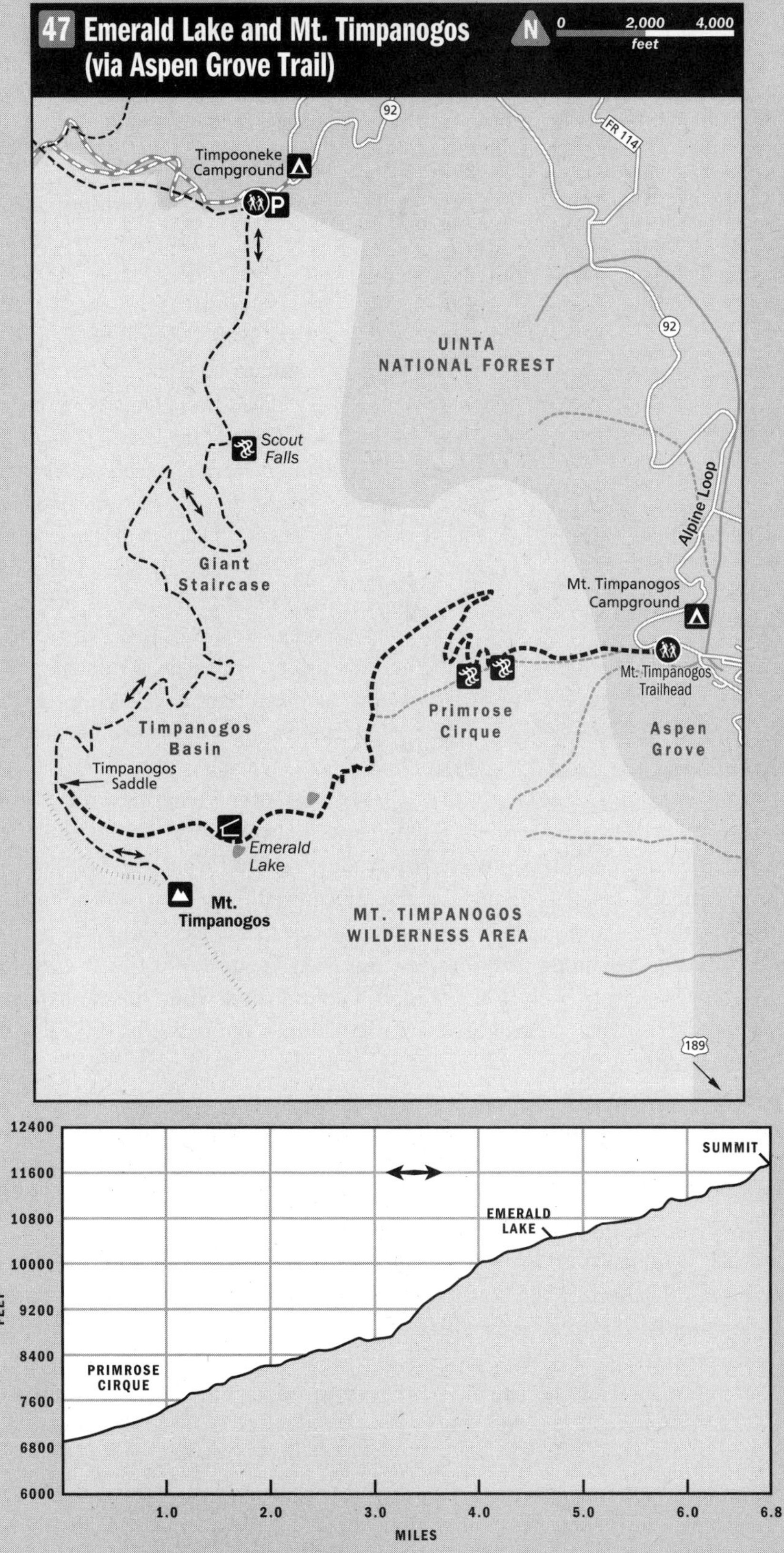
47 Emerald Lake and Mt. Timpanogos (via Aspen Grove Trail)
N
0
2,000
4,000
feet
92
FR 114
Timpooneke Campground
UINTA NATIONAL FOREST
Scout Falls
Giant Staircase
Alpine Loop
Mt. Timpanogos Campground
Mt. Timpanogos Trailhead
Primrose Cirque
Aspen Grove
Timpanogos Basin
Timpanogos Saddle
Emerald Lake
Mt. Timpanogos
MT. TIMPANOGOS WILDERNESS AREA
189
12400
11600
10800
10000
9200
8400
7600
6800
6000
FEET
SUMMIT
EMERALD LAKE
PRIMROSE CIRQUE
1.0
2.0
3.0
4.0
5.0
6.0
6.8
MILES

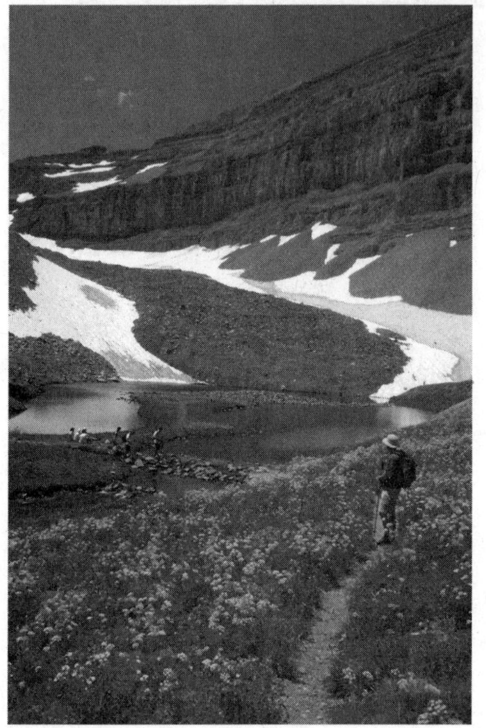

Emerald Lake

has nothing to do with the silly legend contrived in the early 20th century where the image of a lovesick Indian maiden who threw herself off the peak can still be seen in the mountain skyline.

The trail departs from the north side of the large Theater in the Pines parking area and passes a small guard station where you should sign in during the peak summer season. The trail gradually ascends the lower drainage through woods of quaking aspen and Douglas-fir. To the left is a steep avalanche slope where thousands of trees have been leveled and several lives have been lost in recent avalanches.

After entering the Mount Timpanogos Wilderness Area, the trail is paved in asphalt for the next mile. The trail arrives at a waterfall on the left, then makes a sharp turn to the right and into some switchbacks before arriving at a second waterfall. Here the asphalt ends and the trail begins a giant, gradually ascending sweep to the east along the partially shaded south-facing slope of Primrose Cirque. At about 8,000 feet in elevation, the trail turns sharply back to the west and continues its climb of the expansive cirque. Along the way, the trail traverses rocky slopes and passes by several waterfalls and small runoffs.

This section of trail can be particularly treacherous in the spring and early summer, as melting snowfields form ice bridges across the flowing water. Falling through these snowfields to the rocks and rushing water below has resulted in injuries and deaths for unprepared hikers. Use extreme caution when crossing some of the steep snowfields in this section of the trail.

After winding your way up the limestone terraces at the top of Primrose Cirque, you'll pass through a grove of Engelmann spruce (a popular camping area) at an elevation of about 9,500 feet, then move on to a high meadow laced with streams and small lakes. After several stream crossings, the trail ascends to the crest of a moraine slope and the Timpanogos Shelter comes into view, followed by views of Emerald Lake.

Emerald Lake is a wonderful destination if you've made a late start or want a shorter, less demanding outing. The shelter provides the only shade in the area, and a recently constructed toilet lies along a path to the northeast of the shelter.

The Timpanogos Shelter, just 100 yards to the north of Emerald Lake, was built in 1959 by the Forest Service. From 1959 to 1970 it was used as part of the Timp Hike, a community event that drew thousands to the mountain each year on a single late-July weekend. The hike was discontinued in 1970 in an effort to preserve the delicate mountain environment.

Rising to the west of Emerald Lake toward the ridgeline is the Timpanogos Glacier. Trip reports from the early 20th century note the existence of crevasses, indicative of a true glacier. The Dust Bowl drought of the 1930s diminished the glacier considerably. Throughout most of the 20th century, the "glacier" waxed and waned with variation in annual snowfall and temperatures. But in 1994, the snowfield melted sufficiently to reveal some glacial ice below the talus. Studies were inconclusive, so the debate rages on as to whether it's a glacier, a permanent snowfield, or just a patch of snow. The snowfield can be used for both a summit ascent in the spring (typically requiring ice ax and crampons), and for a glissade descent in the summer. Sliding down the snowfield is a popular, fast, and increasingly dangerous descent route. Examine conditions carefully, and use caution.

The route from the shelter to the saddle crosses the meadow north of Emerald Lake to a boulder field often covered with large patches of snow. The area around Emerald Lake is your best opportunity to spot mountain goats that often graze in the meadow and find an easy retreat to the high rocky ledges of Mount Timpanogos. The mountain goats found in Utah are a nonnative species introduced in 1967 from a herd in Washington's Olympic National Park. In addition to Mount Timpanogos, they have been successfully transplanted to the Cottonwood Canyons, the Uintas, and the Tushar Mountains in southern Utah. The current population statewide is more than 1,000, with about 200 inhabiting the Timpanogos massif.

The most grueling section of trail rises from the boulder field above the Timpanogos Basin and steeply ascends to the north before joining the Timpooneke Trail and continuing to the saddle. From the saddle, it's a demanding, rocky, 0.9-mile climb to the metal shelter at the 11,749-foot summit. There you'll have commanding views of Utah Valley to the west and Heber Valley to the east.

Mount Timpanogos is arguably the best mountain hike in Utah, and certainly a classic that every local hiker should experience. As with most mountains, summit success favors those who get an early start. Once you've returned to Emerald Lake from the summit, the afternoon descent along the sunny slopes of Primrose Cirque can be long and hot, so bring plenty of water and sunscreen.

ADDITIONAL AT-A-GLANCE INFORMATION

MAPS: USGS Timpanogos Cave, Trails Illustrated Uinta National Forest (701)
FACILITIES: Restrooms and water at trailhead
DOGS: On leash
SPECIAL COMMENTS: The Aspen Grove Trail to the summit of Mount Timpanogos lies within the Mount Timpanogos Wilderness Area.

48 STEWART FALLS

KEY AT-A-GLANCE INFORMATION

LENGTH: 3.6 miles round-trip
ELEVATION GAIN: 310 feet
ELEVATION AT TRAILHEAD: 6,889 feet
CONFIGURATION: Out-and-back
DIFFICULTY: Easy
SCENERY: Mountain views and waterfall
EXPOSURE: Mostly shaded for first mile; partially shaded for second mile
TRAFFIC: Busy
TRAIL SURFACE: Dirt
HIKING TIME: 1.5–2.5 hours
WATER REQUIREMENTS: 1 liter. Water in the stream below the falls may be purified.
SEASON: Spring, summer, fall
ACCESS: The Aspen Grove Trailhead parking area lies within a U.S. Forest Service fee access area, while the trail itself is almost entirely on Sundance Resort private property. Stewart Falls is located within the Mount Timpanogos Wilderness Area.
MAPS: USGS Aspen Grove, Trails Illustrated Uinta National Forest (701)

See additional information at end of Description, page 213.

GPS Trailhead Coordinates

UTM Zone (WGS84) 12T
Easting 0448578
Northing 4472873
Latitude N 40° 24' 15.8"
Longitude W 111° 36' 19.4"

IN BRIEF

A tiered wedding cake of cascading water set against a mountain backdrop of aspen and fir, Stewart Falls may be the most picturesque waterfall in Utah. The gentle trail is well suited for families, making this an ideal three-season day hike.

DESCRIPTION

For the thousands of Utah Valley residents living below the western slopes of the Timpanogos massif, it's easy to forget how incredibly beautiful the "backside of Timp" is. They should be required to pay a visit at least twice a year—spring, summer, fall, winter; it doesn't matter—to walk through the aspens, breathe the mountain air, and sit by a mountain stream at the base of a thundering waterfall.

Mount Timpanogos boasts some exquisite waterfalls on all sides, and the falls along both Aspen Grove Trail and the Timpooneke Trail should be on every hiker's must-see list. But Stewart Falls, sometimes referred to as Stewarts Cascades, is the most beautiful and accessible of them all. In less than 2 miles from the trailhead, walking along a well-groomed

Directions

From Salt Lake City, go south on I-15 to Orem 800 North (Exit 272). At the bottom of the off-ramp, turn left and proceed east on 800 North (UT 52) toward the mouth of Provo Canyon for 3.7 miles. Take the left ramp onto East Provo Canyon Road (US 189). Continue up the canyon for 7 miles to UT 92, which is the first left after the tunnel. Continue up UT 92, passing Sundance and the Aspen Grove Family Camp on the left. Pass the Forest Service fee booth at 4.6 miles and enter the trailhead parking lot immediately on the left.

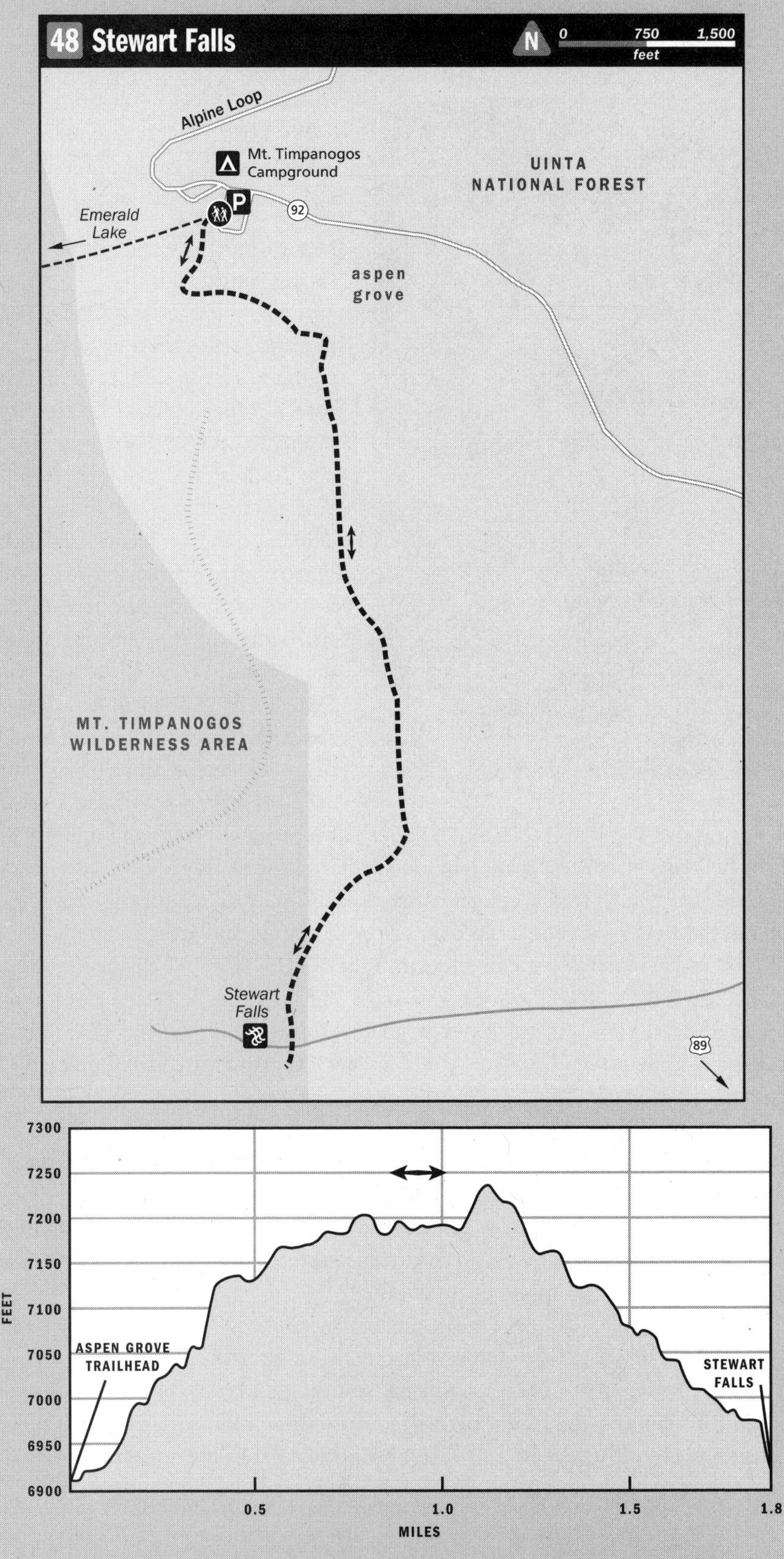
48 Stewart Falls
0
750
1,500
feet
N
Alpine Loop
Mt. Timpanogos
Campground
UINTA
NATIONAL FOREST
Emerald
Lake
92
aspen
grove
MT. TIMPANOGOS
WILDERNESS AREA
Stewart
Falls
89
7300
7250
7200
7150
7100
7050
7000
6950
6900
FEET
ASPEN GROVE
TRAILHEAD
STEWART
FALLS
0.5
1.0
1.5
1.8
MILES

Stewart Falls

wooded slope, you find yourself face-to-face with tiers of cascading spring water.

From the large trailhead parking area, take the trail to the right of the restroom that leads up Primrose Cirque. Follow the sign that points to Stewart Falls, Trail 56. As you look at the slope in front of you to the left, you can see the damage done by recent avalanches that resulted in the loss of several lives. At 0.1 mile, the trail takes a sharp turn to the left and ascends the hillside through a forest of Douglas-fir and aspen. At 1.2 miles, the path passes through the middle of an avalanche slope where hundreds of aspens have been leveled.

Along the way you'll find a rich variety of birds in the trees and underbrush. Yellow-bellied sapsuckers, mountain bluebirds, yellow warblers, and western tanagers are just a few of the colorful varieties you may see. Squirrels make their home in the underbrush of scrub oak, bigtooth maple, and Oregon grape.

The trail reaches a peak elevation of 7,200 feet before beginning its descent toward the falls. Soon, the roar of the falls can be heard even before they come into view. At 1.5 miles from the trailhead, as you come around a bend, your first view of Stewart Falls awaits. Another cascade plunges down the slope to the right.

At 1.7 miles from the trailhead, you'll come to a shale outcropping that serves as a great falls overlook. From there, take the marked trail that descends to the left. A few short switchbacks lead you to the stream level at the base of the falls. Plenty of great vantage points below the falls offer places to play in the water or enjoy a snack. However, the barren slope to the right and in front of the falls is steep and dangerous—best to avoid.

As you approach the falls from the north, you may look across the stream and see others arriving from the south. Here's an alternative approach for your next visit: during most of the late spring, summer, and fall, the Sundance chairlift takes hikers and mountain bikers from the base elevation of 6,100 feet to the summit at 7,150 feet in a matter of minutes. From the summit, a pleasant downhill stroll leads to Stewart Falls at 6,800 feet, then back to Sundance. This loop hike is especially enjoyable in fall as the hillside blazes with autumn colors.

ADDITIONAL AT-A-GLANCE INFORMATION

FACILITIES: Restrooms and drinking water at trailhead parking area
DOGS: Permitted on leash
SPECIAL COMMENTS: Sections of this hike are avalanche prone and should not be hiked in winter.

NEARBY ACTIVITIES

Nestled at the base of Mount Timpanogos and adjacent to Stewart Falls, Sundance Resort offers a diverse mountain recreation experience year-round. Skiing, snowboarding, or cross-country skiing in winter, and biking and hiking in summer, all take place against a backdrop of breathtaking scenery. Lodging, fine dining, theater, and conference facilities make Sundance a favorite choice for an afternoon visit or an extended vacation.

49 BATTLE CREEK FALLS

KEY AT-A-GLANCE INFORMATION

LENGTH: 1.6 miles round-trip
ELEVATION GAIN: 450 feet
ELEVATION AT TRAILHEAD: 5,221 feet
CONFIGURATION: Out-and-back
DIFFICULTY: Easy
SCENERY: Deep-canyon waterfall and valley views
EXPOSURE: Mostly shaded
TRAFFIC: Moderate
TRAIL SURFACE: Dirt and rocks
HIKING TIME: 45 minutes–1.5 hours
WATER REQUIREMENTS: 0.5 liters
SEASON: Year-round. Minimal avalanche risk in winter
ACCESS: Located in Uinta National Forest. No fees or permits required. Open year-round. Horses and mountain bikes also use this trail.
MAPS: USGS Orem, Trails Illustrated Uinta National Forest (701)
FACILITIES: Water and vault toilet near trailhead
DOGS: On leash
SPECIAL COMMENTS: Especially beautiful in autumn with colors and a trailbed of fallen leaves

GPS Trailhead Coordinates

UTM Zone (WGS84) 12T
Easting 0440516
Northing 4468287
Latitude N 40° 21' 47.35"
Longitude W 111° 42' 02.52"

IN BRIEF

A popular, family-friendly route along a creekbed in a deep canyon. The hike's payout: a 50-foot waterfall spraying down the side of a rock cliff.

DESCRIPTION

The Timpanogos massif, which dominates the eastern skyline of Utah County, has several canyons along its foothills that provide water to the towns below and access to the mountain's higher slopes. From the valley, you can most easily identify Battle Creek Canyon as the one immediately to the right (or south) of the *G* on the side of the mountain. Battle Creek supplies the water that fills the large tank and irrigates the orchards you pass on the way to the trailhead. In this area on February 28, 1849, a band of Ute Indians fought Captain John Scott and his men, pursuing Scott's party into the canyon.

Arriving at the parking area, walk toward the blue metal arch over the bridge that leads into Kiwanis Park. Find the unmarked trailhead by walking up the steep slope to your

Directions

From Salt Lake City, go south on I-15 to Highland/Alpine (Exit 284). At the bottom of the off-ramp, turn left and take UT 92 east 7.4 miles toward the mouth of American Fork Canyon. As UT 92 enters the canyon, take UT 146 to the right and up the hill. Continue south on UT 146 (Canyon Road) for 4.8 miles to 200 South in Pleasant Grove. Turn left onto 200 South and continue east for 1.8 miles. As the pavement ends, continue up the wide, dirt road for another 0.3 miles, passing the large water tank on your way to the parking area next to Kiwanis Park.

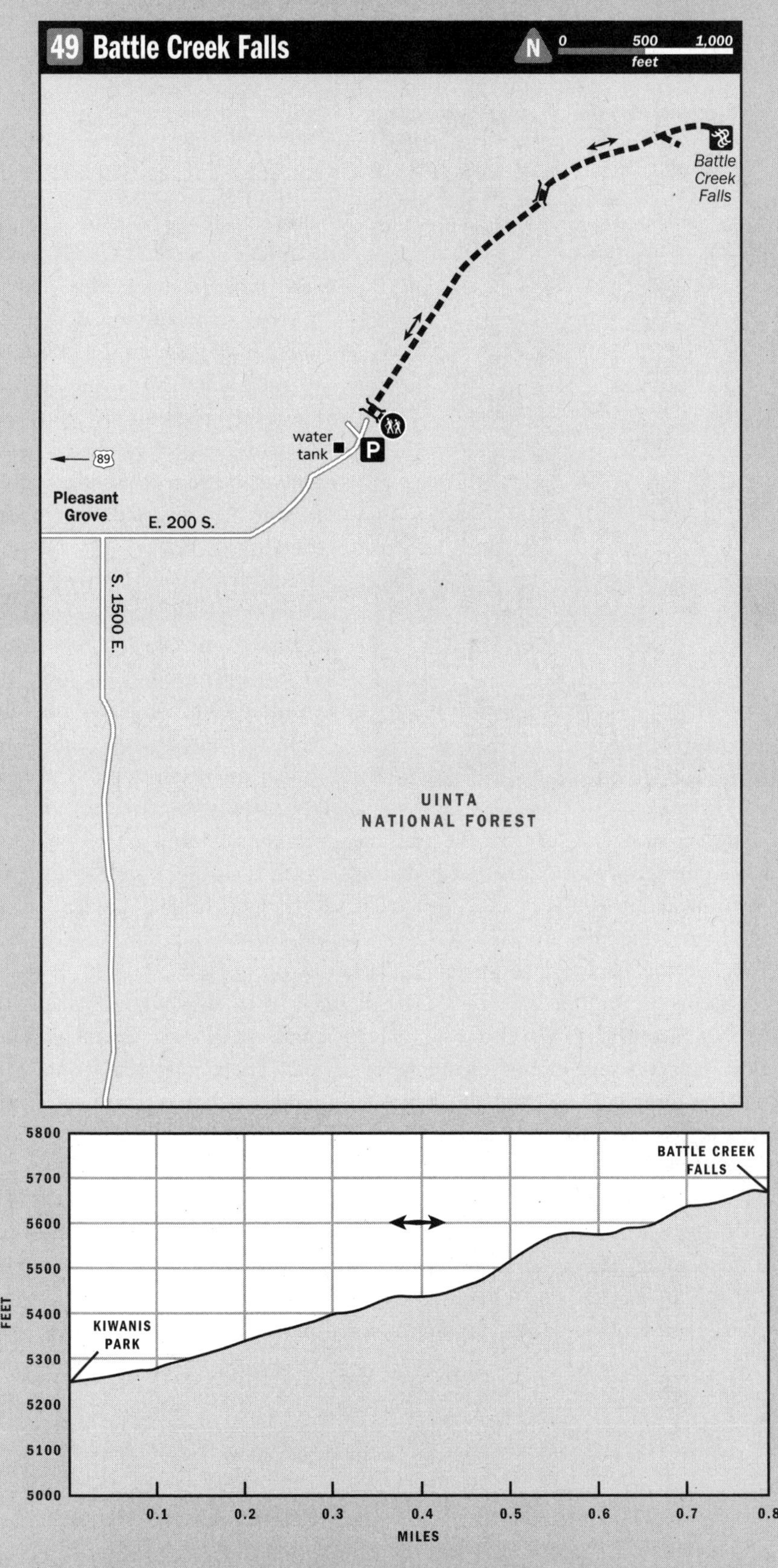

49 Battle Creek Falls
N
0
500
1,000
feet
Battle
Creek
Falls
water
tank
P
89
Pleasant
Grove
E. 200 S.
S. 1500 E.
UINTA
NATIONAL FOREST
5800
5700
5600
5500
5400
5300
5200
5100
5000
FEET
KIWANIS
PARK
BATTLE CREEK
FALLS
0.1
0.2
0.3
0.4
0.5
0.6
0.7
0.8
MILES

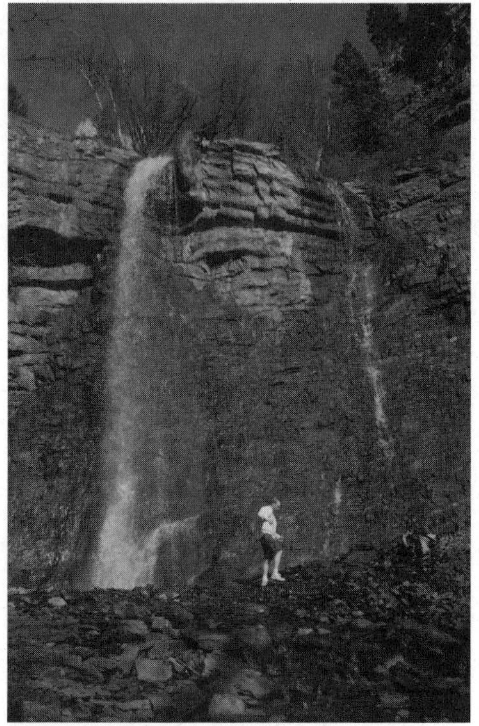

Battle Creek Falls

right just a few feet before crossing the bridge into the park. Note the park's large picnic pavilion, drinking water, and vault toilet, all under the shade of giant cottonwoods. As the trail climbs the hillside, it soon joins a Jeep road on the right.

Don't expect to see any water in the creekbed to your left. Because the water is diverted into underground pipes just up the canyon, it remains dry throughout the year. At 0.3 miles, you'll see a water diversion basin where Battle Creek begins its life underground. Beyond this diversion basin, follow the tumbling creek for another 0.2 miles and cross to the north side of the creek over a sturdy wooden footbridge.

After crossing the bridge, the trail steepens considerably. Shards of shale from the cliffs above cover the trail's dirt base. Still, the trail provides sure footing. Within about 100 feet after you cross the bridge, the falls appear. About 50 feet before the falls, the trail divides. The right spur descends to the base of the falls and the main trail to the left leads to the top.

A natural spring feeds Battle Creek, augmented by snowmelt. So while the falls' spray becomes heaviest in spring, the creek and the falls are perennial. Battle Creek Falls serves as a popular escape from summer's heat, with visitors enjoying the cooling spray near its base. The water falls gently enough so that even young children can safely walk and play under the main channel of water as it bounces off the rock wall. Local adventurers often rappel down the falls in summer.

The trail leading to the top of the falls continues up the canyon and joins the Great Western Trail, which surrounds much of Mount Timpanogos and connects all of the canyon trails on Timpanogos's western slopes.

At the lower elevations, below the falls, the vegetation consists of Gambel oak, sage, and cottonwoods. Conifers and aspens grow at higher elevations near the falls and above. You'll often spot pinyon jays, but scrub jays—while common—prove to be a bit more elusive.

Along the way, you're likely to see more people than animals. Families out for a day hike will find the trail suitable for children, while young couples and older adults can get some exercise just minutes from the neighborhoods in the valley below.

NEARBY ACTIVITIES

The U.S. Forest Service Pleasant Grove Ranger Station is located on the way to the trailhead at 390 North 100 East (UT 146). The office offers maps and publications about recreation in the Uinta National Forest.

50 PROVO RIVER PARKWAY

KEY AT-A-GLANCE INFORMATION

LENGTH: 15 miles

ELEVATION GAIN: –702 feet (from Vivian Park to Utah Lake)

ELEVATION AT UTAH LAKE TRAILHEAD: 4,498 feet

ELEVATION AT VIVIAN PARK TRAILHEAD: 5,200 feet

CONFIGURATION: One-way or out-and-back

DIFFICULTY: Easy

SCENERY: Deep canyon, mountain streams, waterfalls, towering peaks, pastures, wetlands—an amazing variety for an essentially urban trail.

EXPOSURE: Partially shaded

TRAFFIC: Busy

TRAIL SURFACE: Paved

HIKING TIME: Varies greatly based on distance selected

WATER REQUIREMENTS: 1 liter. Drinking fountains are located along the trail, as are parks, restaurants, and convenience stores.

SEASON: Year-round

ACCESS: Hikable year-round. No access fees or permits required.

See additional information at end of Description, page 221.

GPS Trailhead Coordinates

UTM Zone (WGS84) 12T

Easting 0451265

Northing 4467374

Latitude–longitude: See page 221

IN BRIEF

The Provo River Parkway is a community treasure, connecting residents with the river, mountains, waterfalls, parks, shopping, work, and Provo's history. As the parkway follows the course of the river, you're constantly exposed to the life of the river—trout fishing, waterfowl, and riparian plants. Take the trail in bite-size pieces and enjoy.

DESCRIPTION

The Provo River Parkway stretches from a deep mountain canyon through shopping centers, business parks, and neighborhoods to the shores of Utah Lake. Along its course, the trail passes through a national forest, two county parks, 14 city parks, and a state park.

While it's certainly possible to walk the trail from top to bottom, or vice versa, most choose to enter the parkway from one of dozens of access points and enjoy the scenic array found within just a mile or two in either direction. Officially designated as a nonmotorized multiuse trail, the parkway is widely used by families, seniors, and students as Provo's most popular venue for outdoor recreation and exercise.

On any given day you can see hundreds of people on the trail. But think of it as a highly social trail—not a crowded one. Inline skaters, skateboarders, kids on scooters, babies in strollers, cyclists, runners, and walkers all coexist happily, with pedestrians having the right of way.

The most scenic section of the trail may be the upper 5 miles from Vivian Park to the mouth of Provo Canyon (intersection of US 189 and Orem's 800 North). In addition to these two locations you can also enter the trail

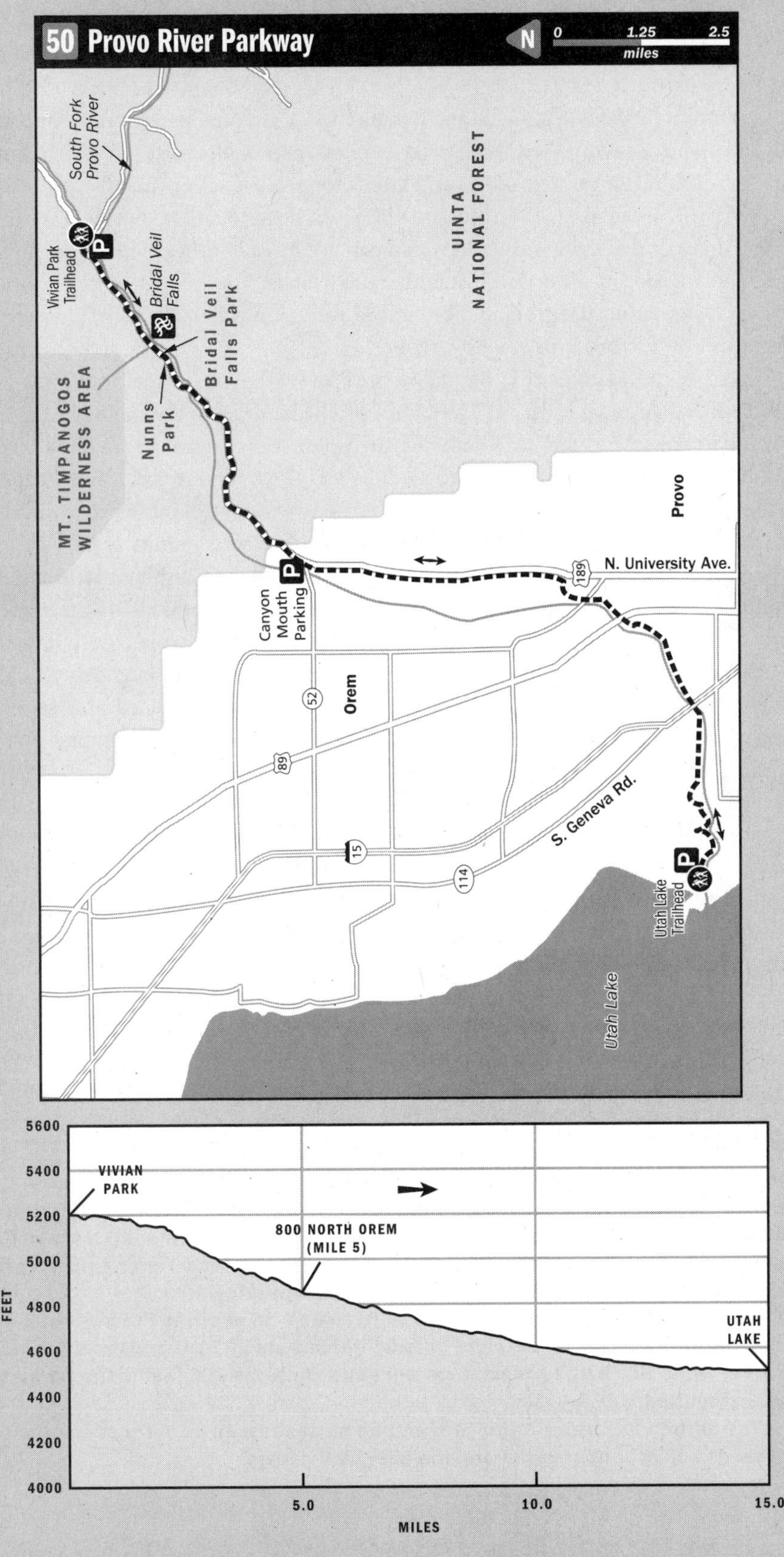

50 Provo River Parkway
N
0
1.25
2.5
miles
South Fork Provo River
Vivian Park Trailhead
Bridal Veil Falls
Bridal Veil Falls Park
Nunns Park
MT. TIMPANOGOS WILDERNESS AREA
UINTA NATIONAL FOREST
Provo
N. University Ave.
189
Canyon Mouth Parking
Orem
52
89
15
114
S. Geneva Rd.
Utah Lake Trailhead
Utah Lake
5600
5400
5200
5000
4800
4600
4400
4200
4000
FEET
VIVIAN PARK
800 NORTH OREM (MILE 5)
UTAH LAKE
5.0
10.0
15.0
MILES

at many points in between, including Nunns Park, Canyon Glen, Mount Timpanogos Park, and Canyon View Park. These access points also offer drinking water and restroom facilities, plus tables and grates for a picnic after the hike.

Within this section, the trail and the river flow together, never more than 20 feet apart and always within view and earshot of each other. The steep canyon walls and wooded canyon floor offer abundant shade. You'll have multiple opportunities to stop and dangle your feet in the water or watch fly fishermen try to snag a trophy cutthroat or rainbow trout.

Among the many scenic highlights in Provo Canyon, Bridal Veil Falls is a perennial crowd-pleaser. At 607 feet, this double cataract is the highest waterfall in Utah. In the spring and early summer, the water sprays onto the trail and hikers play in the runoff. In winter, the frozen falls and the Stairway to Heaven seepage to the right of the falls provide some of Utah's favorite ice-climbing routes. From Nunns Park or Bridal Veil Falls Park, the falls are just a 10-minute walk.

About 100 feet downstream from Bridal Veil Falls is a display of old mining equipment in front of an abandoned mine entrance, a reminder of the mining operations that played such an important role in the canyon's development. Another 100 yards downstream at Nunns Park are the remnants of an early hydroelectric plant built in 1897. At the time, the plant produced almost three times the voltage of any existing line in the nation and powered mining operations 32 miles to the west.

Throughout Provo Canyon you're likely to see raptors circling above, while belted kingfishers and yellow warblers flit along the riverbanks. Young children always seem fascinated by the snake grass (or horsetails), a tall, dark-green, tubular grass growing along the banks.

The lower section of the trail, from Geneva Road to Utah Lake, is every bit as beautiful as the Provo Canyon section, but in a very different way. You might even think you're on a different river in another state. As the river approaches the lake, it widens and slows. Whitewater kayaks are the upriver conveyance of choice, while below it's canoes or rowboats.

Directions

Vivian Park trailhead: From Salt Lake City, go south on I-15 to Orem 800 North (Exit 272). At the bottom of the off-ramp, turn left and proceed east on 800 North (UT 52) toward the mouth of Provo Canyon for 3.7 miles. Take the left ramp onto East Provo Canyon Road (US 189). Go 5.8 miles to Vivian Park. Turn right on South Fork Road. Cross over railroad tracks and enter the parking area.

Utah Lake trailhead: From Salt Lake City, take I-15 south to Provo/Center Street/Airport (Exit 265). Turn right onto Center Street (UT 114) and continue west for 2.5 miles to North 4200 West. Turn right and continue 200 feet to the parking area on the right.

In addition to these starting and ending trailheads, an additional 15 official trailheads with public parking provide easy trail access.

In this final 2.5 miles of the trail, the river meanders through a tunnel of mature cottonwoods. On the trail's north side are protected pastures frequented by egrets and warblers. To the south, the river and marshy lowlands host ducks, geese, and a wide variety of migrating waterfowl. You can easily reach this wetlands section of the trail from Fort Utah Park, Oxbow Park, or Utah Lake State Park.

Between the canyon and the wetlands, the Provo River Parkway passes through neighborhoods and busy shopping centers, and under city streets and I-15. While this center section of the trail lacks the scenic beauty of the canyon and the rural appeal of the lowlands, it does offer a safe, convenient place for local residents to get outdoors and enjoy a walk along the river.

Although cyclists have a 15 mph speed limit and pedestrians enjoy the right of way, you still need to keep to the right or in the marked pedestrian lane and be on guard for cyclists approaching from behind. Access to the swift-moving river is never fenced or protected, so keep young children under careful supervision at all times. Throughout its 15-mile length, the trail is entirely paved and well marked. The almost imperceptible incline rarely varies, so you can enter at any point for a leisurely stroll or a vigorous workout.

ADDITIONAL AT-A-GLANCE INFORMATION

MAPS: USGS Bridal Veil Falls, Orem, Provo

FACILITIES: Restrooms, water, telephone, and other services are available at the trailhead and throughout the hike.

DOGS: Permitted on leash

SPECIAL COMMENTS: Upper 3 miles of trail from Vivian Park to Bridal Veil Falls Park is not maintained from November 1 to March 31 due to avalanche and rockfall hazard.

UTAH LAKE TRAILHEAD LATITUDE–LONGITUDE: N 40° 14' 16.6"; W 111° 43' 55.3"

VIVIAN PARK TRAILHEAD LATITUDE–LONGITUDE: N 40° 21' 19.6"; W 111° 34' 26.9"

NEARBY ACTIVITIES

If just walking along the banks isn't enough excitement for you, try rafting the Provo River. High Country Rafting at Frazier Park (just downstream from Vivian Park) offers exciting trips down the Provo River on mild (Class II) whitewater during the summer season. Trips down the river last about two hours and can be guided or unguided in a raft, tube, or kayak. Call (801) 224-2500 for information and reservations.

51 BIG SPRINGS HOLLOW

KEY AT-A-GLANCE INFORMATION

LENGTH: 5 miles

ELEVATION GAIN: 554 feet

ELEVATION AT TRAILHEAD: 5,796 feet

CONFIGURATION: Out-and-back with loop

DIFFICULTY: Easy

SCENERY: Mountain views to the west and natural springs with perennial flow. Trail follows creek.

EXPOSURE: Mostly shaded

TRAFFIC: Moderate. Go midweek for more solitude.

TRAIL SURFACE: Dirt, moderate incline

HIKING TIME: 1.5–2.5 hours

WATER REQUIREMENTS: Carry 1 liter. Water at springs is generally safe at the source.

SEASON: Year-round. Ideal snow-shoe or ungroomed cross-country ski trail in winter.

ACCESS: Hikable year-round. No fees for parking or park access.

MAPS: USGS Bridal Veil Falls, Trails Illustrated Uinta National Forest (701)

FACILITIES: Restrooms and drinking water are available in the park. Closed in winter.

DOGS: Permitted on leash

GPS Trailhead Coordinates

UTM Zone (WGS84) 12T

Easting 0455511

Northing 4464795

Latitude N 40° 19.523'

Longitude W 111° 31.859'

IN BRIEF

From the city park trailhead, a steady ascent follows a small creek through a broad valley to Big Springs, a natural spring flowing from the mountainside. Mountain views, abundant valley vegetation, and frequent wildlife sightings make this a popular and accessible family adventure.

DESCRIPTION

Take everything you ever imagined about a city park—the crowds, passing cars, cityscapes. Now throw it all out the window. True, the land in Big Springs Hollow is largely owned by the city of Provo, and the trailhead starts in the city park parking lot. But in less than a minute, the parking lot is out of sight and suddenly you're enveloped in a secluded mountain valley in search of the natural springs that feed the meandering creek at your side.

The main trail follows the south side of this wide, slope-sided valley as the creek crisscrosses the trail several times. Sturdy wooden bridges span all of the major creek crossings. For the first 0.7 miles, the trail makes a moderate but steady climb, finally

Directions

From Salt Lake City, go south on I-15 to Orem 800 North (Exit 272). At the bottom of the off-ramp, turn left and proceed east on 800 North (UT 52) toward the mouth of Provo Canyon. Continue to follow UT 52 for 3.7 miles. Take the left ramp onto East Provo Canyon Road (US 189). Go 5.8 miles to Vivian Park. Turn right on South Fork Road. Cross over railroad tracks, pass Vivian Park, and continue up South Fork Canyon for 3 miles. Turn right to enter Big Springs Park. Continue to the upper-level parking area, where you'll find the trailhead in the lot's southwest corner.

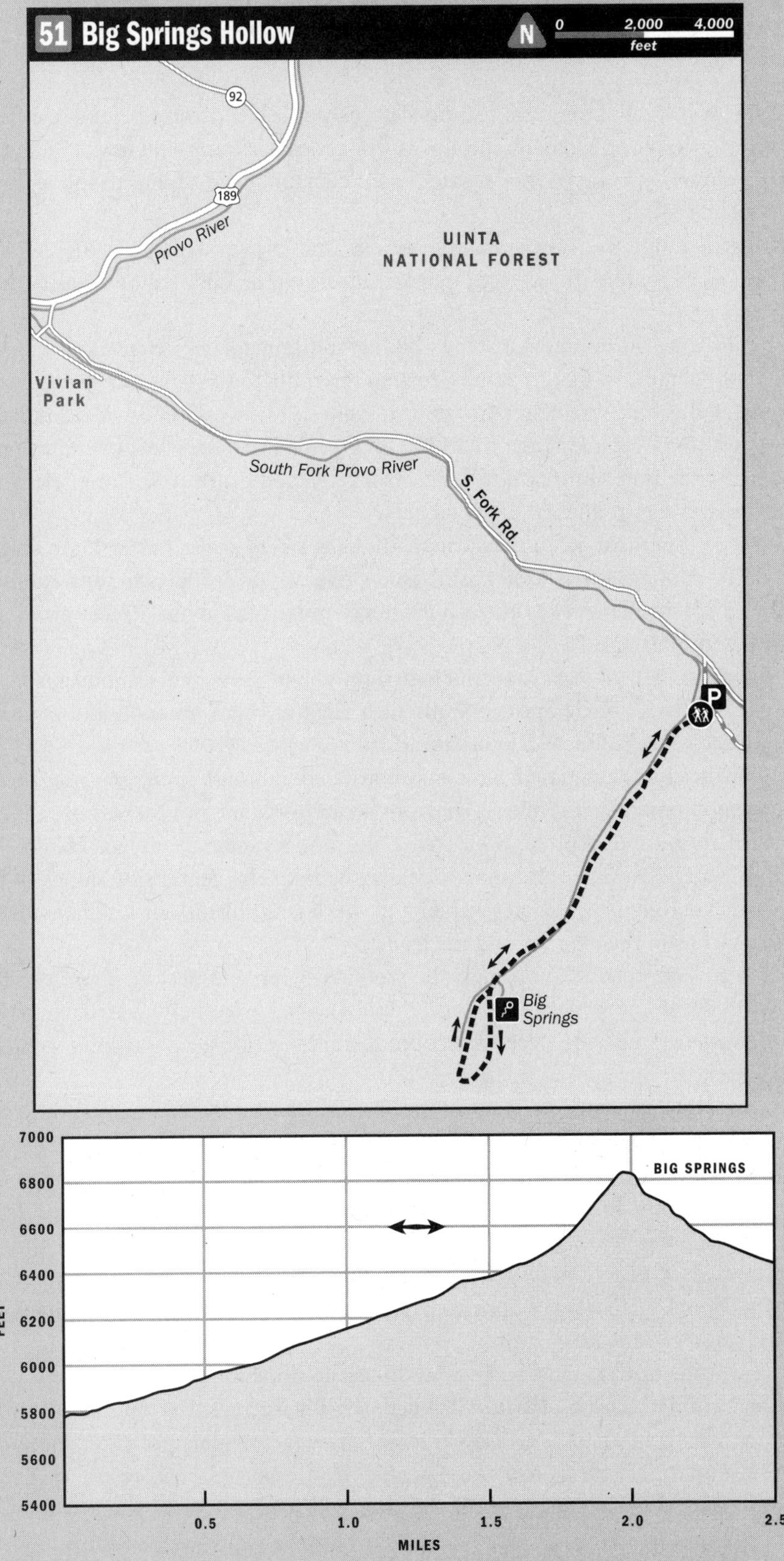
51 Big Springs Hollow
N
0
2,000
4,000
feet
92
189
Provo River
UINTA
NATIONAL FOREST
Vivian
Park
South Fork Provo River
S. Fork Rd.
P
Big
Springs
7000
6800
6600
6400
6200
6000
5800
5600
5400
FEET
BIG SPRINGS
0.5
1.0
1.5
2.0
2.5
MILES

arriving at a knoll where the terrain flattens out a bit. After a brief 0.1 mile of level trail, the slope steepens and the ascent returns. Mountain views of Cascade Peak and the backside of the Wasatch front remain ahead of you to the west for most of the hike.

Throughout the hike, quaking aspens and bigtooth maple provide most of the shade, while thickets of poplar, river birch, and willow cluster near the creek.

Following 30 minutes of steady hiking and immediately after a creek crossing, you'll come to a sign marking a fork in the trail. To the left, another 0.5 miles ahead, is Big Springs. The fork to the right leads to the Cascade Saddle at 4.1 miles. Just after taking the trail's left fork you'll cross the creek over a wooden bridge. By the time you reach the sign, you've gained nearly 500 feet in elevation since leaving the trailhead.

From this point on to the springs, the trail steers closer to the south side of the valley. Along this slope, stands of aspen give way to Douglas-fir, and soon the trail rises above the creek, although it's never more than about 50 feet away, and always within earshot.

Another 0.3 miles beyond the first sign, you'll come to a second sign at the junction of the Cascade Springs Trail. Turn right at this **T**-junction and continue toward Big Springs, just 0.2 miles ahead.

The trail is designated as a nonmotorized multiuse trail, meaning horse riders, mountain bikers, hikers, and—in winter—skiers and snowshoers. They all seem to get along pretty well under the trail's moderate usage. Hikers still predominate in summer and snowshoers in winter. The gentle side slopes of the valley make avalanche risk negligible, and there is no history or visible evidence of avalanches in the area around the trail.

As you approach Big Springs, the woods deepen and become more coniferous with some scrub oak underbrush. The last 0.1 mile before arriving at Big Springs proves to be the steepest section of trail, but not steep enough to require switchbacks or any special treatment.

Cascade Springs flows from several release points on the mountainside and fans down the slope to the left of the trail. A small water diversion culvert at the right of the trail directs some of the water toward the main creek channel. Big Springs marks the high elevation point of the hike at 6,350 feet. The water from Big Springs flows down to South Fork Creek and into the Provo River. Big Springs is the largest of many small springs, seeps, and willow bogs found throughout the canyon. Some of the area's springs have been Provo culinary water sources for more than 60 years.

From Big Springs, follow the trail down the slope to the right and cross over another wooden bridge. About 0.2 miles past Big Springs, the trail merges with the Cascade Trail. This junction represents the turnaround point on the loop. Take a hard right and follow the Cascade Trail east and back to the trailhead parking area. Continuing west on the trail will lead to the Cascade Mountain

Saddle and to Rock Canyon Campground. From this trail junction, ambitious hikers could access a much larger network of trails and actually return to Provo city on foot over the Cascade Mountain Saddle and down Rock Canyon.

On the return, the north side of the loop passes a permanent camp used by the Provo School District as an environmental camp for elementary students in June. You'll find a drinking fountain with chlorinated water at the site during the summer. The trail passes wet and dry grassy meadows with lupine, clover, violets, and mustards. A local rancher still cuts and harvests a spread of alfalfa here.

Throughout the year, hikers can expect to see deer, rabbits, and the occasional moose. Mountain lions roam the hillsides, and you will frequently see their tracks in the winter snow, although you're not likely to actually see this elusive species. Wild turkeys, ruffed grouse, and many songbirds can be spotted in the summer. During one recent summer, a survey of butterflies reported 60 different species in Big Springs Hollow between March and September, with western skippers and western blue tails the most commonly found species.

Weather can change rapidly on the eastern slopes of the Wasatch. Particularly in the fall and winter, once the sun sets or the clouds roll in, afternoon temperatures can drop quickly.

After returning to the parking area, you'll find the tables, fire grates, and covered group sites an inviting spot to relax or enjoy an afternoon picnic or cookout. With their higher elevations, mountain shade, and cooler temperatures, South Fork Canyon and Big Springs Hollow is a popular summer retreat.

Note: Some areas may become boggy in spring. Negligible avalanche risk in winter.

NEARBY ACTIVITIES

Utah County residents use Provo Canyon as a year-round playground. Anglers, river runners, and hikers can find lots to keep them busy through most of the year. In the depths of winter, you'll often spot ice climbers ascending the frozen overspray of Bridal Veil Falls. Vivian Park, at the mouth of South Fork Canyon, is a popular picnic area and serves as the starting point for the historic Heber Valley Railway. The billowing steam engine takes tourists up Provo Canyon from Vivian Park to Soldier Hollow and the Heber Valley. Call (435) 654-5601 or visit **www.hebervalleyrr.org** for schedules, special events, and information.

52 BUFFALO PEAK

KEY AT-A-GLANCE INFORMATION

LENGTH: 1 mile round-trip
ELEVATION GAIN: 287 feet
ELEVATION AT TRAILHEAD: 7,738 feet
CONFIGURATION: Out-and-back
DIFFICULTY: Easy
SCENERY: Sweeping views of Utah Valley and surrounding peaks
EXPOSURE: Partially shaded
TRAFFIC: Light
TRAIL SURFACE: Dirt with shale near the summit
HIKING TIME: 30 minutes–1 hour
WATER REQUIREMENTS: 0.5 liters; no water on or near the trail
SEASON: Late spring through early fall.
ACCESS: No fees for access or parking. The gate near the top of Squaw Peak road is closed from late October to mid-May (depending on weather).
MAPS: USGS Bridal Veil Falls
FACILITIES: No facilities at trailhead or on trail
DOGS: Permitted

GPS Trailhead Coordinates

UTM Zone (WGS84) 12T
Easting 0448429
Northing 4459263
Latitude N 40° 16' 58.4"
Longitude W 111° 36' 18.8"

IN BRIEF

If you're after a great view with very little effort, Buffalo Peak is the easiest, most accessible summit on the Wasatch Front. Within minutes of the trailhead you're overlooking Utah Valley from an elevation of more than 8,000 feet. And you'll likely have the trail and the summit to yourself.

DESCRIPTION

If you were to fill Provo's LaVell Edwards Stadium to capacity with 65,000 local residents, then ask them where Buffalo Peak is, you might find only a handful who could point it out. From the valley floor, Buffalo Peak is a fairly nondescript rounded knoll, north of the more striking Squaw Peak and west of Cascade Peak. It doesn't appear in the USGS Geographic Names Information System database, yet at 8,025 feet elevation, it's higher than many popular peaks on the Wasatch Front. It's unfortunate this peak has gone unrecognized for so long, because Buffalo Peak stands out as one of the best short hikes in Utah

Directions

From Salt Lake City, go south on I-15 to Orem 800 North (Exit 272). At the bottom of the off-ramp, turn left and proceed east. Travel east on 800 North (UT 52) toward the mouth of Provo Canyon for 3.7 miles. Take the left ramp onto East Provo Canyon Road (US 189). Drive 1.8 miles to Squaw Peak Road and turn right. Continue up Squaw Peak Road for 4 miles to the intersection of Squaw Peak Road and Forest Service Road 027. Turn left on FS 027 toward Hope Campground. At 0.4 miles, the pavement ends. Continue on the dirt road for another 2.9 miles to the unmarked trailhead, with a log-rail fence on the right and fire prevention sign on the left side of the road.

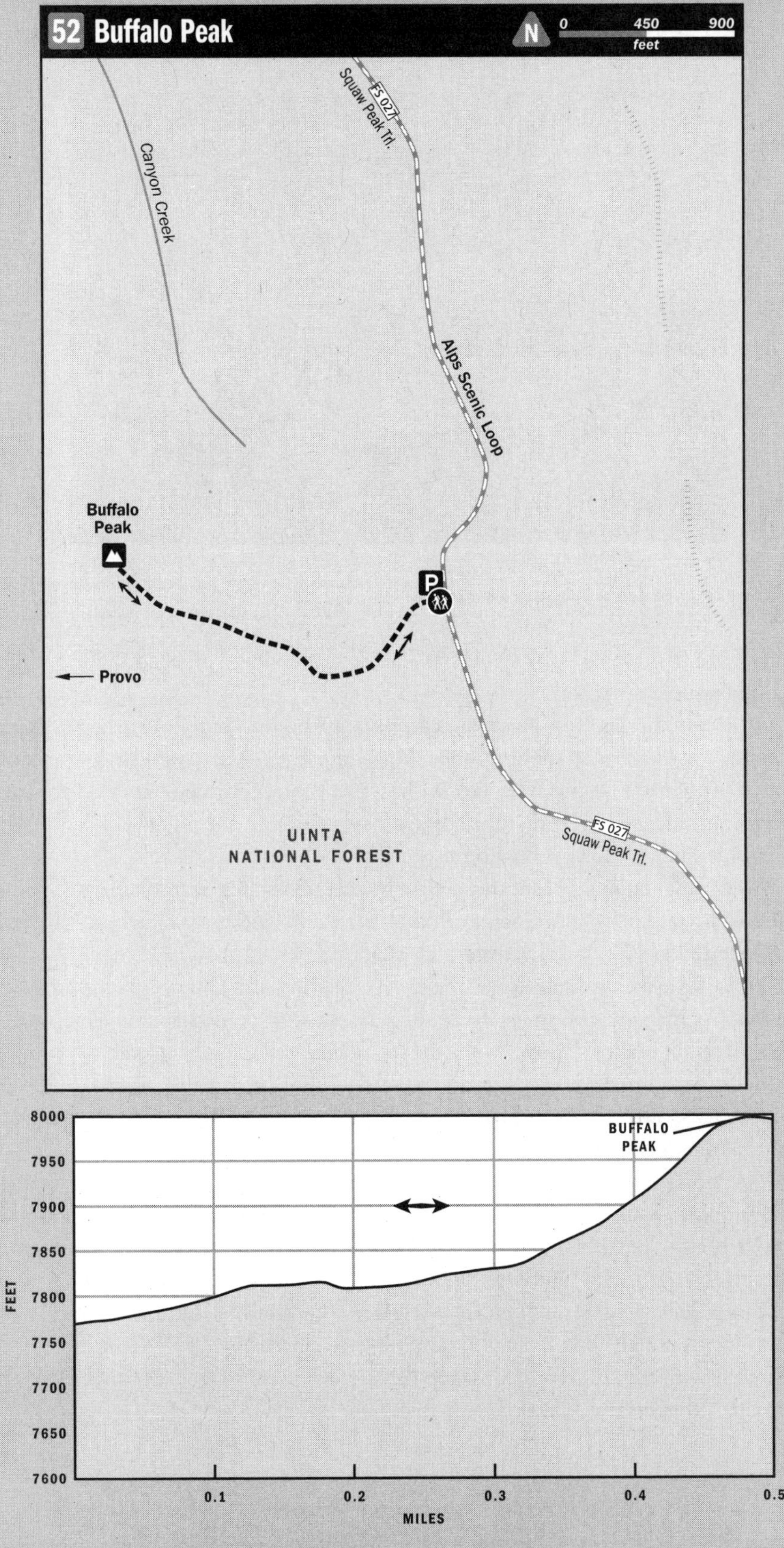

52 Buffalo Peak
N
0
450
900
feet
Squaw Peak Trl.
FS 027
Canyon Creek
Alps Scenic Loop
Buffalo
Peak
P
Provo
UINTA
NATIONAL FOREST
FS 027
Squaw Peak Trl.
8000
7950
7900
7850
7800
7750
7700
7650
7600
FEET
BUFFALO
PEAK
0.1
0.2
0.3
0.4
0.5
MILES

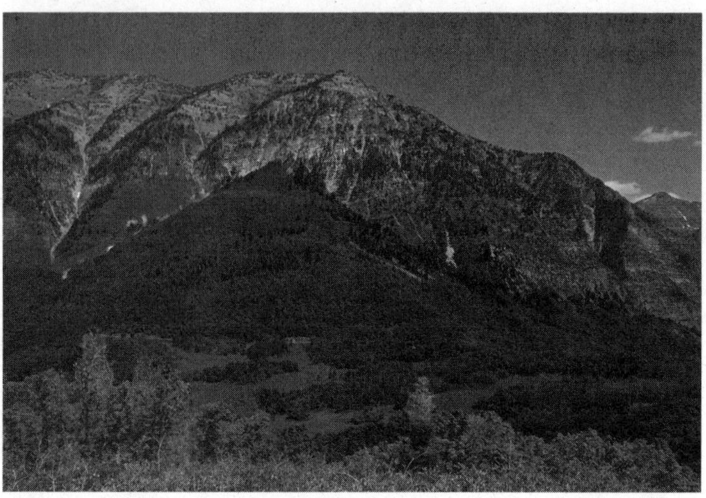

Buffalo Peak, with Cascade Peak as a backdrop

County. You'll enjoy an easy stroll to some dazzling views, all against the solitude of a mountainous backdrop.

At the unmarked trailhead you can park at the side of the dirt road and easily crawl over or under the log fence. You almost feel like you're sneaking onto private property, but the hike lies within the Uinta National Forest. From the fence, continue up the trail through a grassy meadow sprinkled in spring with violet-blue larkspur and yellow bursts of mulesear wyethia.

Deer and cougars visit these dry mountain slopes infrequently. Ground squirrels prove to be more active inhabitants, and with some luck you'll see a black-headed grosbeak or mountain chickadee.

At 100 yards, the trail leaves the grassy clearing and enters a clump of aspen and oak. As the trail continues its gradual ascent, you come to some early partial views of Utah Valley below, with the trail laid out clearly ahead of you. At 0.3 miles, a trail forks to the right, but your summit lies directly ahead. Soon the trail steepens, as the path is sprinkled with chips of shale. The final 0.1-mile push to the summit requires you to negotiate a steep slope of shale and dirt.

After just 0.5 miles of walking from the trailhead, you come to the Buffalo Peak summit, a balding shale outcropping crowned with curly-leaf mountain mahogany, maple, and Gambel oak. In autumn, these hillsides take on the look of a patchwork quilt with lemon-colored aspen, fiery maples, and golden oaks. Take in the excellent views stretching from Mount Nebo on the south to the Salt Lake Valley on the north. You overlook Squaw Peak (elevation 7,877 feet) directly to the south, with the summit of Cascade Peak (elevation 10,760 feet) directly to the east, just 1.6 miles away as the crow flies.

Note: You'll enjoy this trail most on a clear day in late spring with wildflowers in bloom, or in early fall as trees start to turn colors at high elevations. Bring a camera or binoculars.

NEARBY ACTIVITIES

Utah Valley's traditional lover's lane, the Squaw Peak Overlook is a mandatory stop on your way to or from Buffalo Peak. At an elevation of 6,707 feet, it's the perfect drive-to viewpoint for day or evening views of the valley below. From the intersection at the top of Squaw Peak Road and FS 027, turn right and continue 0.3 miles to the overlook parking area.

53 SQUAW PEAK

KEY AT-A-GLANCE INFORMATION

LENGTH: 7 miles
ELEVATION GAIN: 2,709 feet
ELEVATION AT TRAILHEAD: 5,167 feet
CONFIGURATION: Out-and-back
DIFFICULTY: Moderate
SCENERY: Rock formations, canyon, hillside forest, mountain meadow, and panoramic views at summit
EXPOSURE: Mostly shaded
TRAFFIC: Busy
TRAIL SURFACE: Paved for first 0.4 miles, rocky for next 1.2 miles, then dirt to the summit
HIKING TIME: 3.5–5 hours
WATER REQUIREMENTS: 1.5–2 liters, depending on heat
SEASON: Spring, summer, fall
ACCESS: Year-round access; no parking or access fees
MAPS: USGS Bridal Veil Falls
FACILITIES: Restrooms and water at trailhead
DOGS: On leash
SPECIAL COMMENTS: The mouth of Rock Canyon provides a great place to watch or participate in rock climbing.

GPS Trailhead Coordinates

UTM Zone (WGS84) 12T
Easting 0446452
Northing 4457315
Latitude N 40° 15' 52.73"
Longitude W 111° 37' 47.46"

IN BRIEF

One of the most popular summit hikes in Utah County, the climb to the top of Squaw Peak offers memorable highlights such as the dramatic rock walls of Rock Canyon, a climb through a wooded hillside, and panoramic views from the summit. You'll particularly enjoy the hike after the aspens have leafed out in the spring or when they turn a fiery yellow in the fall.

DESCRIPTION

At just 7,876 feet in elevation, Squaw Peak may be considered one of the lesser peaks of the Wasatch Range. But it cuts an unmistakable profile as it rises above the craggy cliffs on Provo's east bench. It's also one of the most deservedly popular day hikes on the Wasatch Front.

The trail to the summit can be broken into three distinctive chunks—the canyon approach, the hillside ascent, and the summit stretch. Each section has a characteristic appeal, and they combine to form a challenging hike offering varied features and highlights. The first 1.5 miles follow the Rock Canyon Trail

Directions →

The trail begins at the mouth of Rock Canyon behind the LDS Temple in Provo. From Salt Lake City take I-15 south to Orem University Parkway (Exit 269). Exit to the left and continue east on University Parkway (UT 265) for 5 miles to 900 East in Provo. Turn left on 900 East and continue north for 0.4 miles, then turn right on Temple View Drive. Continue up Temple View Drive to East 2300 North. Turn right on East 2300 North and continue east for 0.4 miles to the trailhead parking lot straight ahead.

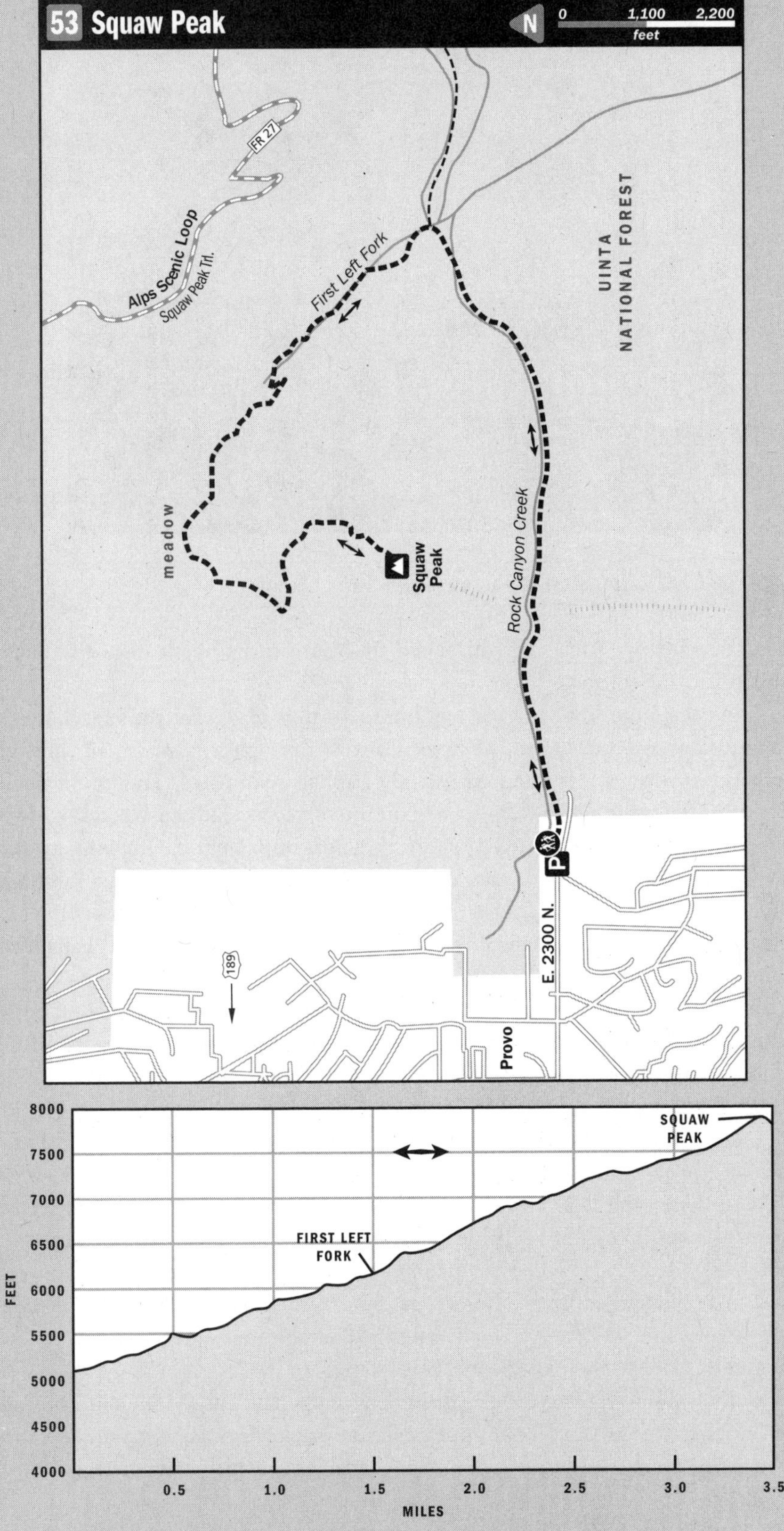
53 Squaw Peak
N
0
1,100
2,200
feet
FR 27
Alps Scenic Loop
Squaw Peak Trl.
First Left Fork
UINTA
NATIONAL FOREST
meadow
Squaw
Peak
Rock Canyon Creek
189
E. 2300 N.
Provo
8000
7500
7000
6500
6000
5500
5000
4500
4000
FEET
SQUAW
PEAK
FIRST LEFT
FORK
0.5
1.0
1.5
2.0
2.5
3.0
3.5
MILES

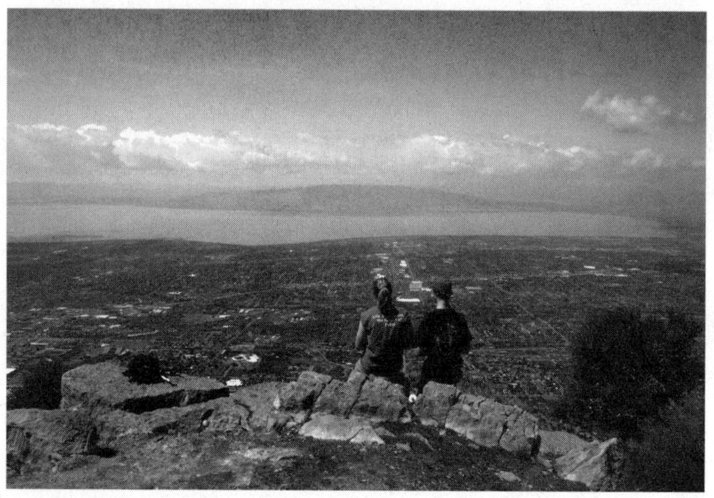

Hikers take in the views from Squaw Peak's summit.

(060) eastward up Rock Canyon. Then the route turns north onto the Squaw Peak Trail to the summit.

From the large trailhead parking lot, the trail is paved for the first 0.4 miles as it leads toward the mouth of Rock Canyon through a covering of sage and Gambel oak. After a few hundred feet, the asphalt road forks. They soon rejoin, but bear to the right if you want to stay on the surfaced road. Easy access to some great routes makes Rock Canyon one of the most popular rock-climbing areas in Utah County. The first rock face on your right is the popular Black Rose wall with Red Slab to the right. Just after the pavement ends, the trail passes through a metal gate and leads to a small cove of climbing faces on the right called The Kitchen.

Beyond the gate, the rocky trail steadily ascends the dry creekbed and passes through a wide canyon. At 0.5 miles past the gate, you'll come to the first of five wooden footbridges crossing the creek. At this point, with the higher elevation, conifers first appear.

On the north side of the creek, at 1.1 miles past the Kitchen gate, you'll come to a brown plastic flap-pole Forest Service sign indicating a trail up the hillside draw to the left, known as the First Left Fork. This begins the second chunk of the hike—the hillside ascent—which begins at an elevation of 6,100 feet. After 1.1 miles of steady climbing, you'll reach a meadow at 7,240 feet. No switchbacks offer relief. But the trail surface is well worn and smooth, and the setting is a thick forest of Gamble oaks and quaking aspens. The climb is steep; the experience, rewarding.

In the hillside forest you may spot deer and small cats. Mountain lions and even bears make an occasional appearance in Rock Canyon, but they are rare. You're much more likely to see mountain chickadees—which often nest and breed

Squaw Peak looms large over the trailhead.

above 8,000 feet—along the hillside trail in spring and summer.

Crossing the high meadow begins the third chunk of the hike—the summit stretch. The trail curves to the left along the southern rim of the meadow through a stand of aspens. Leaving the meadow, the path now heads south toward the summit ahead. You'll climb steadily, but the trail is not quite as steep as the hillside section behind you.

On the way to the summit, the oak cover becomes shorter and juniper dots the hillside. Here you'll first glimpse both the valley to the east and the higher peaks to the west (which are snowcapped well into June). Deer often graze above the meadow; you may even spot them at or near the summit.

Generally, Utah Valley to the west provides the most popular view from the summit. You may feel like you're looking straight down at the trail below, and interestingly, the trail near the mouth of the canyon is about 2,500 feet to the south, with a vertical drop of 2,700 feet. On most days, you can see Mount Nebo to the south and Mount Timpanogos to the north.

As long as you're taking in the panorama, don't forget the peaks behind you to the east. Cascade Mountain (10,908 feet) is the rounded peak with the striated face to the northeast. Lightning Peak is the triangular (11,044) peak in the background to the east, and Provo Peak (11,068) is in the forefront to the southeast. Squaw Peak's summit offers plenty of large, flat rocks that make the perfect table for a summer picnic with a view.

NEARBY ACTIVITIES

With its steep ascents, Squaw Peak supplies a good workout in spring, summer, and fall. During the winter, you may be relegated to Brigham Young University's indoor jogging track in the Smith Fieldhouse. Located near the corner of 1060 North and 150 East in Provo, the Smith Fieldhouse also hosts BYU volleyball games and other events.

54 Y MOUNTAIN

KEY AT-A-GLANCE INFORMATION

LENGTH: 2.4 miles

ELEVATION GAIN: 1,102 feet

ELEVATION AT TRAILHEAD: 5,164 feet

CONFIGURATION: Out-and-back

DIFFICULTY: Moderate

SCENERY: Continuous views of Utah Valley below

EXPOSURE: Completely exposed; no shade

TRAFFIC: Busy

TRAIL SURFACE: Compacted dirt and rock

HIKING TIME: 1–2 hours

WATER REQUIREMENTS: Carry 1 liter. Water at trailhead; none on trail.

SEASON: Year-round. Trail may have snow in winter.

ACCESS: Accessible year-round, day or night. Ample free parking at trailhead.

MAPS: USGS Provo

FACILITIES: Restrooms at trailhead

DOGS: On leash

SPECIAL COMMENTS: A popular trail, well worn by local families and students. Short but steep.

GPS Trailhead Coordinates

UTM Zone (WGS84) 12T

Easting 0446685

Northing 4455125

Latitude N 40° 14' 41.40"

Longitude W 111° 37' 37.9"

IN BRIEF

The immense concrete letter *Y* on the mountainside directly east of the Brigham Young University campus in Provo is visible for miles around Utah Valley. The trail to the Y is a series of a dozen switchbacks offering splendid views of the valley along the way. It's a popular workout or training hike.

DESCRIPTION

At 380 feet high and 130 feet wide, the white Y on Y Mountain is the largest collegiate symbol in the United States—even larger than the HOLLYWOOD sign in the Los Angeles hills. While it can be seen throughout much of Utah Valley, it's also a great place from which to view the valley itself.

The trailhead also provides public access to the Bonneville Shoreline Trail and to the extended Y Mountain Trail for those hikers wanting to continue beyond the Y and on to the summit.

Directions

The trail begins in the foothills directly east of the BYU campus in Provo. From Salt Lake City, take I-15 south to Orem University Parkway (Exit 269). Exit to the left and continue east on University Parkway (UT 265) for 5 miles to 900 East in Provo. Turn right on 900 East and continue south for 0.8 miles to 820 North. Turn left onto 820 North and continue east. After 0.5 miles, 820 East veers left and becomes Oakmont Lane. Continue 0.1 mile along Oakmont Lane to Oakcliff Drive. Turn right on Oakcliff Drive and ascend 0.1 mile to 1450 East. Turn right and continue for 0.1 mile to Terrace Drive. Turn right and follow it 0.1 mile. Before reaching the end of the cul-de-sac, turn left onto 940 North, which leads 0.3 miles up the hill to the trailhead parking lot.

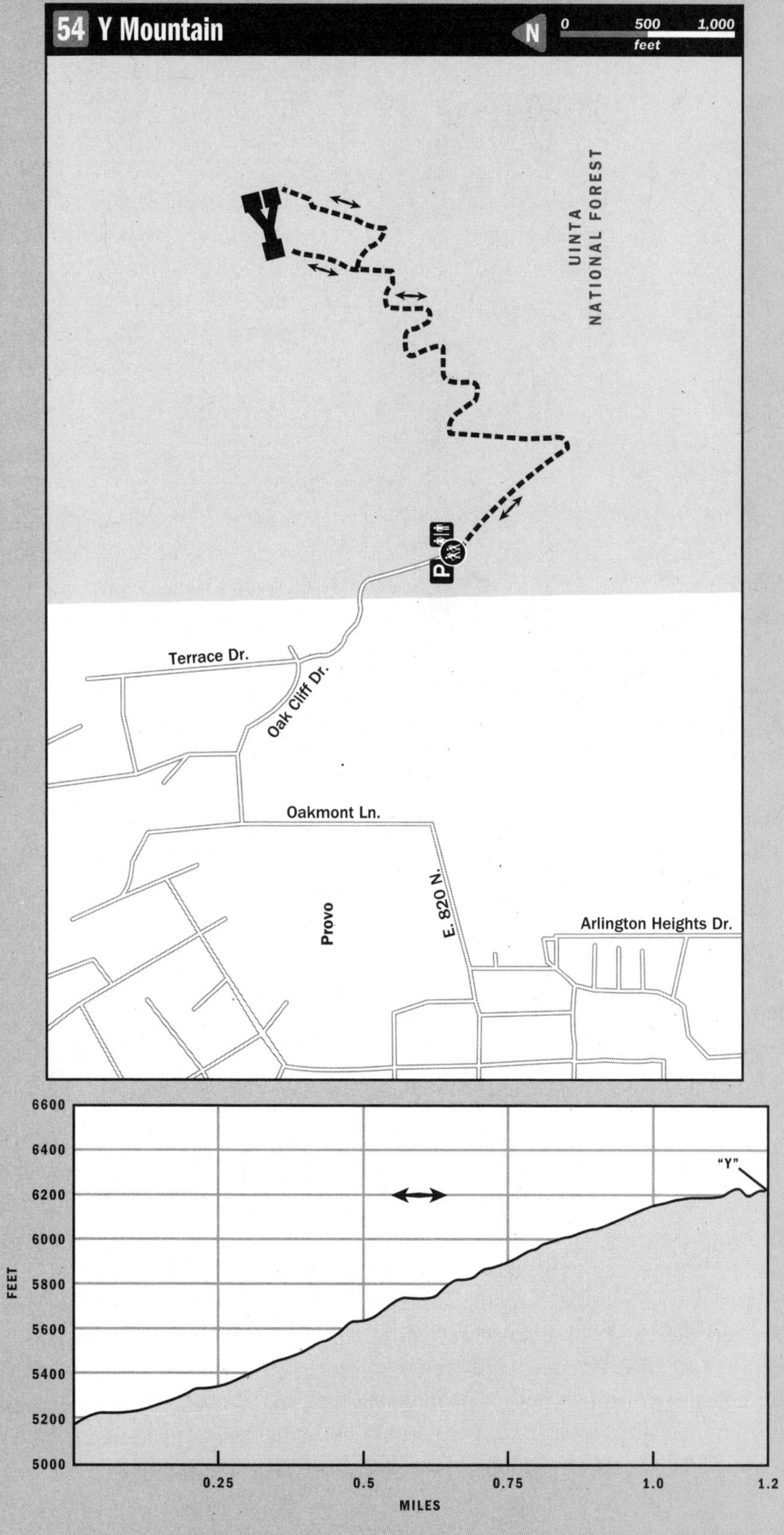
54 Y Mountain
N
0
500
1,000
feet
UINTA
NATIONAL FOREST
Terrace Dr.
Oak Cliff Dr.
Oakmont Ln.
Provo
E. 820 N.
Arlington Heights Dr.
6600
6400
6200
6000
5800
5600
5400
5200
5000
FEET
"Y"
0.25
0.5
0.75
1.0
1.2
MILES

Switchbacks leading up Y Mountain

The wide, well-marked trail is a series of ten steep switchbacks leading to the bottom of the Y, plus two more for those continuing to the top of the Y. The trail is on private land owned by BYU up to the second switchback, after which you enter Uinta National Forest. The city of Provo maintains the trailhead parking area.

Because the trail ascends more than 1,000 feet in just over a mile, this is a popular workout hike, with many residents climbing the path several times a week. No bikes are allowed on the trail, so hikers can move at their own pace and not feel chased. Throughout the hike you have views of the valley below, with no trees to block the view—or the afternoon sun. In the heat of summer you'll see why this hike is popular in the early morning, before the sun crests over the peaks above.

The first two switchbacks are the longest and cover nearly 0.4 miles. For those climbing to the top of the Y, the sign at switchback five marks the halfway point for both distance and elevation gain. Switchback ten is a good rest stop where you can study the photographic panel identifying local peaks and landmarks in the valley below. From this point it's another 0.1 mile to the bottom of the Y. Taking just two more switchbacks 0.2 miles up the mountain leads you to the top of the Y.

Y Mountain juts out from the western slopes of the Wasatch Range to deliver sweeping views of Utah Valley, from Mount Nebo in the south to Lone Peak in the north. Across Utah Lake to the northwest are the Oquirrh Mountains, and the Lake Mountains rise up from the western shores of Utah Lake. The freestanding mountain on the southwest shore of Utah Lake is West Mountain.

The Y was first placed on the mountain in 1906 and enhanced in 1907 with a layer of rock. In 1911 it was enlarged to its present size and made into a block Y with a base of rock, sand, and concrete. Viewed straight-on from the air, the letter appears elongated, but it was designed that way so that it would look normal from the valley floor. In order to reduce both ongoing maintenance costs and the risk of falling, hikers are encouraged not to climb on the surface of the Y.

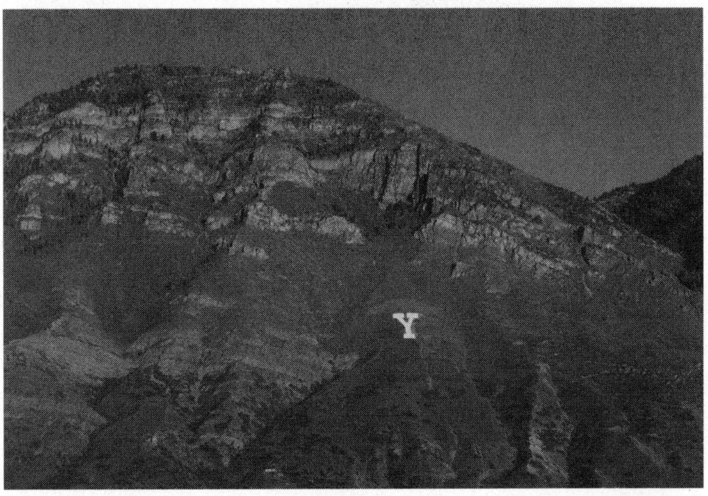

Y Mountain viewed from Orem

Scrubby Gambel oak, sage, and grasses cover the mountain slope. Because the trail is steep and lacks dense vegetation, hikers must stay on the path to minimize erosion. While the trail is steep, it's safe even for young children, with most drop-offs protected by log-rail fencing.

Along the way, chukars frequently cross the trail from their nests in the brush. Magpies and jays appear year-round at lower elevations. Deer graze on the mountain slopes throughout the year, and bighorn sheep occasionally make their way down to the trail area.

Most hikers make the Y their destination and return the way they came up. If you have time, water, and energy to spare, the trail continues from the Y, heading south to Slide Canyon, then north to the summit of Y Mountain at 8,569 feet. It's another 3 miles to the summit (a total of 8 miles round-trip from the trailhead). For those going to the summit, it's nice to know that the steepest part of the trail is all below the Y. If you go just to the Y, you've had a great workout with some well-earned views along the way.

NEARBY ACTIVITIES

The Brigham Young University campus sprawls below the trailhead. After hiking to the Y, a stop at the Creamery on Ninth for an ice-cream cone or shake is a well-deserved guilty pleasure. The Wilkinson Center houses a large food court, the BYU Bookstore, and even a bowling alley on the lower level. The BYU Museum of Art showcases an exceptional permanent collection and plays host to world-class traveling exhibits. The Monte L. Bean Life Science Museum at 645 East 1430 North houses a fascinating and extensive display of animal life. It's a fun place for both adults and children to view both regional wildlife and big game from around the world.

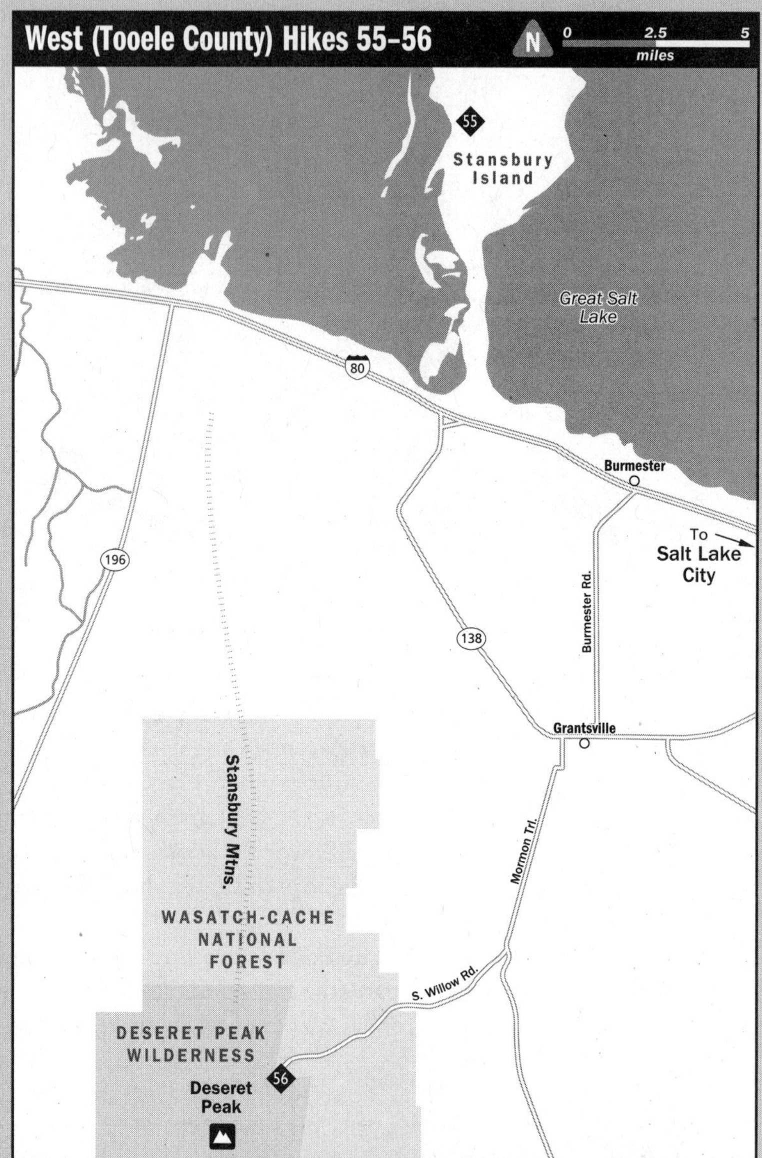
West (Tooele County) Hikes 55–56
N
0
2.5
5
miles
55
Stansbury Island
Great Salt Lake
80
Burmester
To Salt Lake City
196
138
Burmester Rd.
Grantsville
Stansbury Mtns.
Mormon Trl.
WASATCH-CACHE NATIONAL FOREST
S. Willow Rd.
DESERET PEAK WILDERNESS
56
Deseret Peak

WEST (TOOELE COUNTY)

55 STANSBURY ISLAND TRAIL

KEY AT-A-GLANCE INFORMATION

LENGTH: 9.5 miles for the complete loop
ELEVATION GAIN: 619 feet
ELEVATION AT TRAILHEAD: 4,275 feet
CONFIGURATION: Loop
DIFFICULTY: Moderate
SCENERY: Great Salt Lake and geology of Bonneville Shoreline
EXPOSURE: No shade
TRAFFIC: Light
TRAIL SURFACE: Dirt and rock
HIKING TIME: 3.5–4.5 hours
WATER REQUIREMENTS: 1–2 liters, depending on season; no water available on trail
SEASON: Hikable year-round; best in early spring
ACCESS: No fees for access or parking. Trail is managed by the Bureau of Land Management (BLM) and open to hikers, cyclists, and equestrians.
MAPS: USGS Corral Canyon, Plug Peak
FACILITIES: No restrooms or water at trailhead
DOGS: Permitted
SPECIAL COMMENTS: Driving to the trailhead, you'll pass salt evaporation ponds. Morton, Cargill, and other salt companies extract about 2.5 million tons of salt from the lake annually.

GPS Trailhead Coordinates

UTM Zone (WGS84) 12T
Easting 0371743
Northing 4518369
Latitude N 40° 48' 22.6"
Longitude W 112° 21' 14.8"

IN BRIEF

Stansbury Island provides a fascinating glimpse into the geology and natural history of the Great Salt Lake. This loop hike gains all of its elevation in the first mile before following the ancient shoreline of a much larger lake. Solitude, salt, and sweeping lake views define the experience.

DESCRIPTION

When Jim Bridger first saw the Great Salt Lake on an expedition in the winter of 1823–24, he thought it was an arm of the Pacific Ocean. In reality, the Great Salt Lake is the remnant of Lake Bonneville, a much larger prehistoric freshwater lake that was the size of Lake Michigan and covered most of northern Utah. Unless you're armed with some knowledge of the ancient Bonneville shoreline, this could be a fairly mundane desert hike. Let's take a moment to review:

About 15,000 years ago the elevation of Lake Bonneville was about 5,200 feet. This shoreline left a visible "bench," which is prominent along much of the Wasatch Front. Then, about 14,500 years ago, the lake washed away

Directions

From Salt Lake City, take Interstate 80 west to Grantsville/UT 138 (Exit 84). Turn left onto the access road heading west. Continue on this road for 7.1 miles as it curves north onto Stansbury Island, becomes Stansbury Island Road, and heads north along the island's western shore. Turn right and follow a dirt road for 0.2 miles to the BLM trailhead. *Note:* If on the access road you come to a cattle grate followed by a NO TRESPASSING sign, you've gone too far north. Turn around and go back 0.4 miles to the dirt road leading to the trailhead.

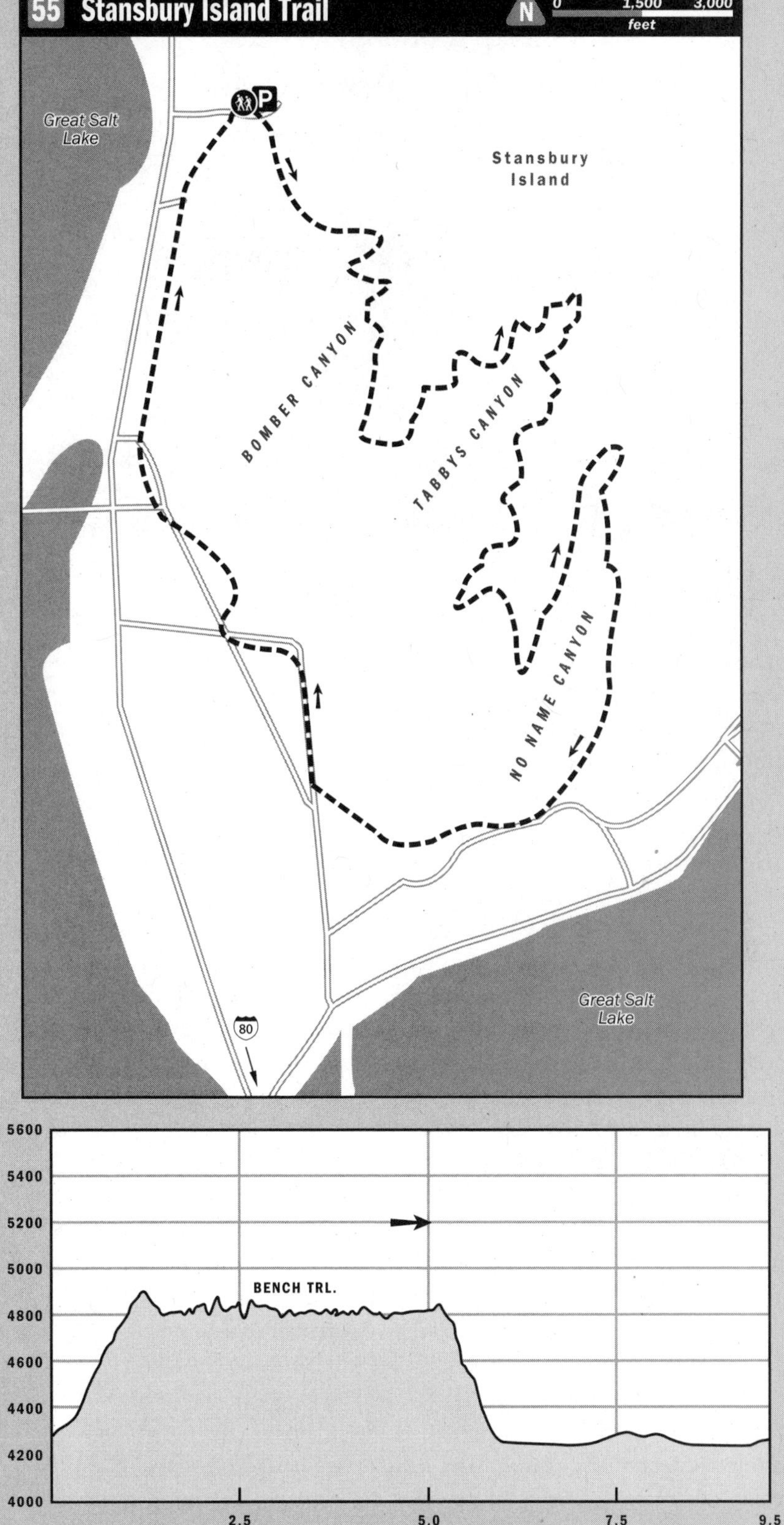

55 Stansbury Island Trail
N
0
1,500
3,000
feet
Great Salt Lake
Stansbury Island
BOMBER CANYON
TABBYS CANYON
NO NAME CANYON
Great Salt Lake
80
5600
5400
5200
5000
4800
4600
4400
4200
4000
FEET
BENCH TRL.
2.5
5.0
7.5
9.5
MILES

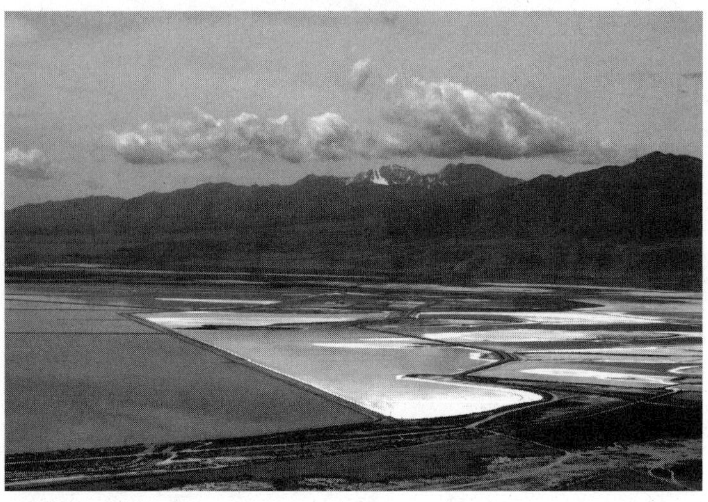

Salt-evaporation ponds to the south with Deseret Peak in the distance

a natural dam near Red Rock Pass in southeastern Idaho, which resulted in a catastrophic flood, draining the lake to a much smaller size. Over the course of a year, the Lake Bonneville shoreline dropped to a lower level, known as the Provo shoreline. The Provo shoreline had an elevation of about 4,840 feet, or 380 feet lower than the earlier Bonneville shoreline. Stansbury Island provides the best preserved and most visible example of the Provo shoreline. This hike follows the Provo shoreline around the southern end of the island as it winds along the level contour of several large canyons.

When Howard Stansbury, a government surveyor, first explored Stansbury Island in 1849, water entirely surrounded it. Since then, the Great Salt Lake has retreated from its 1875 high-water level, leaving Stansbury Island as a peninsula. As you take the road to the trailhead, be sure to watch for the many migratory shorebirds found in the wetlands and pools at the south end of the lake. Once on the island, the shorebirds disappear, replaced by meadowlarks and other range and field birds.

From the trailhead, follow the trail to the south, leading across the alluvial plain and up a rocky slope. At 1.2 miles, you've arrived at the high elevation for the hike, just under 5,000 feet. After crossing the saddle you drop a little more than 100 feet in elevation, and the trail begins its 4-mile love affair with the Provo shoreline. As the contour of the shoreline enters canyons and rounds hillsides, the trail never gains or loses more than 10 feet in elevation. It sticks with the shoreline until making its final descent back to the lake level.

The first canyon you skirt is the fairly small Bomber Canyon. At 1.8 miles you come around the bend to enter Tabbys Canyon, the largest of the canyons and one with dramatic views. After following the deep and clearly visible shoreline contour of Tabbys Canyon for 2.8 miles, you round the hillside to wide-open views of the Great Salt Lake and the Oquirrh Mountains to the east. To the south are the Stansbury Mountains and Deseret Peak. Geologically, Stansbury Island is actually a small northern extension of the Stansbury Mountains.

At 5.2 miles, you'll find yourself at the head of No Name Canyon on the southeast side of the island. At a fork in the trail, take the faint path to the right that descends the slope directly for 0.5 miles to a Jeep road that loops back to the trailhead along the flat-desert terrain just above the lake level. Once you reach the dirt road, the flexipole signs do a good job of guiding you back to the trailhead, although it's a pretty intuitive route. If you want to avoid hiking on Jeep trails, you can leave a shuttle vehicle at the mouth of No Name Canyon and make this a one-way 6.4-mile hike.

Stansbury Island offers a field course in geology. Along the way you'll pass outcroppings of shale, limestone, quartzite, and conglomerates that look for all the world like concrete—but they're not. The calcium carbonate deposits that form much of the Provo shoreline, known as tufa rock, were formed by precipitation from the high dissolved calcium content of Lake Bonneville. You'll find tufa rock used in many early Utah homes in areas such as Bountiful and Pleasant Grove, which are near the Provo shoreline level.

Although the trail is hikable year-round, plan to visit in early spring, when the sheep grass is green and the sage and juniper are aromatic. By mid-May, the range grasses dry and turn brown, and with no shade or water on the trail it can quickly become a hot desert hike.

With every step of the hike you'll have great views of the Great Salt Lake and distant mountains. To the south you'll be looking down on the evaporation ponds used for the commercial production of salt. More than 4.5 billion tons of salt are dissolved and suspended in the Great Salt Lake, which has no outlet. About 2.2 million tons of salt enter the lake annually from surface and groundwater flow, while salt industries extract about 2.5 million tons of salt and other elements from the lake each year. As you look out over a lake that was once 1,000 feet deep, it's interesting to note that today the Great Salt Lake has a maximum depth of only 35 feet, with an average depth of just 14 feet. While no fish live in the lake, abundant brine shrimp serve as a food source for the millions of migratory birds that pass through the area every year.

NEARBY ACTIVITIES

Saltair, a resort on the shores of the Great Salt Lake, features concerts, events, parties, beach access, and showers. Built in 1893 by the Salt Lake and Los Angeles Railroad Company at a cost of more than $350,000, the original pavilion was destroyed by fire in 1971. The current pavilion was built in 1981. To the west of Saltair is the Great Salt Lake Marina State Park, with a well-developed marina, electricity, and a pumpout station.

56 DESERET PEAK

KEY AT-A-GLANCE INFORMATION

LENGTH: 8.5 miles

ELEVATION GAIN: 3,603 feet

ELEVATION AT TRAILHEAD: 7,428 feet

CONFIGURATION: Loop

DIFFICULTY: Difficult

SCENERY: Wooded approach, high-mountain terrain, excellent views

EXPOSURE: Mostly shaded below 10,000-foot level. Fully exposed to sun above 10,000 feet elevation.

TRAFFIC: Light

TRAIL SURFACE: Dirt, rock

HIKING TIME: 5–7 hours

WATER REQUIREMENTS: 2 liters. Water in streams may be purified.

SEASON: Late spring, summer, early fall

ACCESS: Day-use fee payable at self-serve drop box in campground

MAPS: USGS Deseret Peak East, Deseret Peak West

FACILITIES: Restrooms at trailhead

DOGS: Permitted on leash

SPECIAL COMMENTS: Entire hike is within the Deseret Peak Wilderness Area. No motorized vehicles or bicycles permitted.

GPS Trailhead Coordinates

UTM Zone (WGS84) 12T

Easting 0363796

Northing 4482569

Latitude N 40° 28' 58.7"

Longitude W 112° 36' 23.9"

IN BRIEF

At 11,031 feet, Deseret Peak is the highest point in Tooele County and the centerpiece of the Deseret Peak Wilderness Area. It's also a magnificent expanse of both semiarid and alpine scenery—glacial basins, mountain streams, woodland, and high meadows—rising from the middle of the desert. This loop hike captures some of that surprising variety and affords views across the Bonneville Salt Flats and into Nevada.

DESCRIPTION

The Great Basin, which covers western Utah and most of Nevada, consists of dozens of north–south-trending mountain ranges and basins. Best known for their impact on local weather patterns and their jagged profile revealed with each sunset, the Oquirrh Mountains bound the Salt Lake Valley on the west. The Stansbury Mountains, which lie just to the west of the Oquirrhs and Tooele Valley, don't attract as much attention. Wasatch hikers rarely climb Deseret Peak, the jewel of the Stansbury Mountains. And that's a shame, since the area has so much to offer.

Directions

From Salt Lake City, take I-80 west to Grantsville (Exit 84). From the exit, turn left onto the access road, cross under I-80, and continue south on UT 138 for 9.5 miles to Grantsville. Turn right on West Street (400 West), and continue for 5 miles to South Willow Canyon (marked by a sign). Continue west on South Willow Canyon Road for 7.2 miles to the Loop Campground. The last 4 miles of the road are unpaved. You'll find the trailhead at the top of the loop, to the right of the vault toilets.

56 Deseret Peak

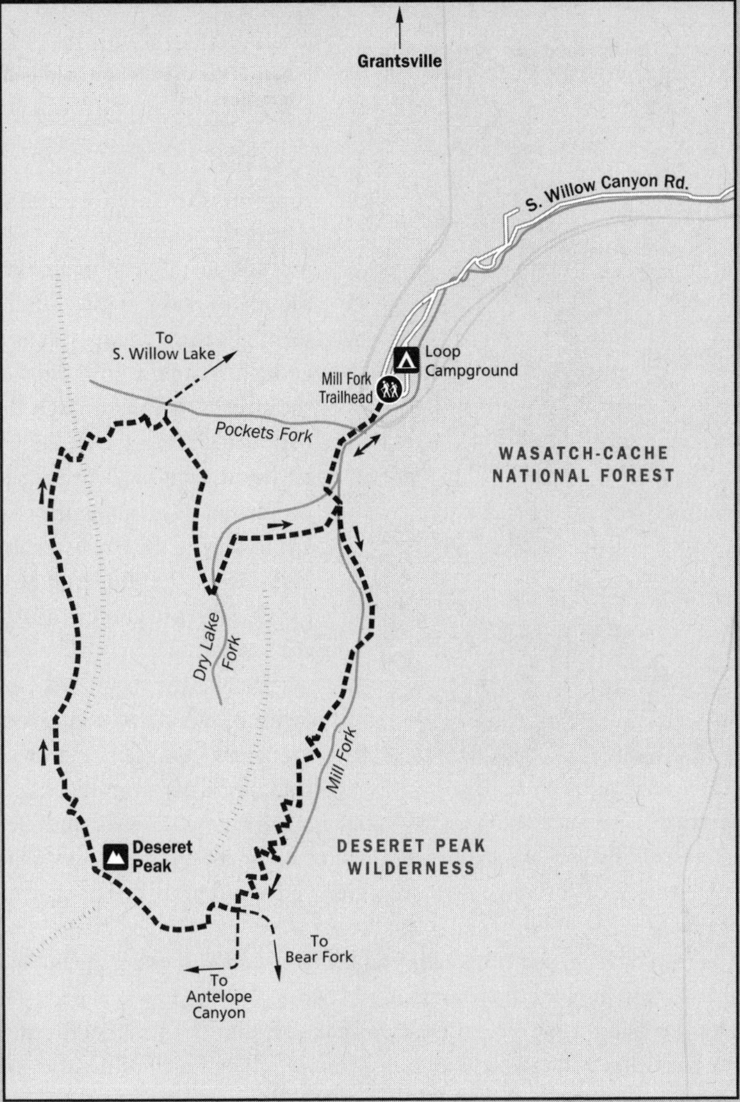

N
0
1,750
3,500
feet
Grantsville
S. Willow Canyon Rd.
To
S. Willow Lake
Loop
Campground
Mill Fork
Trailhead
Pockets Fork
WASATCH-CACHE
NATIONAL FOREST
Dry Lake
Fork
Mill Fork
Deseret
Peak
DESERET PEAK
WILDERNESS
To
Bear Fork
To
Antelope
Canyon

11000
10500
10000
9500
9000
8500
8000
7500
7000
FEET
DESERET
PEAK
MILL
FORK
POCKETS
FORK
2.5
5.0
7.5
8.5
MILES

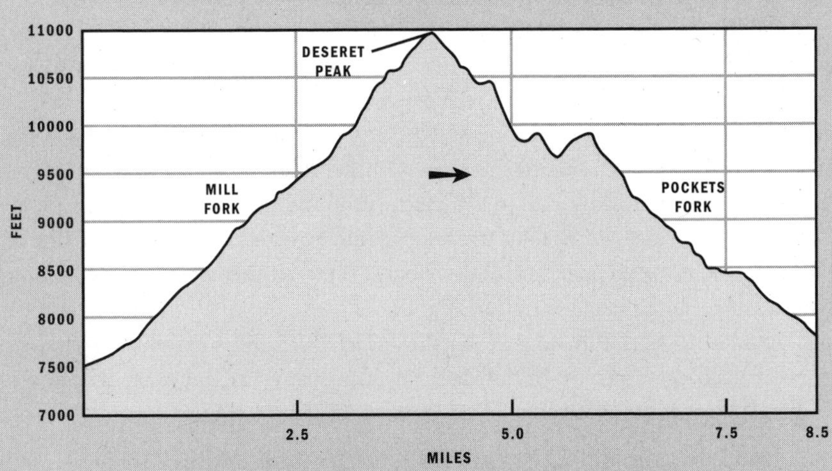

Deseret Peak's trails hold snow well into June.

The drive to the trailhead captures the transformation from desert to mountain as the road ascends an alluvial plain into the mouth of the canyon. You'll drive through two narrows with barely enough room for both the road and the stream to pass through the high rock walls rising above. Nearing the trailhead, you're likely to see wild turkeys and deer along the roadside. On its way to the trailhead, the road gains nearly 2,500 feet of elevation, giving hikers a good head start on the summit.

From the trailhead, a dense forest of aspen and conifers quickly immerses you. This section of the trail provides a vivid example of the aspen-to-conifer succession cycle. Aspen appear early in a woodland life cycle. Conifers, which initially are shaded and protected by aspen, eventually shade out the aspens. Many of the large, mature aspens have fallen in this area, while the conifers remain.

At 0.7 miles from the trailhead, you'll reach a stream crossing. Immediately after the crossing, the trail dips momentarily before coming to a sign and trail junction. Take the trail on the left to Deseret Peak. This junction marks the start of a clockwise loop that will take you up one drainage, along much of the Deseret Peak ridgeline to the summit, and then bring you back by way of another drainage.

At 1.1 miles from the trailhead, you'll enter the lower level of Mill Fork, a large glacial valley ringed by Douglas-fir. The trail leads to the top of a steep glacial bowl, gaining nearly 2,200 feet of elevation in 2.3 miles. After a series of switchbacks near the top of the bowl, you'll arrive at the ridge and enjoy your first views of the Great Basin to the west. On this ridge, at a four-way junction, a sign points the way to Bear Fork on the left, Antelope Canyon directly ahead, and Deseret Peak to your right. Take the trail to the right as it leads almost directly up a shadeless slope to a higher rocky ridge. The trail skirts some false summits before arriving at the true summit nearly a mile from the junction. Along the way, you'll gain an appreciation for the hardy limber pine and subalpine fir that survive a tortured existence at 11,000 feet. In late spring and summer, wildflowers line the rocky trail all the way to the summit.

You'll share the summit with cliff swallows as they swoop and dart around the rocky ledges. Because the Stansbury Mountains are an isolated, stand-alone range, Deseret Peak has nothing nearby to block the view. On a clear day—which in summer is nearly every day—you can see Pilot Peak in Nevada more than 60 miles to the northwest. Mount Nebo is visible to the southeast.

Most Wasatch peak-baggers never see the Bonneville Salt Flats from a summit, but they're easily viewed from Deseret Peak. This 6,000-square-mile bed of salt, known as "the flattest place on earth," is the site of numerous land speed records.

To make the return loop, continue northward as you descend along the summit ridge. After 0.3 miles, the trail drops well below the ridge on the west side. When you've hiked 1.5 miles from the summit, the trail makes a sharp turn to the right and continues its descent of the east side of the ridge in a series of short switchbacks. At 2.2 miles from the summit, having descended Pockets Fork, you'll come to a sign pointing to South Willow Lake to the left and the Loop Campground, your return route, to the right. As the trail sweeps along a bowl, making a gradual descent, you'll have picture-postcard views of the ridge above and to the west. Soon you enter the familiar aspen-and-spruce woodland that leads back to the stream-crossing junction and down to the trailhead.

Not many peaks allow hikers to do a loop and take in such a variety of ecosystems and rough wilderness terrain by means of a well-marked, easy-to-follow trail. A Deseret Peak loop offers hikers abundant scenery, a real appreciation for the immense size of the wilderness area, and a sense of how much is available to explore.

NEARBY ACTIVITIES

Tooele Valley is home to the Deseret Peak Complex, a multipurpose public recreation venue that features one of Utah's largest swimming pools, complete with a waterslide and wading area, professionally designed and maintained tracks for motocross, BMX, ATV, and horse racing. Within the complex, you'll find soccer fields, softball diamonds, pitch and putt golf, playgrounds, an archery park, indoor and outdoor arenas, pavilions, and two museums. For general and special events information, call (435) 843-4000 or visit **www.deseretpeakcomplex.com.**

East (Uintas/Summit Cty.) Hikes 57–60
N
0
1600
3200
feet
To Evanston, WY
Kamas Lake
Picturesque Lake
Butterfly Lake
Butterfly Campground
57
WASATCH-CACHE NATIONAL FOREST
150
Bud Lake
58
Pass Lake
Bonnie Lake
Blythe Lake
Mirror Lake Campground
Bald Mtn.
Moosehorn Campground
Moosehorn Lake
59
150
60
Fehr Lake
Bald Mtn. Pass
HIGH UINTAS WILDERNESS
Murdock Mtn.
To Kamas & SLC
80
40

EAST (UINTAS/SUMMIT COUNTY)

57 NATURALIST BASIN

KEY AT-A-GLANCE INFORMATION

LENGTH: 12–18 miles round-trip
ELEVATION GAIN: 996 feet (low elevation: on trail, near Scudder Lake, 9,950 feet; high elevation: Faxon Lake, 10,946 feet)
ELEVATION AT TRAILHEAD: 10,376 feet
CONFIGURATION: Out-and-back with loop and spur options
DIFFICULTY: Difficult (due to length and elevation)
SCENERY: Lakes and ponds, spruce forests, wildflowers, and surrounding mountains
EXPOSURE: Mostly shaded to Naturalist Basin; full exposure to sun on upper basin above tree line
TRAFFIC: Moderate
TRAIL SURFACE: Dirt and some rock
HIKING TIME: 6–10 hours
WATER REQUIREMENTS: 2 liters. Water in lakes and streams can be purified.
SEASON: Summer
ACCESS: Located within the Wasatch-Cache National Forest fee recreation area. Pick up a recreation pass at the Kamas Ranger Station or at one of the self-service fee stations along the Mirror Lake Highway.

See additional information at end of Description, page 253.

GPS Trailhead Coordinates

UTM Zone (WGS84) 12T
Easting 0511483
Northing 4508023
Latitude N 40° 43' 19.5"
Longitude W 110° 51' 50.5"

IN BRIEF

A rolling trail through a basin of woods, meadows, and scenic lakes, almost entirely above 10,000 feet in elevation. While the complete loop with spur trails to nearby lakes can cover more than 20 miles, it can easily be adapted to a shorter 12-mile hike. But the gentle, flowing nature of the trail makes you want to go on to the next lake or meadow.

DESCRIPTION

The beauty of the Uinta Mountains is as likely to be found in its complex network of basins and drainages as in its quartzite peaks. Unlike the canyons of the Wasatch, you're never quite sure where the water comes from and which direction it's flowing. Naturalist Basin, located east of the Mirror Lake Highway, generally flows south into the Duchesne River. But the rolling, meandering nature of the trail never makes that clearly visible to the hiker.

Naturalist Basin lies to the south of Mount Agassiz, named for the great Swiss-American naturalist, Louis Agassiz. Most of the lakes in Naturalist Basin were named after Agassiz's students at Harvard and Cornell, many of whom went on to become prominent

Directions

From Salt Lake City, take Interstate 80 east to Silver Creek Junction/US 40 (Exit 148). Turn right and go south on US 40 for 3.4 miles to UT 248 (Exit 4). At the end of the off-ramp, turn left and continue on UT 248 for 11.4 miles to South Main Street (UT) in Kamas. Turn left on South Main Street in Kamas and go north for two blocks, then turn right on Center Street (UT 150). Continue on UT 150 for 34.2 miles (just past mile marker 34) to the Hayden Pass/Highline trailhead.

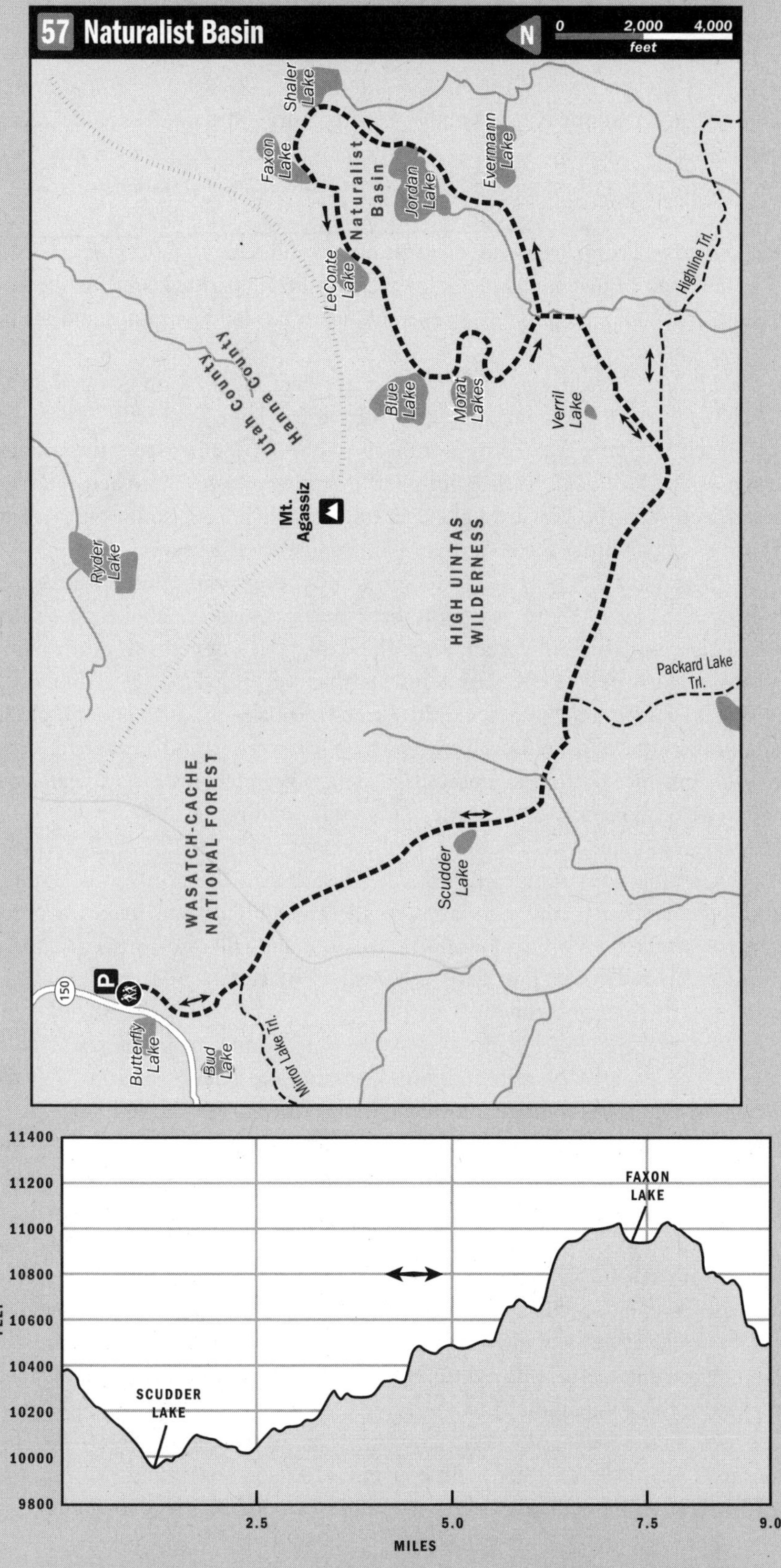

57 Naturalist Basin
N
0
2,000
4,000
feet
Shaler Lake
Faxon Lake
Naturalist Basin
Jordan Lake
Evermann Lake
LeConte Lake
Highline Trl.
Hanna County
Utah County
Blue Lake
Morat Lakes
Verril Lake
Mt. Agassiz
HIGH UINTAS WILDERNESS
Ryder Lake
Packard Lake Trl.
WASATCH-CACHE NATIONAL FOREST
Scudder Lake
150
P
Butterfly Lake
Bud Lake
Mirror Lake Trl.
11400
11200
11000
10800
10600
10400
10200
10000
9800
FEET
FAXON LAKE
SCUDDER LAKE
2.5
5.0
7.5
9.0
MILES

scientists and naturalists, including David Starr Jordan, Nathaniel Shaler, Joseph LeConte, Charles Walcott, and Alpheus Packard. Agassiz's legacy can be found in the names of many American species and natural landmarks.

Naturalist Basin is accessed from the Highline Trail (083), a 60-mile trail that crosses the Uintas from east to west, almost all above 10,000 feet elevation, and much of it above tree line. The large trailhead parking area to the south serves hikers, while the parking area to the north has loading ramps and facilities for horses and stock.

From the trailhead, the trail descends 200 feet in elevation through a forest of Engelmann spruce to a junction with the Mirror Lake Trail at 0.7 miles. Continue on the Highline Trail to the southeast. At about 2 miles from the trailhead, you'll pass Scudder Lake to the south and continue another mile before arriving at a junction with the Packard Lake Trail (059), which leads south on a 1.4-mile optional spur to Wilder Lake, Wyman Lake, and Packard Lake.

In these woods, you're likely to see woodpeckers and pine grosbeaks. One species you're not likely to see is the bark beetle, an insect about the size of a piece of rice; but you will certainly see the damage it's done to trees throughout the Uintas. Bark beetles are native insects that kill individual trees but do not threaten the entire tree species. Healthy trees normally produce enough pitch to flush out the attacking beetles. But when trees are stressed and weakened, they're unable to produce sufficient amounts of defensive pitch. In recent years, more trees have been killed by bark beetles than by forest fires.

Continuing along the Highline Trail for another 1.2 miles, you'll arrive at a marked junction where the trail forks. Go left and to the north into Naturalist Basin. (The Highline Trail continues to the right.) The trail makes a gradual ascent for about a mile into Naturalist Basin, eventually crossing a stream and arriving at an open meadow with a backdrop of Uinta cliffs and 12,428-foot Mount Agassiz to the northwest.

At this point you've hiked a little more than 5 miles from the trailhead and you're at the edge of Naturalist Basin. Jordan Lake (elevation 10,625 feet), a popular fishing destination, is another mile up the trail to the northeast. Morat Lakes (10,757 feet), about a mile to the northwest, also attract the anglers. But if you got off to an early start and still have plenty of energy, consider taking the loop to the upper basin. Few hikers take this loop, since it ascends beyond the tree line into a more remote and rugged alpine ecosystem, but it is certainly worth the effort. To reach this upper basin, take a faint trail leading from the east side of Jordan Lake up a rocky slope to Shaler Lake (10,920 feet). As you ascend just 300 feet of elevation, you move from a subalpine to an alpine ecosystem, where everything changes. You'll find different animals, birds, wildflowers, and trees as you explore this high alpine shelf.

From Shaler Lake, the loop continues on to Faxon Lake (10,946 feet), LeConte Lake (10,925 feet), Blue Lake (10,945 feet), and Morat Lakes (10,757 feet). Passing Morat Lakes, the trail descends 300 feet to return to the junction and stream crossing where you first entered Naturalist Basin. From here you can pick up the trail that returns you to the Highline Trail and on to the trailhead, another 5 miles to the west.

Naturalist Basin is popular but never really busy. The trail is well traveled but never crowded. It's a relaxing, meandering, therapeutic trail, which in spite of its long distance and high elevation is suitable for hikers of various skill levels. For the most part, the route is intuitive, but you should take a GPS, or a map and compass, and be proficient in their use.

ADDITIONAL AT-A-GLANCE INFORMATION

MAPS: USGS Hayden Peak, Trails Illustrated High Uintas Wilderness (711)
FACILITIES: Restrooms, picnic tables, and drinking water at trailhead
DOGS: Permitted
SPECIAL COMMENTS: Located within High Uintas Wilderness Area

NEARBY ACTIVITIES

The Samak Smoke House is a favorite one-stop shopping destination for visitors to the Mirror Lake Highway. Located just 2 miles east of Kamas at 1937 Mirror Lake Highway, the country store and restaurant is a convenient place to pick up your recreation pass and any provisions you might need for the hike. On the return trip, stop and try their famous jerky, and smoked salmon or trout. Shop for gifts and gourmet foods or dine out on the patio. For orders and information, call (435) 783-4880 or shop online at **www.samaksmokehouse.com.**

58 LOFTY LAKE LOOP

KEY AT-A-GLANCE INFORMATION

LENGTH: 4.1 miles
ELEVATION GAIN: 920 feet (Reids Meadow to the pass east of Lofty Lake)
ELEVATION AT TRAILHEAD: 10,154 feet
CONFIGURATION: Loop
DIFFICULTY: Moderate
SCENERY: Alpine lakes, streams, meadows, mountains
EXPOSURE: Mostly shaded below 10,500 feet. Partially shaded above 10,500 feet.
TRAFFIC: Moderate
TRAIL SURFACE: Rock and dirt
HIKING TIME: 3–4 hours
WATER REQUIREMENTS: 1–2 liters. Water in lakes and streams can be purified.
SEASON: Summer
ACCESS: Located within the Wasatch-Cache National Forest fee recreation area. Pick up a recreation pass at the Kamas Ranger Station or at one of the self-service fee stations along the Mirror Lake Highway.
MAPS: USGS Mirror Lake, Trails Illustrated High Uintas Wilderness (711)

See additional information at end of Description, page 257.

GPS Trailhead Coordinates

UTM Zone (WGS84) 12T
Easting 0509017
Northing 4507020
Latitude N 40° 42' 50.9"
Longitude W 110° 53' 34.9"

IN BRIEF

Lofty Lake Loop has something for everyone—lakes, streams, deep woods, meadows, ridge routes, mountain passes, and scenic views—all within a convenient loop. There are a few steep ascents and descents, but they're never too long. There is some routefinding and map reading required, but never too challenging. The hike is well suited to families and children capable of hiking 4 miles over varied and sometimes rugged terrain. The entire hike is above 10,000 feet elevation, so be on guard for symptoms of altitude sickness.

DESCRIPTION

Lofty Lake Loop is the perfect introductory hike into all the scenic beauty that the Uinta Mountains have to offer. It's a loop hike (as you may have already guessed from its name), so you never retrace your route. New territory, surprises, and fresh sights wait around every corner.

The trail can be hiked in either direction, but the clockwise loop described here seems to be the general preference for several reasons: If you get an early start, the wildlife viewing is likely to be better in the clockwise

Directions

From Salt Lake City, take I-80 east to Silver Creek Junction/US 40 (Exit 148). Turn right and go south on US 40 for 3.4 miles to UT 248 (Exit 4). At the end of the off-ramp, turn left and continue on UT 248 for 11.4 miles to South Main Street (UT 32) in Kamas. Turn left on South Main Street in Kamas and go north for two blocks, then turn right on Center Street (UT 150). Continue on UT 150 for 32 miles to the Pass Lake trailhead. Enter the large loop parking area on the left (west) side of the road.

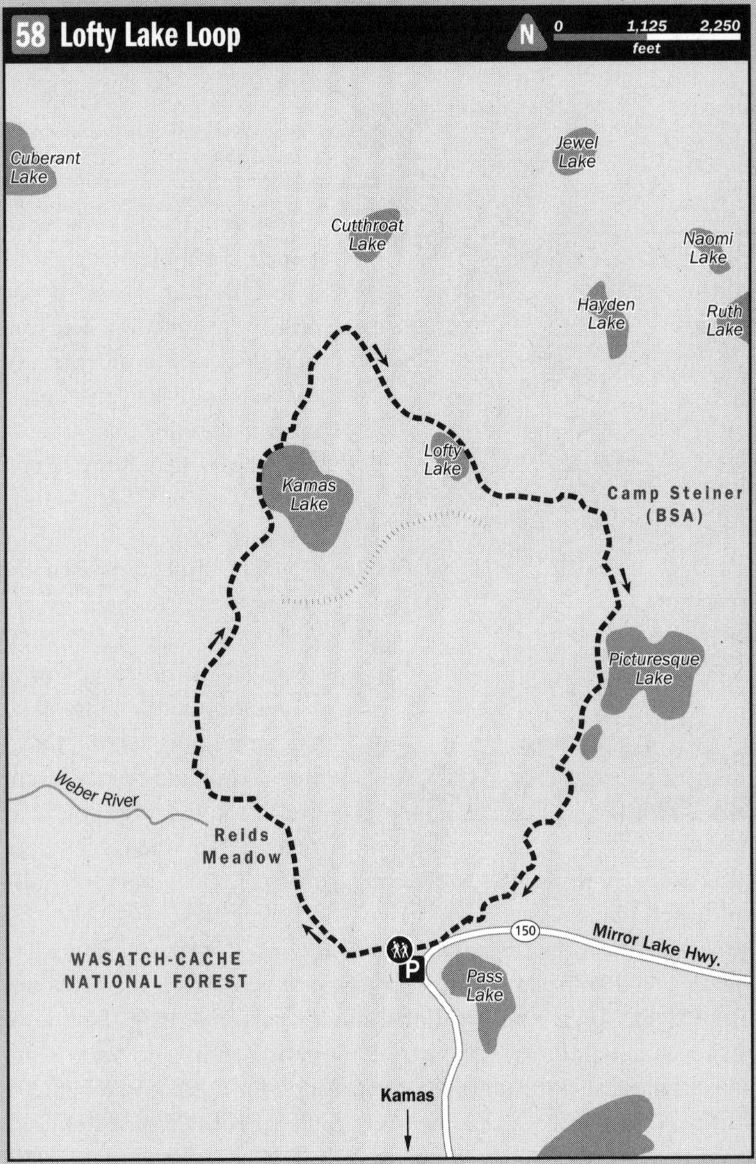

58 Lofty Lake Loop
N
0
1,125
2,250
feet
Cuberant Lake
Jewel Lake
Cutthroat Lake
Naomi Lake
Hayden Lake
Ruth Lake
Lofty Lake
Kamas Lake
Camp Steiner (BSA)
Picturesque Lake
Weber River
Reids Meadow
150
Mirror Lake Hwy.
WASATCH-CACHE NATIONAL FOREST
P
Pass Lake
Kamas

11400
11200
11000
10800
10600
10400
10200
10000
9800
FEET
LOFTY LAKE
KAMAS LAKE
REIDS MEADOW
1.0
2.0
3.0
4.0
4.1
MILES

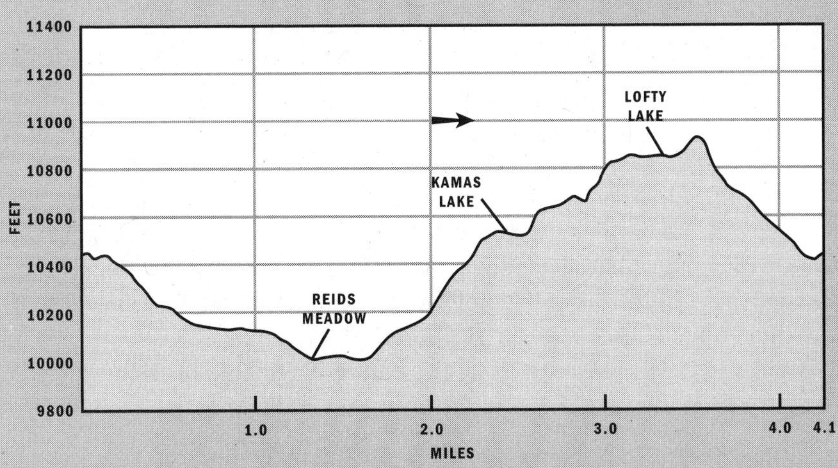

Provo River Falls (see Nearby Activities on facing page)

direction. Also, the steepest sustained grade on the trail occurs as a descent near the end if done in a clockwise direction. The trail leading clockwise from the trailhead to Kamas Lake generally offers more solitude than the section from Lofty Lake back to the parking lot, which passes through the Scout camp.

The trail starts near the restroom at the southwest side of the parking lot and ends just 100 feet away on the north side of the lot. In addition to the Lofty Lake Trail, the trailhead serves the Weber River Trail and the Cuberant Lake Trail. You'll know you're on the right trail when, 50 feet into the woods, you come to a sign directing you to Holiday Park (7 miles) and Cuberant Lake (3 miles).

At this sign, take the trail to Holiday Park and Cuberant Lake to the right. At 0.3 miles you'll come to another fork, where you'll take the Cuberant Lake Trail to the right. You'll find occasional muddy surfaces along these lower sections of the trail. Wildflowers abound all along the trail, with Parry's primrose and alpine asters among the most common. Watch for Queen Anne's lace with its bursts of tiny white flowers; as a member of the carrot family, it has leaves that look just like carrot tops.

At 0.7 miles the trail crosses a small brook, then skirts the north side of a large, open, marshy area known as Reids Meadow. At 0.9 miles you leave the meadow by climbing a rocky slope to the north. At 1.2 miles from the trailhead, you come to another fork in the trail pointing to Cuberant Lake on the left and Kamas and Lofty lakes to the right. Continue up and to the right for another 0.4 miles along a rocky grade made up of chunky quartzite, and you'll soon arrive at a crest with Kamas Lake spread out immediately in front of you. The total distance from the trailhead to Kamas Lake is 1.6 miles. At this point, you've descended just 150 feet from the trailhead to Reids Meadow, yet gained 520 feet in the climb up to Kamas Lake, at 10,520 feet in elevation.

Kamas Lake is a great place to rest before continuing on along the shore leading to a small man-made dam at the northwest end of the lake. From the dam, another steep rocky ascent leads to a high meadow laced with small ponds and brooks, and ringed with fir and spruce. Another steep ascent of a rocky slope leads to a crest above the meadow at an elevation of 10,700 feet and some dreamlike views of Teal Lake, Cutthroat Lake, and Jewel Lake to the north.

At this midpoint, just a half mile beyond Kamas Lake, the trail begins to head south, crossing a high alpine plateau sprinkled with wildflowers and Englemann spruce. At the south end of the plateau you'll come to a small rise before dipping down to Lofty Lake, a shimmering jewel ringed by wildflowers. At an elevation of 10,840 feet, Lofty Lake is 2.5 miles from the starting trailhead.

Leading away from Lofty Lake, the trail rises and peaks at an elevation of 10,920 feet along a rock outcropping. Below is Scout Lake, easily identifiable by the boat dock, which serves the Scouts at Camp Steiner. From this high elevation point, it's just 1.4 miles back to the parking lot, and nearly all of it is downhill. The steepest part is right in front of you as you descend 520 feet in elevation down a rocky slope to the shores of Scout Lake.

The area around Picturesque Lake, which lies immediately south of Scout Lake, can be buggy and is the only portion of the trail where insect repellent may come in handy, especially in July. As with other hikes in the Uintas, afternoon thundershowers can appear quickly. If you see a gathering storm, find the quickest and safest route possible leading away from high, rocky elevations and back to the trailhead.

Leaving Picturesque Lake, the trail crosses a camp service road and continues along a gentle descent back to the parking area, completing the loop in 4.1 splendidly scenic miles.

ADDITIONAL AT-A-GLANCE INFORMATION

FACILITIES: Restroom at trailhead

DOGS: Permitted

SPECIAL COMMENTS: While the hike lies within the Wasatch-Cache National Forest, a section of trail passes through Camp Steiner, the highest-elevation Boy Scout camp in the United States.

NEARBY ACTIVITIES

For visitors on the Mirror Lake Highway, Provo River Falls is a must-see destination waterfall. It is actually a series of three distinct falls separated from each other by about 100 feet. From the parking and picnic area at the upper falls, take the paved trail to the second falls. An easy scramble leads to the river below the third falls. The Provo River Falls parking area is located on the left (west) side of the Mirror Lake Highway, just before milepost 24.

59 FEHR LAKE TRAIL

KEY AT-A-GLANCE INFORMATION

LENGTH: 3.4 miles round-trip

ELEVATION GAIN: 472 feet

ELEVATION AT TRAILHEAD: 10,377 feet

CONFIGURATION: Out-and-back

DIFFICULTY: Easy

SCENERY: Lakes and ponds, spruce forests, wildflowers, and surrounding mountains

EXPOSURE: Mostly shaded

TRAFFIC: Moderate

TRAIL SURFACE: Dirt and some rock

HIKING TIME: 1.5–3 hours

WATER REQUIREMENTS: 1 liter. Water in lakes and streams can be purified.

SEASON: Late spring, summer, early fall

ACCESS: Located within the Wasatch-Cache National Forest fee recreation area. Pick up a recreation pass at the Kamas Ranger Station or at one of the self-service fee stations along the Mirror Lake Highway.

MAPS: USGS Mirror Lake, Trails Illustrated High Uintas Wilderness (number 711)

See additional information at end of Description, page 261.

GPS Trailhead Coordinates

UTM Zone (WGS84) 12T

Easting 0509110

Northing 4504690

Latitude N 40° 41' 34.3"

Longitude W 110° 53' 30.2"

IN BRIEF

The Fehr Lake Trail descends along a route that skirts three alpine lakes and passes through wood and meadows, and along ponds and small streams. You can hike this trail as a short 1-mile stroll to Fehr Lake or continue to Shepard and Hoover lakes for a 3-mile round-trip walk—all in the shadow of Murdock Mountain to the southwest.

DESCRIPTION

This Uintas classic explores descending tiers of jewel-like lakes. The lakes along the Fehr Lake Trail are part of the Duchesne River drainage, which eventually flows into the Green River and on to the Colorado River. The lakes to the south of Bald Mountain summit flow into the Provo River and down to Utah Lake before terminating in the Great Salt Lake. This short hike to three charming lakes can also be used as a starting point or first leg of a longer extended backpacking trip deep into the High Uintas Wilderness.

From the trailhead parking area, the trail departs to the southeast across a small wooden

Directions

From Salt Lake City, take I-80 east to Silver Creek Junction/US 40 (Exit 148). Turn right and go south on US 40 for 3.4 miles to UT 248 (Exit 4). At the end of the off-ramp, turn left and continue on UT 248 for 11.4 miles to South Main Street (UT 32) in Kamas. Turn left on South Main Street in Kamas and go north for two blocks, then turn right on Center Street (UT 150). Continue on UT 150 for 31 miles to a small, unpaved, and unmarked parking area on the right. It's just 100 yards south of the Moosehorn Campground on the west side of the highway.

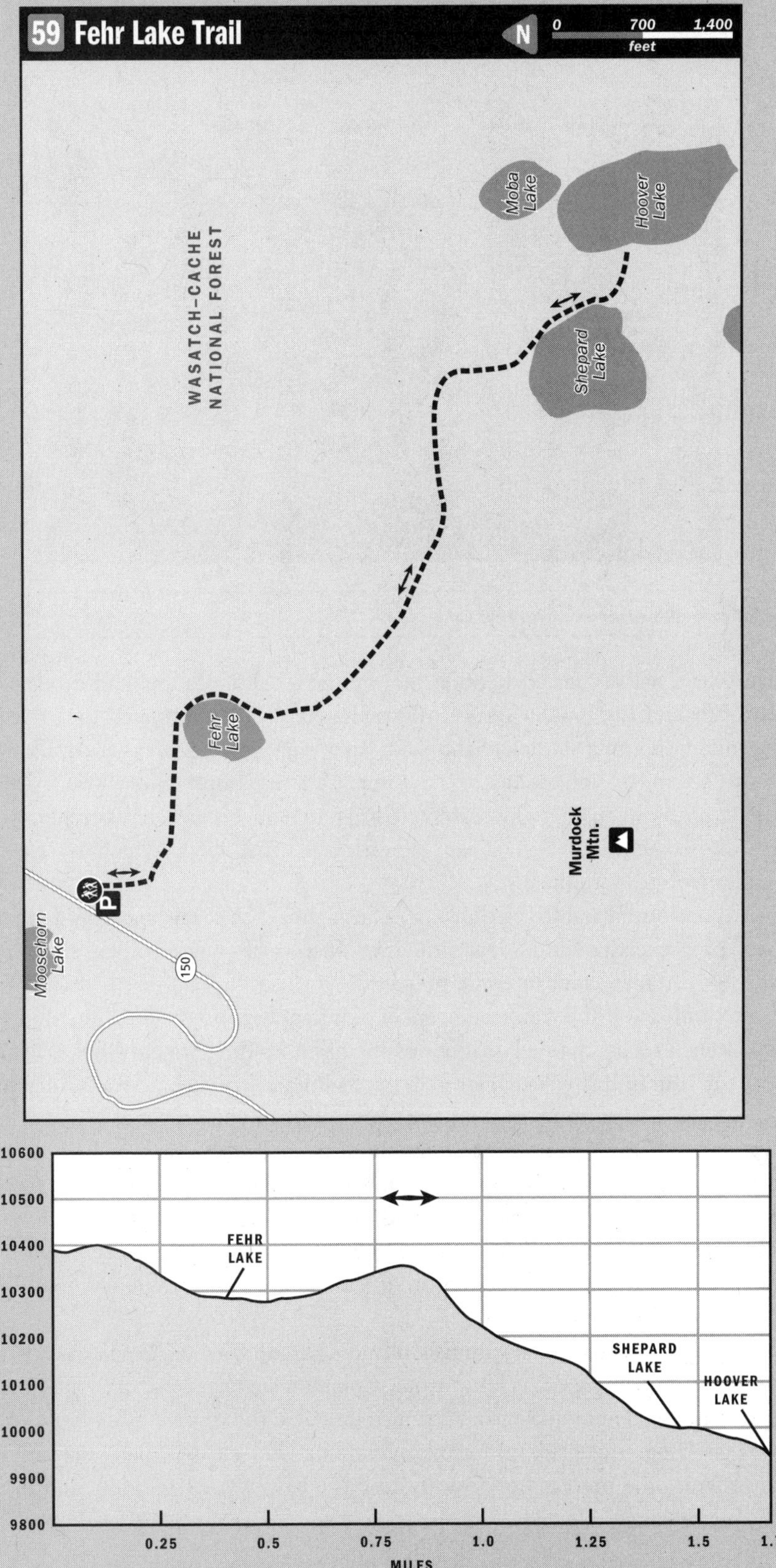

59 Fehr Lake Trail
N
0
700
1,400
feet
WASATCH-CACHE NATIONAL FOREST
Moba Lake
Hoover Lake
Shepard Lake
Fehr Lake
Murdock Mtn.
P
Moosehorn Lake
150
FEET
10600
10500
10400
10300
10200
10100
10000
9900
9800
FEHR LAKE
SHEPARD LAKE
HOOVER LAKE
0.25
0.5
0.75
1.0
1.25
1.5
1.7
MILES

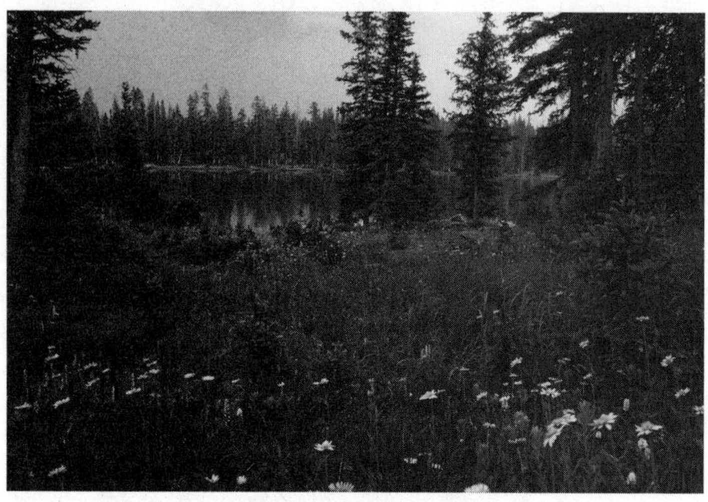

A wildflower-filled meadow near Fehr Lake

bridge over a marshy meadow. Soon the trail leaves the meadow and drops into a forest of fir and Engelmann spruce. Along the way you'll be treated to splashes of blue gentian, shooting star, elephant head, Parry's primrose, and other wildflowers.

At 0.2 miles you come to an unmarked junction, where you continue on the trail as it bears right. After crossing two more wooden bridges, you'll arrive at the shore of Fehr Lake (elevation 10,273 feet), which is less than 0.4 miles from the trailhead.

As you loop around Fehr Lake's eastern shore, the trail becomes faint as it crosses a low meadow and departs the lake. Insects can be a problem early in the season, so you may want to come prepared.

At 1 mile from the trailhead, a small pond appears on the left. The trail soon drops along a rocky channel as it enters the basin holding Shepard Lake. It's easy to lose the trail in this wooded stretch, but as long as you keep descending, you'll be on course. Soon, at 1.4 miles from the trailhead, you arrive at Shepard Lake (elevation 9,987 feet), a body of water about twice the size of Fehr Lake.

As you skirt the northeast shore of Shepard Lake, the trail leaves the lake and, just 100 feet east, rises to a small crest. Looking down the slope, you'll see the largest of the three lakes, Hoover Lake (elevation 9,220 feet), through the trees. Within three minutes you'll be at its shore. At this point you will have hiked 1.7 miles from the trailhead.

The lakes are all stocked with fish, including arctic grayling, brook trout, brown trout, rainbow trout, and cutthroat trout. Common sights around the lakes include deer and moose, chipmunks, ground squirrels, and an occasional black bear.

High Uinta trails are notoriously winding and exceptionally scenic. Fehr Lake provides the perfect opportunity to dip into this lush wooded land of glistening alpine lakes.

ADDITIONAL AT-A-GLANCE INFORMATION

FACILITIES: No facilities at the trailhead, although water and restrooms are available across the highway at the Moosehorn Campground.

DOGS: Permitted

SPECIAL COMMENTS: A rare mountain hike where the trailhead is the high elevation and each lake along the way takes you down the basin to a lower elevation. Save some energy for the hike out.

NEARBY ACTIVITIES

As the Mirror Lake Highway passes through the western Uintas from Kamas, Utah, to Evanston, Wyoming, you'll find dozens of easily accessible developed campgrounds and inviting picnic areas for both day and overnight use. Additionally, you can choose from among hundreds of primitive backcountry campsites throughout the general forest area, many just a mile or two from the highway. For camping reservations, call (877) 444-6777 or visit **www.recreation.gov.**

60 BALD MOUNTAIN

KEY AT-A-GLANCE INFORMATION

LENGTH: 3 miles round-trip
ELEVATION GAIN: 1,179 feet
ELEVATION AT TRAILHEAD: 10,764 feet
CONFIGURATION: Out-and-back
DIFFICULTY: Moderate
SCENERY: Wildflowers, high-alpine vegetation, and exceptional views of the Uintas from the summit
EXPOSURE: No shade on trail
TRAFFIC: Busy
TRAIL SURFACE: Rock and dirt
HIKING TIME: 1.5–3 hours
WATER REQUIREMENTS: 1 liter. There is no water on the trail.
SEASON: Late spring, summer, early fall
ACCESS: Located within the Wasatch-Cache National Forest fee recreation area. Pick up a recreation pass at the Kamas Ranger Station or at one of the self-service fee stations along the Mirror Lake Highway.
MAPS: USGS Mirror Lake, Trails Illustrated High Uintas Wilderness (number 711)

See additional information at end of Description, page 265.

GPS Trailhead Coordinates

UTM Zone (WGS84) 12T
Easting 0508110
Northing 4504253
Latitude N 40° 41' 20.9"
Longitude W 110° 54' 14.3"

IN BRIEF

With a convenient trailhead and a well-groomed trail to the summit, Bald Mountain is an ideal climb, especially for children and inexperienced hikers who want to experience the thrill of climbing a high mountain summit. A National Recreation Trail recognized for its outstanding scenery, the Bald Mountain Trail offers wildflowers and breathtaking views of lakes and surrounding peaks in the High Uintas.

DESCRIPTION

The Uinta Mountains are part of a rare mountain range in the Western Hemisphere that runs east to west, rather than north to south. Bald Mountain, located at the western edge of the Uintas, is a freestanding rounded peak that begs to be climbed. With a summit elevation of 11,943 feet, Bald Mountain is the most easily accessible high peak in Utah, higher than any peak in the Wasatch Range, and well worth climbing. Other Uinta peaks to the east are higher—including the highest point in Utah, 13,528-foot Kings Peak—but none are more suitable for a day hike.

Directions

From Salt Lake City, take I-80 east to Silver Creek Junction/US 40 (Exit 148). Turn right and go south on US 40 for 3.4 miles to UT 248 (Exit 4). At the end of the off-ramp, turn left and continue on UT 248 for 11.4 miles to South Main Street (UT 32) in Kamas. Turn left on South Main Street in Kamas and go north for two blocks, then turn right on Center Street (UT 150). Continue on UT 150 for 29 miles to the Bald Mountain trailhead/picnic area on your left. The trailhead is at the northwest corner of the large loop parking lot.

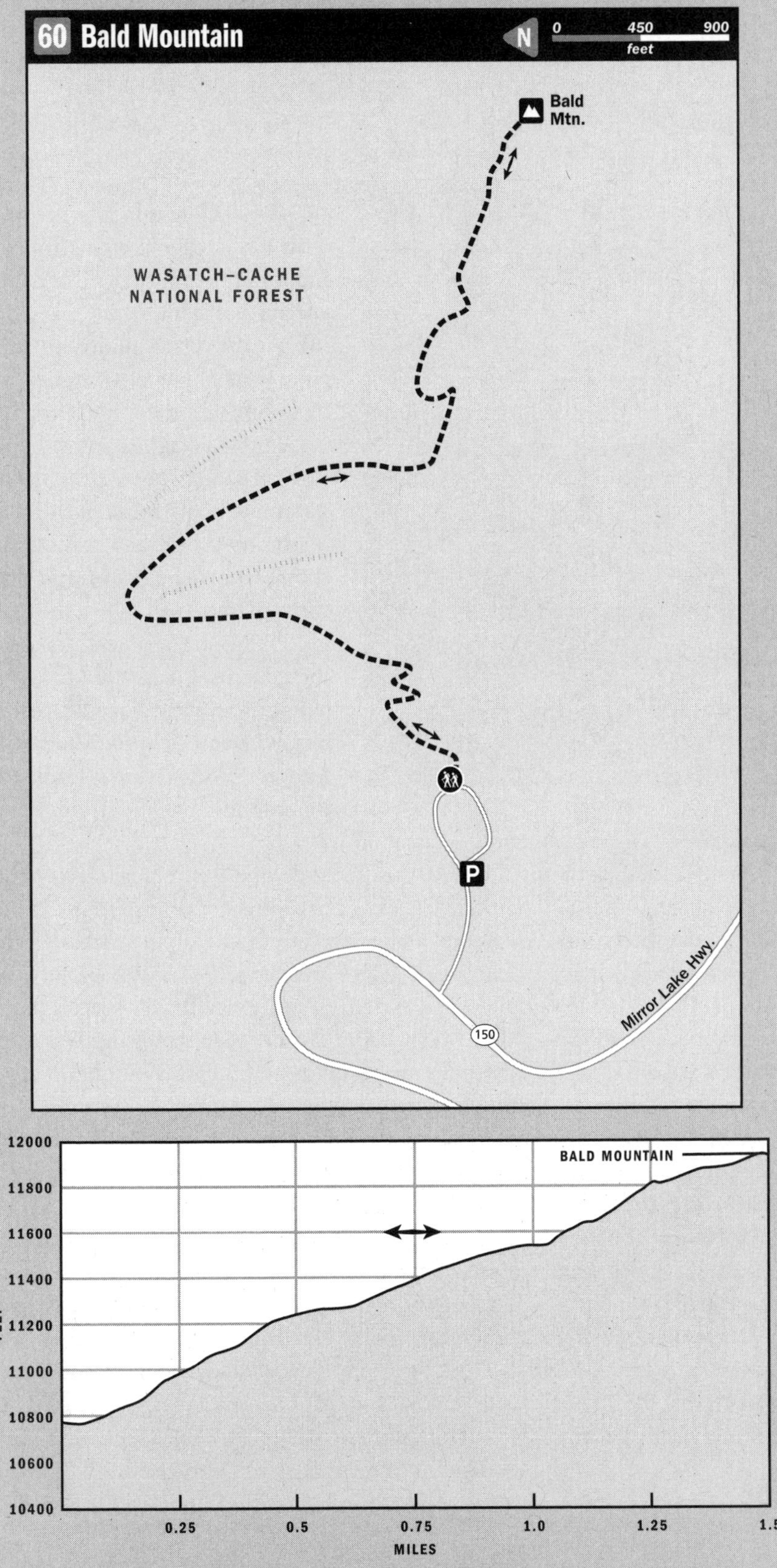

60 Bald Mountain
N
0
450
900
feet
Bald
Mtn.
WASATCH–CACHE
NATIONAL FOREST
P
150
Mirror Lake Hwy.
12000
11800
11600
11400
11200
11000
10800
10600
10400
FEET
BALD MOUNTAIN
0.25
0.5
0.75
1.0
1.25
1.5
MILES

The rock staircase to the Bald Mountain summit

Bald Mountain provides more than just bragging rights for making it to the top, though. It delivers spectacular summit views and gives hikers the opportunity to move from a subalpine environment to a high-alpine zone while experiencing an amazing variety of wildflowers along the way. A herd of mountain goats inhabits the slopes of the mountain and can often be spotted on the plateau and above the tree line.

From the trailhead located at the edge of a meadow of lavender alpine aster, the trail passes through a small stand of spruce before hitting the rocky slope leading up the mountain. The trail, though unmarked, is well traveled and easy to follow.

At 0.6 miles, as the path approaches the tree line, you enter a large, rocky tundra plateau. The trail continues its ascent across this upper shelf, but at a more gentle gradient. As you reach the higher elevation, the alpine asters become noticeably smaller, but just as vibrant. They are joined by moss campion, fiery Indian paintbrush, blue sky pilot, and dozens of other wildflower species. At this high elevation, you'll find wildflowers you're not likely to see in the Wasatch or in other areas of Utah. Subalpine fir makes its last appearance at about 11,400 feet, but the wildflowers continue to the summit.

At 0.9 miles the trail steepens to ascend a false summit. As you crest this mound, the true summit comes in to view just 100 yards ahead. This last section of trail crosses a flat stretch of quartzite before climbing a short stairway of large, angular blocks. You'll encounter some big steps, but no scrambling is required.

Just 1.5 miles from the trailhead, you reach the expansive summit dome, with Reids Peak immediately to the northwest. The large, rounded peak to the east is Mount Agassiz (12,428 feet), while Hayden Peak (12,479 feet) is the jagged peak to the northeast. On a clear day you won't be able to count all of the lakes that lie in the basins below, but Moosehorn Lake lies immediately below, between the highway and the eastern slopes of Bald Mountain. Mirror Lake is the larger lake to the north, on the east side of the highway.

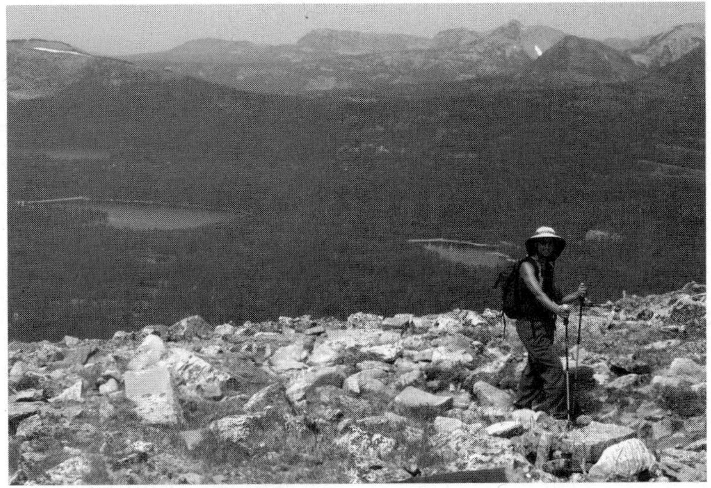

Bald Mountain offers great views into the basins below.

Climb Bald Mountain early in the day. During the short summer season, afternoon thundershowers and lightning commonly occur in the Uintas. If such a storm appears to be brewing, you'd be wise to turn around and make a quick retreat to the parking area.

ADDITIONAL AT-A-GLANCE INFORMATION

FACILITIES: Restrooms and picnic area at trailhead. Nearest water is at Mirror Lake Campground.

DOGS: Permitted

SPECIAL COMMENTS: Bald Mountain is the highest peak in this book, yet one of the easiest to climb. It's normal to feel winded at this elevation, but also watch for more severe signs of altitude sickness, which can include headache, nausea, vomiting, and dizziness.

NEARBY ACTIVITIES

The Kamas Ranger Station, located at 50 East Center Street in Kamas, makes an excellent starting point for a trip along the Mirror Lake Highway. The station has an interpretive center and offers an excellent assortment of books, maps, and resource materials for area trails, campgrounds, and activities.

60 HIKES
WITHIN 60 MILES

SALT LAKE CITY

INCLUDING

OGDEN, PROVO,

AND THE UINTAS

APPENDIXES AND INDEX

APPENDIX A: HIKING RETAILERS

Black Diamond
2092 East 39900 South
Salt Lake City, Utah 84124
(801) 278-0233
www.bdel.com

Cabela's
2502 West Grand Terrace Parkway
Lehi, Utah 84043
(801) 766-2500
www.cabelas.com

Hansen Mountaineering
1799 North State Street
Orem, Utah 84057
(801) 226-7498
www.hansenmountaineering.com

Kirkham's Outdoor Products
3125 South State Street
Salt Lake City, Utah 84115
(801) 486-4161
www.kirkhams.com

Out N Back
1797 South State Street
Orem, Utah 84097
(801) 224-0454
www.outnback.com

Patagonia
2292 South Highland Drive
Salt Lake City, Utah 84106
(801) 466-2226
www.patagonia.com

Recreation Outlet
615 East State Road
American Fork, Utah 84003
(801) 763-7722
www.recreationoutlet.com

3160 South State Street
Salt Lake City, Utah 84115
(801) 484-4800

REI
3285 East 3300 South
Salt Lake City, Utah 84109
(801) 486-2100
www.rei.com

230 West 10600 South, Suite 1700
Sandy, Utah 84070
(801) 501-0850

Sportsman's Warehouse
165 West 7200 South
Midvale, Utah 84047
(801) 567-1000
www.sportsmanswarehouse.com

1075 South University Avenue
Provo, Utah 84601
(801) 818-2000

1137 West Riverdale Road
Riverdale, Utah 84405
(801) 334-4000

APPENDIX B:
HIKING CLUBS AND TRAILS ORGANIZATIONS

Mountain Trails Foundation
P.O. Box 754
Park City, Utah 84060
(435) 649-6839
www.mountaintrails.org

Outdoors Unlimited
Brigham Young University
1151 Wilkinson Student Center
Provo, Utah 84602
(801) 422-2708
outdoors.byu.edu

Serac Mountaineering Club
P.O. Box 1997
Orem, Utah 84059
(801) 226-7498
www.seracclub.org

Sheryl's Adventure Club
Sheryl McGlochlin, Director
Salt Lake City, Utah
(801) 278-5313
www.crazysheryl.com
smcgloch@yahoo.com

Sierra Club, Ogden Group
P.O. Box 1821
Ogden, Utah 84402
utah.sierraclub.org/ogden

Sierra Club, Utah Chapter
2159 South 700 East, Suite 210
Salt Lake City, Utah 84106
(801) 467-9297
utah.sierraclub.org

University of Utah Outdoor Recreation Program
2140 East Red Butte Road, Building 650
Salt Lake City, Utah 84112
(801) 581-8516
www.utah.edu/campusrec

Utah Valley University Outdoor Adventure Center
800 West University Parkway
SC103H
Orem, Utah 84058
(801) 863-7052
www.uvu.edu/oac

Wasatch Mountain Club
1390 South 1100 East, Suite 103
Salt Lake City, Utah 84105
(801) 463-9842
www.wasatchmountainclub.org

Weber Pathways
P.O. Box 972
Ogden, Utah 84402
(801) 393-2304
www.weberpathways.org

Weber State University Wilderness Recreation Center
4022 Taylor Avenue
Ogden, Utah 84408
(801) 626-6373
www.weber.edu/wrc

APPENDIX C: GLOSSARY OF SALT LAKE CITY-AREA HIKING TERMS

Alpine Relating to mountains; often descriptive of plants, animals, and scenery found in mountainous regions.

Alpine zone Life zone found in regions above 11,500 feet; characterized by arctic-alpine tundra.

Avalanche A mass of snow, ice, and accompanying debris sliding down a mountain or over a cliff.

Berm A natural or man-made raised bank of earth that forms a low ridge.

Bonneville Shoreline, or **Bench** The geologic features visible at the 5,090-foot level on the mountains surrounding Salt Lake City. These deposits were left by the shoreline of ancient Lake Bonneville 15,000 years ago.

Boulder-hopping Hiking that involves walking and sometimes jumping across sections with large rocks.

Bowl A large depression left in the earth by a retreating glacier, often part of a cirque.

Bushwhack To clear a path through thick woods or undergrowth where no trail exists.

Cairn A stack of rocks created as a trail marker. Hikers often construct cairns to mark the way on faint trails.

Canopy A layer formed by the leaves and branches of the forest's tallest trees.

Cirque A deep-walled, glacier-carved basin on a mountain usually forming the blunt upper end of a valley.

Conifer Trees and shrubs that are typically cone-bearing and evergreen. In Utah, common conifers are spruce, fir, pine, and juniper.

Couloir A steep mountainside chute or gully that often retains snow late in the season.

Drainage An area (basin) generally bounded by ridges or slopes, encompassing a watershed.

Exposure Vulnerability; used to describe the potential for physical harm in the event of a fall.

Forb A broad-leaf plant other than grass, often found growing in fields and meadows.

Glacier A large body of ice moving down a slope or mountain.

Glissade To slide in a standing or sitting position down a snow-covered slope without the use of skis.

Knife-edge A mountain ridge, often close to the summit, characterized by a narrow passage and slopes that drop sharply on both sides.

APPENDIX C: (CONTINUED) GLOSSARY OF SALT LAKE CITY-AREA HIKING TERMS

Krummholz Trees and other wooded vegetation found near tree line that have been twisted and stunted by wind and severe weather.

Massif A compact portion of a mountain range containing one or more summits. Mount Timpanogos, for example, is a massif within the larger Wasatch range.

Montane zone Life zone found at elevations from 8,000 to 9,500 feet and characterized by aspen and Douglas-fir.

Moraine The rocks and soil carried and deposited by a glacier.

Outcropping The exposed part of a rock formation that can be seen above the ground.

Riparian Located or living along or near a stream or river.

Routefinding Techniques of navigating in a backcountry or wilderness setting without the use of GPS, compass, or maps.

Saddle A ridge between two peaks.

Scrambling A type of climbing that does not entail the use of ropes; instead, hands and legs are used to provide propulsion and balance.

Scree Debris consisting of small loose rocks, usually fist-size or smaller.

Side canyon A tributary or branch of a larger canyon. Broads Fork and Mineral Fork are side canyons of Big Cottonwood.

Snowfield An expanse of snow cover that can be either permanent or last well beyond the winter season. The accumulation above Emerald Lake on Mount Timpanogos is considered a permanent snowfield.

Subalpine zone Life zone found at elevations from 9,500 feet to tree line (about 11,000 feet) and characterized by spruce forests.

Switchback A zigzagging trail up the side of a steep slope or mountain. Allows for a more gradual and less strenuous ascent.

Talus A sloping mass of rock debris at the base of a cliff.

Tarn A mountain lake formed by a glacier.

Technical climbing Rock or mountain climbing involving the use of ropes and protective equipment.

Transition zone The foothills at an elevation of 5,500 to 8,000 feet characterized by oak and maple shrublands.

APPENDIX C: (CONTINUED)
GLOSSARY OF SALT LAKE CITY-AREA HIKING TERMS

Traverse A section of trail that moves across a slope or ridge in a horizontal direction.

Tree line (also ***timberline***) The elevation where the trees end and subalpine or alpine vegetation begins. The elevation of tree line varies with latitude and climate. In northern Utah, the tree line is around 11,000 feet.

Tundra The treeless vegetation found in high-alpine and arctic terrain, consisting of lichens, mosses, grasses, and low shrubs.

Watershed The land area that drains water into a river system or other body of water.

INDEX

FROM MENASHA RIDGE PRESS!

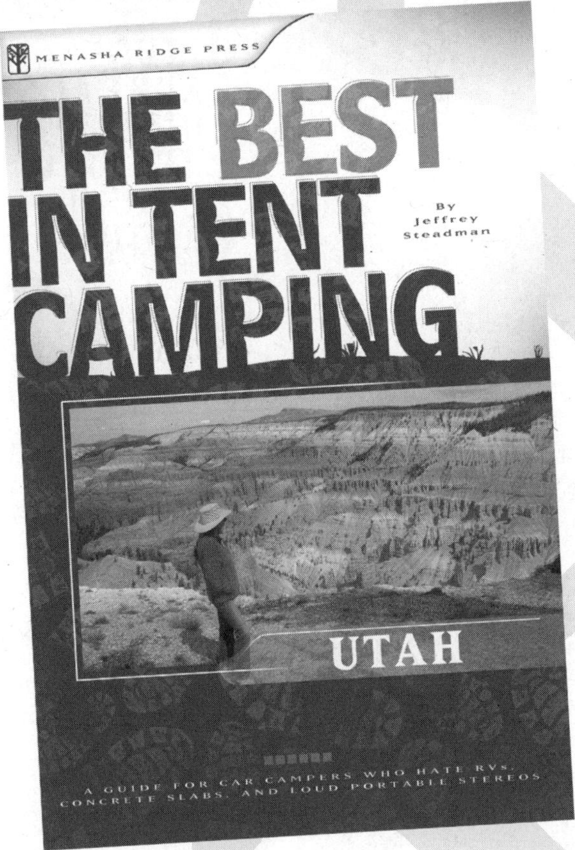

BEST IN TENT CAMPING: UTAH

by Jeffrey Steadman

ISBN: 978-0-89732-647-6

$14.95; 208 pages

From over 400 campgrounds statewide, the author has culled the 50 best places to pitch your tent and steer clear of those frantic and bustling campgrounds full of RVs, concrete slabs, and loud portable stereos.

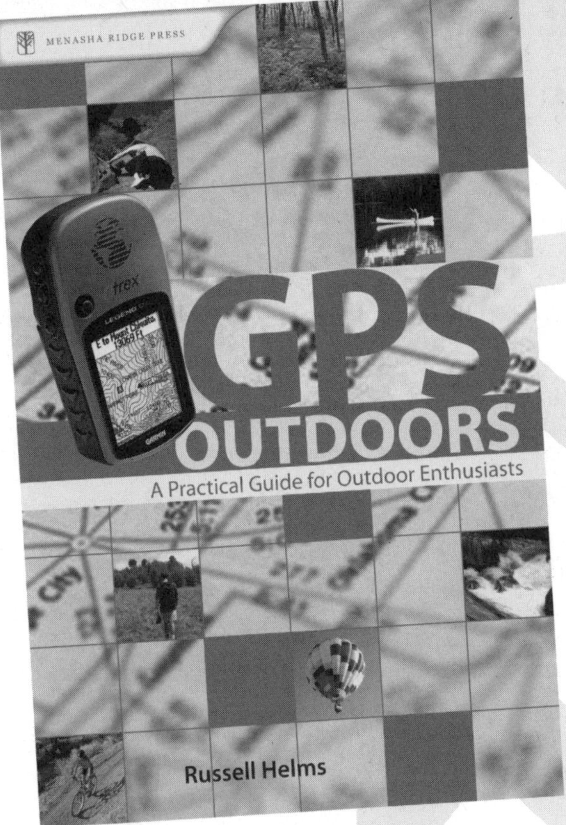

GPS OUTDOORS

by Russell Helms
ISBN 10: 0-89732-967-8
ISBN 13: 978-0-89732-967-5
$10.95
120pages

Whether you're a hiker on a weekend trip through the Great Smokies, a backpacker cruising the Continental Divide Trail, a mountain biker kicking up dust in Moab, a paddler running the Lewis and Clark bicentennial route, or a climber pre-scouting the routes up Mount Shasta, a simple handheld GPS unit is fun, useful, and can even be a lifesaver.

FROM MENASHA RIDGE PRESS!

COMPLETE BOOK OF FIRE

by Buck Tilton

ISBN 10:0-89732-633-4
ISBN 13: 978-0-89732-633-9
$12.95 • 6 x 9 • pb
104 pages • illustrations

In addition to the comforts of a campfire, a life may often hang in the balance. When a campfire becomes a matter of life or death, there is no room for error. This book provides the knowledge and fosters the confidence to successfully stay alive.

Looking for more info?

Menasha Ridge Press has partnered with Trails.com to provide additional information for all the trails in this book, including:

- Topo map downloads
- Real-time weather
- Trail reports, and more

To access this information, visit:
http://menasharidge.trails.com

In Partnership With

DEAR CUSTOMERS AND FRIENDS,

SUPPORTING YOUR INTEREST IN OUTDOOR ADVENTURE, travel, and an active lifestyle is central to our operations, from the authors we choose to the locations we detail to the way we design our books. Menasha Ridge Press was incorporated in 1982 by a group of veteran outdoorsmen and professional outfitters. For 25 years now, we've specialized in creating books that benefit the outdoors enthusiast.

Almost immediately, Menasha Ridge Press earned a reputation for revolutionizing outdoors- and travel-guidebook publishing. For such activities as canoeing, kayaking, hiking, backpacking, and mountain biking, we established new standards of quality that transformed the whole genre, resulting in outdoor-recreation guides of great sophistication and solid content. Menasha Ridge continues to be outdoor publishing's greatest innovator.

The folks at Menasha Ridge Press are as at home on a white-water river or mountain trail as they are editing a manuscript. The books we build for you are the best they can be, because we're responding to your needs. Plus, we use and depend on them ourselves.

We look forward to seeing you on the river or the trail. If you'd like to contact us directly, join in at www.trekalong.com or visit us at www.menasharidge.com. We thank you for your interest in our books and the natural world around us all.

SAFE TRAVELS,

Bob Sehlinger

BOB SEHLINGER
PUBLISHER